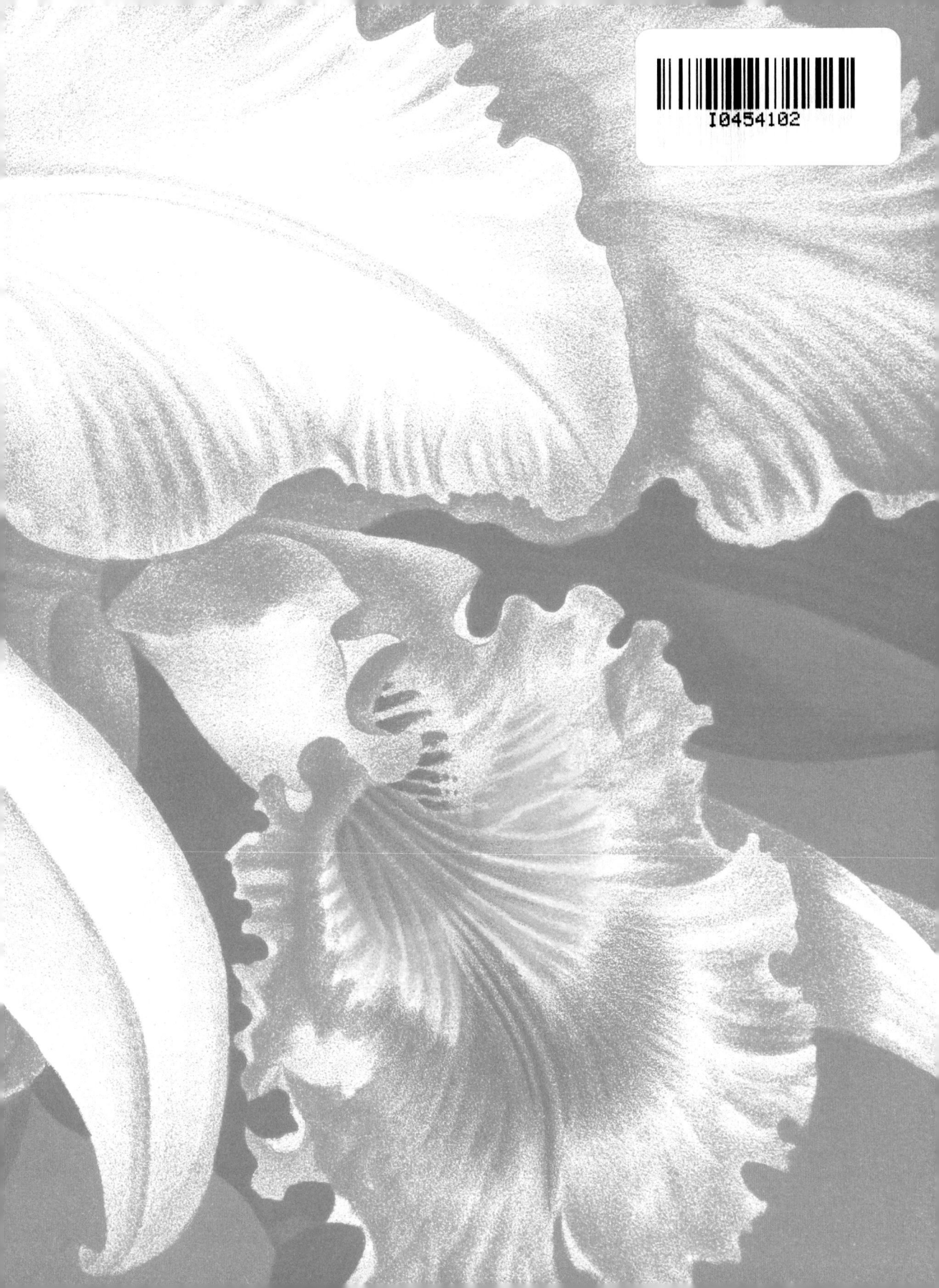

THE

ORCHID

LAUREN GARDINER was Curator of the Cambridge University Herbarium and member of the RHS Orchid Committee. She previously worked at the Royal Botanic Gardens, Kew, where she specialized in the systematics and conservation of orchids and palms.

PHILLIP CRIBB is a leading specialist on the taxonomy and conservation of orchids, and a member of the RHS Orchid Committee. He was Deputy Keeper of the Herbarium and Curator of the Orchid Herbarium at the Royal Botanic Gardens, Kew until his retirement in 2006.

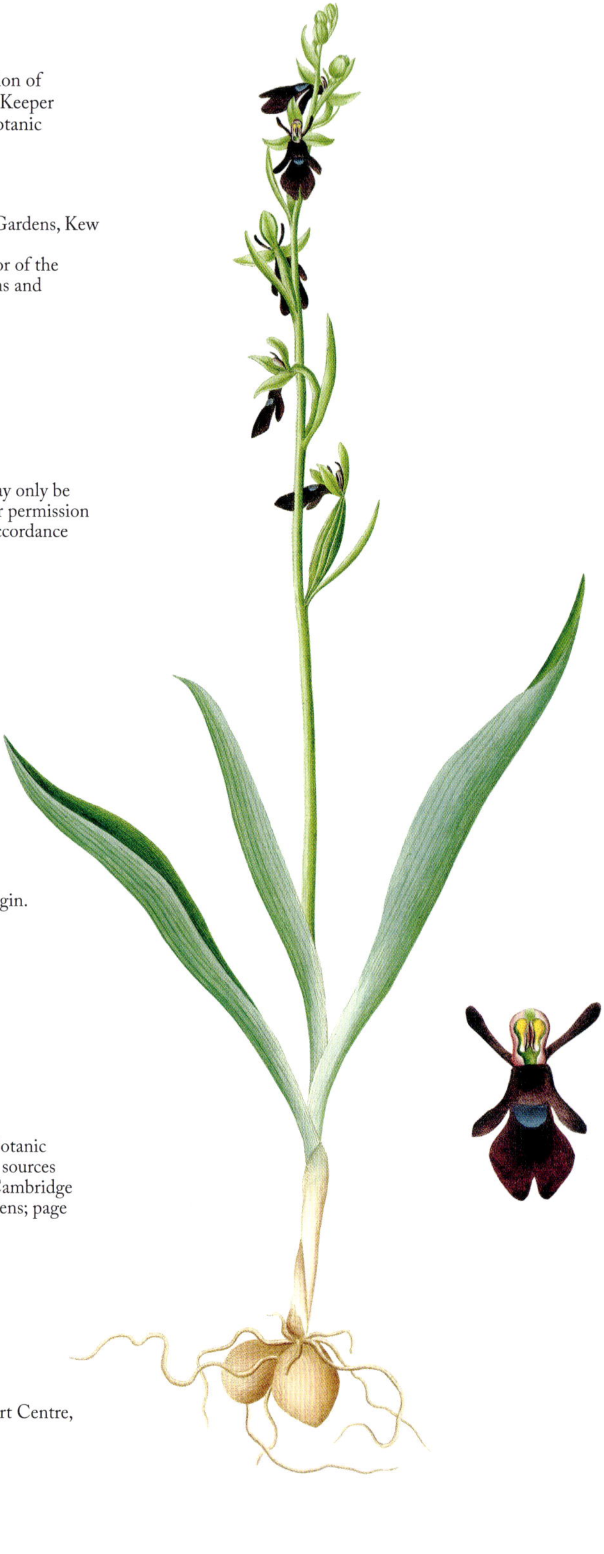

First published in 2018 by André Deutsch Limited

This edition published in 2026 by Welbeck
An Imprint of HEADLINE PUBLISHING GROUP LIMITED

1

Cataloguing in Publication Data is available from the British Library

ISBN 978 1 03542 772 7

Printed and bound in Dubai

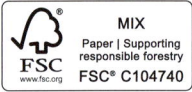

Headline's policy is to use papers that are natural, renewable and recyclable products and made from wood grown in well-managed forests and other controlled sources. The logging and manufacturing processes are expected to conform to the environmental regulations of the country of origin.

Publishing credits
Kew Project Manager: Lydia White
Picture research: Lauren Gardiner, Phillip Cribb, Lydia White
Photography: Paul Little
Editor: Alison Moss, Ellie Jardine
Design: Katie Baxendale
Production: Arlene Lestrade

Picture credits
All images unless otherwise stated © The Board of Trustees of the Royal Botanic Gardens, Kew. The publishers would like to thank the following additional sources for their kind permission to reproduce the pictures in this book: page 14, Cambridge University Library (DAR 115:141); page 106, Marie Selby Botanical Gardens; page 192, Carol Woodin.

HEADLINE PUBLISHING GROUP LIMITED
An Hachette UK Company
Carmelite House
50 Victoria Embankment
London EC4Y 0DZ

The authorised representative in the EEA is Hachette Ireland, 8 Castlecourt Centre, Dublin 15, D15 YF6A, Ireland (email: info@hbgi.ie)

www.headline.co.uk
www.hachette.co.uk

Royal Botanic Gardens **Kew**

THE

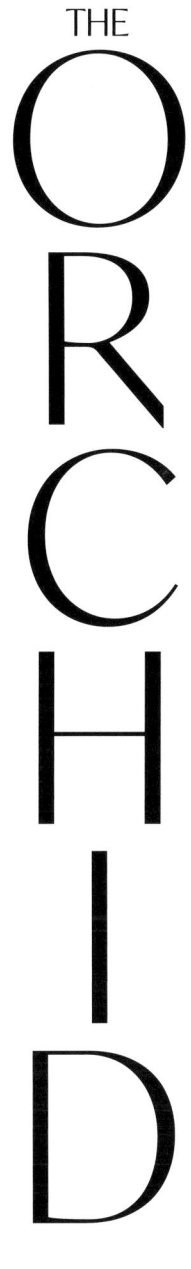

ORCHID

A celebration
of the
world's most
charismatic
flower

Lauren Gardiner
& Philip Cribb

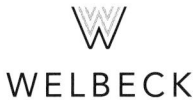

WELBECK

CONTENTS

INTRODUCTION

The orchid family (Orchidaceae) is the most diverse group of flowering plants in the world with some 30,000 distinct species and an enormous range of different flowers. Orchids are found on every continent of the planet, except Antarctica, and in nearly all terrestrial habitats, from sea level to high-altitude alpine vegetation, only excluding true desert and frozen land. The tropical and subtropical forests of the world contain the largest number of orchid species, many of which are epiphytes, living on the trunks and branches of trees, from the lowland rainforests of Borneo, to the high-elevation cloud forests of the Andes. Yet temperate parts of the world, including Europe, North America and non-tropical parts of Australia, all play host to thousands of terrestrial orchid species, often emerging only periodically after years and sometimes hidden underground.

Artists have long been attracted to capture orchids in their work, using a wide range of techniques and media. In this book, we present a selection of this remarkable diversity using works from the Archives of the Royal Botanic Gardens, Kew. Forty charismatic orchid species have been chosen, from around the world, from the extravagant and colourful to the understated and subtle, from the more traditionally and flamboyantly striking to some of the more strange and quirky species. All are beautiful, and all have evolved in synchronization with their animal pollinators and associated plants, animals and fungi, to result in the extraordinary flowers and vegetative structures we see and enjoy today.

Kew's Library and Archives contains one of the greatest collections of botanical artwork in the world, with over 200,000 pieces, many of which are original works, collected together over the last 200 years. Works held by Kew include many by the masters of botanical illustration from the eighteenth century to the present day, including Georg Dionysius Ehret, Pierre-Joseph Redouté, the Bauer brothers, Franz and Ferdinand, and Walter Hood Fitch; modern works by the likes of Christabel King, Pandora Sellars and Margaret Stones for journals such as *Curtis's Botanical Magazine* and *Kew Bulletin*. Kew is home to the only two purpose-built galleries in the world dedicated entirely to botanical art. The Marianne North Gallery was designed, built and filled with 833 paintings by the intrepid artist, and opened in

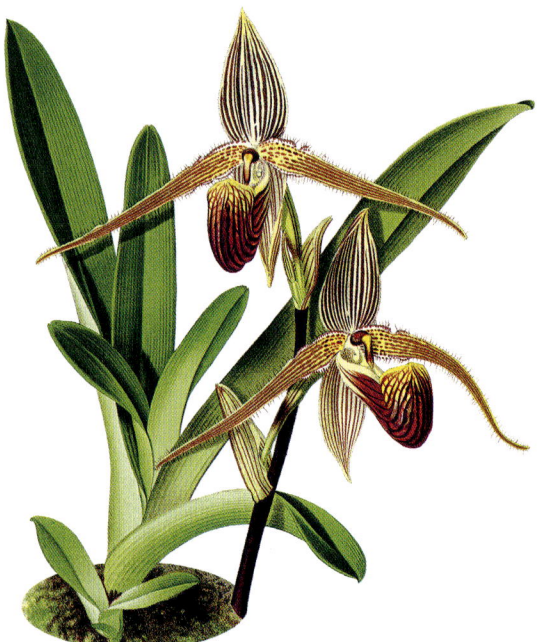

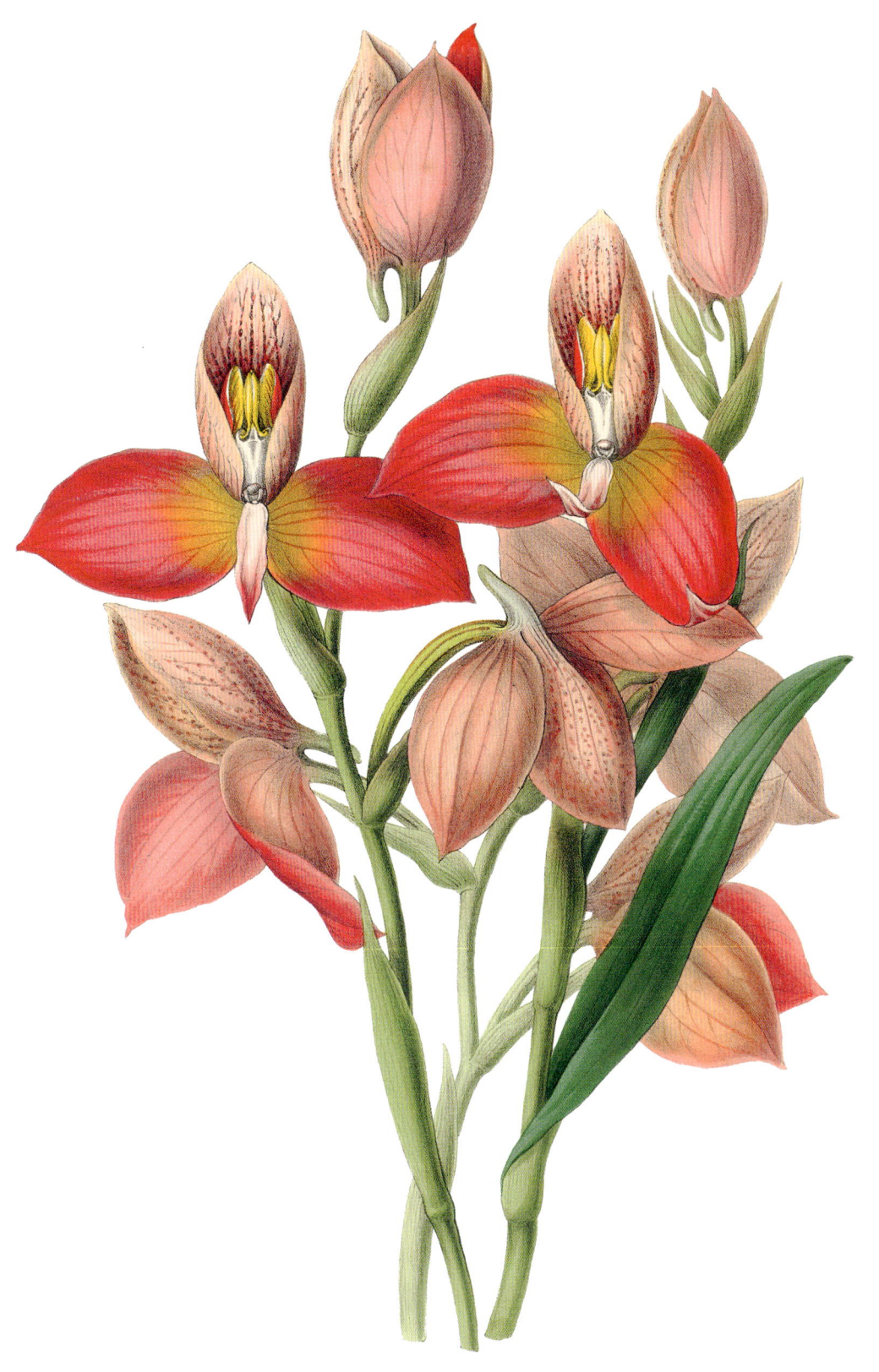

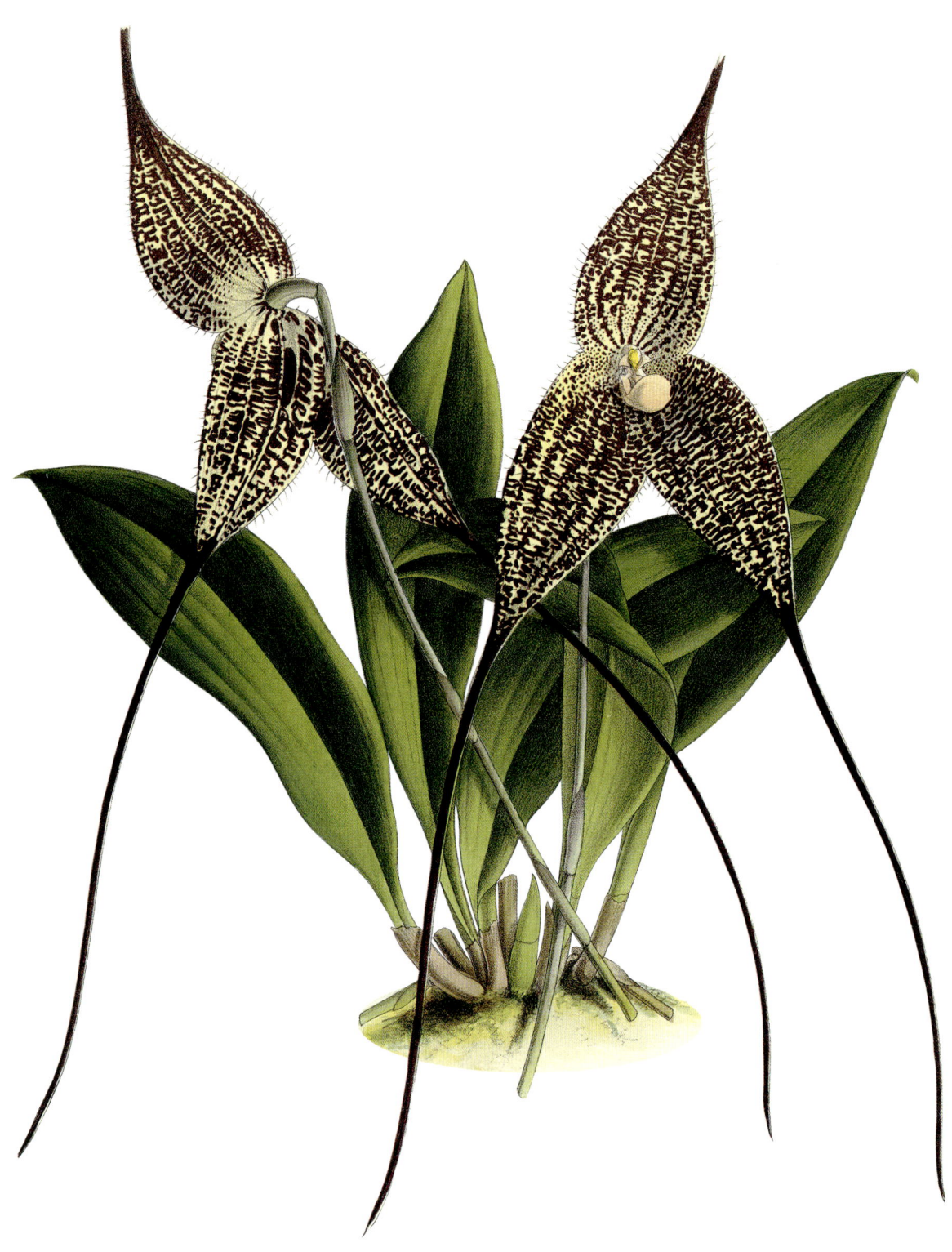

1882. The Shirley Sherwood Gallery of Botanical Art opened in 2008 and displays a range of works from the private collections of Dr Shirley Sherwood and the Royal Botanic Gardens, Kew in several different exhibitions and installations each year.

Kew has a long history of botanical art and illustration focusing specifically on orchids, and a unique collection of work, which continues to grow each year. These were not only produced and/or purchased for aesthetic appreciation, celebrating the beauty and wonder of this huge group of plants, but much of the collection has primarily scientific purposes – a practice which continues to be extremely important today.

Woodcut illustrations of orchids appeared in the European "Herbals" of the fifteenth to seventeenth centuries depicting terrestrial species with medicinal properties, and their identifying features. Orchid species new to science started to enter Europe in the eighteenth and nineteenth centuries, brought back from South America, Southern Africa, South East Asia, China and Australia, and were grown in the British orchid nurseries of Loddiges, Low, Sander and Veitch, and botanical gardens at Kew, Glasnevin, Edinburgh, Glasgow and the (later, Royal) Horticultural Society of London at Chiswick. The Kew collection is the oldest surviving living orchid collection in the world, dating back to the 1770s when William Aiton began to grow orchids introduced from the Caribbean and tropical Asia. The plants that first survived the long sea journey to Europe and the smoky "stove-houses" in which they were grown – in attempts to mimic the supposedly hot and steamy climes of their native habitats – would, by Victorian times, lead to a frenzy of "orchidmania" in well-to-do society. Botanical artists, such as Walter Hood Fitch, Sarah Drake and Matilda Smith, were employed to illustrate the thousands of new orchids and other plants being described, often in beautifully produced volumes such as

John Lindley's *Sertum Orchidaceum* (1837–41) and James Bateman's *The Orchidaceae of Mexico and Guatemala* (1837–43), and in periodicals such as *Curtis's Botanical Magazine* and *Edwards' Botanical Register*.

Kew's interest in the orchid family was nurtured by Sir Joseph Banks, who was fascinated by the tropical orchids that he saw when he accompanied Captain James Cook on his first voyage to Australia. Banks, unofficial director of Kew, was the first person to grow epiphytic orchids in hanging baskets to mimic their native habitat. The living collection grew rapidly with the appointment of Sir William Hooker as the first Director of Kew in 1841. He had a lifelong interest in the family, a fascination inherited by his son, Joseph, who also published extensively on the family and encouraged Charles Darwin when his interest turned to orchid pollination. In 1865 the elder Hooker purchased John Lindley's important orchid herbarium upon his death in 1865. Lindley's herbarium includes the type collections of nearly all the new species that arrived in England between 1820 and 1865 and remains of critical importance to orchid studies. Sir Joseph succeeded his father at Kew and, in 1880, appointed Robert Allen Rolfe as Kew's first orchid specialist. In 1893, Rolfe founded the *Orchid Review*, the world's oldest surviving orchid journal and, later, with Charles Curtis, produced the first listing of artificial orchid hybrids. Kew continues to excel as a centre of orchid cultivation, science and conservation, and the living orchid collection continues to grow, providing plants for research and conservation projects.

We hope that this book will delight those who already have a passion for orchids, and entrance and intrigue those whose interest is just beginning.

LG, Cambridge
PC, Kew

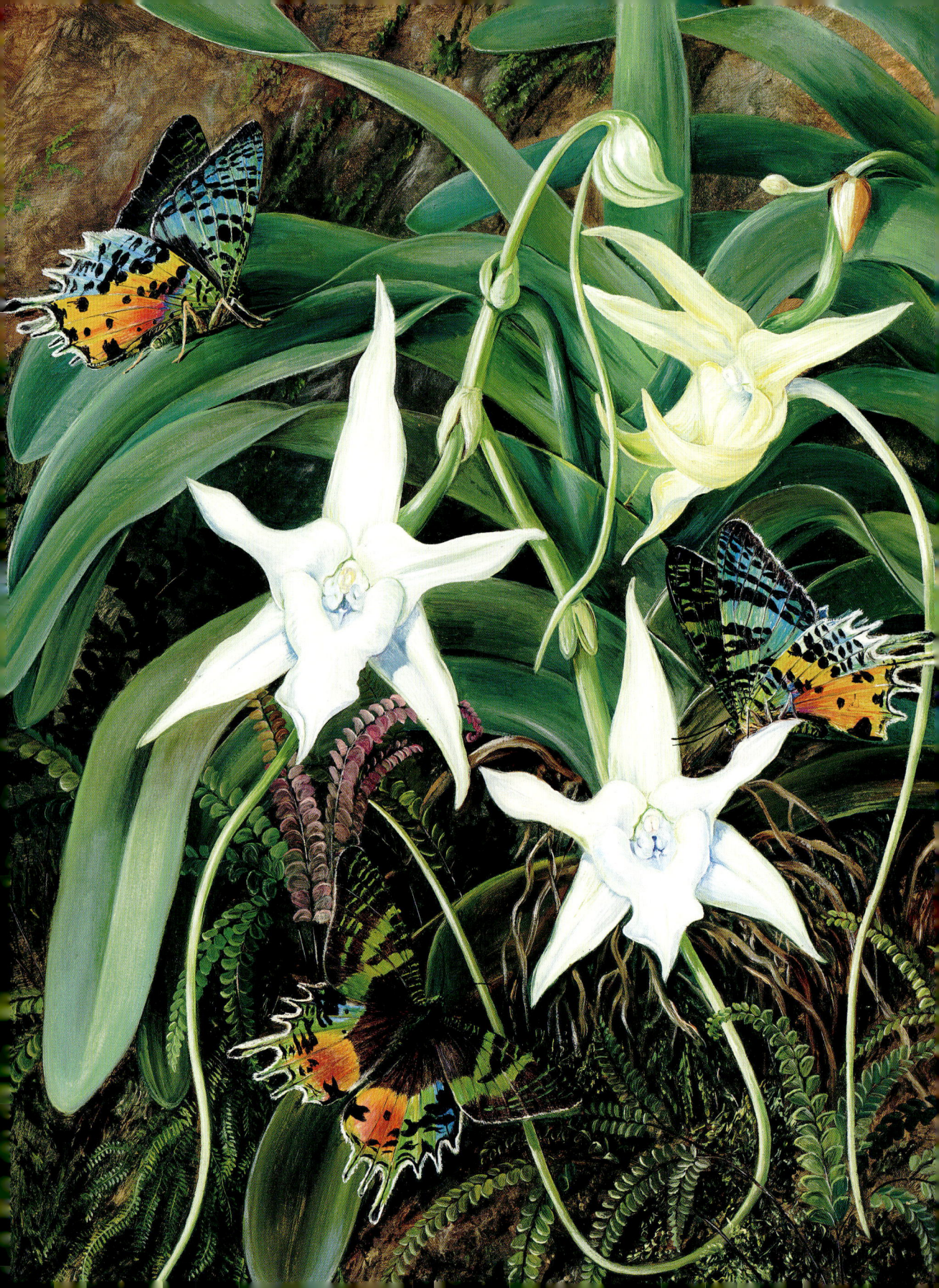

DARWIN'S COMET ORCHID

ANGRAECUM SESQUIPEDALE

"Good Heavens what insect can suck it?" wrote Charles Darwin in his January 1862 letter to Joseph Dalton Hooker, Director of the Royal Botanic Gardens, Kew. The orchid he was describing was *Angraecum sesquipedale*, an epiphytic species in the Vandeae tribe, endemic to the lowland forests of Madagascar. Collected by the French botanist Louis-Marie Aubert du Petit-Thouars in 1798, though Thouars did not formally publish the species until 1822. A plant had been sent to Darwin by James Bateman, the author of the monolithic tome *The Orchidaceae of Mexico and Guatemala* (1837–43) and later *A Monograph of the Genus Odontoglossum* (1874), and just one of a number of well-connected orchidophiles in the UK who would send Darwin interesting species to study at his home, Down House, in Kent.

A. sesquipedale has large, star-like, waxy, night-scented flowers which change colour from greenish white to creamy or pure white as they open and mature, but it was the extremely long thin spur, which reaches up to 30 cm (11½ in) in length, that really intrigued Darwin.

Writing about it in his book *On the Various Contrivances by which British and Foreign Orchids are Fertilized by Insects* (published in 1882 and the follow-up to his famous 1859 work *On the Origin of Species*), Darwin hypothesized that "in Madagascar there must be moths with prosces capable of extension to a length of between ten and eleven inches!" – as only such an insect would be able to access the supply of nectar at the far end of the spur, and in doing so pick up and/or deposit the orchid's pollen (packaged into two balls of pollen called pollinia).

Translating from the Latin, *sesquipedale* means "one and a half feet long", and although the spur of *A. sesquipedale* is not quite as long as this, it is one of the longest known floral spurs in the plant kingdom. Darwin went on to describe how such extraordinary organs as the long spur in the orchid, and the enormous proboscis of the insect, could come into existence, and further developed his theories of descent with modification and differential survival originally presented in *On the Origin of Species*, to explain the mechanism by which

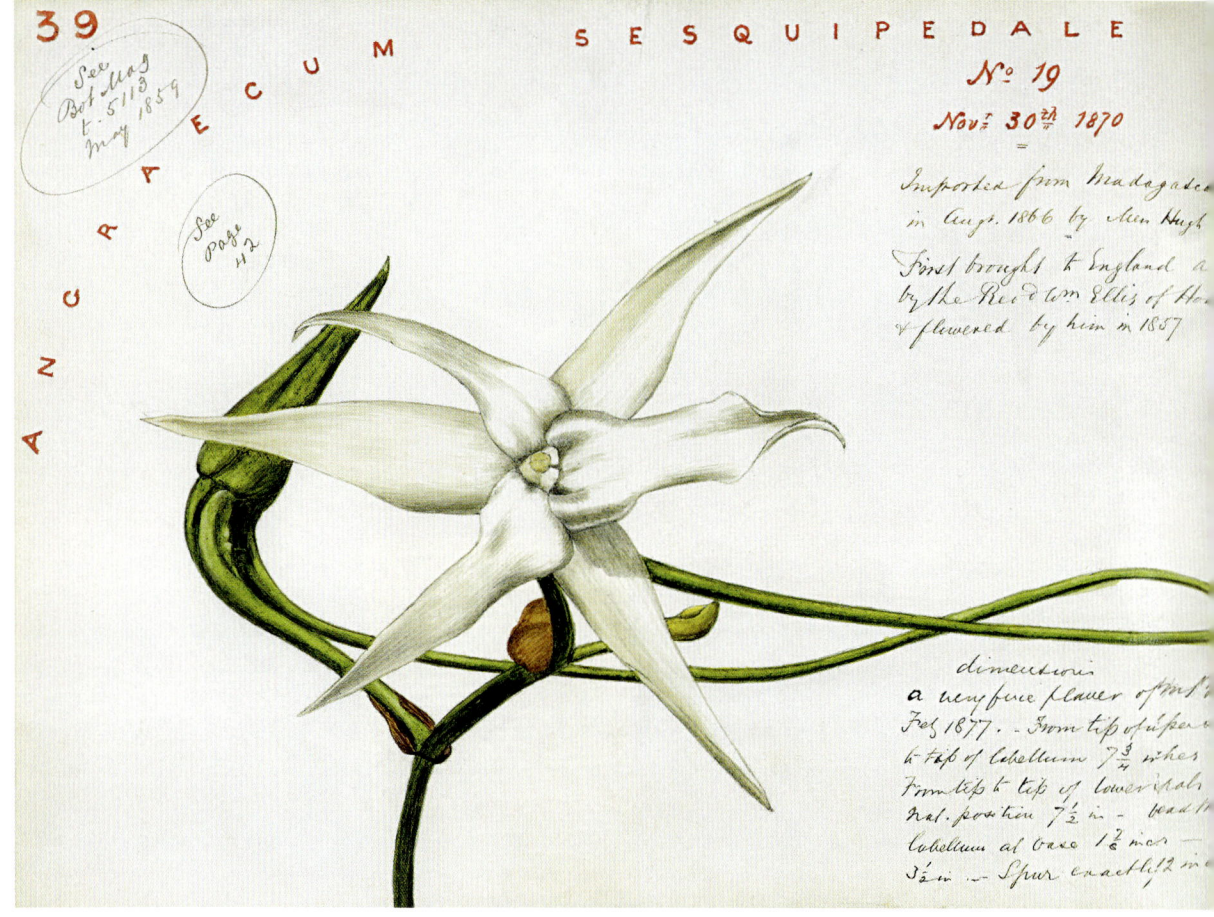

The handwritten annotations on the illustration read:

39

SESQUIPEDALE

No 19

Nov. 30th 1870

See Bot Mag t. 5113 May 1859

See page 42

A N Z A C R A E C U M (vertical letters at left)

Imported from Madagascar in Augt. 1866 by Mess Hugh

First brought to England a by the Revd Wm Ellis of Ho & flowered by him in 1857

dimensions a very fine flower of Mr Feb 1877. — From tip of upper to tip of labellum 7¾ inches From tip to tip of lower petals nat. position 7½ in — head of labellum at base 1½ in or 3 in — Spur exactly 12 in

Above: *Angraecum sesquipedale* by John Day, 1870.

"there would in each generation be on the average an increase in the length of the nectaries [spur], and also an increase in the length of the proboscis of the moths." The rest of the book develops these ideas on the co-evolution of orchids and their pollinating insects, citing temperate and tropical orchids that Darwin had observed, including *Ophrys apifera* and *Catasetum* species, many of which were sent to him at Down House by his wide circle of correspondents and confidantes.

However, the missing link for Darwin's theory regarding *A. sesquipedale* was the absence in Madagascar of any known moth with such a long proboscis. It was not until 41 years later, in 1903 (21 years after Darwin's death), that a likely candidate was discovered, namely the hawkmoth *Xanthopan morganii praedicta*, and it was not until the 1990s that conclusive photographic evidence was obtained of this moth extending its extensive (albeit somewhat ungainly) proboscis, delicately manoeuvring it into the mouth of the spur, reaching the nectar right down at the base and picking up the pollinia in the process. Another member of the *Angraecum* genus that has an interesting and unique pollinator is *Angraecum cadetii*, from the

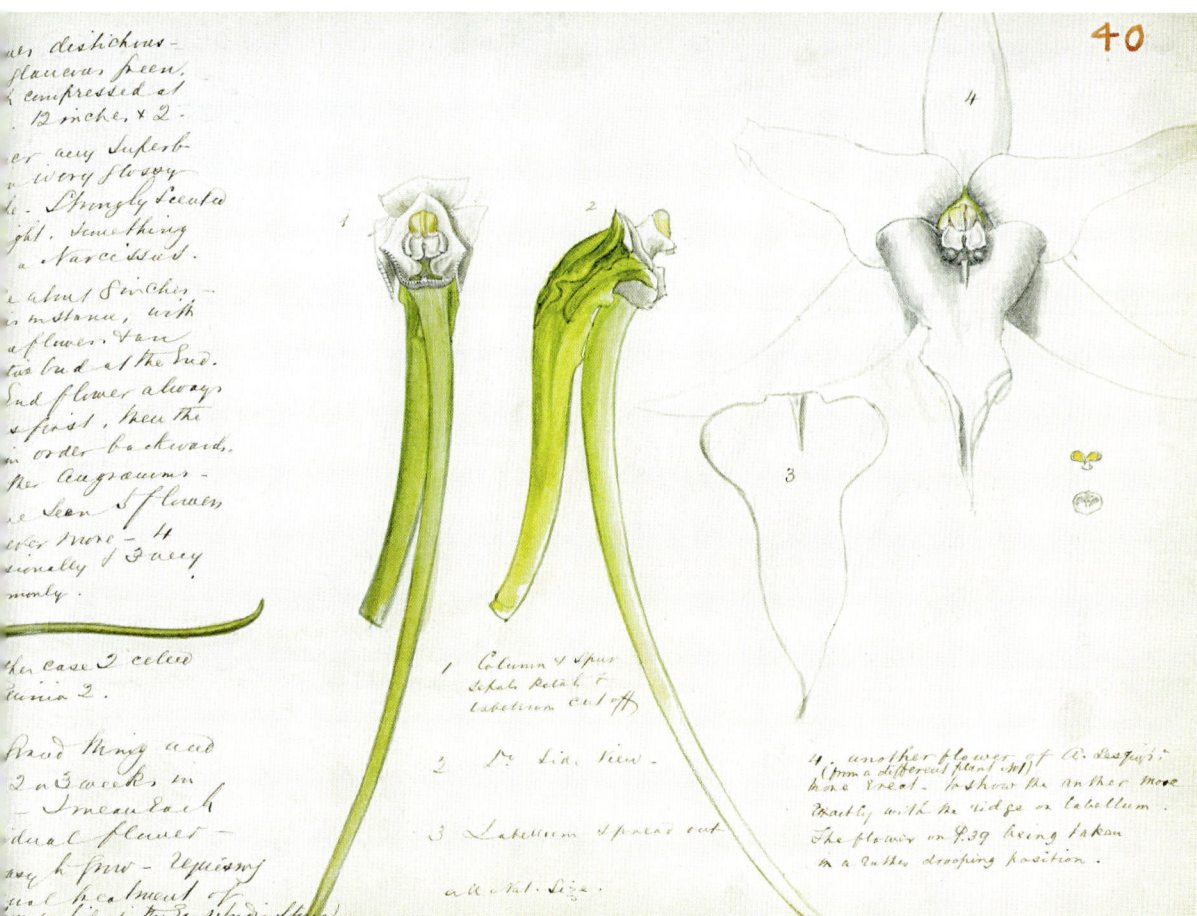

islands of Mauritius and Réunion, which in 2008 was discovered to be the first reported instance of a species of cricket (specifically, *Glomeremus orchidophilus*) pollinating a plant.

Interestingly, in *Various contrivances* Darwin made another important prediction about *A. sesquipedale*, this time with a conservation message, stating, "If such great moths were to become extinct in Madagascar, assuredly the *Angraecum* would become extinct." This is exactly what is thought to have happened to a related species in the same genus, *Angraecum longicalcar*, which has an even longer spur, at around 40 cm (15 in) in length. The pollinator for this species, a hawkmoth with a proboscis of similar length, has never been identified, and seed pods do not seem to be produced by wild plants unless the flowers are deliberately pollinated by hand. Without human help through *in situ* and *ex situ* conservation efforts, this species faces a severe threat of extinction in the wild. Luckily *A. sesquipedale* is currently not thought to be at a particularly elevated risk of extinction, with its moth pollinator still surviving and enabling the orchid to reproduce in the wild naturally.

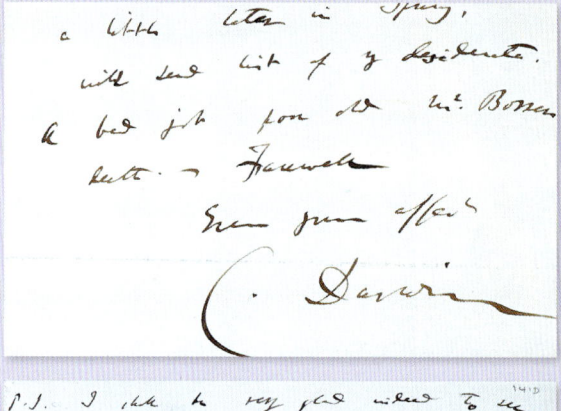

Opposite: *Angraecum sesquipedale* in R. Warner and B. S. Williams, *The Orchid Album*, 1887.

Extracts from a letter from Charles Darwin to Joseph Dalton Hooker, Down House, 25 January 1862

In 1862 Charles Darwin included a postscript note at the end of a letter to Joseph Hooker, exclaiming "Good Heavens what insect can suck it?" in reference to the enormously long spur of the striking white orchid that James Bateman had recently sent him.

Darwin and Hooker corresponded throughout their careers and, by the time of this letter several decades after they first became acquainted, had become great friends and confidantes – Darwin addresses his later letters, as he does here, to my "My dear Hooker". Some years before this letter, prior to the publication of his theories on natural selection and knowing these ideas would be extremely controversial, Darwin had written to his friend that "it is like confessing a murder". Both men shared their scientific ideas, discussing theories and evidence, in what now form great archives documenting the evolution of the scientific theories of natural selection and variation, descent with modification, and biogeography during the Victorian age.

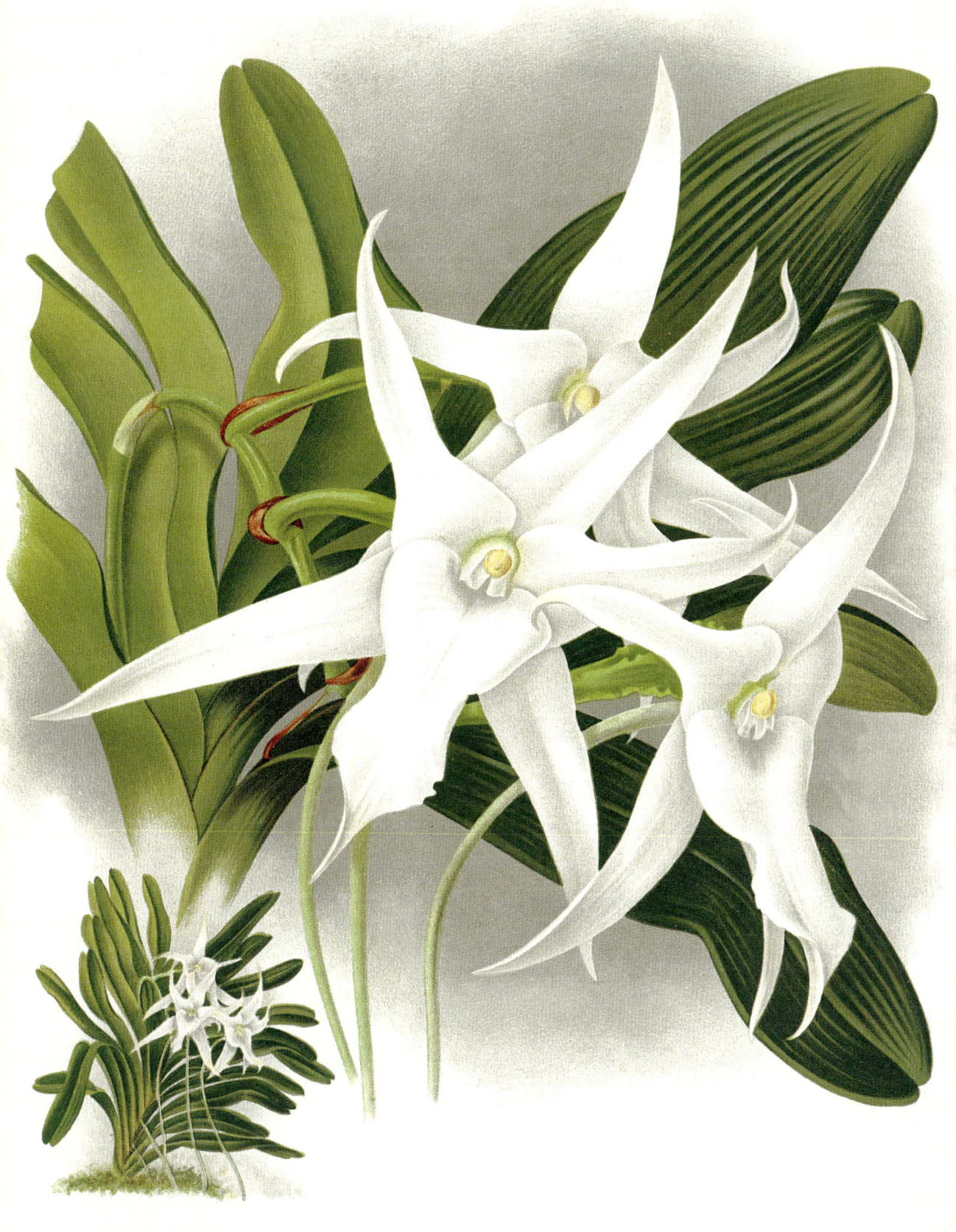

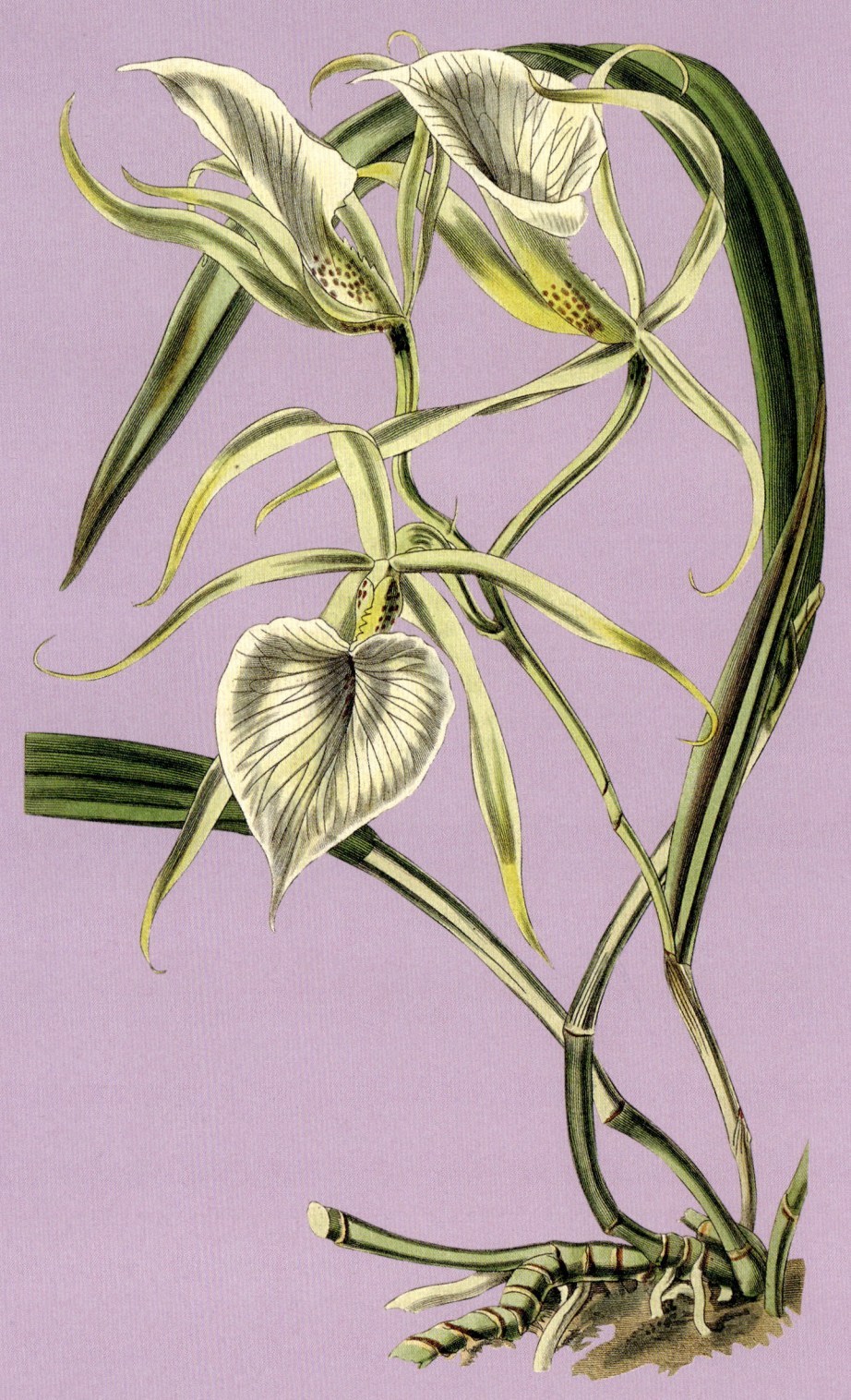

LADY OF THE NIGHT
BRASSAVOLA NODOSA

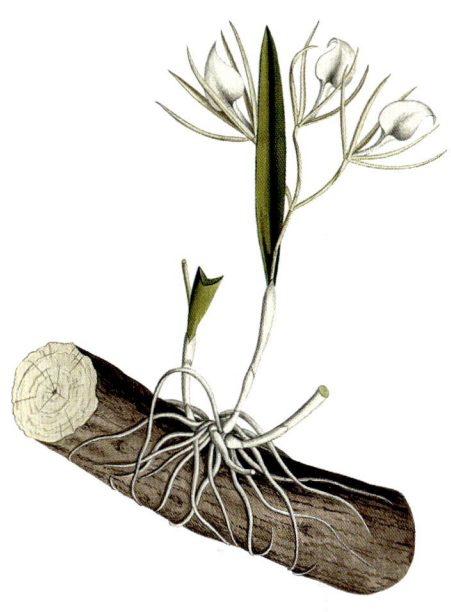

Brassavola nodosa, known as "dama de la noche" (lady of the night) in Guatemala, was one of the earliest tropical American orchids to receive a scientific binomial name. Carl Linnaeus described it as *Epidendrum nodosum* in the first edition of his *Species Plantarum* (1753), the book that is considered to be the starting point of binomial nomenclature. In those days, when only a small number of tropical orchids were known, the orchids were assigned to very few genera, with most American species being placed in *Epidendrum*, a genus that has a more restricted circumscription today.

The orchid was transferred to *Brassavola* by the eminent British botanist Robert Brown when he established the genus in 1825. The genus is characterized by its stems bearing a single slender, cylindrical leaf and a short inflorescence of showy flowers with slender white, pale yellow or green sepals and petals, and a large white trumpet-shaped lip with a tapering point. *Brassavola nodosa* has the largest flowers in the genus. It is widely, albeit sparsely, distributed from Mexico throughout Central America to Panama, the West Indies and Venezuela. It is found growing on the roots of mangroves along the sea shore, and on rocks or trees in open fields and woodland up to 500 m (1,600 ft) above sea level.

The earliest drawing of this orchid is in Nikolaus Jacquin's collection of West Indian plants published in 1763 in *Selectarum Stirpium Americanarum Historia* (see image, above). Sarah Drake's illustration in 1832 for *Edwards' Botanical Register* (see page 21) is probably the first coloured illustration of it. Sarah Drake was the nursemaid to John Lindley's family before her artistic talent was discovered.

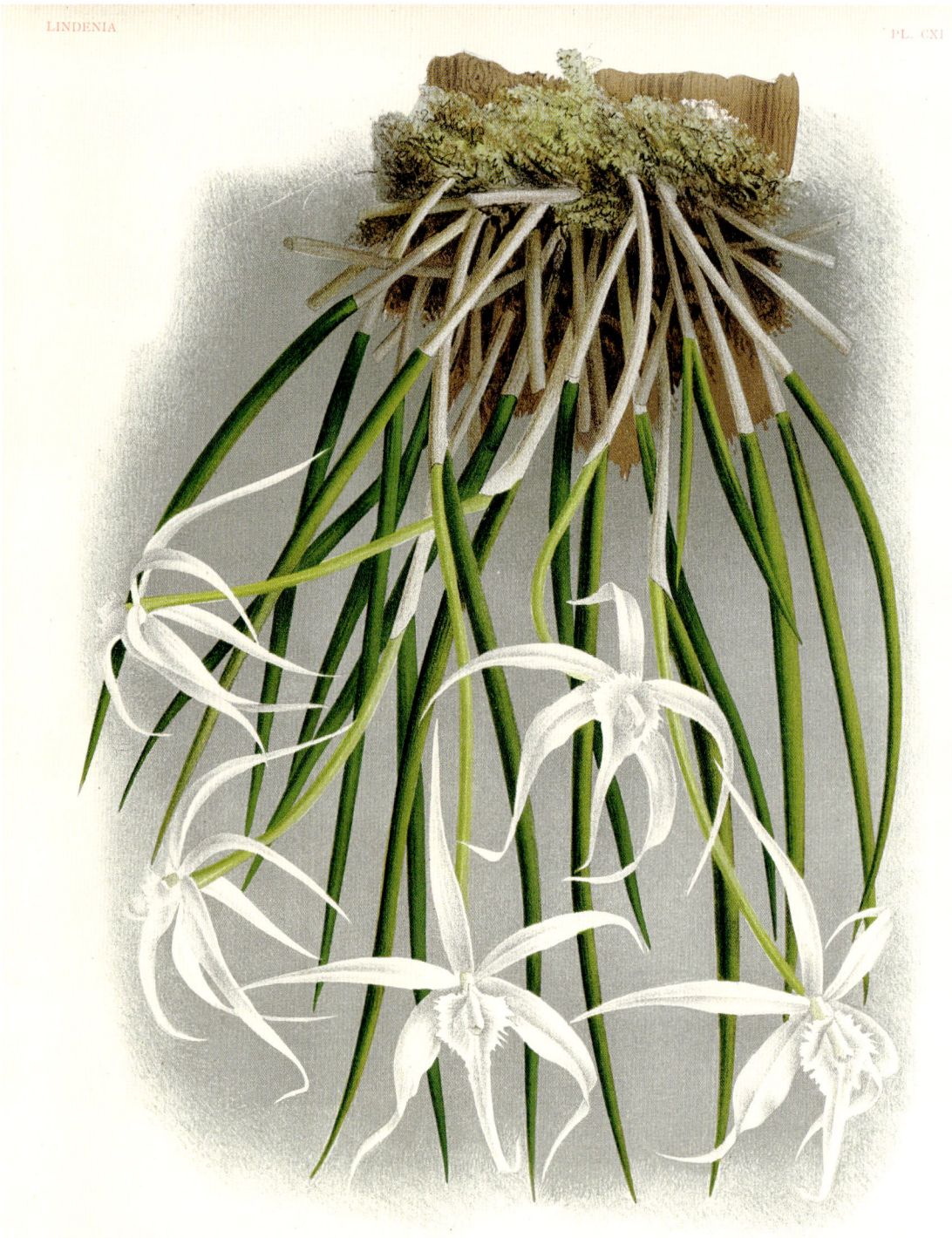

BRASSAVOLA CUCULLATA R. BR. var. CUSPIDATA HOOK.

P. De Pannemaeker ad nat. del. et pinx.

18   Lady of the night   *Brassavola nodo*

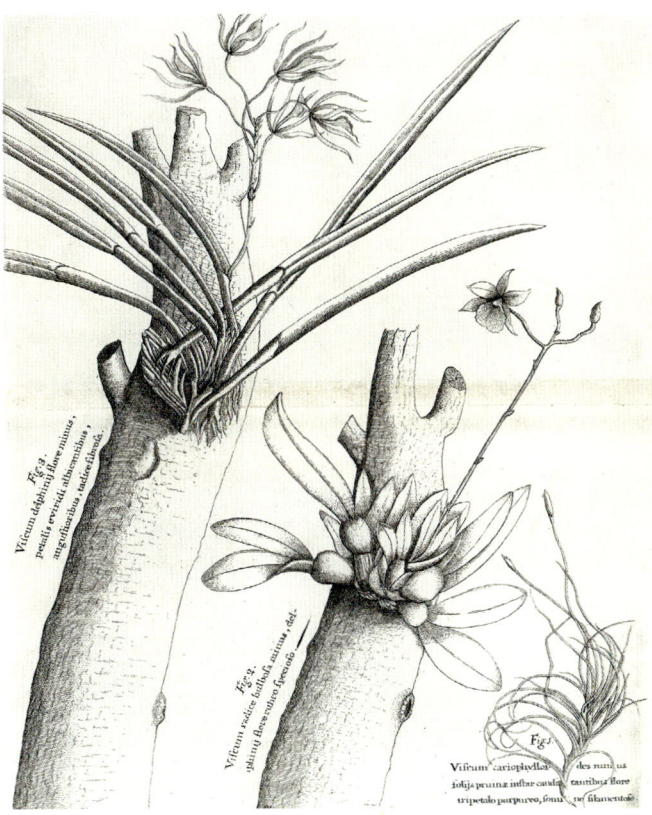

Fig. 3.
Viscum delphinii flore minus, pendulis viridi albicantibus, augustioribus radice lunula.

Fig. 2.
Viscum radice bulbata minus, det. gining flore cados species.

Fig. 1.
Viscum cariophyllat...
folia pruinae instar caulis... des minimus
tripetalo purpureo, limi... caulibus flore...
... int filamentosa.

Opposite: *Brassavola cucullata* var. *cuspidata* flowered at the Linden nursery in Ghent and drawn by Pieter de Pannemaeker for J. J. Linden, *Lindenia: Iconographie des Orchidées*, 1887.

Above: *Brassavola cordata* (as *Viscum delphinii*) drawn by Sir Hans Sloane for his *A Voyage to the Islands Madeira, Barbados, Nieves, S. Christopher and Jamaica*, 1707–25 (Fig. 3). Because of its epiphytic habit, Sloane named this a mistletoe rather than an orchid.

Brassavola is a small genus of about 24 species with a distribution that ranges from Mexico, Central America and the West Indies throughout tropical South America as far south as northern Argentina and Paraguay. Seven species are found in Mexico and Central America, six in both the West Indies and northern South America and ten in Brazil. A surprising number of species were grown in Victorian England. One of the earliest of these, drawn by Sydenham Edwards for his *Botanical Register*, was the sweetly scented *Brassavola cucullata*, probably the most distinctive species in the genus, easily distinguished by its lip with fimbriate lateral margins. It is widely distributed from Mexico and the West Indies to northern South America. Both Walter Hood

Fitch and William Hooker drew it for *Curtis's Botanical Magazine*. The Jamaican species, *B. subulifolia*, has been illustrated a number of times, notably by Sarah Drake in the *Botanical Register* and by Fitch in the *Botanical Magazine* (mistakenly as *B. cordata*) and in Hooker's *Century of Orchidaceous Plants*. Mrs Horsfall's painting in the Kew collection may have been the model for Fitch's work.

A number of South American species have attractive flowers that have been the focus of horticultural interest. Lady Barklay drew the Brazilian species, *B. martiana*, in January 1852, and that painting is now in the Kew collection. Fitch drew *B. perrinii* ranging from Argentina across to Bolivia for the *Botanical Magazine*, while Janet Ross painted a plant flowering in her husband's collection in Florence in February 1892. A number of Brazilian species, most notably *B. gardneri* and *B. martiana*, were drawn for Martius's *Flora Brasiliensis*.

Brassavola species have been crossed in cultivation with species in several allied genera, such as *Cattleya, Laelia, Rhyncholaelia* and *Epidendrum*, to produce a wide variety of popular artificial hybrids. Their popularity is due both to their dwarfing effect on larger orchids, and to their scented flowers that have a tubular lip. The two species of *Rhyncholaelia – R. digbyana* and *R. glauca –* were originally assigned to *Brassavola*, but are distinguished by their larger flowers, distinctive habit and broad leathery leaf. The influence of *R. digbyana* (see page 223) can be seen in many of its hybrids with *Cattleya*, which notably inherit the latter's large flowers with a fimbriate margin to the lip.

Facsimile of Linnaeus's Species Plantarum page 953

Linnaeus's description of Epidendrum nodosum (now *Brassavola nodosa*) from his *Species Plantarum* of 1753.

Species Plantarum by Linnaeus (Carl Linné), published in 1753, represents the starting point for binomial botanical nomenclature. Previously, plants were provided with Latin names that were descriptive of the species and were seldom binomials. Linnaeus, using an idea first used by Caspar Bauhin many years earlier, standardized all plant names, the first word representing the genus to which all closely related species belong, the second word an adjective that distinguished the particular species from others.

He scanned all of the existing literature and collected all of the published polynomial names used by other authors. Thus, his *Epidendrum nodosum*, featured here on page 953 of *Species Plantarum*, garnered names from the works of Herman, Plukenet and Sloane which all referred to this species. The generic name he chose was *Epidendrum* and the epithet or adjective was *nodosum*, so that the species name became *Epidendrum nodosum*. This was later transferred to the genus *Brassavola* by Robert Brown.

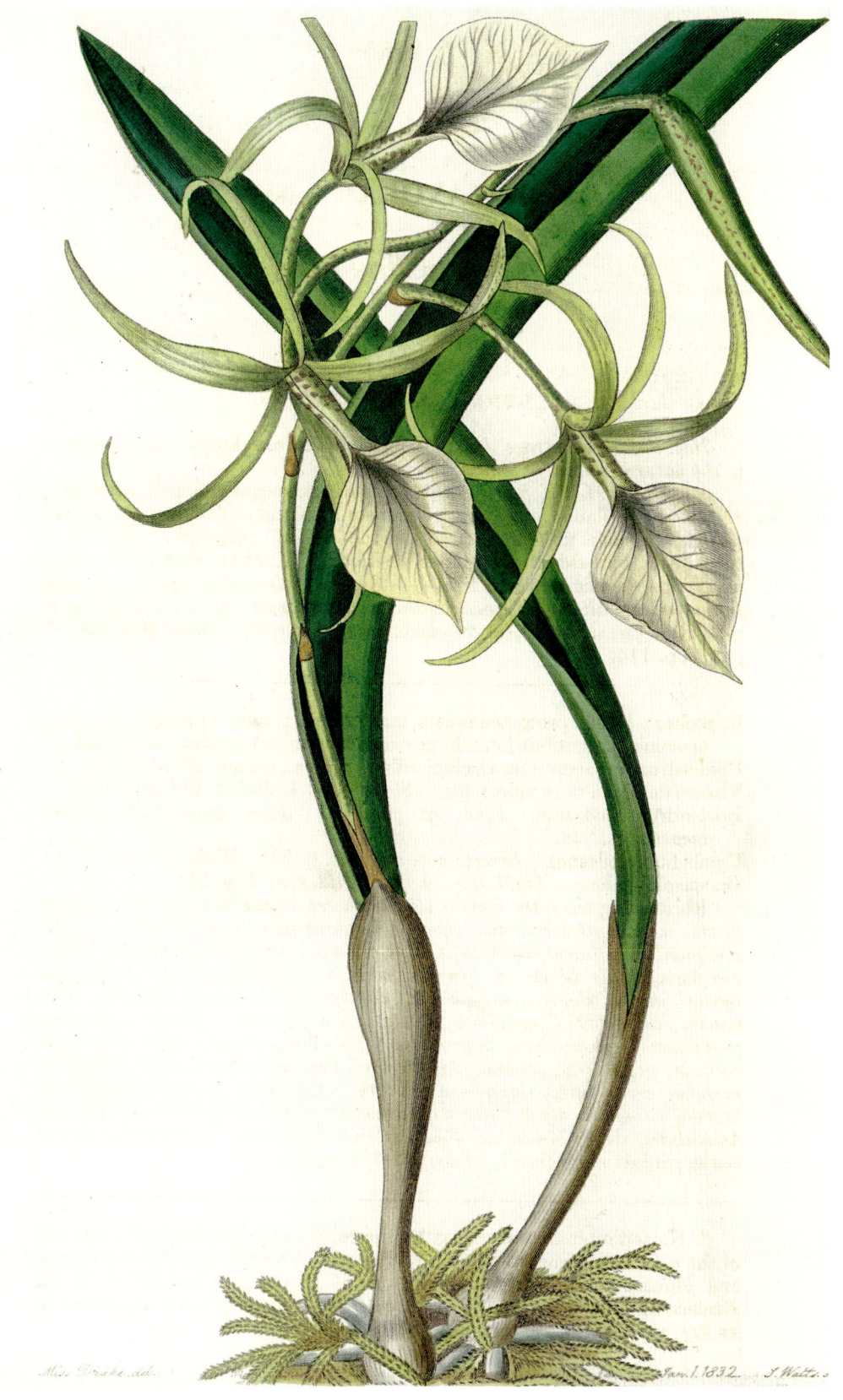

Jan. 1. 1832. S. Watts.

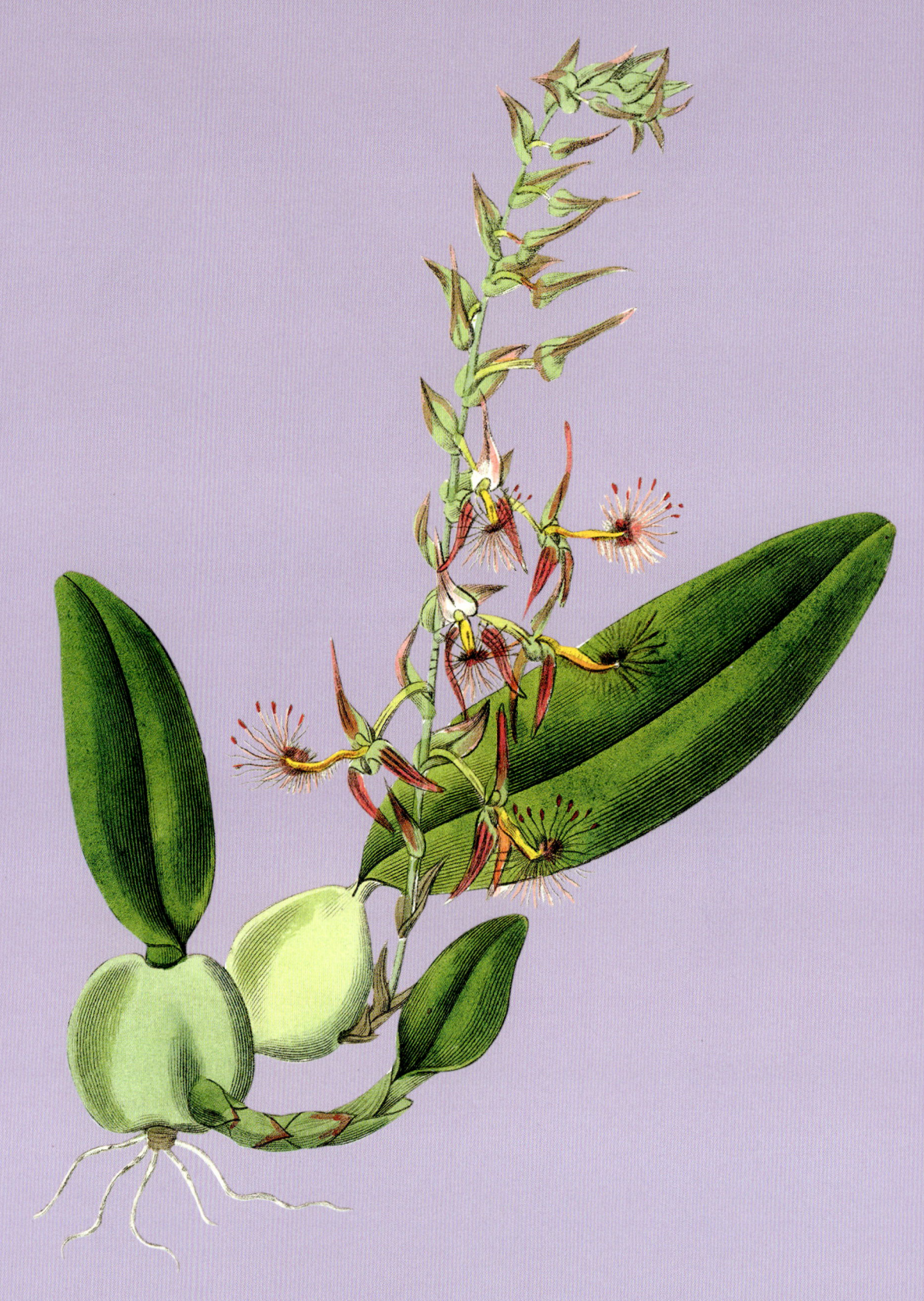

BEARDED BULBOPHYLLUM
BULBOPHYLLUM BARBIGERUM

Opposite: Miss Sarah Drake's fine illustration of the Loddiges' plant of *Bulbophyllum barbigerum drawn* for *Edwards' Botanical Register* in 1837 which accompanied John Lindley's original description of the species (see page 25).

Right: *Bulbophyllum barbigerum* flowered at Kew, from a plant donated by Loddiges, who had imported it from Sierra Leone, and drawn by Walter Hood Fitch for *Curtis's Botanical Magazine*, 1861.

*B*ulbophyllum is perhaps the largest genus in the orchid family, and is estimated to contain over 2,500 species, with more being described every year. It is a pantropical genus that occurs in Asia, Australasia, Africa, Madagascar and the Americas, but the majority of the species are found in tropical and subtropical Asia. *Bulbophyllum* species are epiphytes that grow on trees or lithophytes that grow on rocks. They have a distinctive habit, usually with a chain of one-noded egg-shaped to cigar-shaped one- or two-leaved pseudobulbs borne on a short to long rhizome. Thus some form clumps while others extend along branches or stems. These plants can form extensive colonies in suitable habitats. The inflorescence can be very varied, ranging from one-flowered to many-flowered racemes or false umbels, the latter resembling daisies when in flower.

Bulbophyllum barbigerum, which is one of the many African species, is a distinctive epiphytic orchid found across tropical Africa from Sierra Leone to the Central African Republic and Zaire. It is distinctive in having discoid one-leaved pseudobulbs and a spreading to erect raceme of small, deep purple, somewhat fly- or gnat-like flowers characterized by a highly motile slender lip with a dense tuft of long deep purple hairs at its tip. In a breeze the lip moves rapidly, and this fluttering is thought to attract flies. The visiting insect picks up the pollen

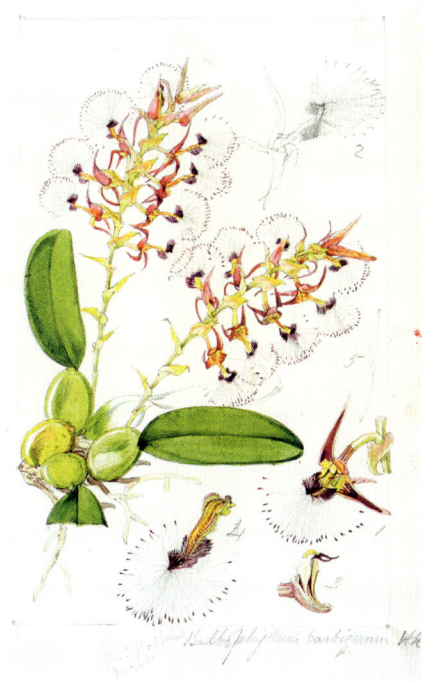

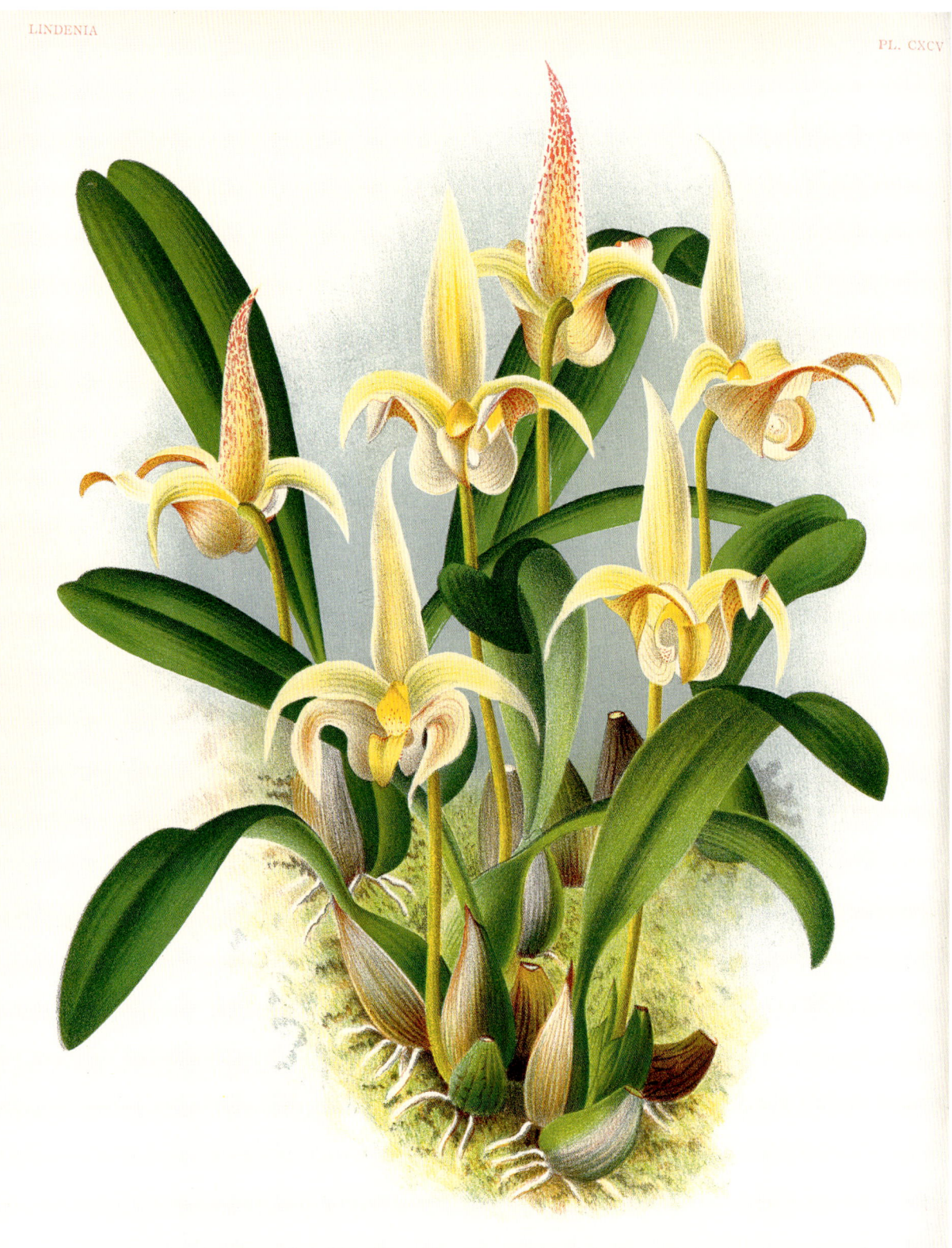

BOLBOPHYLLUM LOBBI LINDL.

1942

* BOLBOPHYLLUM barbigerum.

Bearded Bolbophyllum.

GYNANDRIA MONANDRIA.

Nat. Ord. ORCHIDACEÆ.

BOLBOPHYLLUM, Thouars. Sepala erecta, acuminata, subæqualia, lateralibus cum pede columnæ connatis et basi obliquis. *Petala* nana (rarissimè sepalis subæqualia). *Labellum* cum pede columnæ articulatum, unguiculatum, sæpiùs integrum et posticum. *Columna* nana, anticè bidentata et bicornis. *Anthera* 1-2-locularis. *Pollinia* 4, libera, valdè inæqualia, nunc in uno connata, nunc per paria cohærentia, altero cujusvis paris minuto lobuliformi.—— Herbæ *epiphytæ*, rhizomate repente *pseudobulbifero*. Folia coriacea, avenia. Racemi *radicales*. Lindl. Gen. & Sp. Orch. p. 47.

B. *barbigerum*; pseudobulbis lenticularibus, foliis solitariis racemo erecto brevioribus, bracteis ovatis amplexicaulibus ovario subæqualibus, sepalis lineari-lanceolatis acuminatis, petalis subulatis columnâ brevioribus, labello lineari-lanceolato acuminato villoso apice stuposo-barbato.

A most curious plant introduced from Sierra Leone, by Messrs. Loddiges, with whom it flowered in June 1836. It grows pretty freely under the hot damp system of cultivating epiphytes.

That a drawing is altogether incapable of representing so strange a conformation as exists in this species, will be evident in the course of the following description. The pseudo-bulbs are small, lenticular, very pale green bodies, from one edge of which springs an oblong, firm, smooth, veinless leaf. From the opposite edge of the pseudo-bulb there rises a raceme of flowers, about six inches long, the base of which is protected by brown, narrow, imbricated scales. The number of flowers in each raceme is from 15

* From βολβος a bulb, and φυλλον a leaf, in allusion to the leaves universally arising from a bulb-like stem or pseudo-bulb.

to 20. The bracts are, for the size of the flowers, rather large, broad, ovate, a little stem-clasping, very pale green, and stained with crimson at the points. The three sepals are narrow and taper to a point, pale green externally, dull chocolate brown in the inside (*fig. 2. a. a. a.*). The petals are minute, slender-pointed scales, shorter than the column, and not discoverable without disturbing the sepals. The column is dwarf, and terminated in part by two long curved horns (*fig. 1. a. a.*, and *fig. 2. c.*). The anther is a little round lid, beautifully studded with crystalline points (*fig. 1.*). The lip (*fig. 2. b.*) is one of the most extraordinary organs known even among Orchidaceous plants; it is a long, narrow, flexuose, sharp-pointed body, closely covered with a yellow felt; just within its point there is a deep purple beard of exceedingly fine compact hairs; on the under side, at a little distance from the point of the lip, is another such beard; and besides these there is, at the end of the lip, a brush consisting of very long, purple threads, so excessively delicate, that the slightest disturbance of the air sets them in motion, when they wave gently to and fro, like a tuft of threads cut from a spider's web; of the last mentioned hairs some are of the same thickness throughout, others terminate in an oblong club, so that when the hairs are waving in the air, and I do not know that they ever are at rest, a part float along gracefully and slowly, while the others are impelled by the weight of their glandular extremities to a more rapid oscillation.

Nor is this all; the lip itself, with its yellow felt, its two beards, and its long purple brushes, is articulated with the column by such a very slight joint, that to breathe upon it is sufficient to produce a rocking movement, so conspicuous and protracted, that one is really tempted to believe that there must be something of an animal nature infused into this most unplant-like production.

Messrs. Loddiges possess another species, with similar habits.

John Lindley's original description of *Bulbophyllum barbigerum* in *Edwards' Botanical Register*, 1837

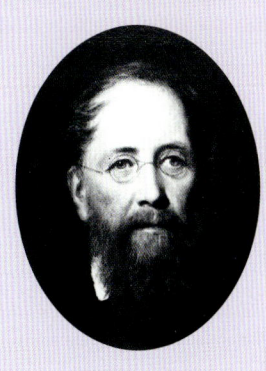

John Lindley (1799–1865) was Professor of Botany at King's College, London and Assistant secretary (later Secretary) of the Royal Horticultural Society. In the latter role he had first access to plants collected around the world by the Society's plant collectors. His orchid herbarium, including nearly 2,000 types, came to Kew after his death, while his main herbarium was purchased by Cambridge University. Lindley's description of *Bulbophyllum barbigerum* was published in *Edwards' Botanical Register*, a journal that he wrote and edited.

masses when it comes into close contact with the flower. With the pollen masses now attached to its thorax, the fly can visit and then pollinate another flower of the same species.

This pretty orchid was an early introduction (in 1836) into cultivation from Sierra Leone in West Africa by the orchid nursery of Loddiges of Hackney, London. It was described in the following year by John Lindley, the "father of orchidology", in *Edwards' Botanical Register*.

The French explorer and botanist Louis-Marie Aubert du Petit Thouars established the genus *Bulbophyllum* in 1822 based upon material from Madagascar and the Mascarene Islands. Since then, species of the genus have been found throughout the tropics and subtropics of Africa, Asia, Australia and the Americas, and into the Pacific Islands as far east as Tahiti. Some of the showiest species are found in Asia and the Malay Archipelago. *Bulbophyllum lobbii* from the Malay Peninsula and the western Malay Archipelago has a solitary large flower borne on a long flower stalk. Even larger flowers are found in the remarkable species *B. echinolabium*, from Sulawesi, which has a long inflorescence that produces several spectacular flowers in succession.

Many bulbophyllums are fly pollinated, and for this reason some of them have extremely unpleasant-smelling flowers. When in flower, the New Guinea species *B. macrobulbum*, *B. fletcherianum* and *B. phalaenopsis* can be detected dozens of metres away, as their flowers smell of decaying flesh. These species are also notable for their large pseudobulbs and for their strap-like, leathery leaves, which in the latter two species can reach up to 1 m (3 ft) in length, and are the largest leaves in the genus. The Bornean species *B. beccarii* has similarly foul-smelling pungent flowers. The eminent botanical artist Matilda Smith was asked to illustrate it for *Curtis's Botanical Magazine* when it first flowered at Kew more than a century ago, but she refused to enter the glasshouse because of the stench emanating from within. She eventually painted the orchid while sitting outside the glasshouse.

In contrast to these large-flowered species, the genus *Bulbophyllum* also contains some of the smallest orchids. A flowering growth of the Australian miniature orchid, aptly named *B. minutissimum*, is smaller than a fingernail. In the wild it usually grows in colonies covering rocks in the mountains of eastern Australia.

For many growers, the stars of the genus are found in section *Cirrhopetalum*, long considered to be a separate genus. Species such as *B. longiflorum*, *B. rothschildianum*, *B. medusae* and *B. mastersianum* bear their flowers in a false umbel at the apex of a long slender flower stalk, in an arrangement that somewhat resembles a daisy. The flowers of these species are also distinguished by their very long and partly connate lateral sepals, which are many times longer than the dorsal sepal. *Bulbophyllum longiflorum* has a remarkable distributional range, being found in tropical Africa, Madagascar, tropical Asia, the Malay Archipelago, tropical eastern Australia, New Guinea and the Pacific islands.

Bulbophyllum species new to science continue to be described at a rate of up to 50 a year, which suggests that there may be many more.

Opposite: *Bulbophyllum weberi* (mistakenly as *Cirropetalum thouarsii*) drawn by Walter Hood Fitch for *Curtis's Botanical Magazine* in 1846.

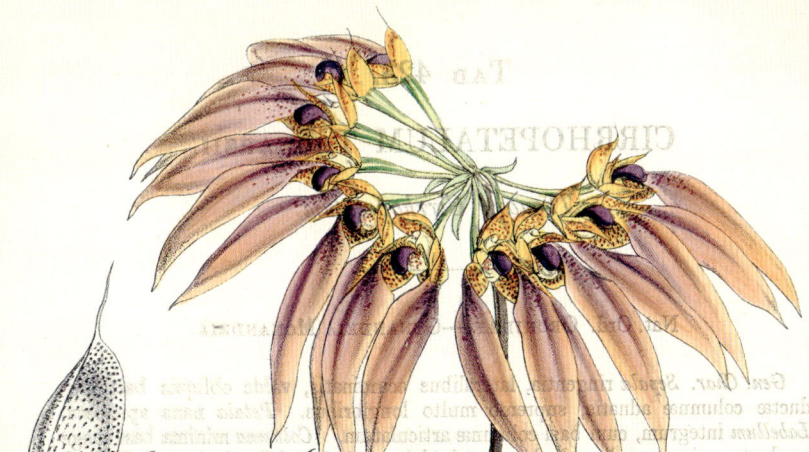

1

2

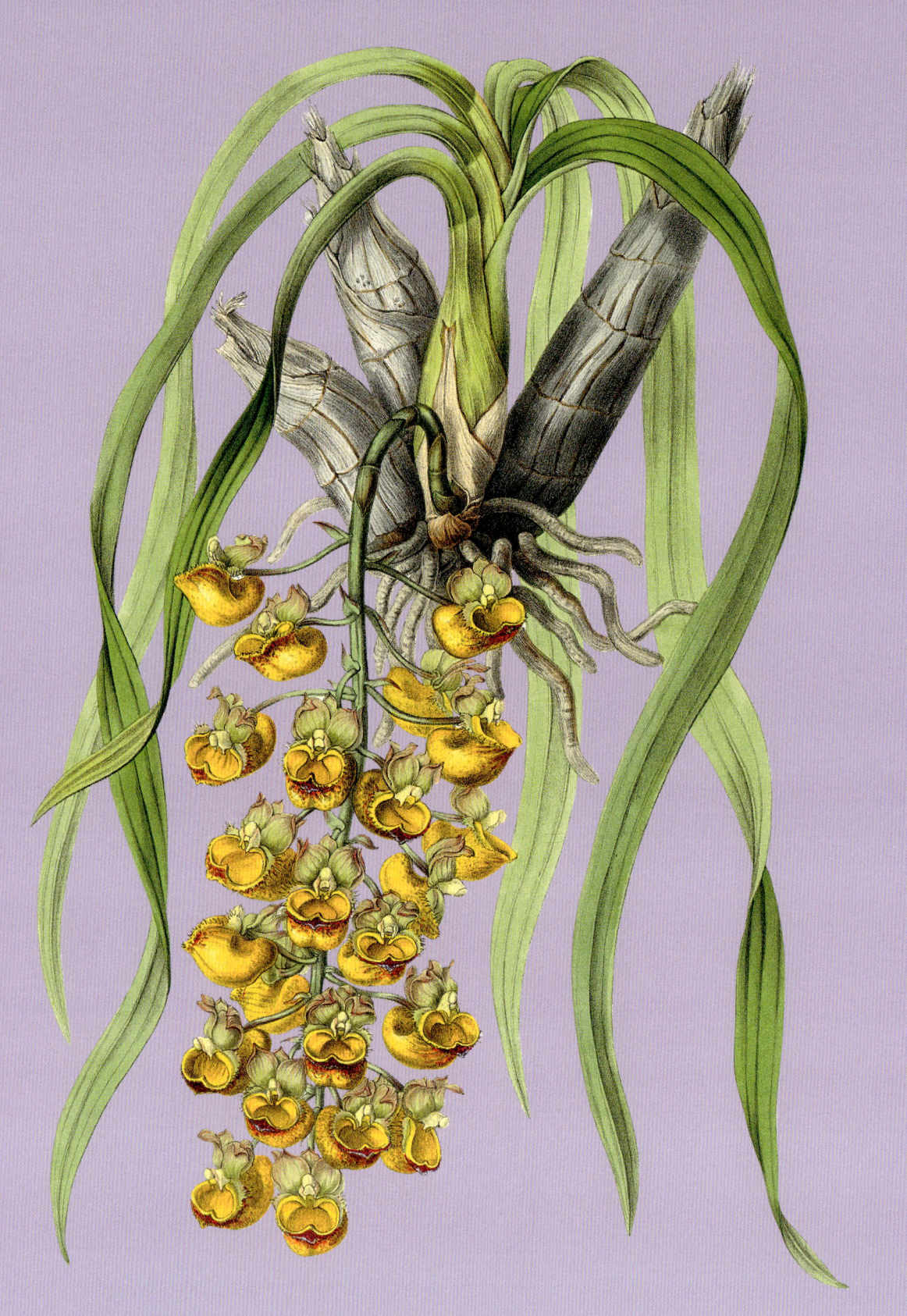

CATASETUM
CATASETUM SPP.

The genus *Catasetum* is interesting to an unusual degree in several respects. The separation of the sexes is unknown amongst other orchids, except perhaps in the allied genus *Cycnoches*. In *Catasetum* we have three sexual forms, generally borne on separate plants, but sometimes mingled together on the same plant; and these three forms are wonderfully different from one another, much more different than, for instance, a peacock from a peahen. ... This genus is still more interesting in its manner of fertilisation.

Charles Darwin,
On the various contrivances by which ... orchids are fertilised by insects (1862)

Charles Darwin's interest in orchids and their fertilization began with observations on the chalk hillside near his house at Downe in Kent, but his studies soon expanded to include tropical orchids that, at the time, were being cultivated in increasing numbers in English greenhouses. His extensive network of contacts allowed him to solicit flowers of tropical species as they bloomed, with small parcels arriving regularly at his home for him to dissect and ponder their methods of reproduction. He received flowers of several species of *Catasetum*, and devoted a 30-page chapter of his book to their morphology and pollination.

As noted in the quote above, Darwin recognized that *Catasetum* flowers came in three distinct forms – male, female and hermaphrodite. Each of these forms looked quite different from the others, to the extent that earlier botanists had believed that each belonged not only to a distinct species but also to one of three distinct genera, named *Catasetum*, *Monacanthus* and *Myanthus*, respectively. All are now placed in *Catasetum*, the first of these genera to be described. Darwin's examination of these flowers confirmed earlier observations by John Lindley, and field observations by Dr Crüger in Trinidad and Robert Schomburgk in British Guyana, that the male flowers have an anther but the stigma is not functional, whereas the female flowers have a functional stigma but lack an

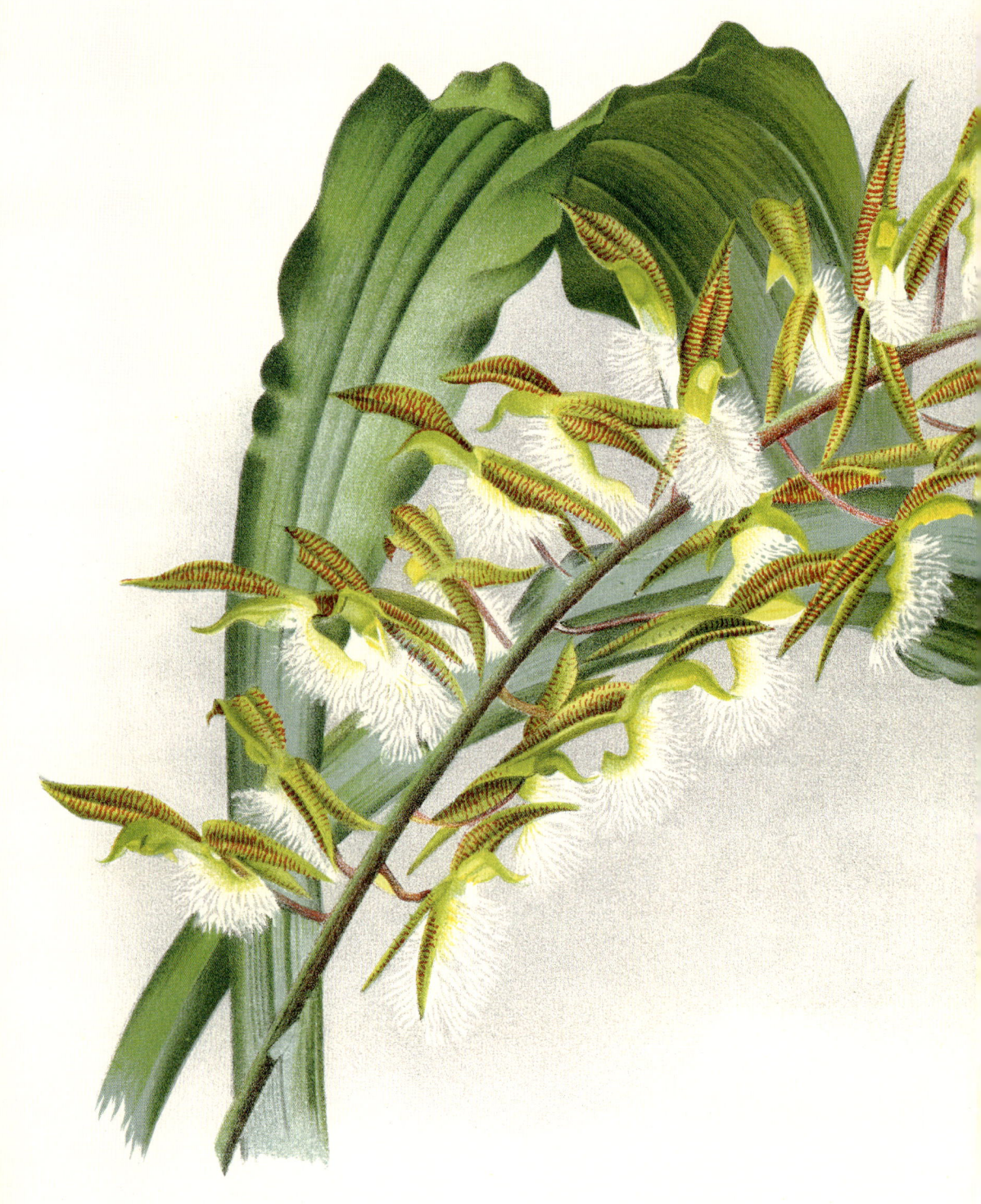

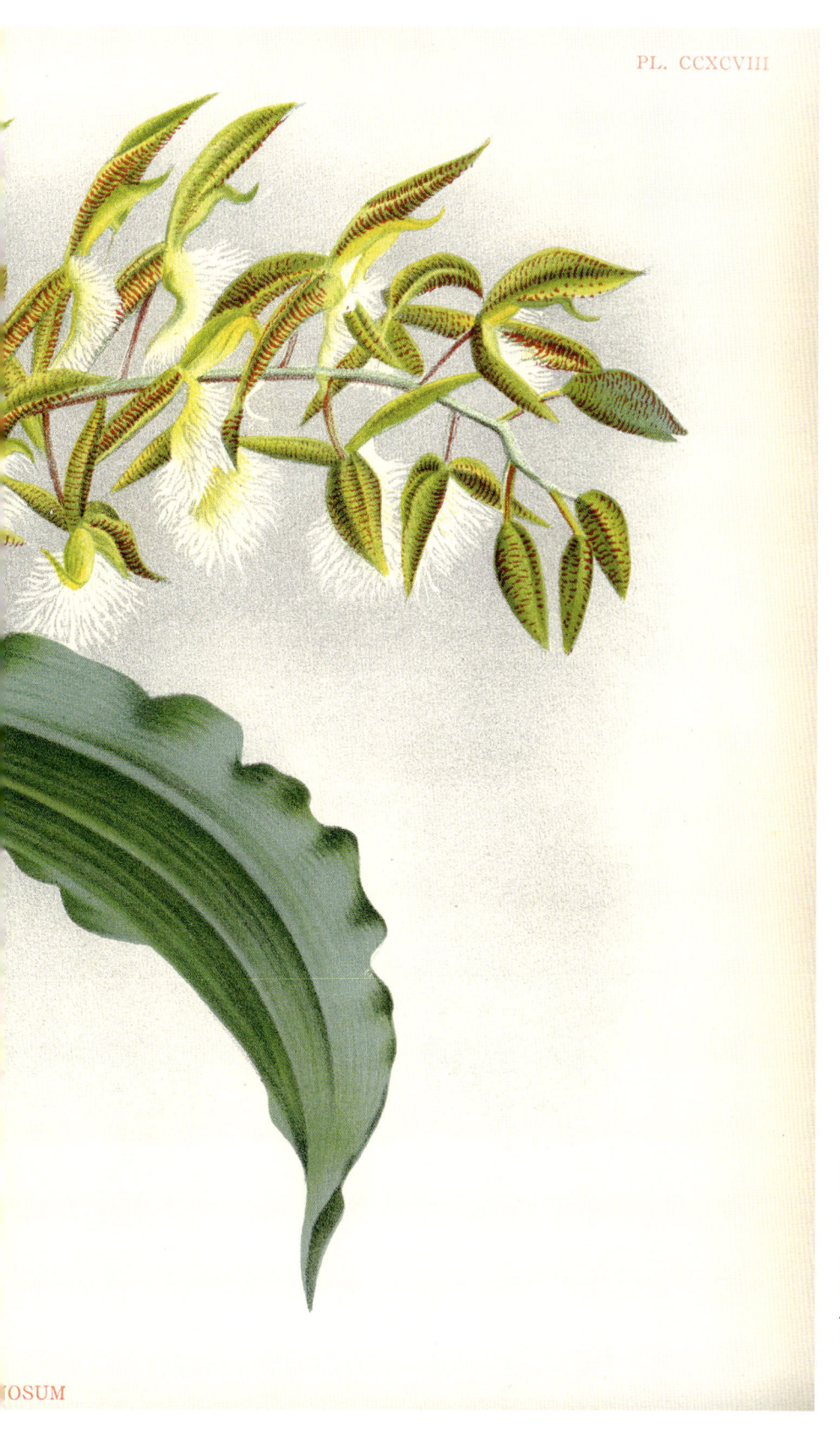

OSUM

Left: A male
inflorescence of
Catasetum barbatum
var. *spinosum*
drawn by Pieter de
Pannemaeker for
J. J. Linden, *Lindenia:
Iconographie des
Orchidées*, 1891.

Fig. XXVIII.

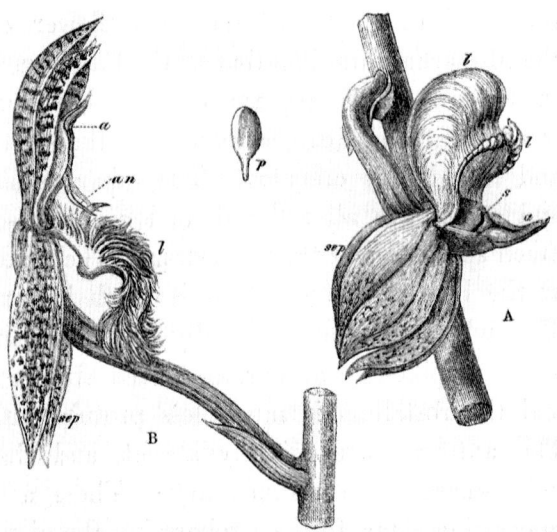

MYANTHUS BARBATUS.   MONACHANTHUS VIRIDIS.

a. anther.
an. antennæ.
l. labellum.

p. pollen-mass, rudimentary.
s. stigmatic cleft.
sep. two lower sepals.

A. Side view of Monachanthus viridis in its natural position.
    (The shading in both drawings has been added from
    M. Reiss' drawing in the ' Linnæan Transactions.')
B. Side view of Myanthus barbatus in its natural position.

With respect to Monachanthus viridis and Myanthus barbatus, the President and officers of the Linnæan Society have kindly permitted me to examine the spike bearing these two flowers, preserved in spirits, and sent home

Myanthus barbatus and _Monacanthus viridis_ by George Sowerby

George Sowerby's detailed woodcuts of _Myanthus barbatus_ and _Monacanthus viridis_ for Charles Darwin's _On the various contrivances by which British and foreign orchids are fertilised_ (1862). Darwin realized that these were the male and female flowers respectively of the orchid now known as _Catasetum barbatum_.

anther. The male flowers also often have a complex lip with a sticky basal cavity and marginal lobes or fringes, whereas the lip of the female flowers is simpler and often deeply concave. Furthermore, Darwin realized that the male flowers possess an elaborate trigger mechanism in the form of two long slender tapering extensions of the base of the column that, when touched, allow the explosive release of the pollen masses, which are under tension in the anther. The pollen masses are attached by a thin strap of tissue to a sticky basal blob, which cements them on to the body of any bee that touches the trigger. If that bee then visits a female flower, the pollen masses will be transferred to the stigma of the flower,

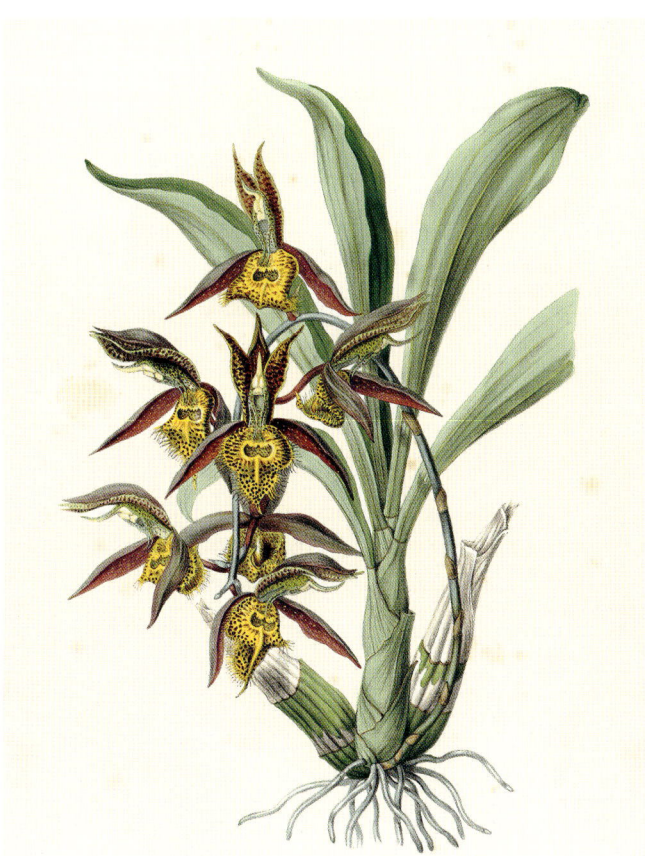

and fertilization will occur as a result.

The female flowers are usually borne in short erect inflorescences, whereas the showier male flowers are borne on arching or pendent inflorescences. The female flowers are less frequently seen than the male ones, and in some species only male or female inflorescences have been described. Of course, further study occasionally showed the female flowers to correspond to male ones given a different name. Darwin studied several species of *Catasetum*, namely *C. barbatum, C. saccatum, C. tabulare, C. tridentatum* (= *C. macrocarpum*), *C. callosum* and *C. planiceps.*

The generic name *Catasetum* refers to the trigger antennae (from the Greek words *kata*, meaning "downward", and *seta*, meaning "bristle"). The genus was established by the German botanist Carl Sigismund Kunth (1788–1850) based upon *Catasetum macrocarpum,* a name coined but not published by the French botanist Achille Richard. Kunth achieved lasting fame for publishing the tropical American botanical discoveries of Alexander von Humboldt and Aimé Bonpland, made during their pioneering expedition between 1799 and 1804. Today, we know that the genus comprises 178 species with a distribution in Mexico and throughout Central and tropical South America.

Catasetum barbatum was collected by John Henchman along the Mazaruni River in British Guyana (now Guiana) and introduced by him into cultivation. It flowered for the first time in 1835, and was described in the same year by John Lindley as *Myanthus barbatus.* However, in 1844, Lindley transferred it to the present genus when he realized that *Catasetum* species had dissimilar male and

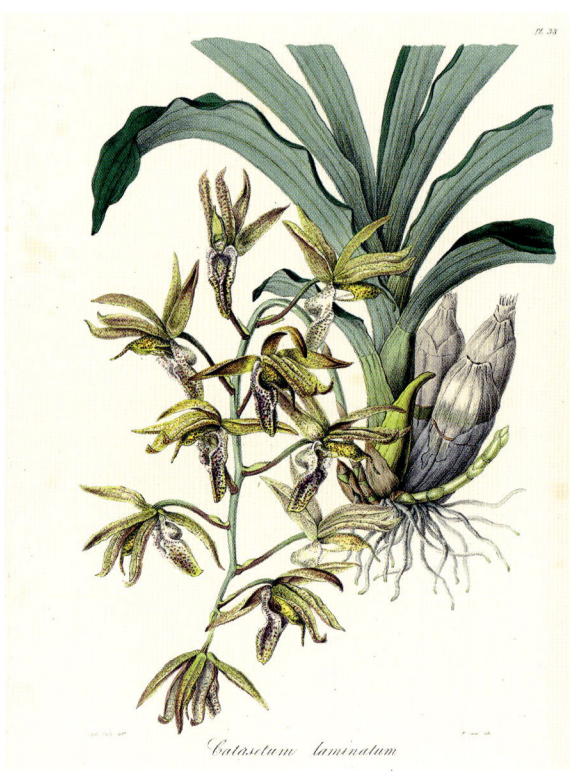

Catasetum laminatum

female flowers. This species is widespread throughout the Guianas, Amazonian Brazil, Colombia and Venezuela, usually growing as an epiphyte, but occasionally growing terrestrially in rainforest at altitudes below 300 m (1,000 ft).

Some *Catasetum* species have particularly beautiful male flowers. The Venezuelan species, *C. pileatum*, bears large white, pale yellow or pale greenish male flowers with an almost circular lip. Characteristically the antennae at the base of its column are crossed rather than parallel. Some forms of *C. pileatum* have flowers heavily marked with reddish-purple spots.

Catasetum species fall into three groups, namely those with parallel antennae at the column base (such as *C. barbatum*), those with crossed antennae (such as *C. saccatum*) and those with vestigial antennae (such as *C. discolor* and *C. tabulare*).

Many beautiful illustrations have been made of various *Catasetum* species, and among the finest are those by Sarah Drake of *C. laminatum*, *C. longifolium* and *C. saccatum* for Lindley's *Sertum Orchidaceum* (1840).

From a horticultural point of view, *Catasetum* flowers do not last long but are highly scented (to attract pollinating bees). However, their artificial hybrids do have longer-lasting flowers, and have begun to gain in popularity.

Clowesia species were until recently also included in the genus *Catasetum*, but differ in having perfect (hermaphrodite) flowers. *Clowesia rosea* and *C. russelliana* are common in cultivation, as is their artificial hybrid, which is particularly easy to grow and flower.

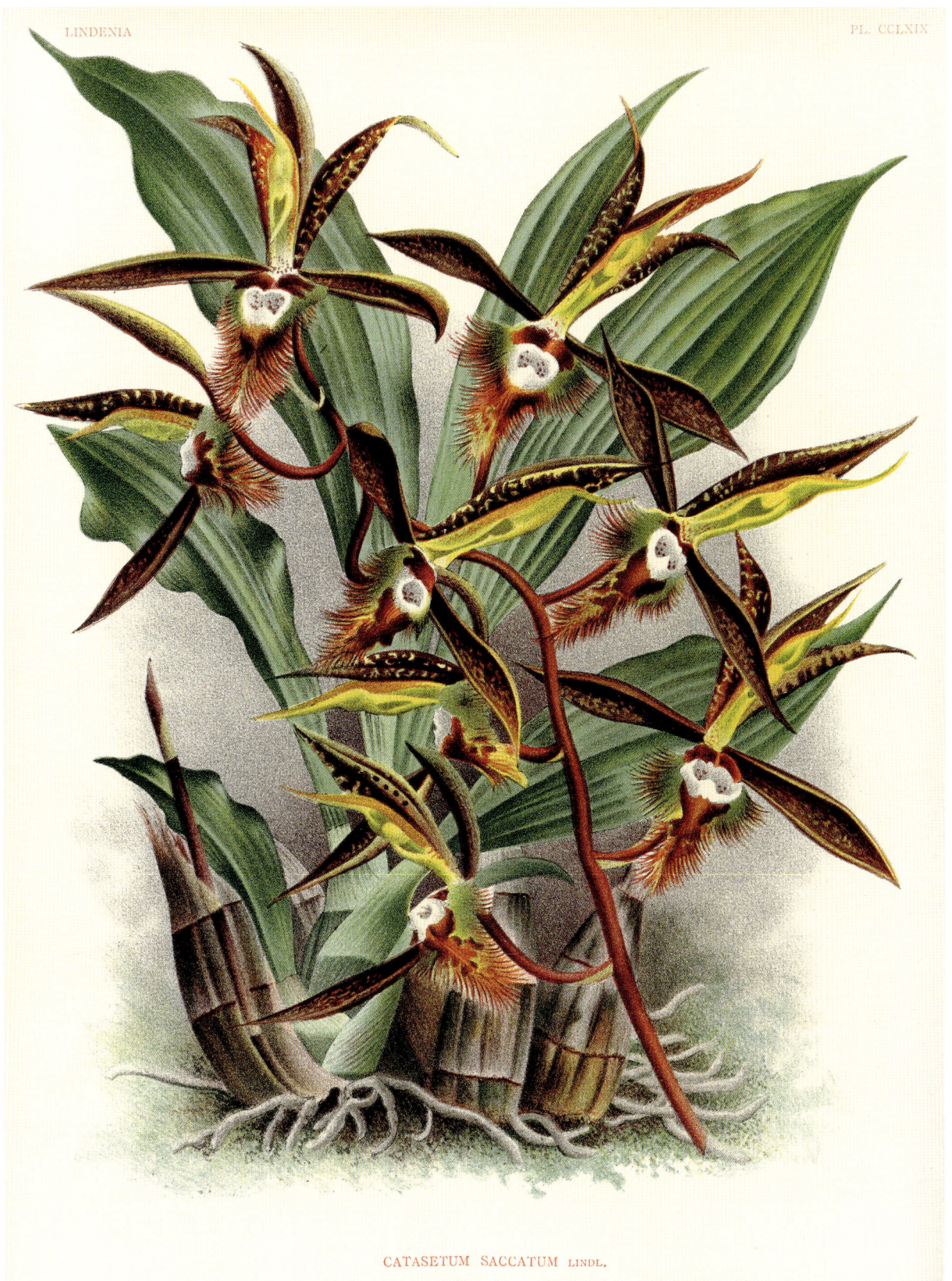

CATASETUM SACCATUM LINDL.

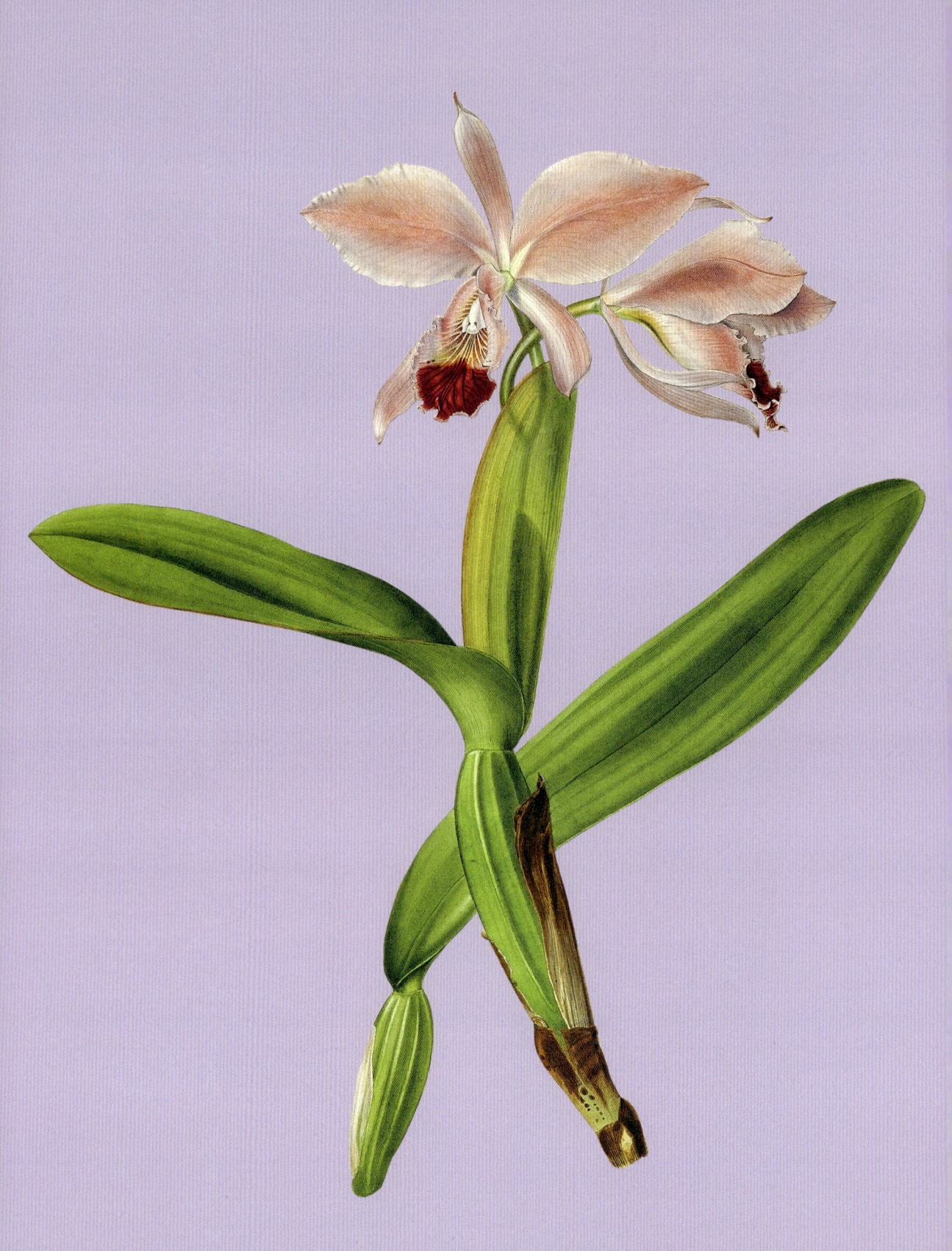

RUBY-LIPPED CATTLEYA
CATTLEYA LABIATA

Opposite: The original illustration of *Cattleya labiata* which accompanied John Lindley's description of the genus and species in his *Collectanea Botanica* or *Figures and Botanical Illustrations of Rare and Curious Exotic Plants*, 1821.

In June 1817, the naturalist William Swainson sent a consignment of "mosses and parasites" from Pernambuco in Brazil to William Hooker, then Professor of Botany at the University of Brazil. Hooker sent part of the consignment on to William Cattley, a wealthy English merchant and patron of horticulture with a penchant for exotic plants. Cattley mounted the orchid and it flowered in the November of the same year, producing large, spectacular lilac-pink flowers with a dark purple-marked lip. He wrote of "The most splendid, perhaps, of all Orchidaceous plants, which blossomed for the first time in Britain in the stove [glasshouse] of my garden in Suffolk, during 1818, the plant having been sent to me by Mr W Swainson, during his visit to Brazil." John Lindley, then a young man and writing *Collectanea Botanica* (1821), an account of Cattley's tropical plant collection, described it as *Cattleya labiata*, naming the genus for his patron. Later, Swainson travelled to Rio de Janeiro and from there returned to England with a much larger batch of plants and animals (which did not include *C. labiata*). This second shipment led to confusion about the origin of the original plants, thought to have been imported from Rio de Janeiro.

In 1836, William Gardner caused further confusion about the origin of *C. labiata* when he found *C. lobata* growing on large rocks in Rio de Janeiro and thought that he had rediscovered *C. labiata*. The latter had long been thought to be extinct until this magnificent orchid was rediscovered in Pernambuco in 1889 in a batch of 50 plants sent to M. Moreau, an amateur orchid grower in Paris. Sadly, today the "Mata Atlantica" forests of the eastern seaboard of Brazil are reduced to less than 5 per cent of their former extent, and their flora is greatly endangered.

Surprisingly, *C. labiata*, although the type of the genus, was not the first *Cattleya* species to be described. *C. forbesii* was the first species of the genus to be identified, when Frei Mariano Conceição Vellozo described it in 1790 as *Epidendrum pauper* in his *Florae Fluminensis* (about the flora of Rio). Due to lack of funds, this book was not published until 1825.

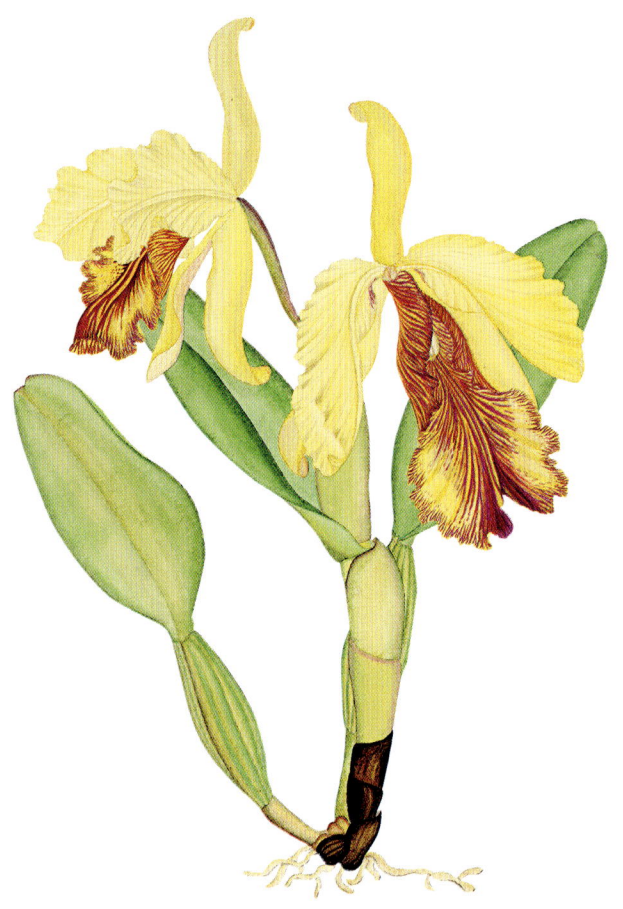

Above: The Colombian *Cattleya aurea*, a close ally of the Costa Rican *Cattleya dowiana*. These two species are the only large-flowered species with yellow sepals and petals.

Cattleya loddigesii was the first *Cattleya* species to be introduced into cultivation, in 1812. Mr Shepherd, a gardener at the Liverpool Botanic Garden, had been sent the plant from Rio de Janeiro by a Mr Woodeford. It thrived but remained undescribed until 1819, when Loddiges flowered it at their famous nursery in Hackney, London. It was illustrated for Loddiges' *The Botanical Cabinet*, where it was described as *Epidendrum violaceum* (a name that was never transferred to *Cattleya*).

Cattleya labiata is a member of the select group of beautiful tropical orchids that led to a rapid rise in the popularity of orchid growing in Europe – a hobby which in some respects paralleled the "tulip mania" that had occurred in the Netherlands a century earlier. The Loddiges establishment was the first English nursery to specialize in tropical orchids, but it was rapidly followed by many others, notably those of Low & Co. of Upper Clapton, Veitch & Sons of Exeter and Chelsea, Sander & Sons of St Albans and Bruges, and the Brussels nursery of Jean Linden, a former orchid hunter in tropical South America. These nurseries employed orchid hunters who were sent to the tropics to find novelties, often with astounding success. Unfortunately, the best localities proved to be magnets for collectors, who stripped them of many thousands of plants.

Brazil has also yielded many other large-flowered *Cattleya* species, namely *C. aclandiae*, *C. amethystoglossa*, *C. guttata*, *C. harrisoniana*, *C. leopoldii*, *C. schilleriana*, *C. violacea* and *C. wallisii*. However, collectors hit the jackpot in the Andes of Venezuela, Colombia, Ecuador and Peru and in Costa Rica. Here they found many *C. labiata* allies, including the Costa Rican *C. dowiana* and the similar Colombian *C. aurea*, both having golden-yellow flowers with a lip veined and marked with royal purple, as well as *C. mossiae*, *C. lueddemanniana*, *C. percivaliana*, *C. lawrenceana*, *C. jenmannii*, *C. trianae*, *C. quadricolor*, *C. mendelii*, *C. gaskelliana* and *C. schroderae*, all of which had pink or purple flowers.

Nowadays, all *Sophronitis* species and many Brazilian *Laelia* species, both distinguished from *Cattleya* by the fact that they have eight rather than four pollinia in their anther, have been added to the genus *Cattleya*. In addition, *Sophronitis* had a distinctive habit and flower colour, usually red or bright orange.

Cattleya species hybridize freely with each other and also with species of *Brassavola*, *Epidendrum*, *Laelia* and *Rhyncholaelia*. They were first successfully hybridized in cultivation in the late nineteenth century, and have gone on to produce a vast array of artificial hybrids. This rich palette of species formed the basis of many of the large-flowered hybrids that are so popular today. In particular, *Cattleya* (formerly *Sophronitis*) *coccinea*, although it is a small plant, has bright orange-red flowers and, when hybridized with the large-flowered species, introduces its spectacular colour to its progeny.

Below: *Cattleya labiata* drawn by John Day, 1882.

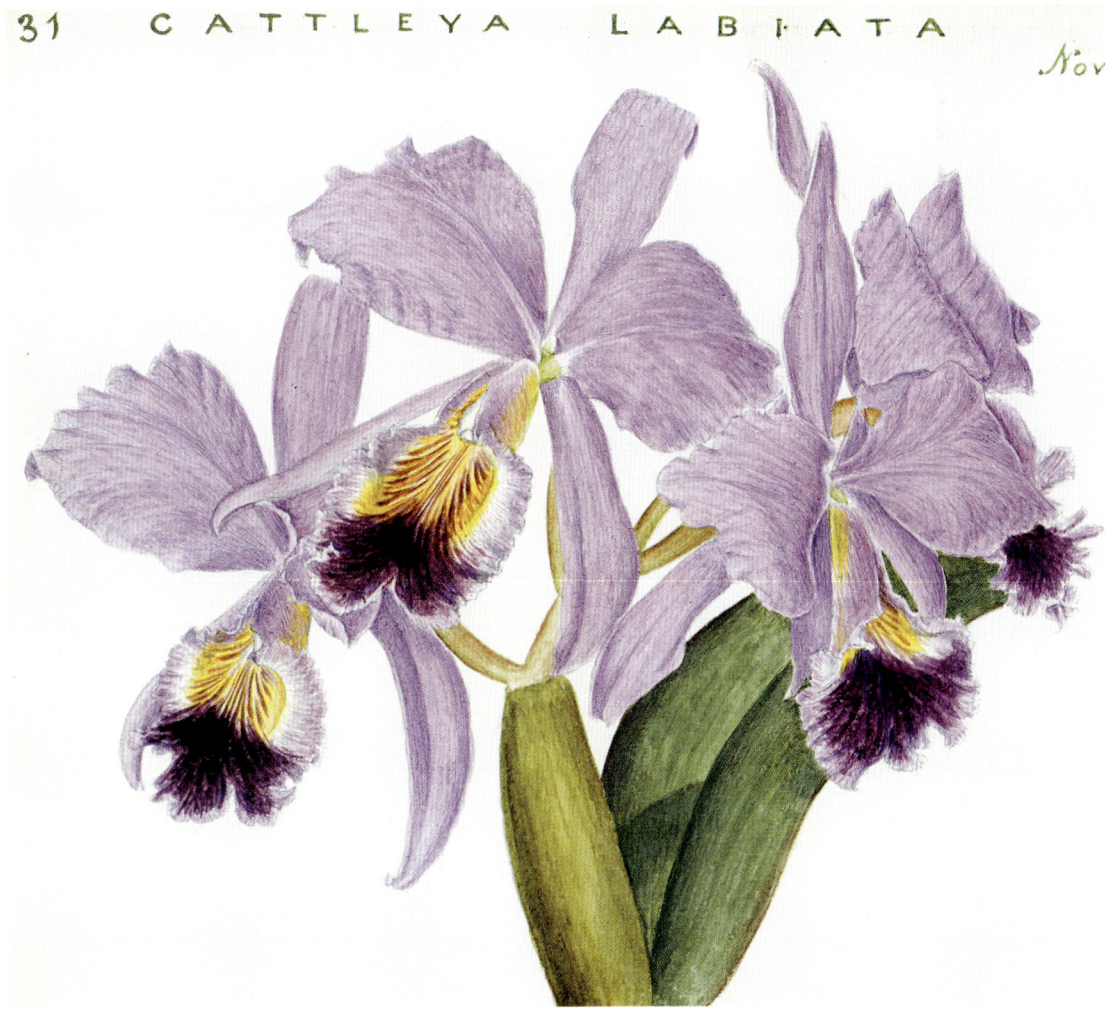

31   C A T T L E Y A   L A B I A T A

Nov

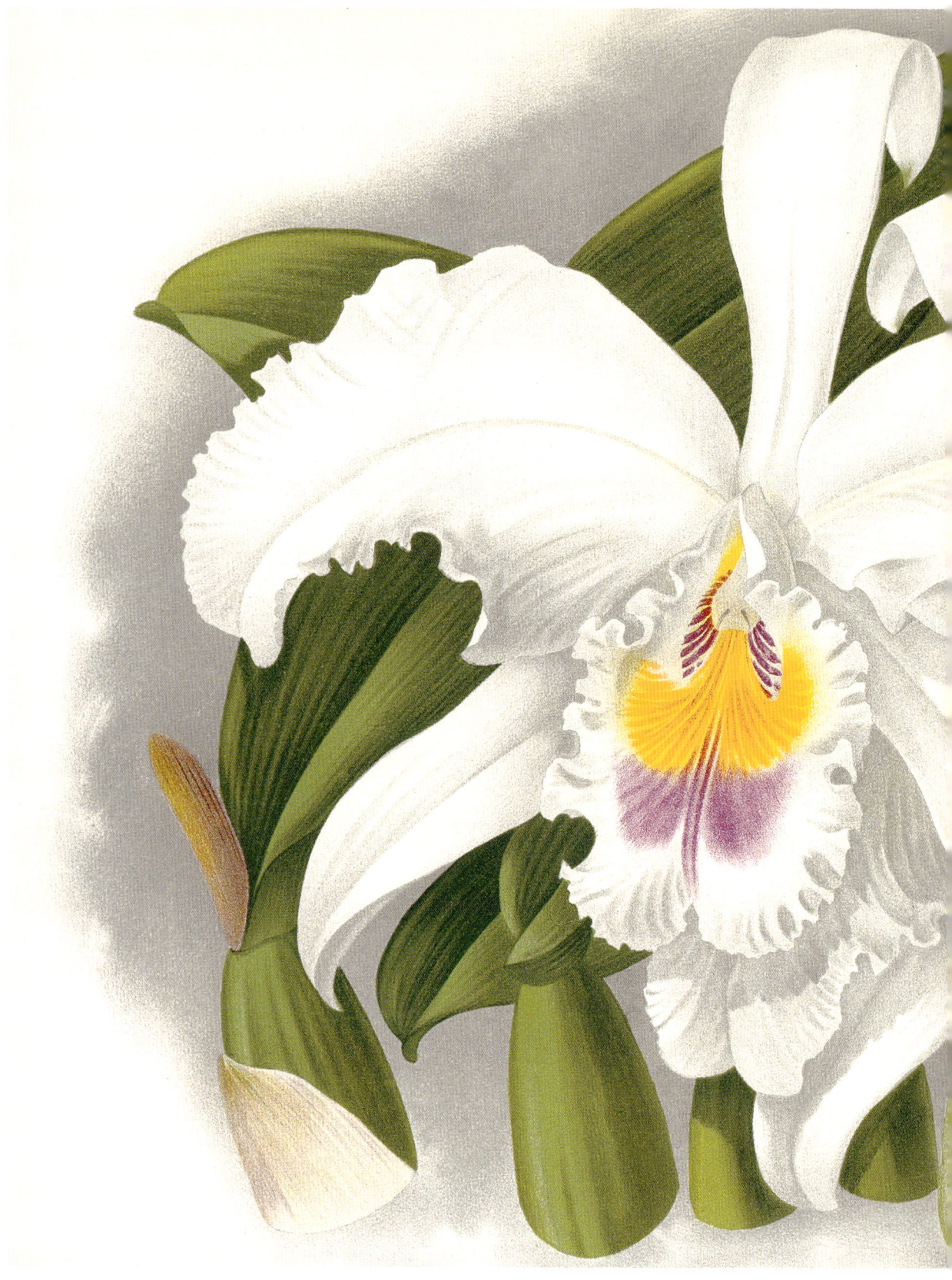

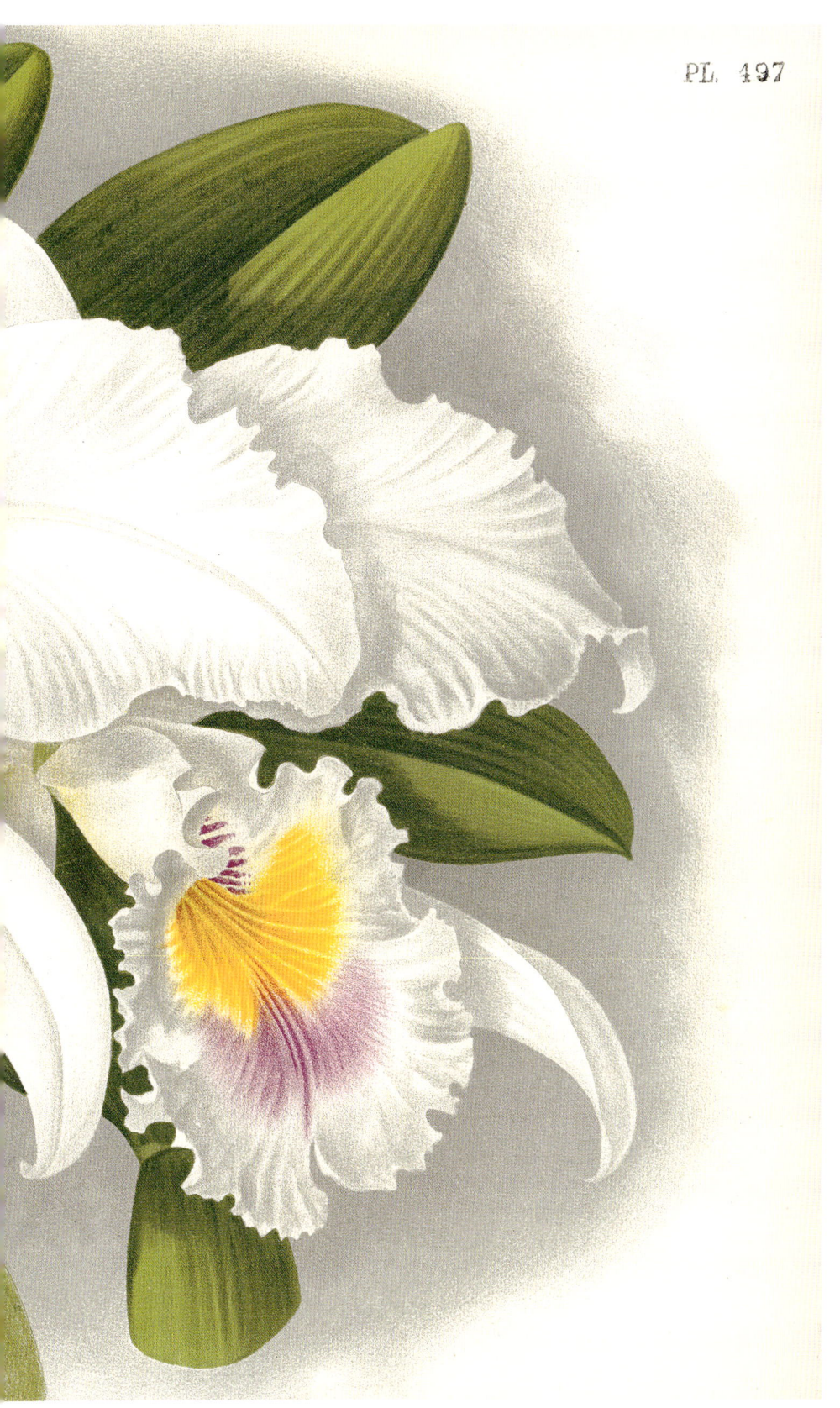

Left: A semi-alba
form of *Cattleya
labiata* var.
foleyana flowered
by Admiral Foley
of Fordingbridge,
Hampshire, and
drawn for R. Warner
and B. S. Williams,
The Orchid Album,
1893.

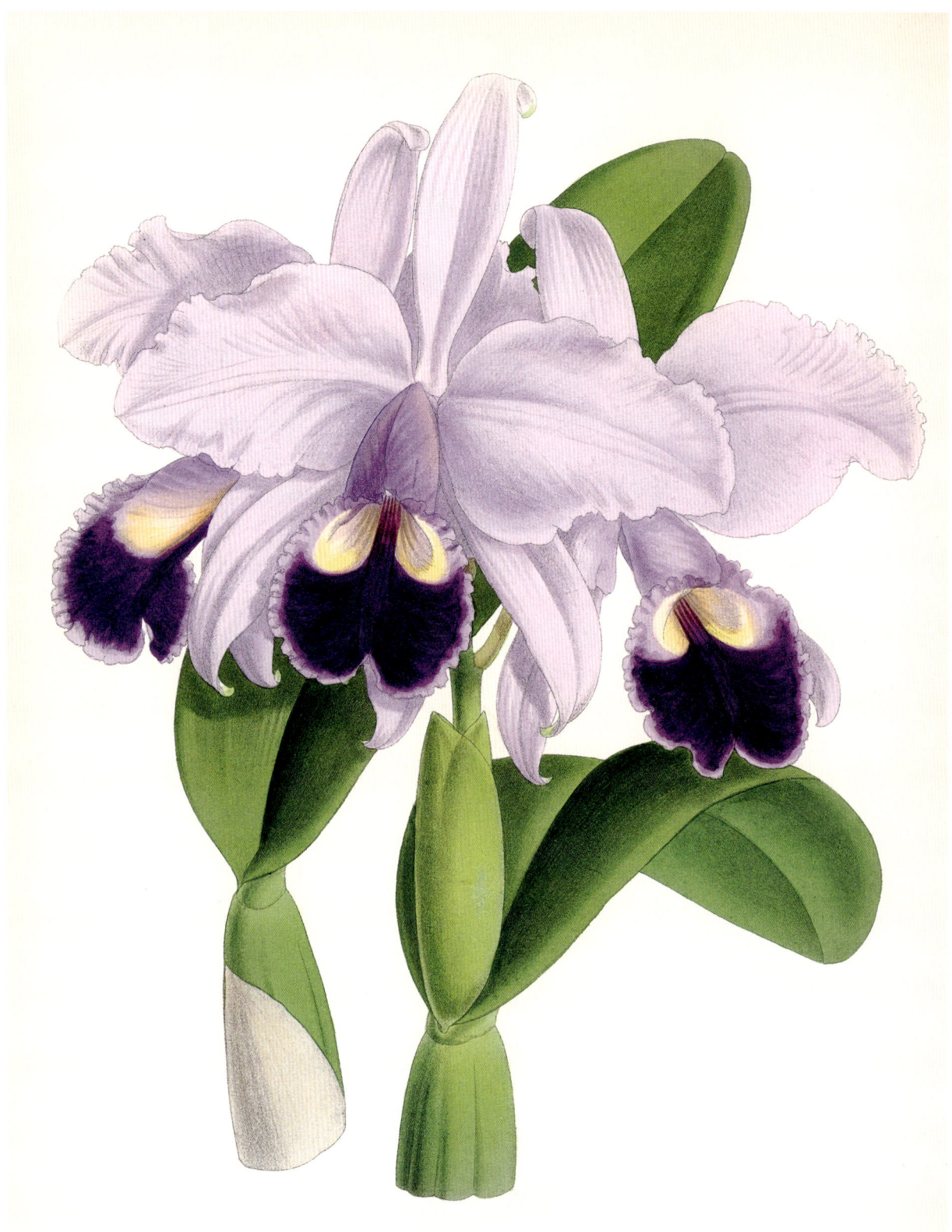

CATTLEYA LABIATA

Cattleianæ.

Tab. 33.

CATTLEYA LABIATA.

Nat. Ord. Orchideæ. Sect. 5. *Br.* Linn. Syst. Gynandria Monandria.

CATTLEYA. Perianthium resupinatum patens : laciniis subæqualibus. Columna libera semiteres, labello eroso cucullato amplexa. Anthera infrà-apicilaris, opercularis persistens, columnæ apice subulato supertecta 4-locularis : septis completis membranaceis marginatis. Massæ pollinis 4 lenticulares per pares filo elastico granulato in ipsis reflexo connexæ.—*Herbæ parasiticæ (Americæ æquinoctialis)* ; *bulbis fasciculatis* ; *foliis solitariis carnosis, enervibus* ; *floribus terminalibus geminis grandibus subodoris.*

Cattleya perianthii laciniis exterioribus lineari-lanceolatis acutis, quàm interiores 3-plò angustioribus, labello indiviso.

Descr. *Bulbi* fasciculati, epigæi, oblongi, suboctogoni, vestigiis folii primarii sphacelatis vestiti. *Folia* solitaria, lanceolata, retusa, plana, cartilaginea, enervia, atro-viridia, rubro marginata, ascendentia. *Spatha* duplex ; exterior maxima, foliorum ferè longitudine, acinaciformis, hinc fissa, colorata ; interior multoties minor. *Scapus* 1-2-florus, intra spatham inclusus, teres, glaber. *Flores* resupinati, suavissimè lilacini, odori. *Perianthii* patentis *laciniæ* 3 exteriores, lanceolatæ, acuminatæ, interiores patentes, ovato-lanceolatæ, margine crispæ, exterioribus multoties latiores. *Labellum* obovatum, cucullatum, carnosum, porrectum, limbi margine eroso, undulato, intùs pulcherrimè luteo et rubro venosum, versus apicem intensè purpureum. *Columna* directione labelli, libera, semiteres, clavata, alba, ultra cardinem antheræ posticè in apiculo in antheram incumbente elongata, anticè bicornis. *Anthera* gibba, 4-locularis, septis membranaceis, undulatis, completis ; in singulo loculo jacet massa pollinis una, lenticularis, coriacea, integra, per processum filiformem, granulatum, in ipsâ deflexum in clinandrio incumbens. *Gynizus* cavus, secernens, apice retuso, luteolo, deorsùm flexo ad antheram recipiendam. Rarò (vide fig.) è basi anteriore gynizi producitur processus subulatus enervis, versus apicem luteolum tendens.

This is another of the fine Orchideous plants that were collected with our *Oncidium barbatum* by Mr. Swainson in the Brasils, and sent by him to Dr. Hooker. Our drawing was made by Mr. Curtis from a specimen which flowered in Mr. Cattley's stove last November. Without exception, it is the handsomest species of the order we have ever seen alive : and we have on that account the greater pleasure in publishing it, as it has given us an opportunity of paying a compliment to a gentleman, whose ardour in the collection, and whose unrivalled success in the cultivation, of the difficult tribe of plants to which it belongs, have long since given him the strongest claims to such a distinction. The only other species of the genus with which we are acquainted, is one which has been published by Mr. Loddiges, with the name of *Epidendrum violaceum.* We propose to call it *Cattleya Loddigesii,* and to define it thus :—

Cattleya (*Loddigesii*) perianthii laciniis subæqualibus obtusis, labelli trilobi lobo medio sellæformi.

EPIDENDRUM VIOLACEUM. *Loddiges Bot. Cab.* 337.

The only genus with which it is necessary to compare *Cattleya,* is *Broughtonia* of Mr. Brown, which agrees with it in many important particulars, but is essentially distinguished by its labellum being produced into a spur, connate with the ovarium. The habit of the two genera is also somewhat different.

Among the figures of Orchideous genera in the *Flora Peruviana,* is one called by the authors of that work *Sobralia* ; which in general appearance bears so much resemblance to *Cattleya,* that we formerly believed them to be the same. Fortunately, however, specimens of *Sobralia* from Pavon exist in Mr. Lambert's invaluable herbarium, which we have been liberally permitted to analyse. It proves to be a genus different from any before published ; and may be distinguished by the following characters, obtained from *S. dichotoma.*

SOBRALIA, *Ruiz et Pav.*

Perianthium resupinatum patens laciniis subæqualibus. Columna libera semiteres labello cucullato amplexa. Anthera terminalis opercularis persistens 2-locularis : septis carnosis. Massæ pollinis ——. *Herbæ (Americæ æquinoctialis) terrestres virgatæ, foliis vaginantibus nervosis acutis. Flores terminales, sæpius racemosi.*

We possess specimens, sent by Dr. Wallich from Nepal, of two plants resembling *Cattleya* in habit, but in fact more nearly related to *Cymbidium,* in which it is probable that some similar species are included ; they are, however, to be distinguished from that genus by having an unilocular anther inserted below the summit of a winged column ; and in their peculiar gynizus, which is precisely the same as that of *Arethusa, Calopogon,* &c. Their habit too is totally dissimilar to *Cymbidium,* of which *C. sinense* must be considered the type. We therefore would consider them a distinct genus, which may be called *Cælogyne,* with the following characters.

CÆLOGYNE.

Perianthium resupinatum patens. Labellum trilobum cucullatum cum columnâ articulatum. Columna alata ultra antheram producta. Anthera lateralis opercularis unilocularis. Massæ pollinis duæ bipartitæ. Gynizus infundibularis bilabiatus. *Herbæ parasiticæ (Indiæ orientalis) bulbosæ ; foliis coriaceis glabris nervosis. Flores pauci racemosi e spathâ squamosâ radicali.*

1. Cælogyne (*punctulata*) bulbis fasciculatis, foliis lanceolatis basi attenuatis, perianthii laciniis lanceolatis crebrò punctatis, labelli lobo medio acuto : cristâ oboletâ.
   Hab. In Nepaliâ, *Wallich.* (*v. s. sp.*)
2. Cælogyne (*cristata*) caudice serpente, bulbis solitariis, foliis lineari-lanceolatis, perianthii laciniis labellique lobo medio obtusis : cristâ fimbriatâ.
   Hab. In Nepaliâ, *Wallich.* (*v. s. sp.*)
? 3. Cymbidium nitidum, *Wallich.*

EXPLANATION OF THE PLATE.

1. Columna seen in front. 2. The same from behind. 3. The same from the side. 4. The same in front without the anther. 5. A longitudinal section of the last. 6, 7, 8. Various views of the anther. 9, 10. Pollen masses.

John Lindley's original description of *Cattleya* in *Collectanea Botanica* (1821)

John Lindley's original description of the genus *Cattleya* (and illustration, see page 39) of *Cattleya labiata* for his *Collectanea Botanica* (1821). This fine tome commemorated the tropical plants flowered by William Cattley of High Barnet, who was Lindley's patron. Cattley's wealth came from the Russian trade through St Petersburg in the Baltic, where his partner John Prescott was based.

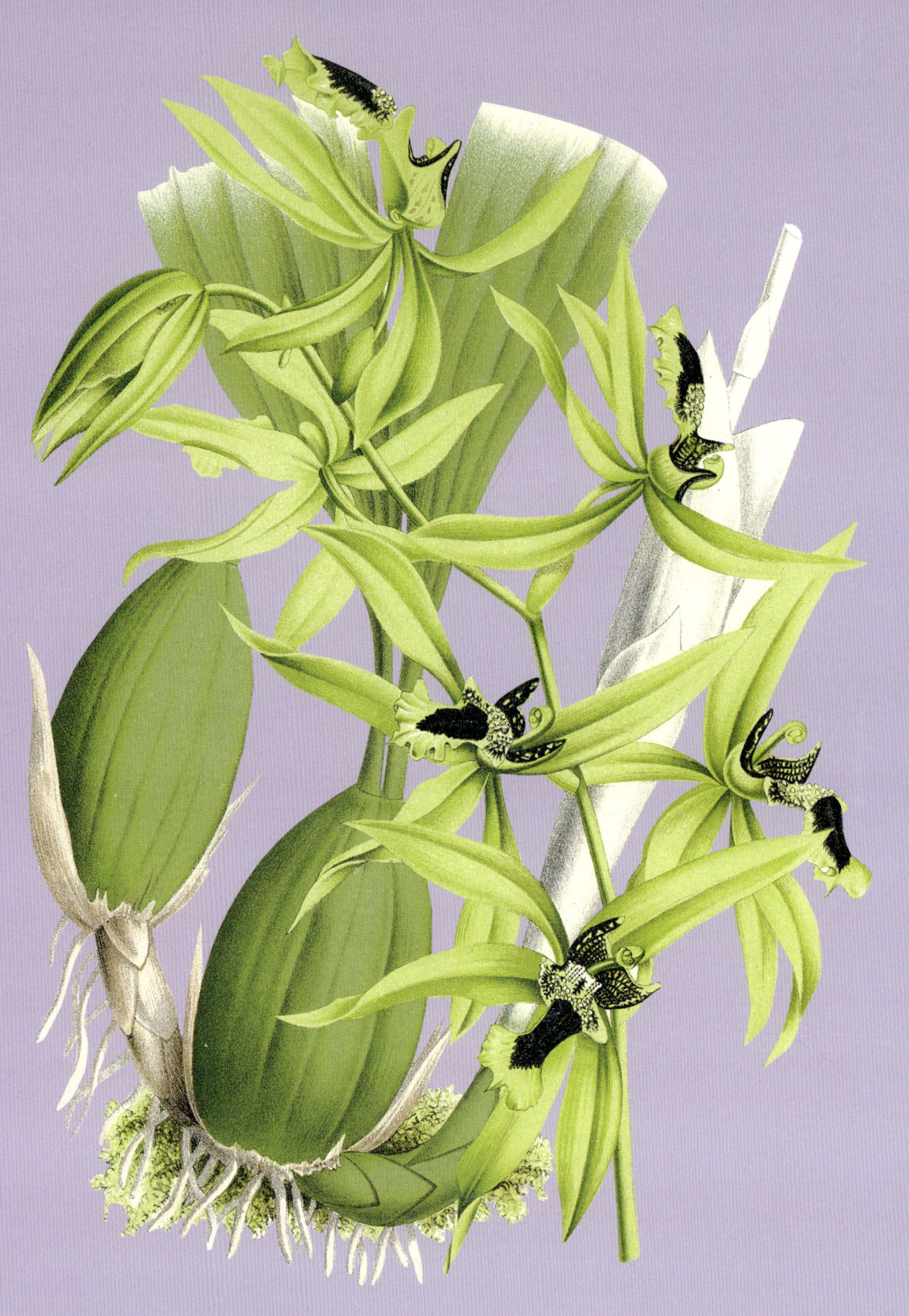

BLACK-LIPPED ORCHID
COELOGYNE PANDURATA

True black is a colour rarely encountered in the plant kingdom. Different flower colours are produced in one of two ways – either through structural features that alter the reflectance or absorption of light, or as a result of pigments within tissues. The presence or absence of particular pigments results in different wavelengths of light being transmitted, absorbed, or reflected back to the observer. If all of the light is absorbed by the pigments, and none of it is reflected, the flower will appear black. This situation is extremely rare, and virtually all "black" coloured flowers, such as black pansies, tulips, dahlias and calla lilies, are in fact very dark red, purple or brown.

Truly black-flowered orchids are even more unusual, although in this family of around 30,000 species there are a number of candidates. Two species described elsewhere in this volume have very dark-coloured flowers. In *Dracula vampira* (see page 108) the dark striations on the sepals are so close together that they give the appearance of a solid black background, and in *Prosthechea cochleata* (see page 202) the enlarged hood-like labellum can be extremely dark in colour and may thus appear to be black. However, it is the flowers of *Coelogyne pandurata* that are thought to be the closest to "true" black. The background of clear bright green tepals surrounds and contrasts strikingly with the deeply undulating and keeled labellum of white and "black" ridges and frills.

Named in 1853 by John Lindley, the "father of modern orchidology", this species was introduced into cultivation by Loddiges in Hackney, London, after being collected in Borneo by Mr Hugh Low, who was there on behalf of his father's nursery, the Low nursery of Upper Clapton. Loddiges' establishment, like many other nurseries of the day, sent out its own collectors to bring back exciting orchid novelties, which would not only cause a sensation in Europe, but also command exclusivity and fetch high prices. Low (later Sir Hugh) was an extremely successful senior administrator in colonial Britain, initially in Borneo in the mid-1800s, and later in the nineteenth century in the Malay Peninsula. Despite his responsibilities, Low still found time to make the first

CHAPTER VII

BORNEO AND JAVA

AFTER a fortnight at Government House, Sir William wrote me letters to the Rajah and Rani of Sarawak, and I went on board the little steamer which goes there every week from Singapore. After a couple of pleasant days with good old Captain Kirk, we steamed up the broad river to Kuching, the capital, for some four hours through low country, with nipa, areca, and cocoa-nut palms, as well as mangroves and other swampy plants bordering the water's edge. At the mouth of the river are some high rocks and apparent mountain-tops isolated above the jungle level, covered entirely by forests of large trees. The last mile of the river has higher banks. A large population lives in wooden houses raised on stilts, almost hidden in trees of the most luxuriant and exquisite forms of foliage. The water was alive with boats, and so deep in its mid-channel that a man-of-war could anchor close to the house of the Rajah even at low tide, which rose and fell thirty feet at that part. On the left bank of the river was the long street of Chinese houses with the Malay huts behind, which formed the town of Kuching, many of whose houses are ornamented richly on the outside with curious devices made in porcelain and tiles. On the right bank a flight of steps led up to the terrace and lovely garden in which the palace of the Rajah had been placed (the original hero, Sir James Brooke, had lived in what was now the cowhouse). I sent in my letter,

and the Secretary soon came on board and fetched me on shore, where I was most kindly welcomed by the Rani, a very handsome English lady, and put in a most luxurious room, from which I could escape by a back staircase into the lovely garden whenever I felt in the humour or wanted flowers.

The Rajah, who had gone up one of the rivers in his gun-boat yacht, did not come back for ten days, and his wife was not sorry to have the rare chance of a countrywoman to talk to. She had lost three fine children on a homeward voyage from drinking a tin of poisoned milk, but one small tyrant of eighteen months remained, who was amusing to watch at his games, and in his despotism over a small Chinese boy in a pig-tail, and his pretty little Malay ayah. The Rajah was a shy quiet man, with much determination of character. He was entirely respected by all sorts of people, and his word (when it did come) was law, always just and well chosen. A fine mastiff dog he had been very fond of, bit a Malay one day. The man being a Mahomedan, thought it an unclean animal, so the Rajah had it tried and shot on the public place by soldiers with as much ceremony as if it had been a political conspirator, and never kept any more dogs. He did not wish to hurt his people's prejudices, he said, for the mere selfish pleasure of possessing a pet.

He had one hundred soldiers, a band which played every night when we dined (on the other side of the river), and about twenty young men from Cornwall and Devonshire called "The Officers," who bore different grand titles,—H. Highness, Treasurer, Postmaster-General, etc.,—and who used to come up every Tuesday to play at croquet before the house. Some of them lived far away at different out-stations on the various rivers, and had terribly lonely lives, seldom seeing any civilised person to speak to, but settling disputes among strange tribes of Dyaks, Chinese, and Malay settlers.

The Rajah coined copper coins, and printed postage-stamps with his portrait on them. The house was most comfortable,

---

Extract from *Recollections of a Happy Life, Being the Autobiography of Marianne North,* **by Marianne North, 1893**

Marianne North was an extraordinary woman, travelling the world extensively between 1871 and 1885 and producing over 800 oil paintings of plants from across the globe, in all manner of habitats. Her style was strikingly bold and vivid for its time and is quite distinctive. During her lifetime North funded the world's first purpose-built gallery for botanical art, at the Royal Botanic Gardens, Kew, and bequeathed the building and 833 of her paintings (covering nearly every inch inside) to Kew upon her death.

full of books, newspapers, and every European luxury. The views from the verandah and lovely gardens, of the broad river, distant isolated mountains, and glorious vegetation, quite dazzled me with their magnificence. What was I to paint first? But my kind hostess made me feel I need not hurry, and that it was truly a comfort and pleasure to her to have me there; so I did not hurry, and soon lost every scrap of Japanese rheumatism, the last ache being in the thumb which held my palette—it is usually the limb that does most work which suffers from that disease. Every one collected for me as usual. Orchids and pitcher-plants were pulled for me most ruthlessly, the latter being of several varieties, from the tiny little plants which grew in the meadow near, and whose pitchers were not half the size of thimbles, to trailing plants of six or eight feet long. The common pepper-plant, too, was much cultivated and very elegant, as well as gambier and other dyes, sago, and gutta-percha, the former growing thirty feet high, with grand terminal bunches of flowers from the centre of the crown (very unlike the small Cycads people had called the Sago palm in other countries). It takes fifteen years before it flowers; then, before the fruit has time to ripen, the whole tree is cut down and the pith taken out and washed. Wallace says one tree could supply a man with food for a whole year. The gutta-percha trees were fast disappearing. They ought to have been protected by law, and the people compelled to bleed them as in other countries, not to sacrifice the great trees for one crop—trees which had been a hundred years growing, and could not be quickly replaced.

Nearly every evening I used to go for a row up and down the river with the Rani. It was quite alive with canoes and other picturesque boats, from good-sized merchant vessels to mere hollowed logs of wood, so small that the paddlers seemed to sit on the water, and might easily be snapped up by alligators; but they did not often come so high up the river. When they did there was an immediate crusade; traps were

baited with monkeys or cats, and the beast was caught. The Rajah gave a large reward for one, and a still larger sum if, after a *post-mortem* examination, the brute was proved to be a man-eater. It was always buried under one of the garden trees, to the great improvement and delight of the latter.

The little town was full of life and civilisation, the bazaars and houses gay with colour, porcelain panels with raised flowers and griffins being let into the walls. At night the lights got so magnified in reflection that one could fancy oneself almost at Cologne or Mayence. Above and below for miles the semi-amphibious Malays had built their basket-like dwellings on stakes in the mud or on the banks above—thatched, walled, and floored with the leaf-stalks of the nipa palm, which delights in growing in brackish water, being almost drowned at high tide and almost dry at low. The Malays get wine, salt, and sugar from its juice, and oil from the nuts, which are contained in a cone as big as a cannon-ball. The sunsets were superb on the river. When the tide was very high we used to go up some of the small side-streams, and push our way under arches of green tangle, which broke off bits of our boat's roofs, as well as the rotten branches over our heads. We watched troops of monkeys gambolling in the trees, chattering and disputing with one another as to who we were, and what we came for. One day we were overtaken by darkness in one of these expeditions, and made a short cut home overland, with a native to guide us by an almost invisible path through the bush, very suggestive of snakes, but we saw none. The wild jungle came close up to the garden on three sides, and none but native eyes could discover paths beyond or through it.

There were acres of pine-apples, many of them having the most exquisite pink and salmon tints, and deep blue flowers. These grew like weeds. They were merely thinned out, and the ground was never manured. They had been growing on that same patch of ground for nine years. They were wonderfully good to eat. We used to cut the top off with a knife

North included many orchids in her compositions, sometimes as the main focus of the work and other times as parts of landscapes or compositions of multiple plants.

In this extract from her autobiography she describes staying with the Rajah and Rani of Sarawak and being overwhelmed by the number of orchids and other tropical plants collected from the surrounding forests and presented to her to paint. "What was I to paint first?" she exclaims.

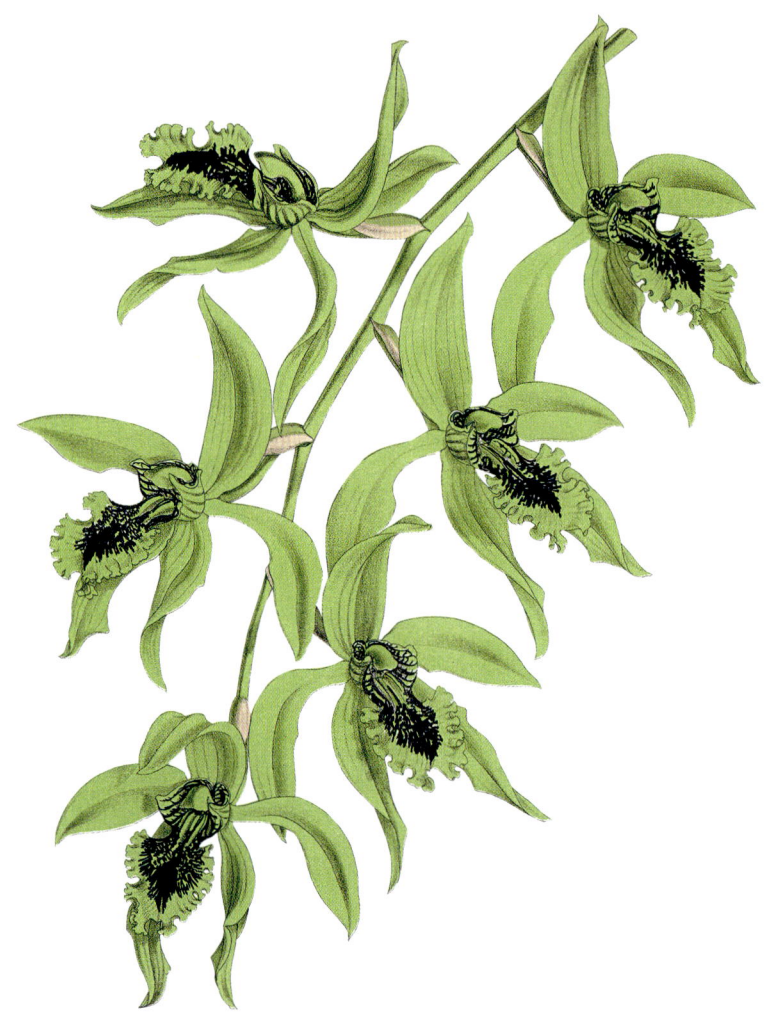

documented ascent of Mount Kinabalu, and discovered and collected a huge number of species new to science on his travels. Many of these, including *Dendrobium lowii* and *Paphiopedilum lowii*, were later named after him.

The colour of the labellum is so unusual that when the orchid grower and illustrator John Day painted *Coelogyne pandurata* he commented that "I like it very much – it is so peculiar. I think it is almost the only thing I ever used lampblack for." Day's series of 53 "scrapbooks" recorded nearly 3,000 orchid species in finely detailed illustrations, with his annotated

observations and descriptions of the plants further embellishing each page. Over the course of 40 years, Day acquired, grew and flowered each plant – this often being the first time that the species had ever bloomed in the UK – and recorded the blooms for posterity in his delightful scrapbooks.

Unfortunately, it is not just the colour of this species that is rare. The peat swamp forests of Peninsular Malaysia, Sumatra, Java, Borneo and the Philippines, where *Coelogyne pandurata* grows in the wild, are being severely threatened by tree felling for timber and development, and by the burning of the thick peat below.

Above: *Coelogyne pandurata* by John Nugent Fitch, in R. Warner and B. S. Williams, *The Orchid Album*, 1883.

Opposite: *Coelogyne pandurata* in *Orchids and Other Flowers of Sarawak, Borneo* by Marianne North, 1882. The scarlet creeper is an *Aeschynanthus* (Gesneriaceae) and the white-flowered orchid is *Coelogyne swaniana*.

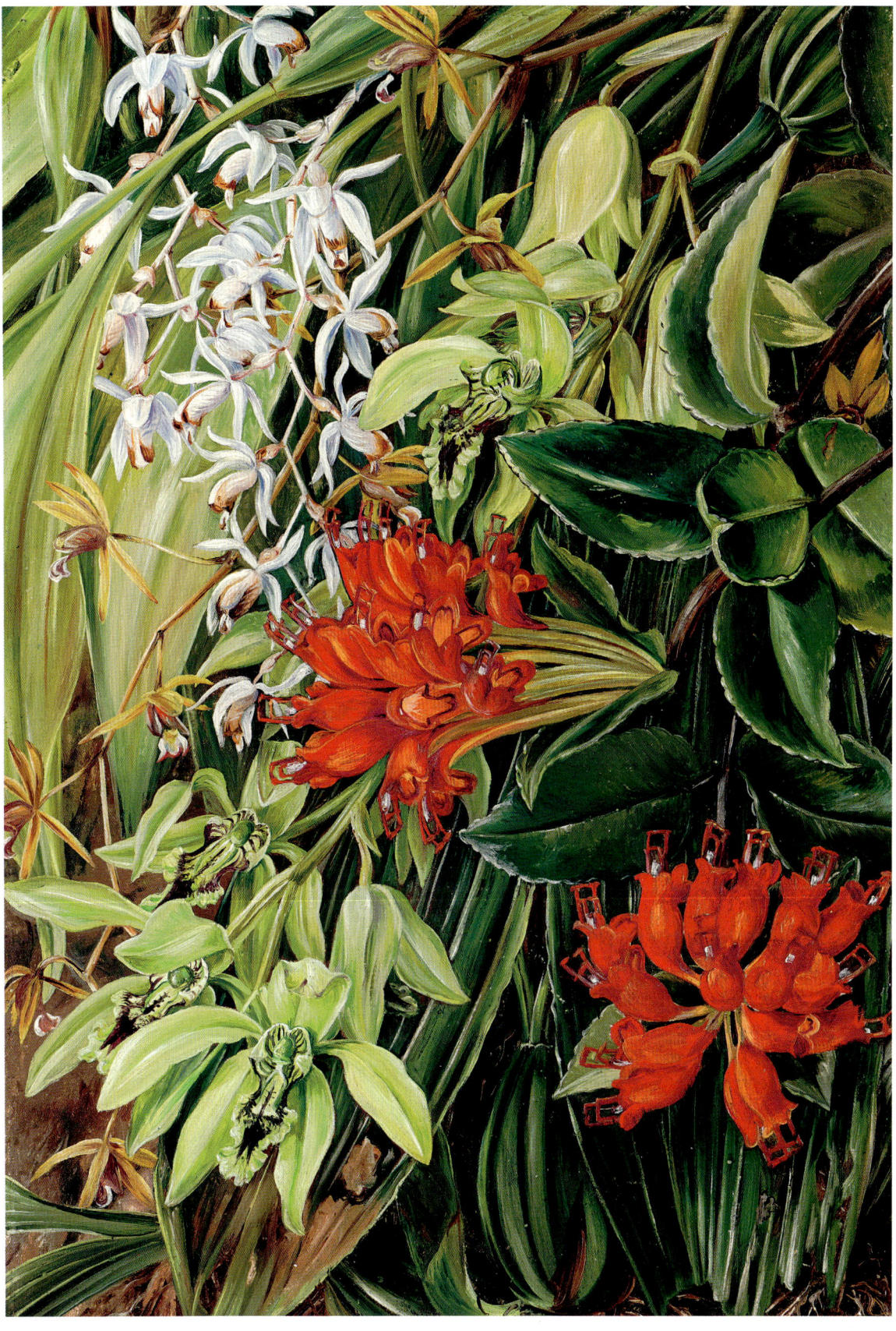

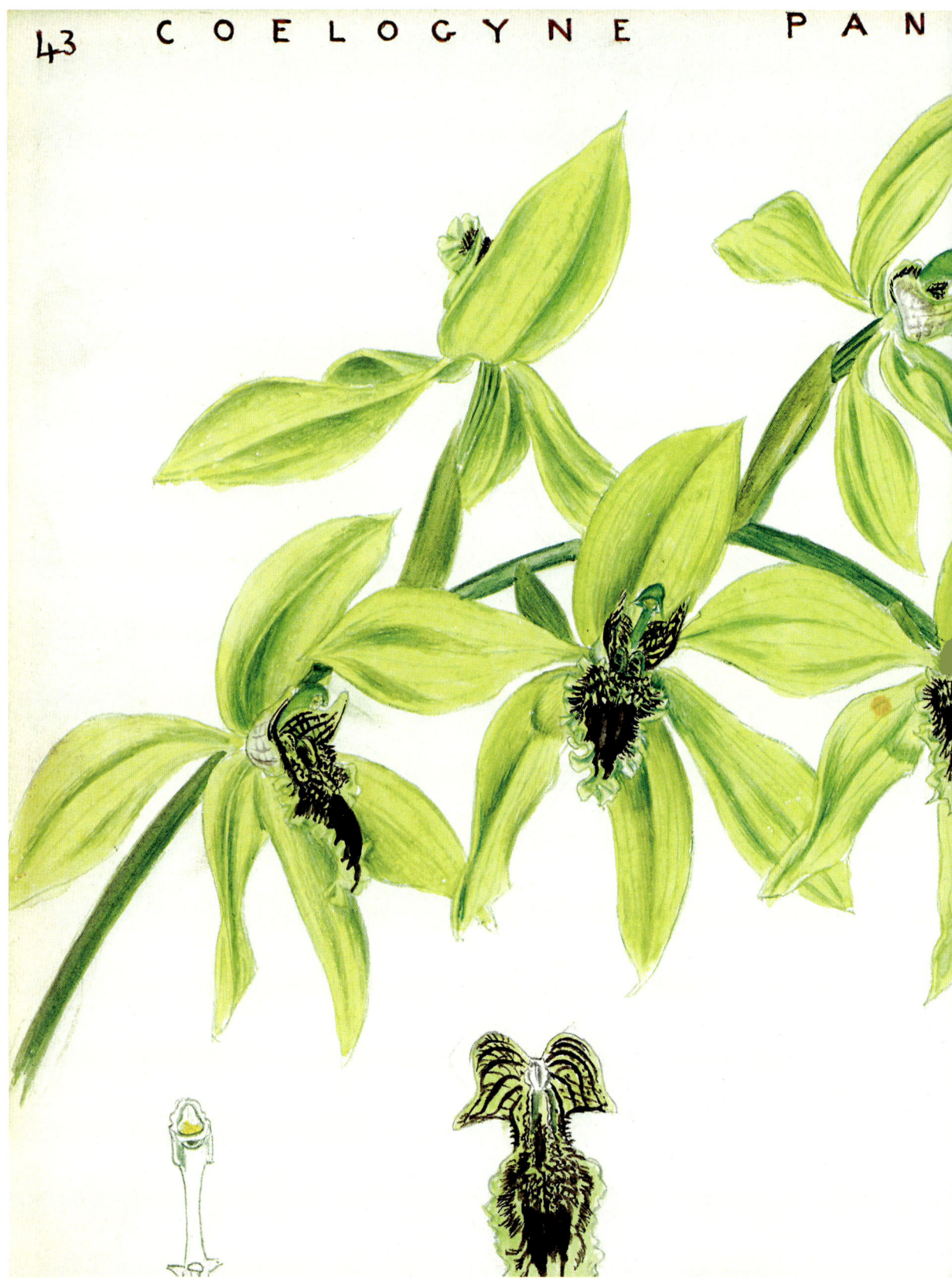

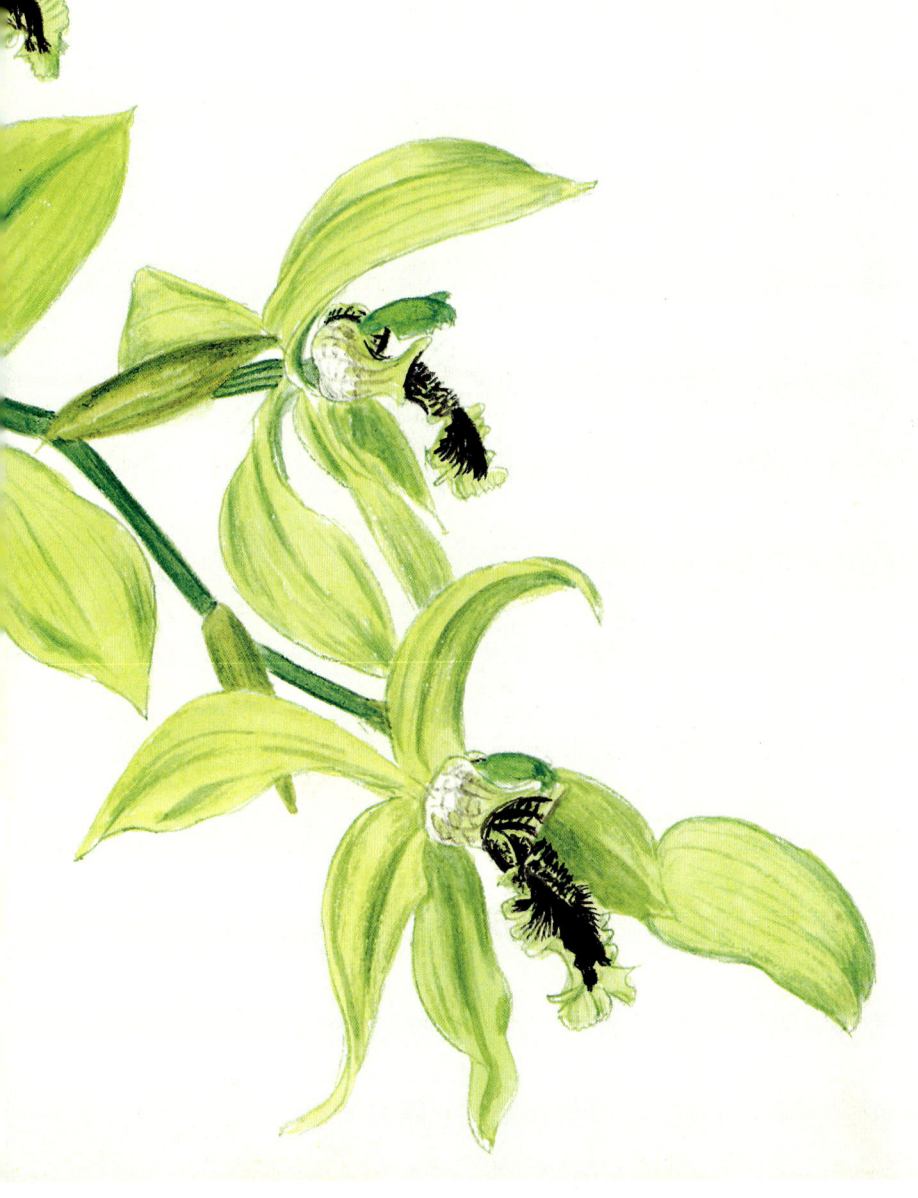

July 4th 1884

Left: *Coelogyne
pandurata* by John
Day, 1884.

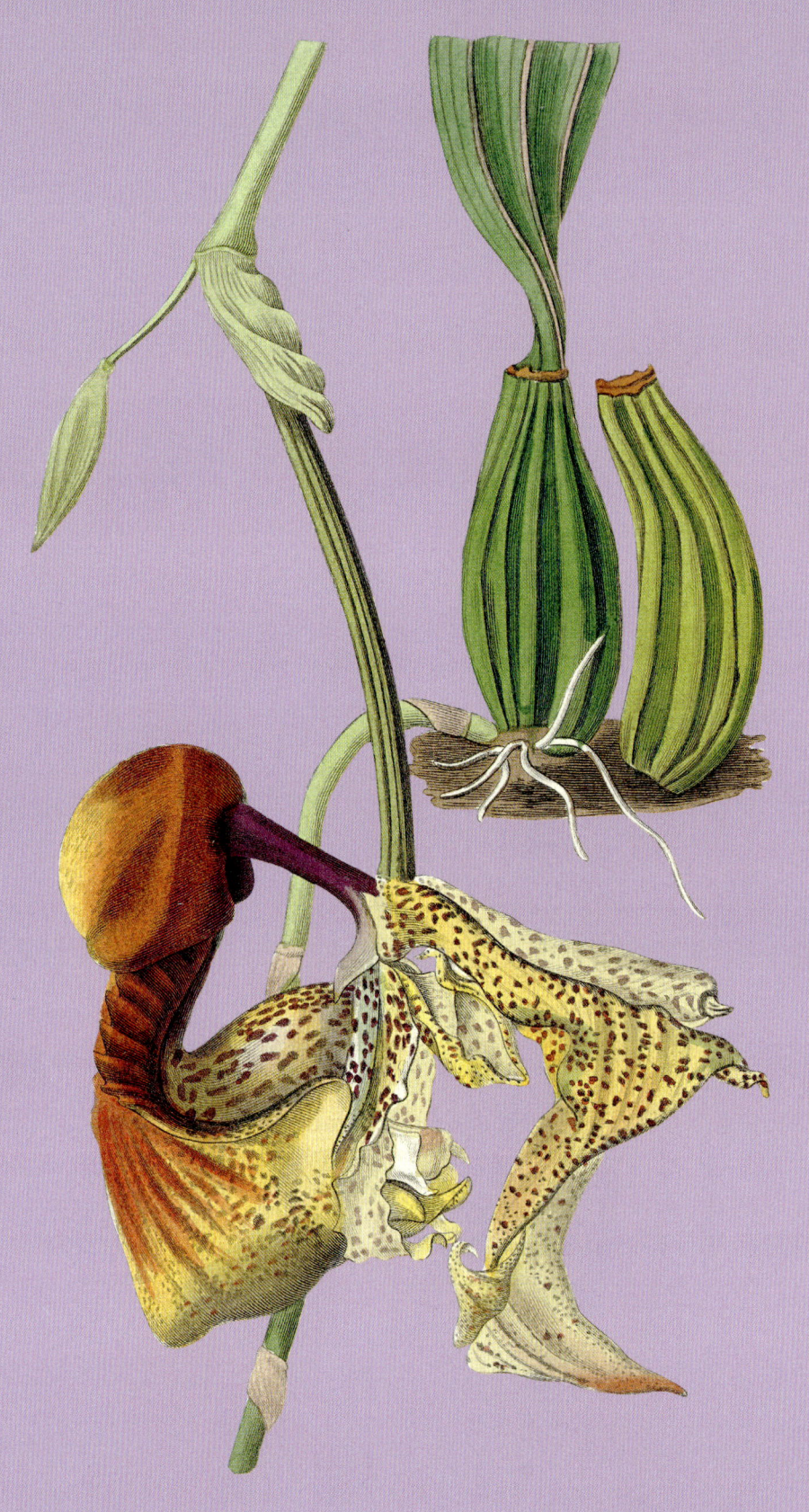

LARGE-FLOWERED BUCKET ORCHID
CORYANTHES MACRANTHA

Accustomed as we are now become to strange forms amongst orchideous plants, I doubt whether any species has yet been seen more remarkable for its unusual characters than *Coryanthes macrantha*.

John Lindley (1836), in *Paxton's Magazine of Botany, and Register of Flowering Plants, vol. 3*

Found growing in the wild in Trinidad, Brazil, Venezuela, Colombia, Peru, Suriname, Guyana and French Guiana, *Coryanthes macrantha* has a truly strange-looking flower. William Hooker, the first official director of the Royal Botanic Gardens, Kew, named the genus *Coryanthes* based on the Greek words *corys*, meaning "helmet", and *anthos*, meaning "flower". Charles Darwin was intrigued by one of these species, the yellow-orange freckled *Coryanthes macrantha*, with its large, waxy, fragrant flowers hanging below the plant, and was particularly fascinated by the description of bees scrabbling on the surface of the helmet-shaped upper portion of the flower (known as the hypochile).

Orchids are well known in the plant world for having co-evolved alongside other organisms in order to grow, survive and reproduce. Many of these distinctive and mutually beneficial relationships involve the evolution of highly specialized flowers and pollination mechanisms, which often allow either only one or a limited range of (usually, but not always) insects to transfer pollen from one flower to another. This exchange results in the pollination of the recipient flower and ensures that genetic material from one flower recombines with that from another flower. Commonly, and usually ideally, pollen is transferred from another plant of the same species rather than one from the same plant, as combining genetic material from two parents ensures that the seed produced are more genetically distinct from either parent. Offspring from such pairings tend to survive better than those from self-pollinated flowers, and it is more likely that novel combinations of characteristics will arise which may be better adapted to survival and be passed on to future generations.

The euglossine bees of which Darwin wrote were collecting oils from the

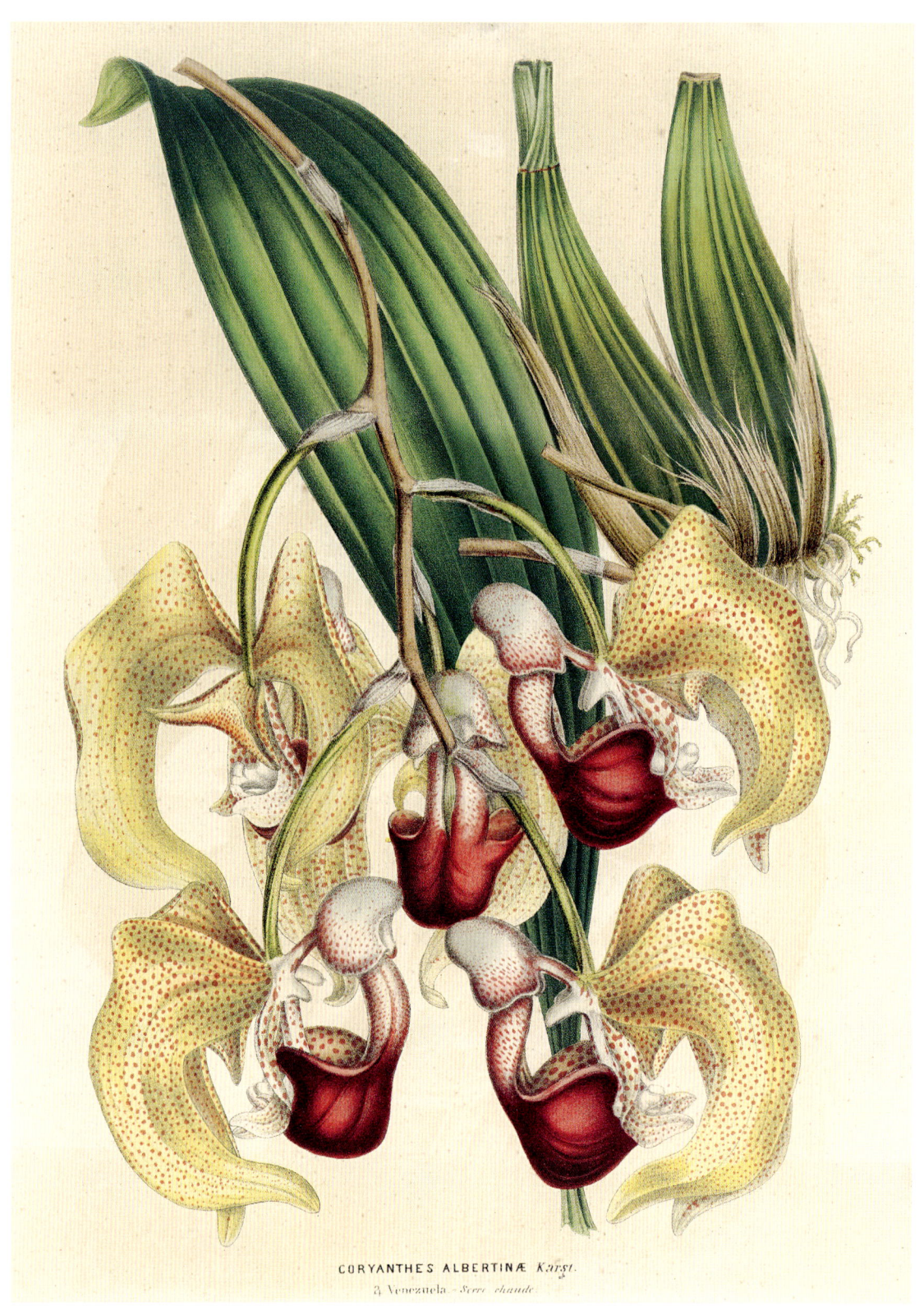

CORYANTHES ALBERTINÆ *Karst.*

Venezuela - *Serre chaude*

Large-flowered bucket orchid   *Coryanthes macrantha*

[handwritten letter, partially legible]

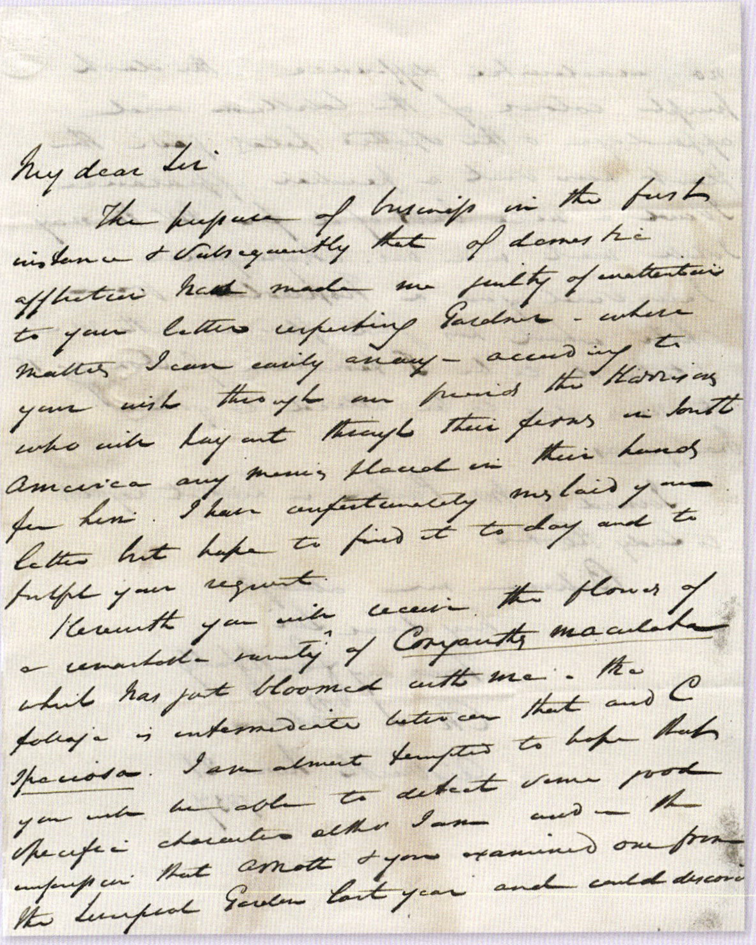

My dear Sir

The purpose of business in the first
instance & subsequently that of domestic
affection had made me guilty of inattention
to your letters respecting Gardner — where
matters I can easily arrange — according to
your wish through our friend the Harrisons
who will lay out through their firms in South
America any monies placed in their hands
for him. I have unfortunately mislaid your
letter but hope to find it to day and to
fulfil your request.

Herewith you will receive the flower of
a remarkable variety of *Coryanthes maculata*
which has just bloomed with me. The
foliage is intermediate between that and *C.
speciosa*. I am almost tempted to hope that
you will be able to detect some good
specific characters altho' I am — and — the
impression that Arnott & you examined one from
the Liverpool Garden last year and could discover

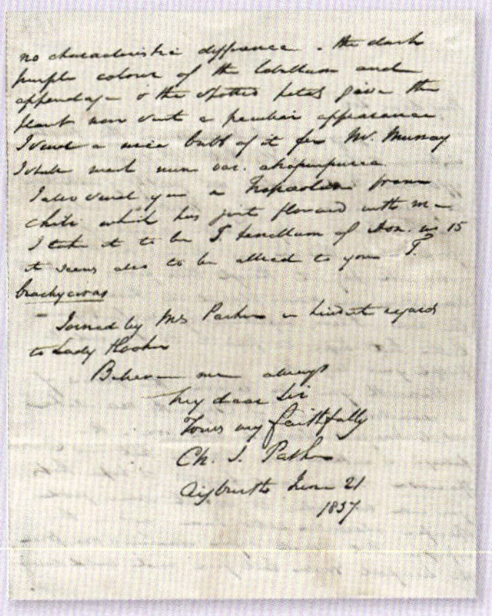

[second smaller page of the letter]

no characteristic difference. The dark
purple colour of the labellum and
appendages & the spotted fields give the
flower an exceedingly peculiar appearance.
I send a nice bulb of it for Mr Murray
& take much more care of herbarium.
I also send you a *Tropaeolum* from
Chile which has just flowered with me —
I take it to be a handsome of Serra no 15
it seems also to be allied to your *Tropaeolum*.
brachyceras
— Sends by Mr Parker — kind regards
to Lady Hooker

Believe me always
my dear Sir
Yours very faithfully
Ch. S. Parker
Aigburth June 21
1837

Letter from Charles Parker to Sir William Jackson Hooker, from Aigburth (Liverpool), 21 June 1837

Charles Parker discusses a favour respecting Gardner and their friends
the Harrisons. Parker has mislaid Hooker's last letter but hopes to find
it today and fulfil Hooker's request. He notes that Hooker will receive
the flower of remarkable novelty, *Coryanthes maculata*, which has just
bloomed with him and has foliage "intermediate with *C. speciosa*". He
discusses the foliage of this plant and sends a bulb of it to Murray. He
also sends a *Tropaeolum* from Chile which has just flowered with him.

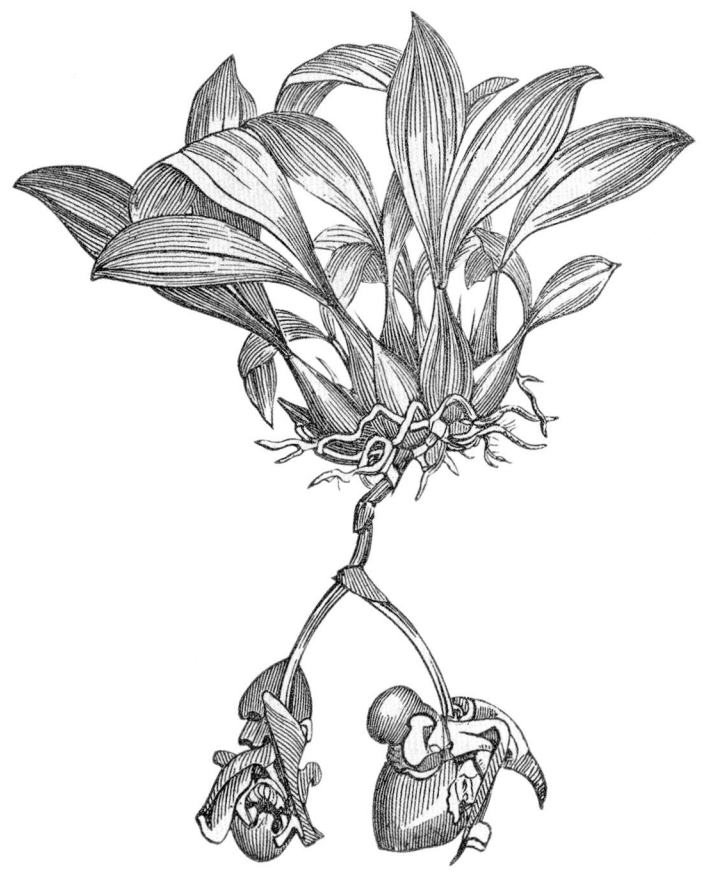

Above: *Coryanthes macrantha* in *Paxton's Magazine of Botany, and Register of Flowering Plants*, 1839.

Opposite: *Coryanthes macrantha* by Maubert, in J. J. Linden *Pescatorea*, 1860.

surface of the hypochile, and we now know that they use these oils as pheromones to attract females for mating. In their endeavours, the male bees may slip and fall into the deep bucket-shaped structure below, called the epichile. The latter is filled with a clear liquid that is secreted from glands and has steep slippery sides. Once its wings are soaked with this liquid, the bee can neither fly nor climb directly out to safety. The only way it can exit the epichile is by squeezing through the

narrow tunnel between the epichile and the apex of the column. As it does so, small parcels of pollen called pollinia become attached to its body, ready to be deposited at the next flower into which the insect accidentally falls.

Another species in the genus, *Coryanthes vasquezii*, is an integral part of the complex life cycle of the Brazil nut tree, *Bertholletia excelsa*. In the Amazon rainforests of South America where these two species grow, male euglossine bees collect fragrant waxy oils from the flowers of *Coryanthes vasquezii*, in order to attract the female bees for mating. When collecting the oils, the bees inadvertently pollinate the orchid flowers. Meanwhile, only large-bodied female euglossine bees can push open the flowers of the Brazil nut tree and feed on the nectar within them. After the resulting fruits have developed for over a year and the seeds inside are mature, the Brazil nut tree relies on one final animal – a small rodent called an agouti – in this mutualistic ecological web of food and reproduction. The agouti is able to open the large round fruits, which can contain up to 24 individual seeds (each of which is what we call a single "Brazil nut"), and will eat some of these and bury others for future consumption. A proportion of these buried seeds will never be recovered by the agouti, and so may germinate and develop into the next generation of trees. If just one of the plant or animal species in this interdependent network is not present, the remaining species cannot survive.

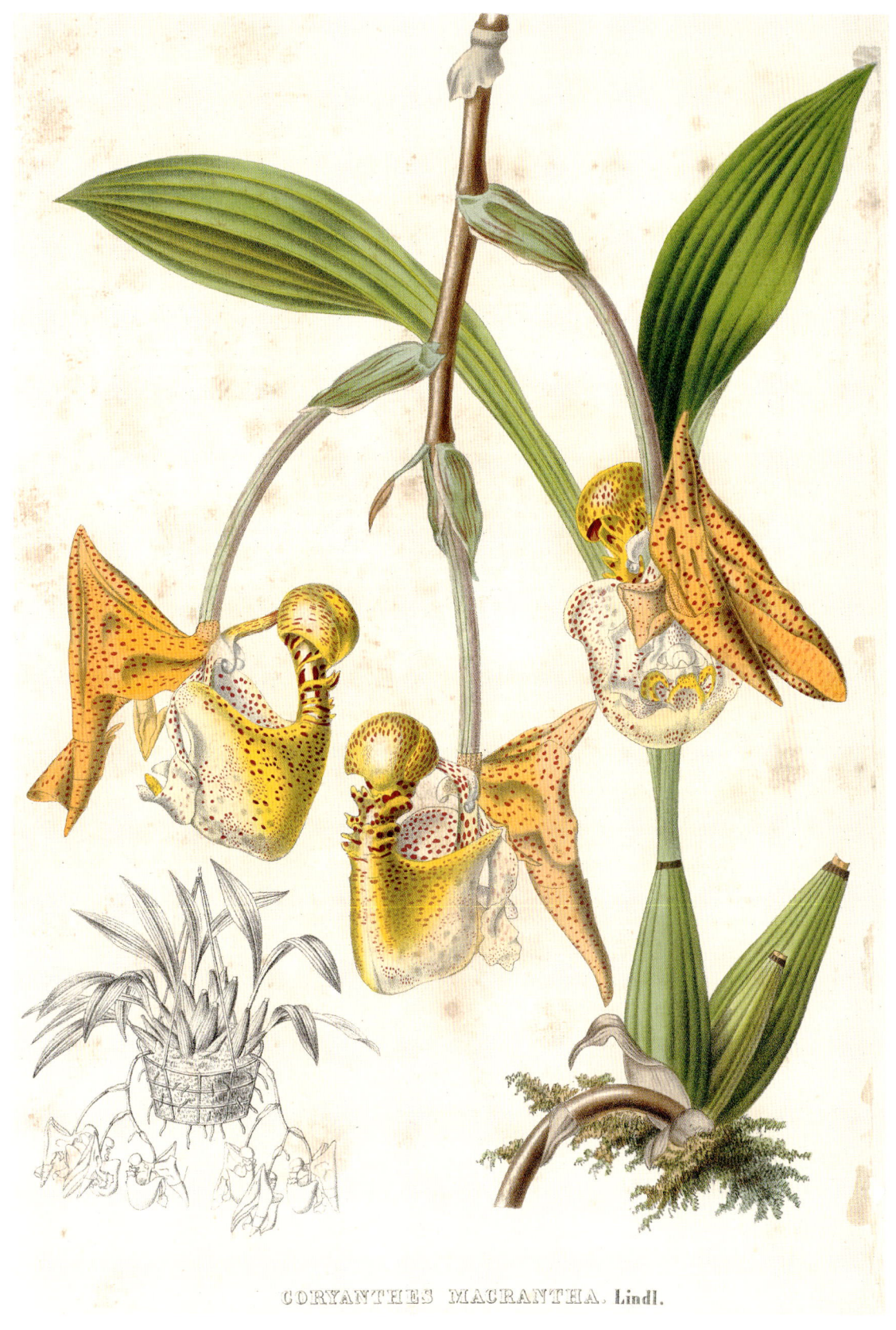

CORYANTHES MACRANTHA. Lindl.

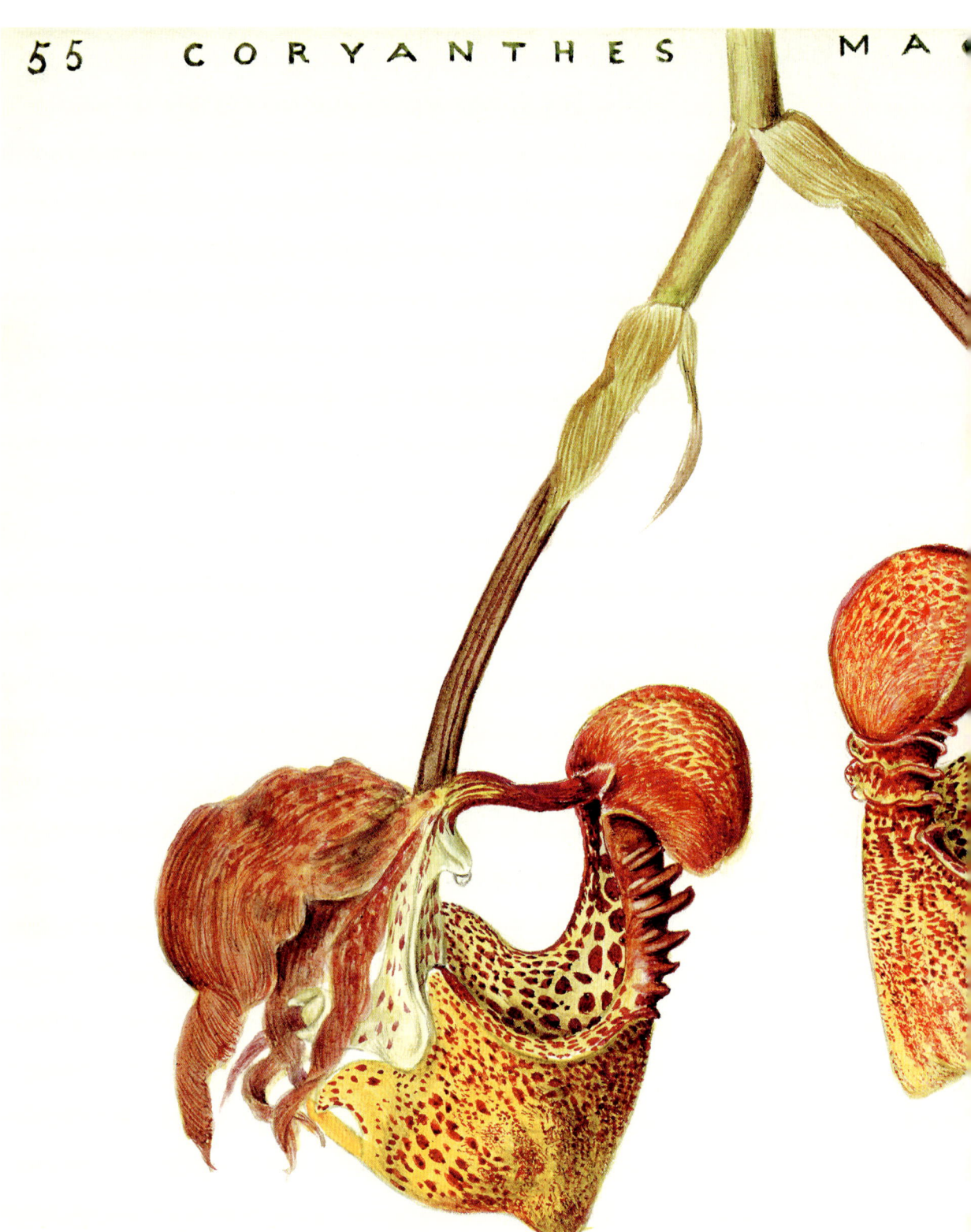

June 19th 1886

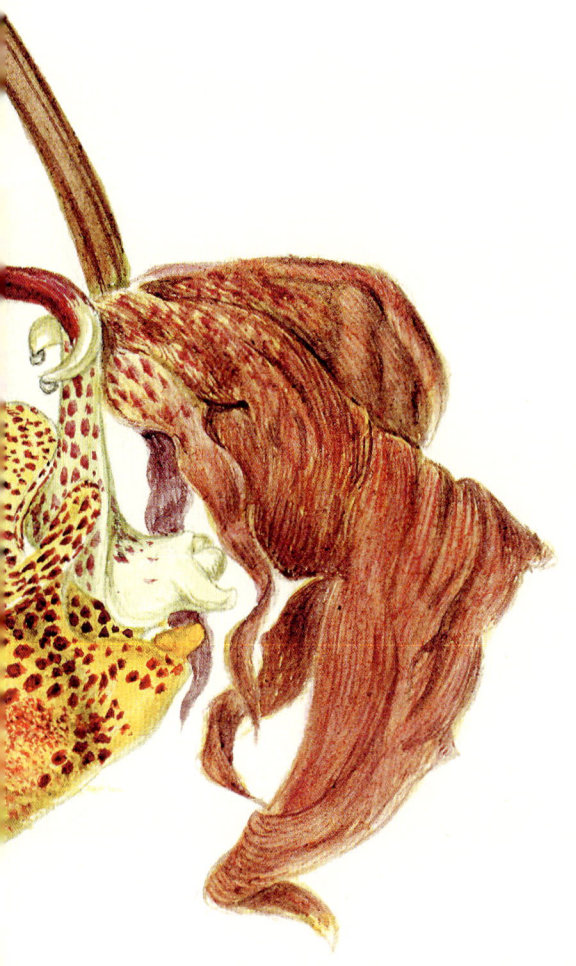

See next page

Left: *Coryanthes macrantha* by John Day, 1886.

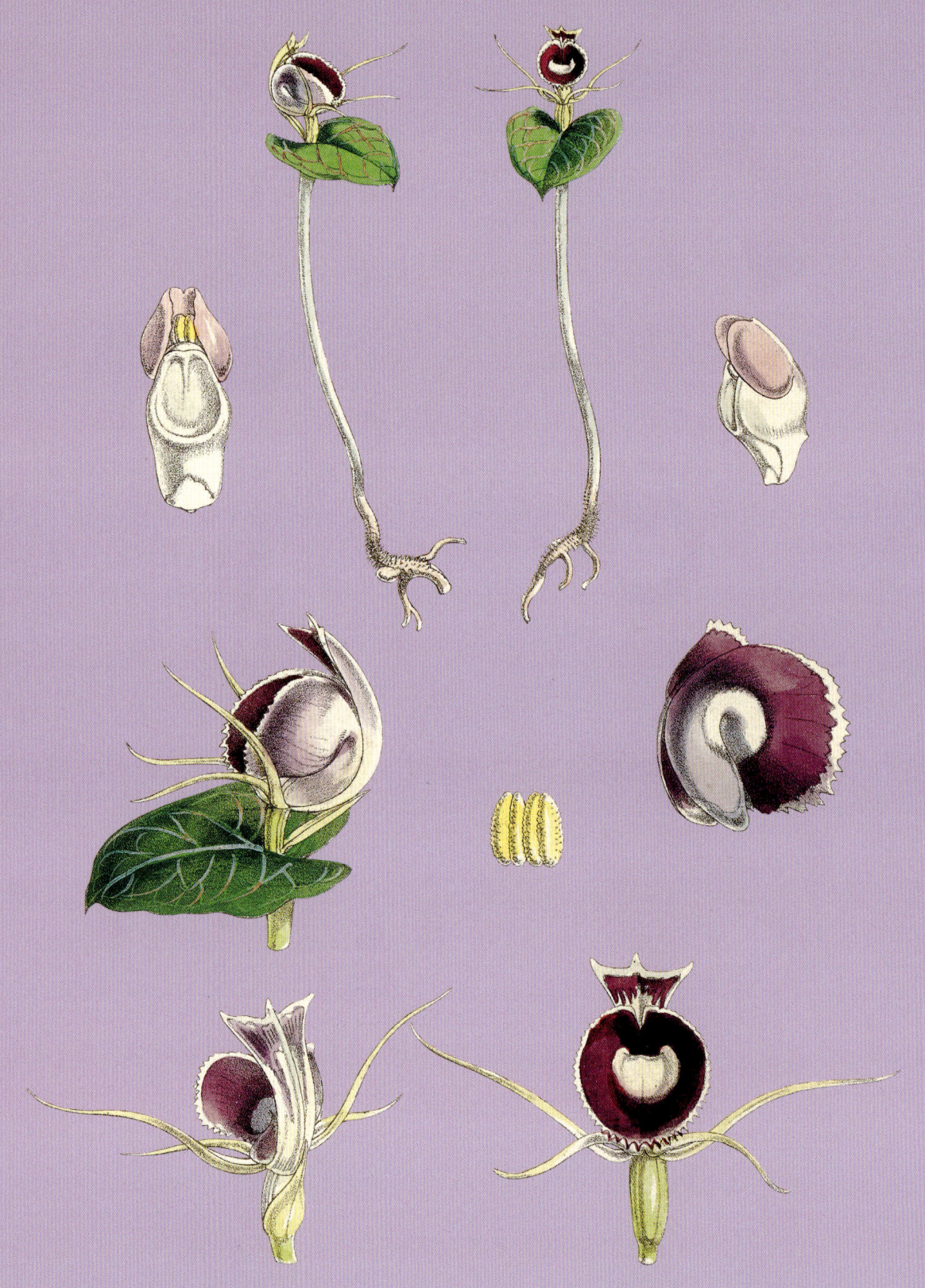

PAINTED HELMET ORCHID
CORYBAS PICTUS

*C*orybas orchids are a group of enigmatic, terrestrial orchids that grow close to the ground and have curiously shaped flowers thought to resemble the fruiting bodies of basidiomycete fungi. Usually fairly well hidden in thick undergrowth, these orchids are found growing as colonies of plants on mossy ground, rocks and tree boles in dense shade, in mid- to lower montane forests from Australia and New Zealand through New Guinea, Borneo, Indonesia and Indo-China to the eastern Himalayas and southern China. Members of the genus *Corybas* have a round fleshy underground tuber and a single heart-shaped, kidney-shaped or almost round leaf, with a short single-flowered stem above. *Corybas* species are relatively poorly known, as their short-lived flowers are inconspicuous and hidden among other vegetation, but species new to science are discovered fairly regularly, with 26 species having been described since 2000.

The name of the genus is derived from the Greek word for male dancers, *korybantos*, who wore crested helmets and worshipped the female god Cybele.

The dorsal sepal of the single flower is much larger than the other sepals and the petals, and forms a hood-shaped "helmet" that curves over the column, which bears the fertile parts of the flower. The large deeply concave labellum curves up around the other side of the column, and the remaining petals and sepal are much reduced and may even be thread-like.

Carl Ludwig Blume was the second director of the Bogor Botanic Gardens in Java (then known as Buitenzorg Botanic Gardens, the foremost botanical centre for the Dutch East Indies), and later the first director of the Rijksherbarium in Brussels and then Leiden in the Netherlands. During his tenure in Bogor, Blume spent considerable time and effort documenting the enormous number of orchids found on the island of Java and its neighbouring islands. He described many species for the first time, including four species now placed in the genus *Corybas*, one of which was *Corybas pictus*, which he described in 1825 as *Calcearia picta*. *Calcearia* was later determined to be synonymous with the earlier named genus *Corybas*, and all species within the former were transferred to the latter.

LXXXIII.

CORYBAS ACONITIFLORUS.

Aconite-flowered Corybas.

ORDO NATURALIS.

Orchideæ. *Juss. Gen. p.* 64.

═══════════

Sect. 1. Monandræ.

Pericarpium membranaceum. Petalorum supremum, galeæ instar, fornicatum : Labellum grande, supremo connivens, compressum, margine nunc pectinatum : reliqua longe minora. Stylus apice lateribusque dilatatis 3-lobus, cui infra stigma pulvinar subrotundum apponitur. Anthera dorso styli infra marginem inserta, mobilis, 2-locularis. Pollen granulosum. *Herbæ pulchellæ*. *Radix tuberosa, superne fibras paucas succulentas exserens. Caulis circiter pollicem longus. Folia 3, medium tantummodo completum reliquis bracteæformibus. Flores solitarii. Nomen a floribus* Κορυβαντος *velatum caput simulantibus. Character ad exemplar fere defloratum cum sicco alius speciei collatum, itaque recognoscendus.*

C. folio medio reniformi acuminulato : labelli margine valde revoluto.

Sponte nascentem in *New Holland*, legit ALEXᴿ. GORDON.

Floret apud nos *Julio*.

For this curious plant, Mr. HOOKER is indebted to the Countess of ESSEX, whose collection at *Cashiobury*, will soon be, like every thing else there, truly princely and magnificent. The specimen was much decayed when it reached me, but by comparing it with a dried one both of this and another species, liberally given to me by E. J. A. WOODFORD, Esq. I am enabled to draw up the following description.

Root whitish, spindle-shaped with one short fibre at the top, its base terminating in a bulb about the size of a pea. Stem about an inch long, round, smooth. Leaves 3, of which only the middle one can be called complete: Petiole embracing the stem: Lamina circular, kidney-shaped, very entire, shortly acuminated, bright green on the upper surface, paler underneath, exceeding finely papulose, the two lowest pair of side nerves semi-circular and concentric. Flower solitary, of a dark violet blue colour. Pericarpium while young green and obpyramidal, its alternate angles smaller. Upper Petal large, vaulted over the Labellum which is nearly as large, melliferous on both the internal sides near the base, revolute at the margin and in this species I believe quite entire, but in another indented-ciliate: the remaining Petals very small. Style small, buried within the labellum, behind the anther and at the sides of the stigma dilated into 3 lobes: a whitish tubercle or bolster covers the front below the stigma. Stigma nearly orbicular, concave. Anther yellow, inserted far below the margin of the style, 2-locular. Pollen in the living specimen dissolved upon the stigma : in a dried one of both species moistened by boiling water, apparently consisting of separate grains.

REFERENCES TO THE PLATE.

1. A flower, half of the upper Petal being cut away to show the Labellum. 2. Half of the Labellum shewing one of the Nectariums near the base. 3. Style, natural size. 4. 5. A side and front view of the Style highly magnified, showing the lowest Petals, Bolster, Stigma and Anther.

Original description and publication of the genus *Corybas* by Richard Salisbury, in *The Paradisus Londinensis: or Coloured Figures of Plants Cultivated in the Vicinity of the Metropolis*, vol. 2, t.83 , 1807

Richard Salisbury published the newly described genus *Corybas* in 1807, basing the new group of orchids on the species *Corybas aconitiflorus* from "New Holland" (Australia), in his book *The Paradisus Londinensis*. The description included an illustration of the species by William Hooker, who would later become the first director of the Royal Botanic Gardens, Kew.

Salisbury was elected to be the first honorary secretary of the Horticultural Society of London (which would later become the Royal Horticultural Society), founded in 1804, but was a controversial character in botany during his career, naming and renaming plants according to his own rules, not following Linnean classification, and being accused of plagiarism and unethical behaviour. Although many of Salisbury's genus names are no longer accepted, many of his species names are still used – and in the case of *Corybas aconitiflorus*, both the genus and species names are still accepted.

Found in Malaysia, Java, Sumatra and Borneo, *Corybas pictus* has an attractive pointed heart-shaped leaf with silver-white to pink veins and crisped edges. The single flower is deep red to maroon inside, with a white centre, and has stripes externally, and thin spidery lateral sepals and petals. Tiny fungus gnats pollinate the flowers, and it is thought that they are tricked into visiting the flower because it resembles a fungus on which they usually feed and lay their eggs. After pollination, the stem on which the flower is borne elongates as the fruit develops, presumably to aid dispersal of the seed, and it may lift the seed pod up to 30 cm (1 ft) above the plant.

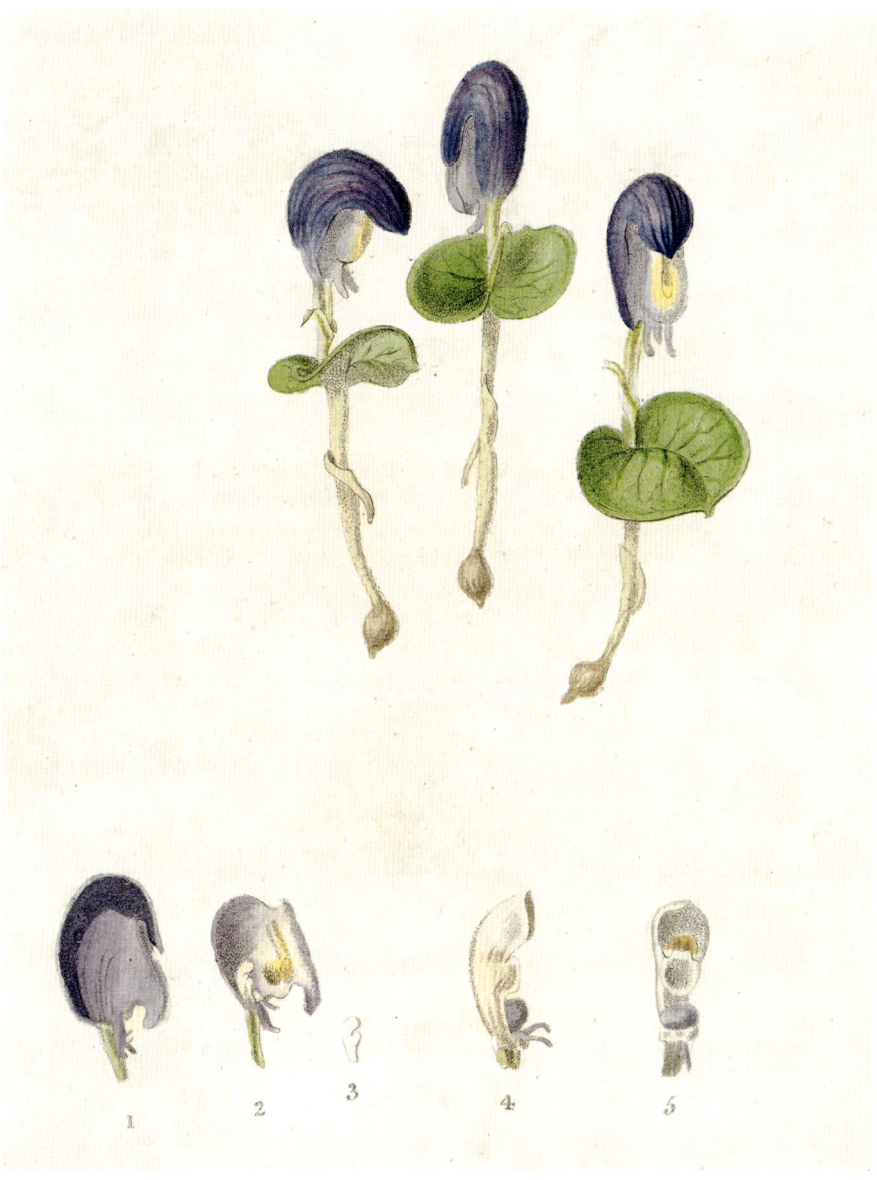

Left: *Corybas aconitiflorus* by William Jackson Hooker, in R. Salisbury, *The Paradisus Londinensis: or Coloured Figures of Plants Cultivated in the Vicinity of the Metropolis*, 1807.

Following pages: *Corybas pictus* (as *Corysanthes picta*) by Latour and A.J. Wendel, in Carl von Ludwig's *Collection des Orchidées les plus Remarquables de l'Archipel Indien et du Japon*, 1859.

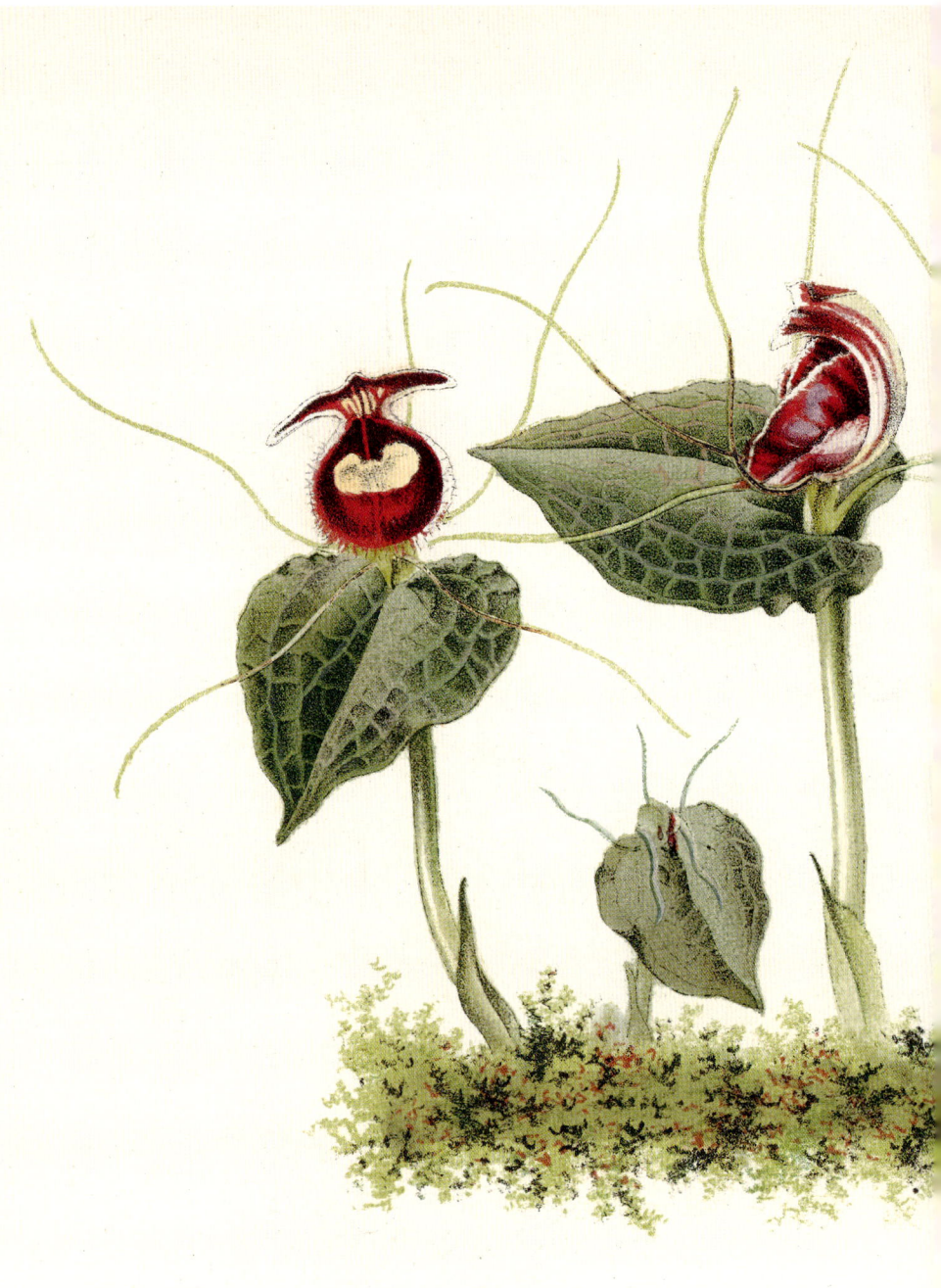

Corysant

Gronin

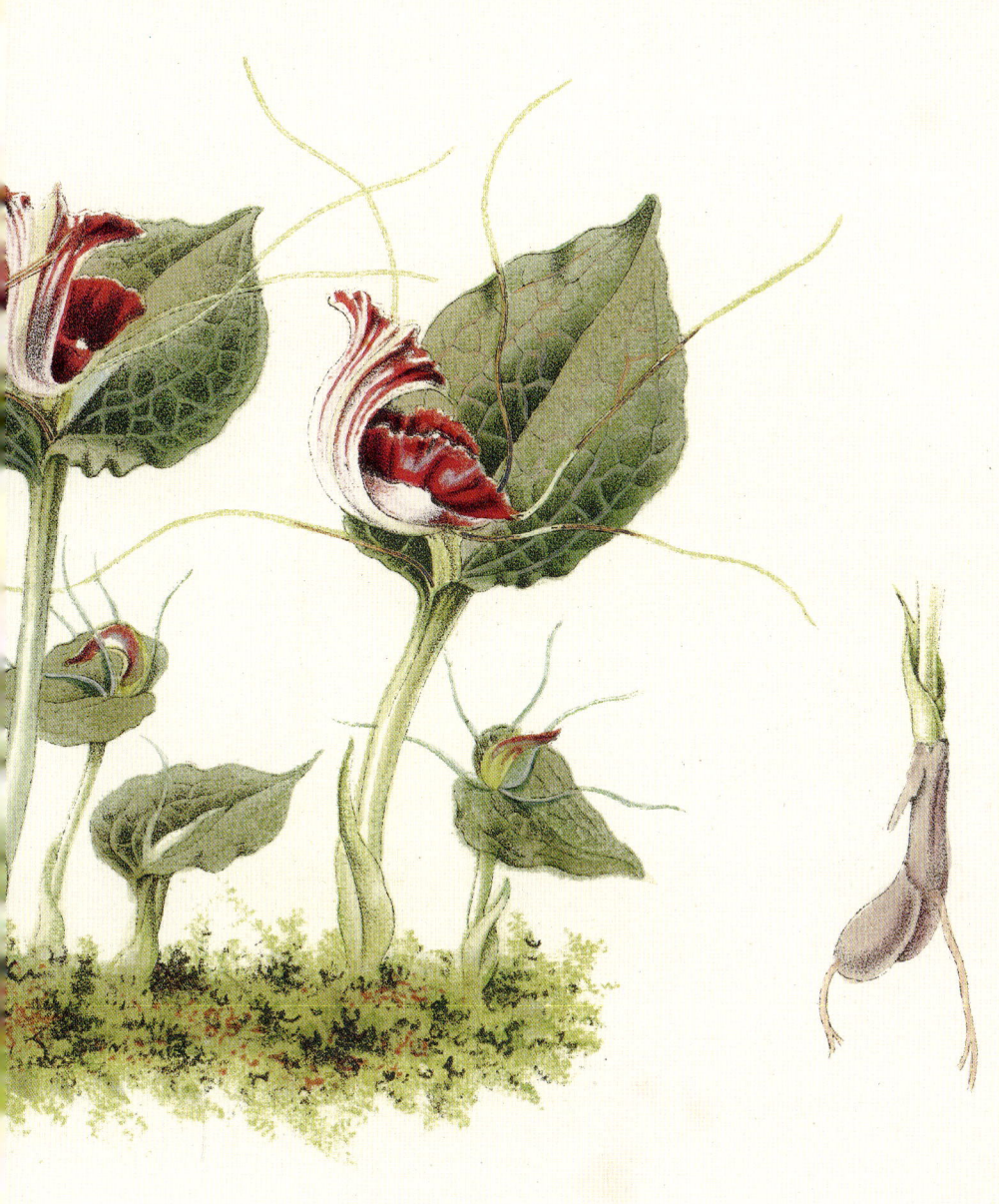

Chromolith. G. Severeyns fils. lith. de l'Acad.

ta Lindl.

lters.

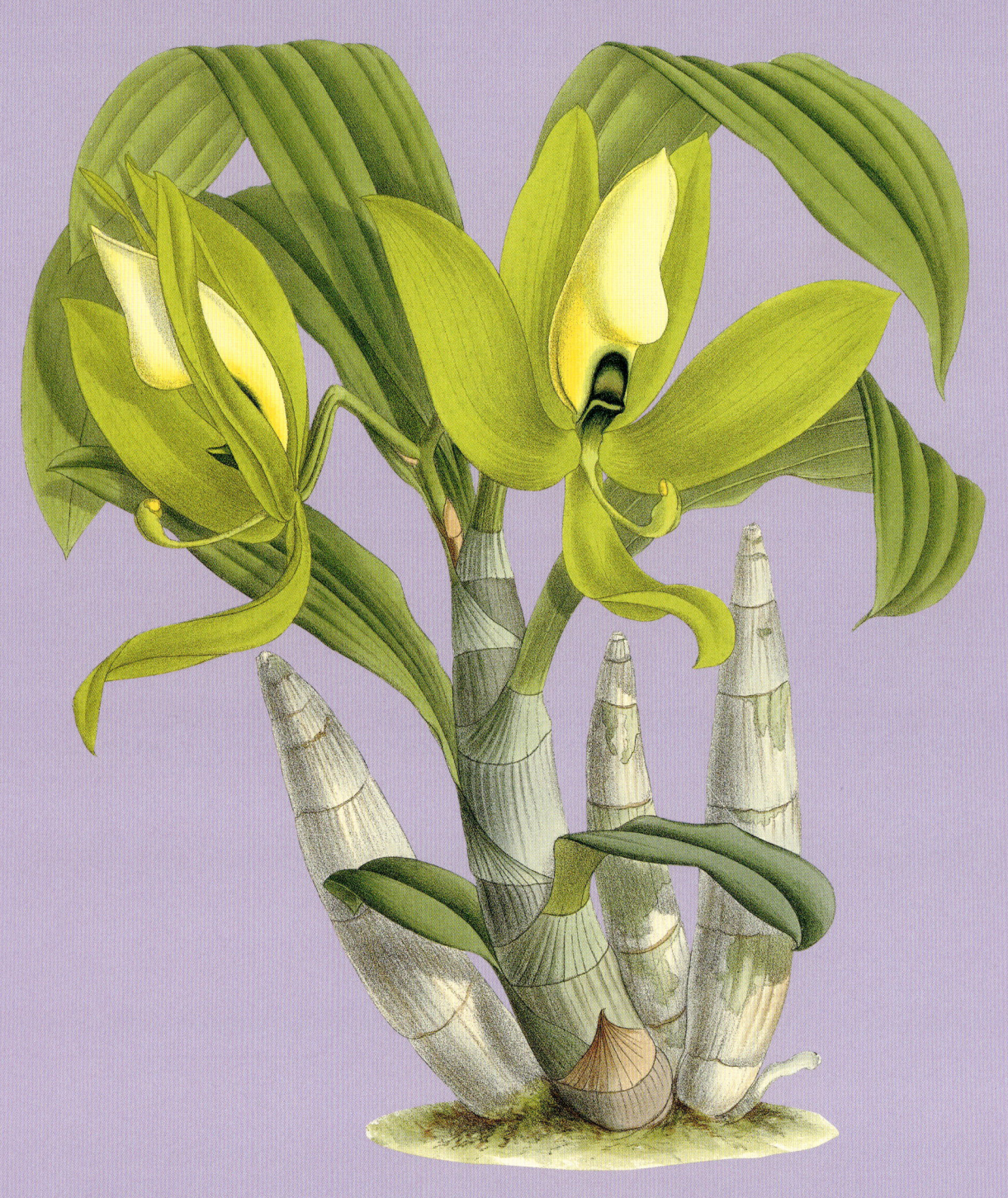

SWAN ORCHID
CYCNOCHES CHLOROCHILON

Cycnoches chlorochilon, the swan orchid, belongs to a small but fascinating genus of tropical American orchids that range from Central America to Brazil, where they grow epiphytically on trees in the rainforest, and are not at all common in nature. The British botanist and orchid specialist John Lindley established the genus *Cycnoches* in 1832 in his *Genera and Species of Orchidaceous Plants*, naming it for its graceful column which resembles the elegantly curved neck of a mute swan (from the Greek words *kyknos*, meaning "swan", and *anchen*, meaning "neck").

Cycnoches species have a cigar-shaped fleshy swollen stem, called a pseudobulb, with several pleated leaves borne towards its apex. The plants have distinct male and female flowers, unlike most orchids, which have bisexual flowers bearing functional male organs (the stamen) and female organs (the stigma). The large, fleshy and pleasantly fragrant flowers are also slightly unusual among the orchids in that the lip (a highly modified petal) is uppermost in the flower. The female flowers of the swan orchid lack a functional stamen and pollen masses but have a column that bears the stigma on its lower (ventral) but upward-facing surface. The male flowers have a more slender and graceful column that lacks a functional stigma but bears a terminal stamen, with the pollen masses lying below the anther cap. Bees attracted by the fragrance of the flowers try to land on the glossy, convex, fleshy lip, but their feet cannot gain purchase, and the insect slips down along the column, taking the pollen masses with it as it passes the stamen. The pollen masses stick to the thorax of the bee and can be transferred to the stigma of a female flower if and when the bee visits.

Cycnoches chlorochilon was described by the German botanist Otto Klotzsch in 1838 based upon a plant collected by Morris from Maracay in coastal Venezuela, and flowered in Germany by Eduard Otto. This species is widely distributed in the lowland and lower hill forests of Panama, Colombia, Venezuela and the Guianas, usually growing by rivers and streams. It has been illustrated many times, although not always accurately. For example, in 1888 a male inflorescence flower was illustrated

Opposite: Matilda Smith's illustration of the Brazilian *Cycnoches haagii* for *Curtis's Botanical Magazine* in 1896. The lithograph was the work of John Nugent Fitch, Walter Hood Fitch's nephew and student.

OCTOBER 18, 1879.] *THE GARDENERS' CHRONICLE.* 493

Notices of Books.

Description of the Glasshouses in the Botanic Garden of the Copenhagen University, *with Plans and Details of the Works Executed in Forming the Gardens from* 1871—1874. Published on the occasion of the Fourth Centenary of the University (June, 1879), by J. C. Jacobsen and Tighe Rothe.

The new garden at Copenhagen is laid out on the site of part of the ancient fortifications of Copenhagen within the city, and close to the University and other scientific institutions, but being surrounded by open spaces, gardens, &c., it has many of the advantages of being in the country. It has a total area of about 21 acres, and is an oblong square in shape. Advantage has been taken of the ramparts, moat, glacis, &c., which formerly occupied the ground, to turn them into sloping banks, terraces, hills and hollows, glass roofing measures about 3470 square yards. There is a wide terrace in front of the main range, with a granite stair about 20 feet wide, leading from the centre of it to the gardens; then there is a range of lean-to houses on either side of this grand stair against the terrace wall and parallel to the main range, facing S.S.E. The main range is about 305 feet long, the centre Palm-house being 100 feet in diameter and 62 feet high; there is at each end of the range a circular house about 60 feet in diameter and 33 feet high, and between those and the Palm-house are two span-roof houses about 65 feet long each by 30 feet wide and 25 feet high. These two houses have each an annexe 13 feet wide lean-to against the south front of them. The back upright of this range is a wall, against which, to the north, are potting and tool-stores, rooms, &c. The lean-to ranges on either side of the granite stair on the low level are each about 130 feet long by 16½ feet wide, in consists in preserving a mean temperature in the intermediate space, so as to prevent the cooling of the interior glass, which would then cool the air inside. The terrace is built on arches, giving an enormous underground chamber with about 775 square yards of floor, which serves to hold a large quantity of fuel, as well as to store in winter plants from the gardens which will not stand frost, also a store for tools, &c. There are stairs leading from the main range down into this subterranean passage, the floor of which is on the same level as the floor of the low ranges in front of the terrace, thus providing a means of communication between the high and low ranges without going into the open air at all. Three ordinary Cornish steam boilers, having internal furnaces with Galloway tubes in them (and having a capacity equal to a 40 horse-power engine) are placed side by side under the terrace in this chamber. The whole of the glasshouses are heated with steam-pipes, viz.,

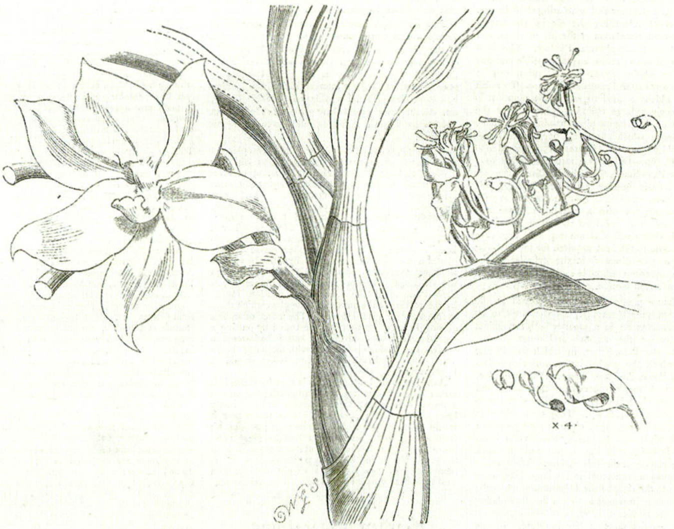

FIG. 78.—CYCNOCHES WARSCEWICZII: WITH MALE AND FEMALE FLOWERS. (SEE P. 505.)

suited for the different species of plants; part of the moat is made into a lake; the result being a very picturesque garden, well adapted to its purpose. The nature of the ground has rendered draining almost superfluous, but has necessitated the placing of stone trenches on the steeper slopes to prevent the soil being carried into the lake during heavy rains. When demolishing the fortifications they came upon a quantity of stable manure, which had been buried under a great heap of earth for nearly two centuries. The water supply is abundant, and provides a continuous flow through the lake. Owing to the climate the glasshouses play an important part in the work of the garden, and are also made a feature in the arrangement, occupying, as they do, a commanding position on an elevated plateau at the northern extremity of the gardens, protected behind by a plantation and by high buildings behind that again. The plantation, when the trees grow taller, will form a fine background to the range. The glasshouses have a superficies occupied by the plants of about 2600 square yards, a capacity of about 13,000 cubic yards, and the three divisions. In front of these two ranges, at a distance of about 20 feet, is a span-roof house about 53 feet long, 19 feet wide, and 10½ feet high. At some distance from this there is an aquarium with a glass roof, about 33 feet in diameter by 18 feet high, having a circular basin in the centre about 18 feet in diameter, 3 feet 3 inches deep at the sides, and 6 feet 6 inches deep in the middle. Behind the aquarium are two low span-roofed houses for propagating and scientific research, each 24 feet by 12 feet, with potting-room and laboratories attached. The whole of the main range (except the two little annexes) is double glazed, as is also the aquarium; the other houses are all single glazed, or the higher half of roof double and the lower half single glazed—all that is single glazed being provided with shutters. The principal uprights and rafters in the main range and aquarium are of iron, but to prevent drip from the cold iron it is nearly all covered with wood to the inside; care has been taken to make the double glazing (especially to the outside) as tight as possible, as the great advantage of this system 1282 yards of 4-inch, 415 yards of 3-inch, and 300 yards of 1½-inch pipes.

It is found that heating by steam has many advantages over heating by hot water, especially in large glasshouses; one advantage is that all the boilers can be placed in one stokehole, and even one boiler and consequently a single fire can be made to heat high and low levels, far and near, where hot water would not circulate. The heat can be got up or let out of any of the branches by simply opening or closing a stopcock, and they give off about 60 per cent. more heat than hot-water pipes. Besides the heating apparatus proper a 2-inch pipe is carried along at the spring of each roof (between the double glazing) to melt the snow and keep a dry atmosphere in between. The square surface of piping allowed per 1000 yards of cubic content of the glasshouses varies from 26 square yards of surface in a temperate-house to 138 square yards in the aquarium to keep it at 20° C., or 32° above the external temperature. The boilers are kept generally at a pressure of three atmospheres, and the smoke is carried under the Palm-

Cycnoches warscewiczii in *The Gardeners' Chronicle*, 18 October 1879

An unattributed engraving of *Cycnoches warscewiczii* showing female and male flowers on the same plant drawn in 1879 for the *Gardeners' Chronicle*, a journal with a wide distribution that included many articles of orchids, including species new to science, culture, famous collections, glasshouse innovation and taxonomy.

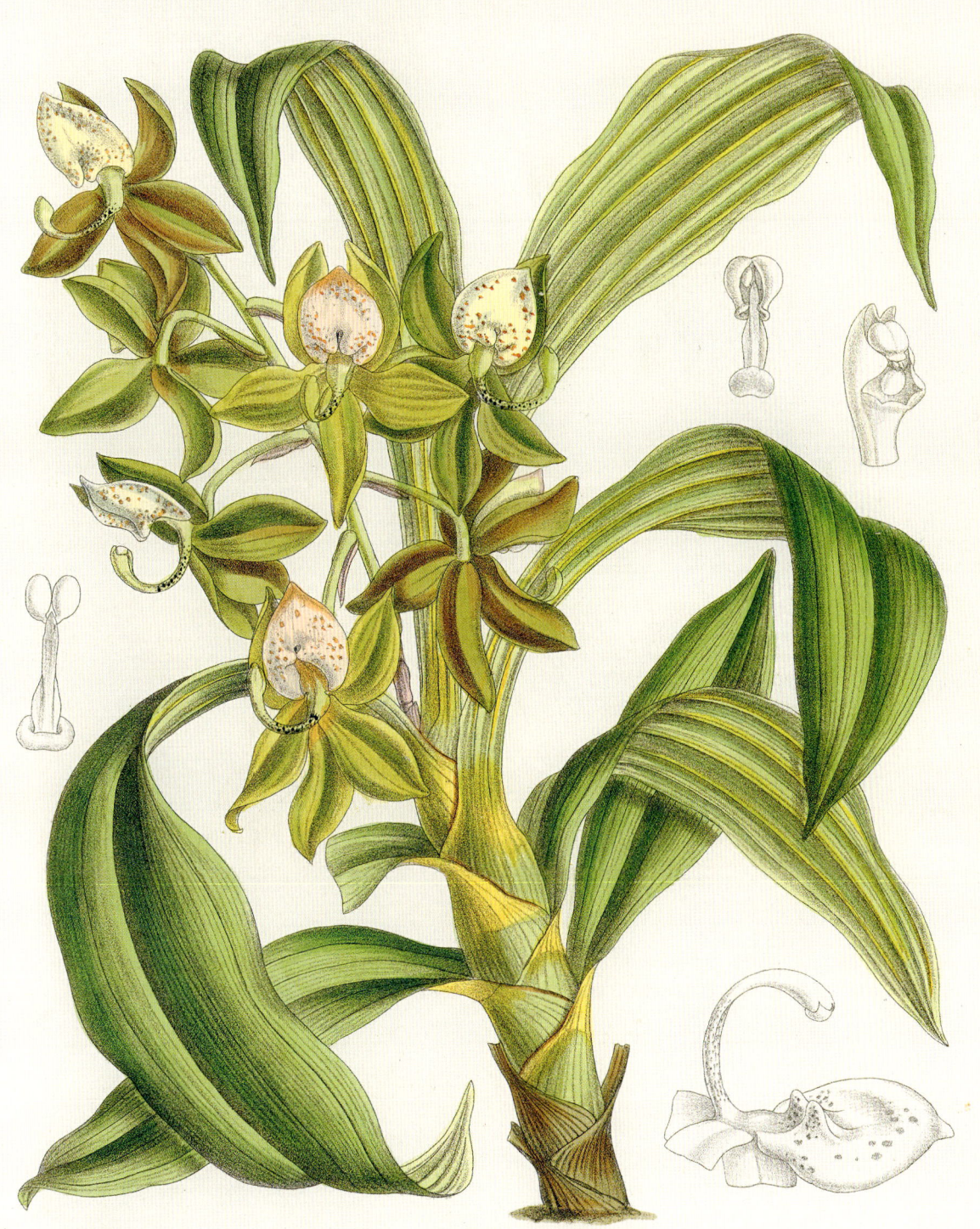

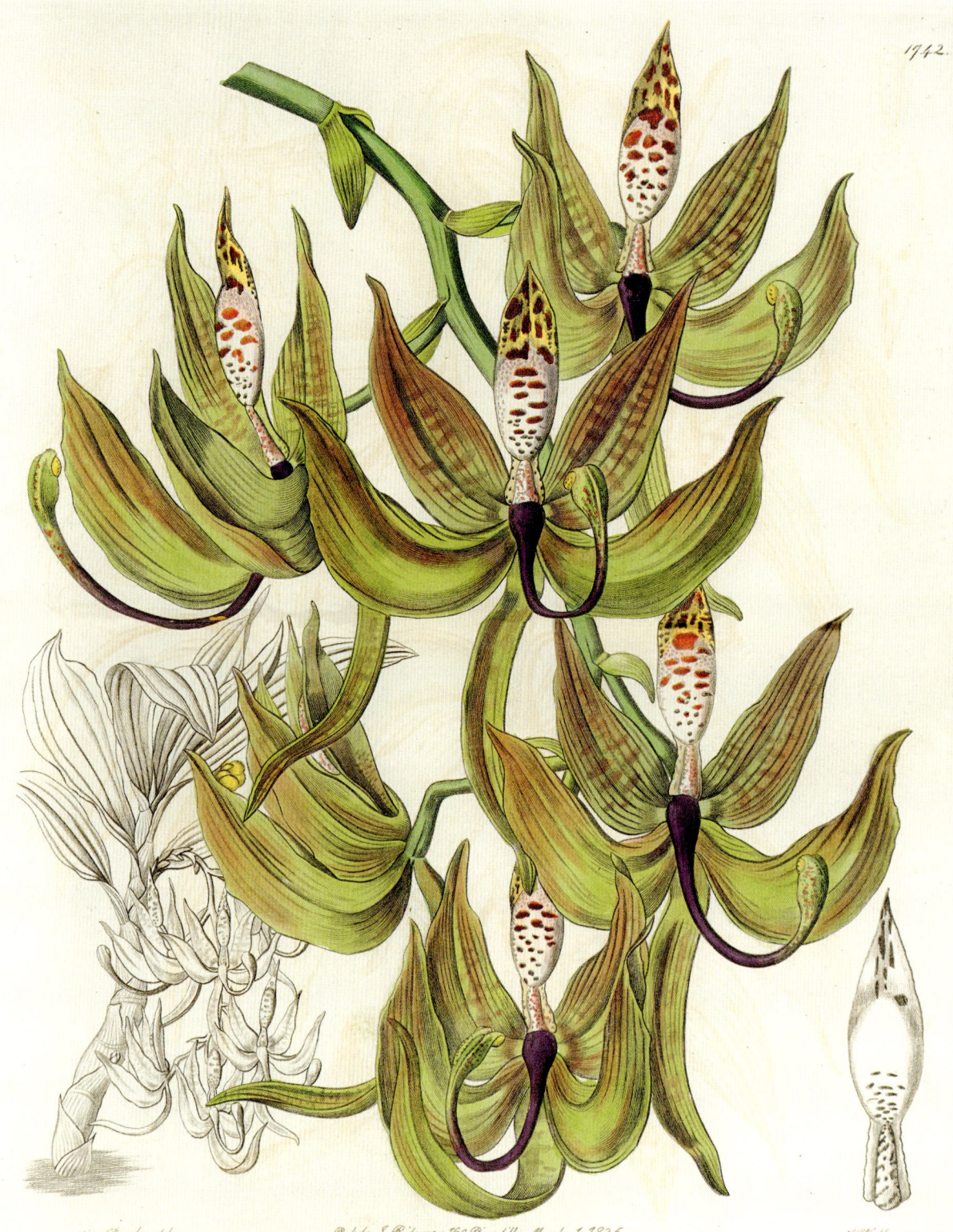

1742.

Miss Drake del.   Pub. by J. Ridgway 169 Piccadilly March. 1. 1835.   J. Watts sc.

Opposite: *Cycnoches loddigesii*, a male inflorescence, drawn by Sarah Drake for *Edwards' Botanical Register* in 1836.

Below: A male inflorescence and plant of *Cycnoches egertonianum* (as *Cycnoches ventricosum* var. *egertonianum*), including details of the lip and column, flowered at the Royal Botanic Gardens, Kew and illustrated by Walter Hood Fitch for *Curtis's Botanical Magazine* in 1843.

correctly orientated in *L'Illustration Horticole* but upside down in *The Garden*.

The genus comprises about 20 species that fall into two distinct groups, namely those in which the male and female flowers are somewhat similar in shape, and those in which they are markedly different. In the first group, which includes *C. chlorochilon*, the male and female flowers more or less resemble each other, but differ in their column structure as explained above. Sarah Drake's wonderful double plate for *Edwards' Botanical Register* of the northern tropical South American species *C. loddigesii* is more colourful than *C. chlorochilon*. It commemorates

Loddiges nursery in Hackney, London, which pioneered the cultivation and sale of tropical orchids in England. Another distinctive species is the Brazilian *C. haagii*, which was drawn for Martius's *Flora Brasilica* and was beautifully illustrated in colour by Matilda Smith for *Curtis's Botanical Magazine*. In particular, Smith included the details of the floral structure which are so important for the accurate identification of the species.

However, in the other group the male and female flowers differ markedly. Thus in *Cycnoches egertoniana* the female flowers are more similar to those of *C. chlorochilon*, but in contrast the male flowers are borne in hanging racemes and have a spoon-shaped lip with a fringe of slender lobes around its margin. Light intensity and nutrition determine the sex of the flowers that are produced by a plant. Walter Hood Fitch drew *Cycnoches egertonianum* for *Curtis's Botanical Magazine*, and Matilda Smith sketched three species as records for the Kew collection, namely *C. maculata* grown by Charlesworth on 22 October 1903, *C. pentadactylon* on 29 August 1904, and *C. densiflora* grown by Mr Birchenak of Alderley Edge, Cheshire on 17 November 1908. However, one of the finest illustrations is that of *C. aureum* by Lilian Snelling on 24 October 1938, probably intended for *Curtis's Botanical Magazine* but never used. It includes a watercolour of the pendent inflorescences, and black-and-white pencil sketches of the habit and details of the flower.

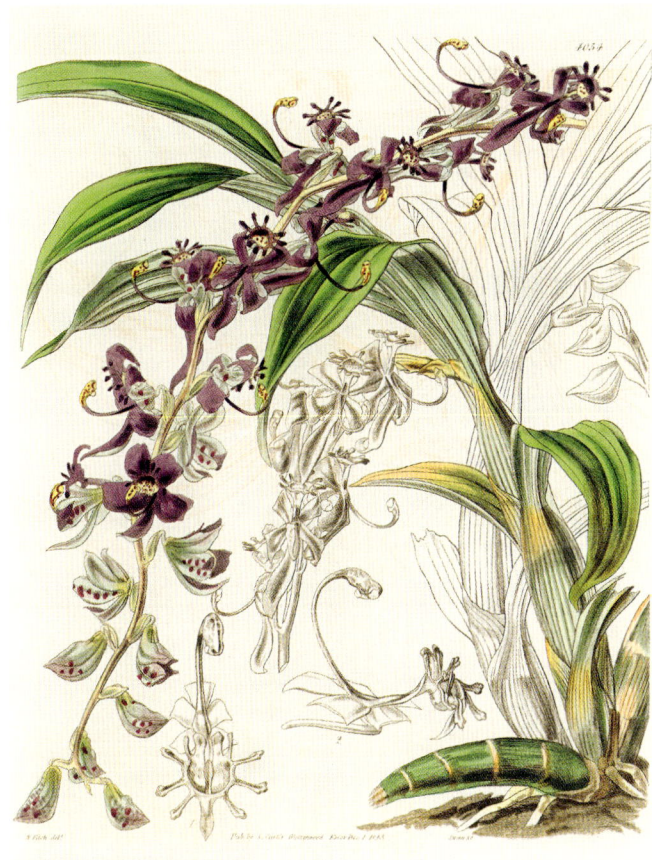

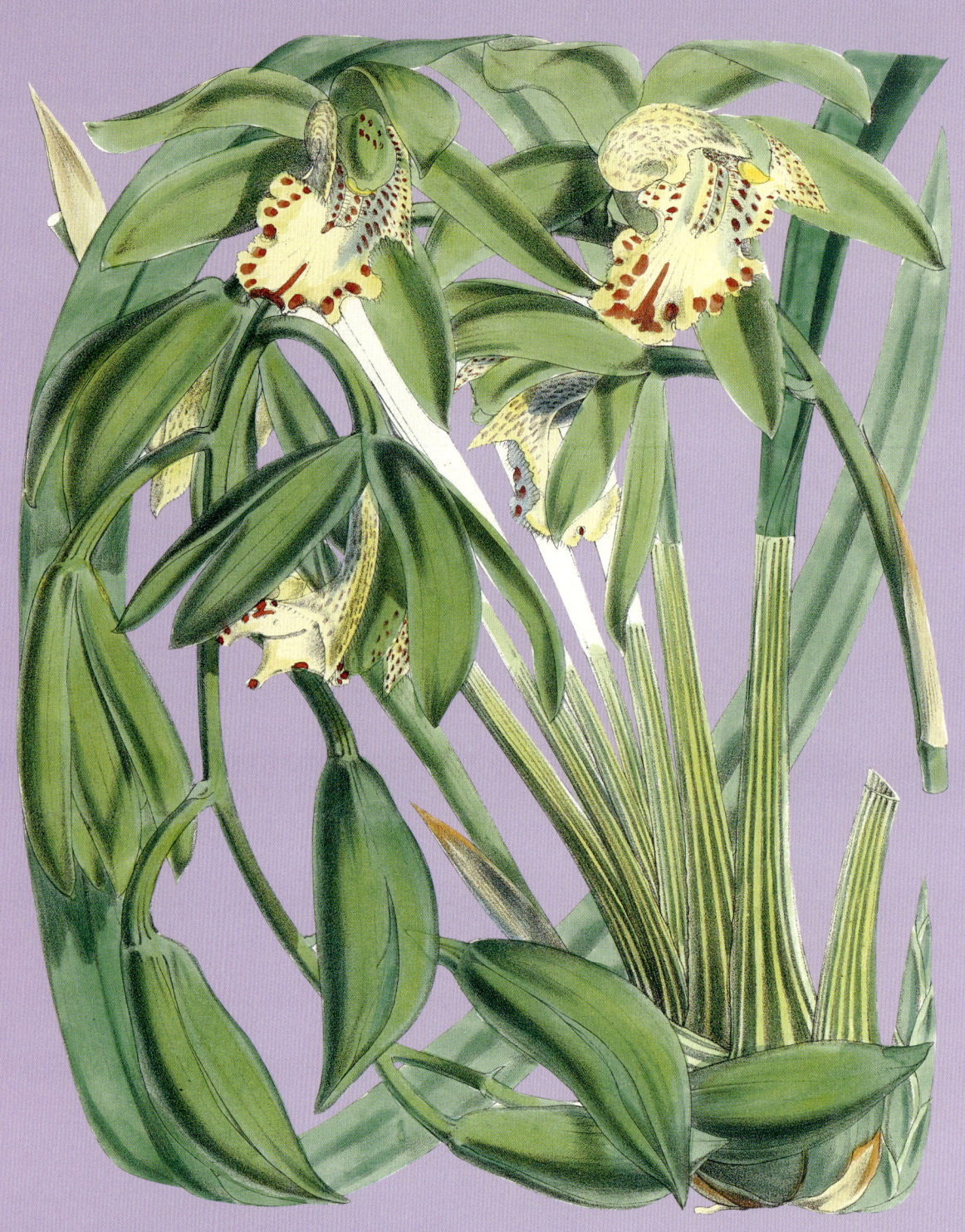

JOSEPH HOOKER'S ORCHID
CYMBIDIUM HOOKERIANUM

Mountains around the world provide ideal habitats for a great many orchid species. The Himalayas and the surrounding ranges and foothills in Nepal, India, Myanmar and south-west China are a repository for some truly spectacular and important orchids, including *Cymbidium hookerianum*, which was named in honour of Joseph Dalton Hooker, the second Director of the Royal Botanic Gardens, Kew. Hooker spent a considerable time in the Indian Himalayas in the late 1840s, collecting many species and bringing them back to Europe for the first time.

Originally the species was named *Cymbidium grandiflorum* in 1851 by the Englishman William Griffith, who collected it in Bhutan, but that name had already been used for another species (now no longer considered to be a *Cymbidium*, but moved to another genus as *Cleistes grandiflora*). Therefore Griffith's use was considered to be "illegitimate" according to the rules of the *International Code of Nomenclature for Algae, Fungi and Plants*. The next validly published name for the species

then took priority – that of the German botanist Heinrich Gustav Reichenbach, who had in 1861 named the same taxon to commemorate Hooker. Reichenbach was one of the foremost orchidologists of the 1800s, succeeding John Lindley as the world's leading authority on orchids after the Englishman's death.

The large flowers of *Cymbidium hookerianum* are borne on a long, arching inflorescence, have a cream or white-coloured lip with dark red markings, and the yellow-green tepals may or may not have red markings as well. The flowers usually have a fresh green apple fragrance. Vegetatively the plants have long grass-like leaves, and given enough time may grow into striking large specimen plants. The large flowers of *Cymbidium hookerianum* and the plant's preference for cool growing conditions have resulted in this species becoming important in the hybridization of orchids. Although the species itself is difficult to bloom because the buds are very sensitive to changes in temperature, hybrids resulting from crosses with other species can be much more easily grown and flowered.

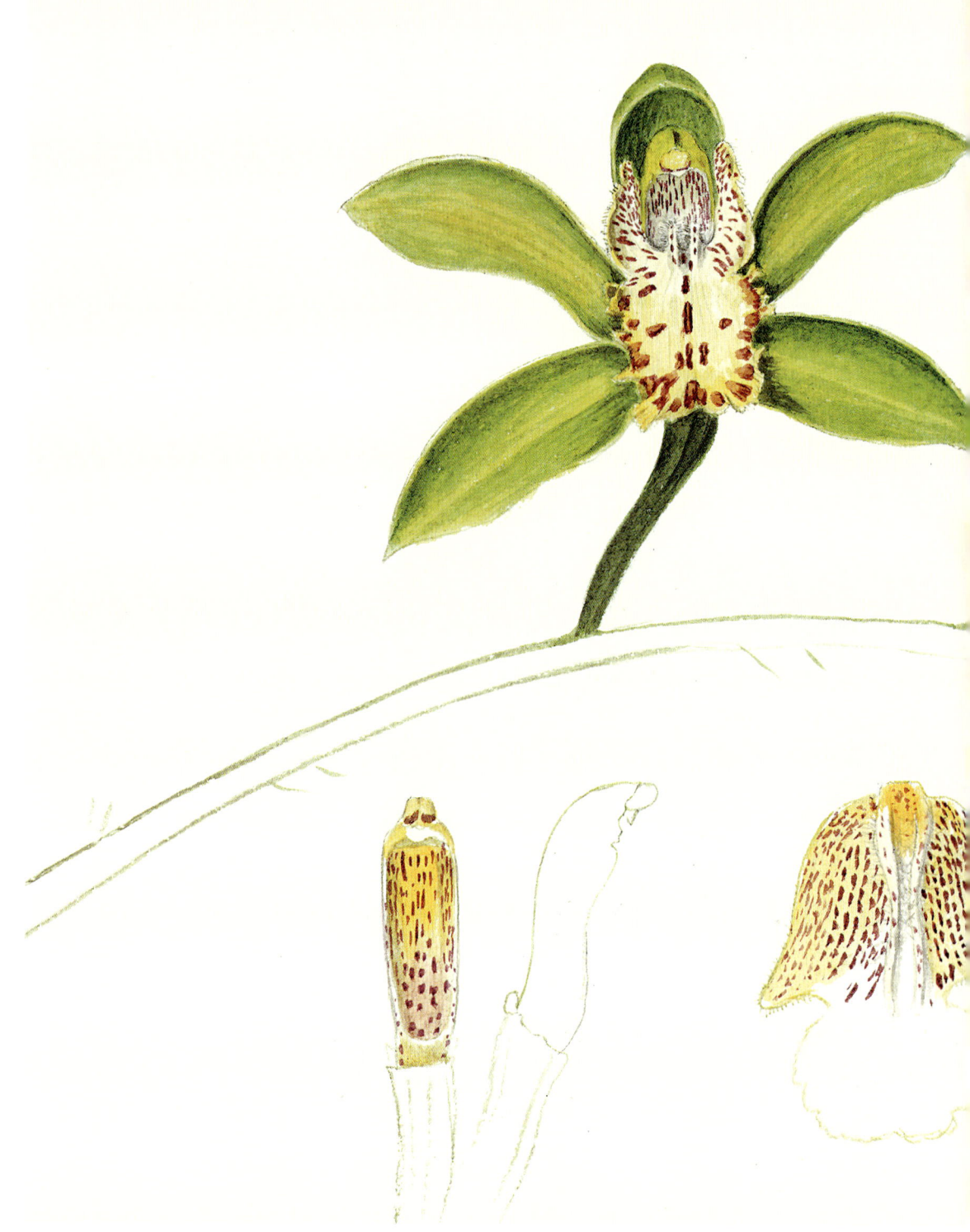

KERIANUM

Febry 22nd 1884

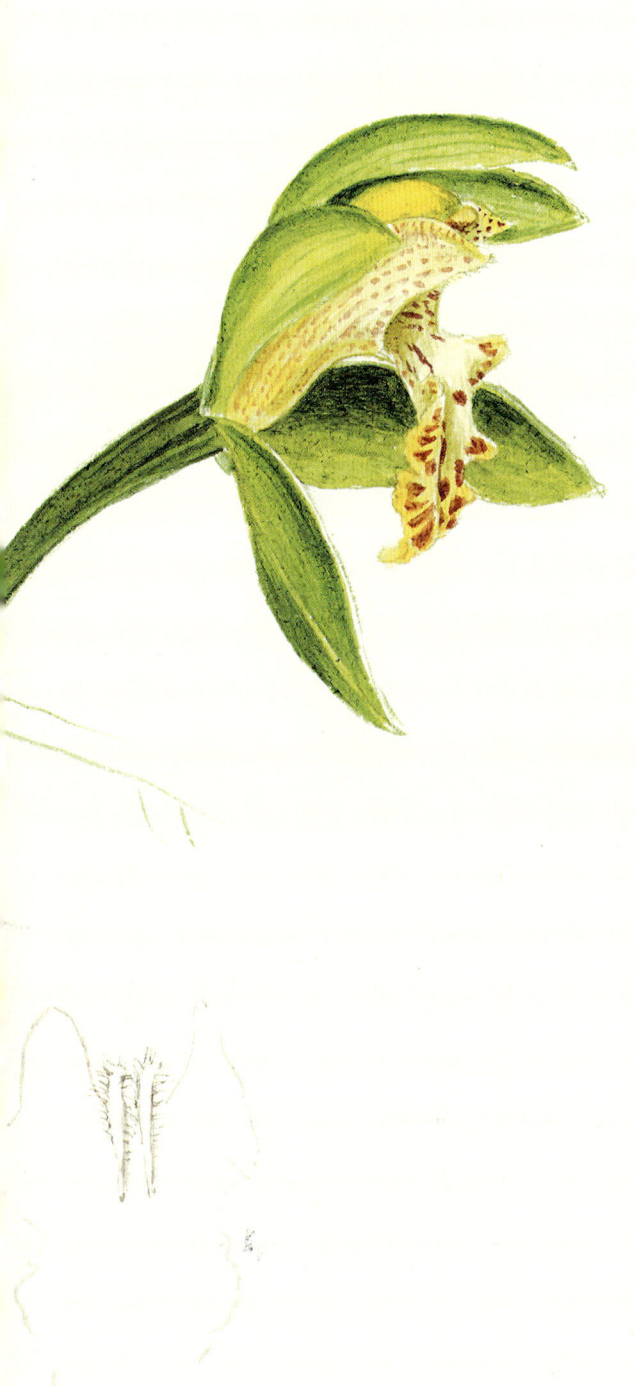

A noble Speci
or varieties
which I have
now seen for
the first time
It was first
described & named
by Prof. Reich:
in S.C. Jnuary 6th/66
(See Le Bk X. 46
& named by him
in compliment to
Dr JJ Hooker of
Kew. It is
a native of
Sikkim. There
is a good figure
of it in Bot. Mag
t. 5574 — May
1866. where
full description
is given — It was
flowered first
in this Country
by Messrs J Veitch'
Sons. but has
very rarely bloom

New Plants.

323. CYMBIDIUM HOOKERIANUM, *Rchb. fil.*

Foliis lineari-ligulatis acutis (bipedalibus), vaginis energice striatis, pedunculo porrecto racemoso grandifloro, floribus illos Cymbidii eburnei æquantibus, sepalis petalisque stellatis, oblongis obtuse acutis, petalis paulo angustioribus, labello trifido, laciniis lateralibus basi subsemicordatis, seu æqualibus, antice angulatis, lacinia antica subcordata ovata transversa lobulosa, lineis geminis velutinis a basi disci in basin laciniæ anticæ, labello ceterum hinc illinc subvelutino. Sepala et petala viridia. Labellum et columna albo-flavida guttis atropurpureis.

A magnificent species, with the habit of Cymbidium giganteum, but with larger flowers of a pale Apple green; the lip and column being whitish, with numerous purple blotches. The delicacy of colours is very beautiful.

What must prove to be this plant, flowered years ago at Exeter with Messrs. Veitch, under Mr. Dominy's care. We saw it with buds at the Royal Exotic Nursery, Chelsea; and we were told the development of flowers was very slow, so that the plant is expected to be one of the grand ornaments of the International Flower Show.

No doubt Messrs. Veitch will be glad to obtain the name before the opening of the flowers—an excellent name too, given with the writer's best wishes as a gratulation for the first new year's day of his Kew directorship, to Dr. Hooker. *Rchb. fil.*

Species description by Heinrich Gustav Reichenbach, in *The Gardeners' Chronicle and Agricultural Gazette*, page 7, 6 January 1866

In the 1800s, enormous numbers of plant species were being collected in the tropics and other distant lands, brought back to Europe and cultivated, flowered and described scientifically in the many horticultural publications of the day, including *The Gardeners' Chronicle*.

The German orchidologist Heinrich Gustav Reichenbach published the species *Cymbidium hookerianum* in this journal, including a botanical Latin "diagnosis" of the species describing the key and distinguishing features of the plant and flowers, and a description in English of how the species came into cultivation and to his attention.

Here we learn that the plant was first cultivated by the great Veitch nursery, which was based in Exeter and Chelsea in the UK, and that Reichenbach is dedicating the species to Joseph Dalton Hooker, for the first New Year's day of his tenure as the second director of the Royal Botanic Gardens, Kew.

Below: *Cymbidium hookerianum* (as *Cymbidium grandiflorum var. punctatum)* by Alphonse Goossens, in J. J. Linden, *Lindenia: Iconographie des Orchidées*, 1893.

Below right: *Cymbidium hookerianum* (as *Cymbidium grandiflorum)* by Robert Pantling, in *Annals of the Royal Botanic Garden, Calcutta*, 1891.

Cymbidium species are not just found in the Himalayas, but are distributed throughout the Indian subcontinent, Indo-China, eastern Asia and south-east Asia, and as far south as northern and eastern Australia. Chinese *Cymbidium* species have been cultivated in China for thousands of years, and it is said that the great philosopher Confucius wrote about the plants, describing *Cymbidium* as the "King of Fragrance". The Four Gentlemen, or the Four Noble Ones, of Chinese Song dynasty Confucianism have *Cymbidium* as the symbol of spring, representing beauty and nobility, but also fragility and humility.

Highly prized for their graceful leaves, delicate flowers and light fragrance, the orchids appear in Chinese artwork and writings from the Song, Ming and Qing dynasties. Fragrance and variegated leaves are highly desirable traits. Indian *Cymbidium* species tend to have larger flowers, and today cultivated hybrids form the basis of a vast cut-flower trade in India and Pakistan. Sprays of *Cymbidium* flowers may last for 2 or 3 months after the first bud opens, and the long-lasting, waxy blooms have an important role in floral decorations, bouquets and corsages at large celebrations such as weddings.

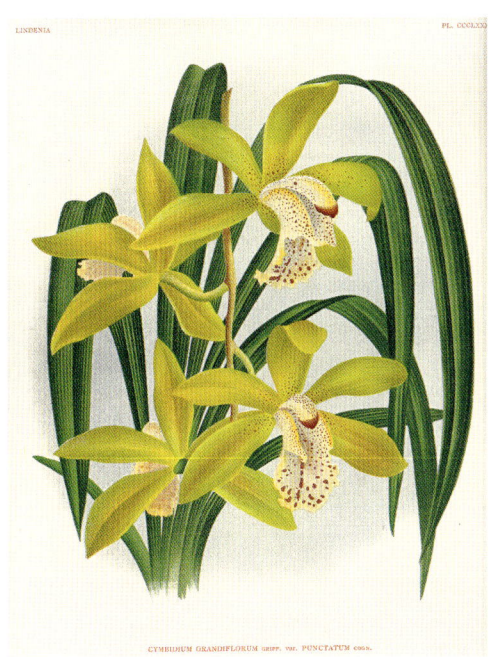

CYMBIDIUM GRANDIFLORUM Griff. var. PUNCTATUM Cogn.

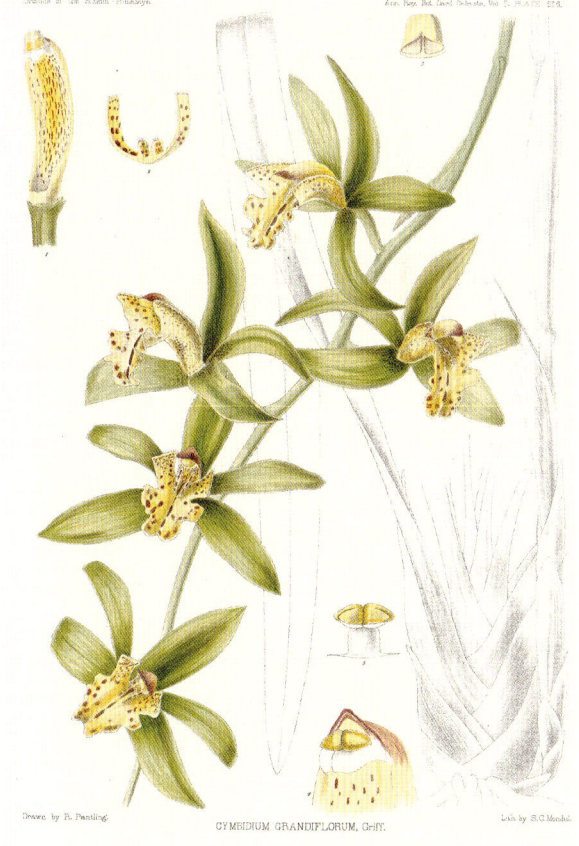

Drawn by R. Pantling.

CYMBIDIUM GRANDIFLORUM, Griff.

Lith by S.C Mondul.

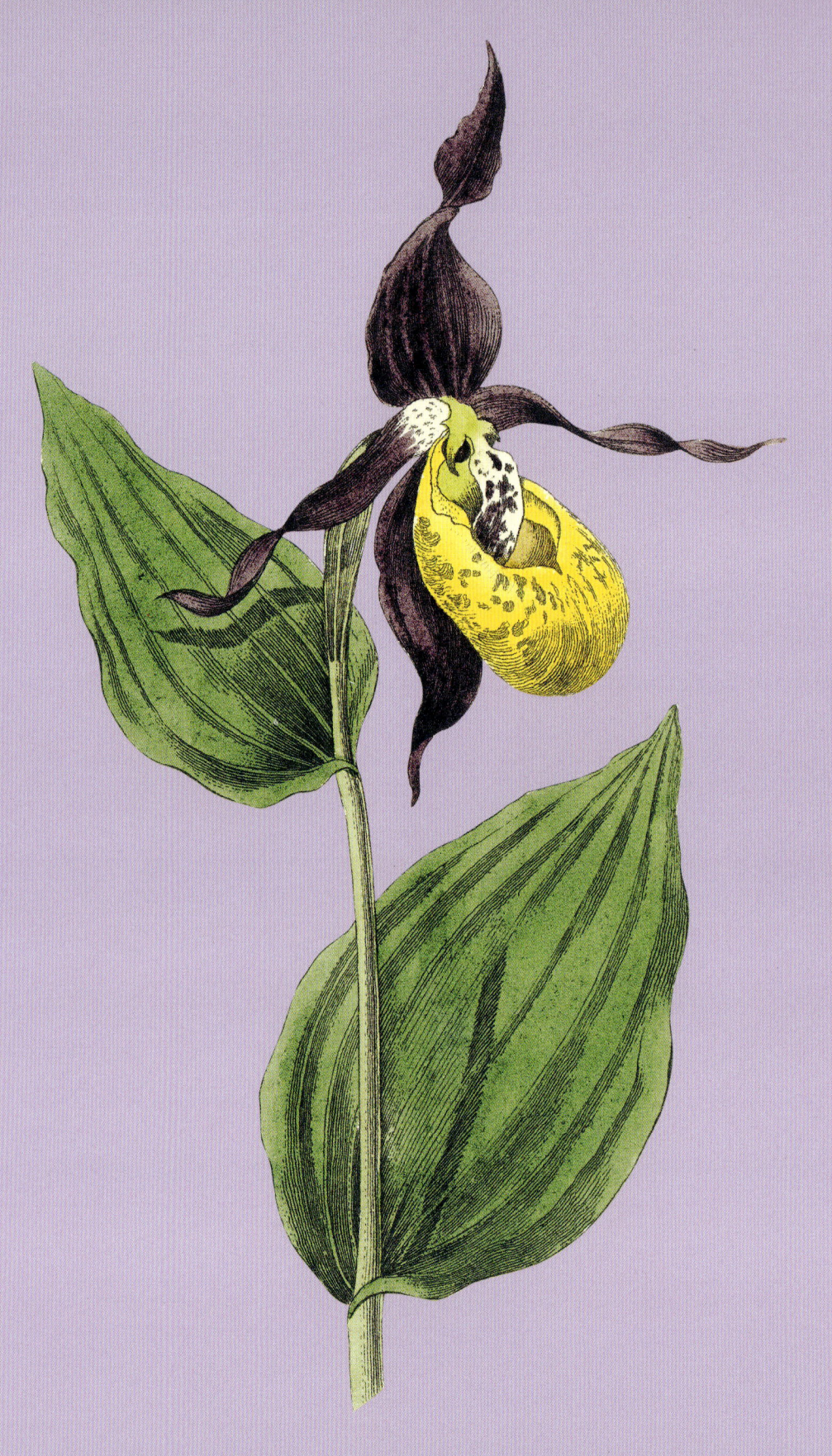

LADY'S SLIPPER ORCHID
CYPRIPEDIUM CALCEOLUS

If the beauty or scarcity of a plant, or the singularity of its structure, entitle it to our notice, the ladies' slipper certainly merits the first place in every collection of British plants. It may, indeed, be reckoned the Queen of all European orchideae. Accordingly, it has not only been admired and cherished by the scientific botanist, but it has, among gardeners, always been sold at the highest price of any British vegetable.

James Sowerby, *English Botany* (1790)

The lady's slipper orchid, *Cypripedium calceolus,* is one of the most recognizable and renowned flowering plants in the European flora. In many countries, including the UK, it is also one of the most endangered, and in some countries, such as Greece, it is already extinct. It has become a symbol for plant conservation in many countries, especially in England, where it was the first plant to have its own Species Survival Programme as part of English Nature's strategy to protect rare and endangered species of fauna and flora.

Carl Linnaeus first used the name *Cypripedium* in 1737 in his *Flora Lapponica* when he described the European species as "*Cypripedium foliis ovato-lanceolatis*". The name *Cypripedium* alluded to Cyprus, the island that was the mythological birthplace of

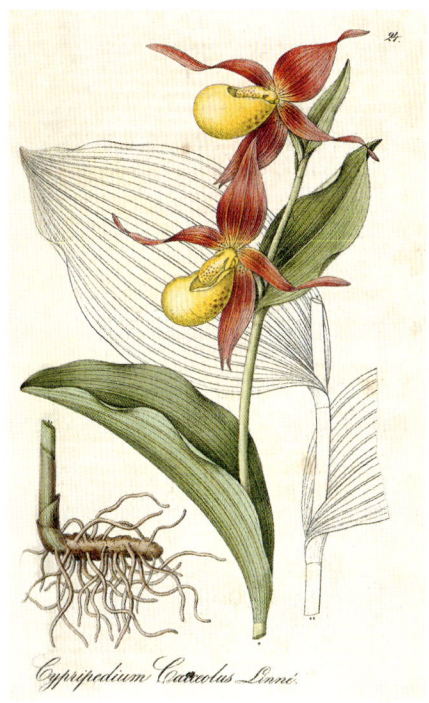

Cypripedium Calceolus Linné.

Aphrodite (Venus), and *pedilum*, meaning a shoe or slipper, referred to the vernacular name ("lady's slipper" in Britain, "Frauenshuh" in Germany and "sabot de Venus" in France). In 1753, Linnaeus named and described *C. calceolus*.

The Flemish botanist Rembert Dodoens published the earliest description of this orchid, under the names "*Calceolus Marianus*", "Pfaffen schuh", "Papen schoen" and "*Calceolus Sacerdotis*", and a simple but accurate illustration of a cultivated plant (the earliest record of its cultivation), in his herbal of 1568. He used it again in his *Stirpium Historiae Pemptades* (1583), together with a more refined illustration originating from Carolus Clusius's herbal, *Rariorum Aliquot Stirpium* (1583), referring to it as "Marienschuh". Clusius observed the plant in the wild in Austria and Hungary, and it seems likely that his illustration was based on a plant from his travels. We now know that the distribution of this orchid is more extensive, ranging from western and northern Europe across to eastern Siberia, north-eastern China and northern Japan.

Dodoens' plate reappeared in John Gerard's *Herball* (1597) and John Parkinson's *Paradisi in Sole Paradisus Terrestris* (1629). Gerard made the earliest reference to its cultivation in the British Isles, but he was unaware that it was a native British plant. It was first recognized as such by John Parkinson in his *Theatrum Botanicum* (1629), where he recorded it growing in "Lancashire, near upon the border of Yorkshire, in a wood or place called the Helkes, which is three miles from Ingleborough", where it has survived until today. Parkinson was an

astute observer and was the first to link *Cypripedium* species with the orchids and to note their tiny seeds. The French botanist Michel Adanson was the first to formally include them in the orchid family, in 1763.

J. P. Cornut reported the North American species *C. acaule*, the Moccasin flower, in 1635 in his *Canadensium Plantarum Historia*, where he listed "*Calceolus marianus canadensis*". The earliest coloured illustration of a North American species is that of "*Calceolus flore maximo rubente*" (*C. acaule*) by

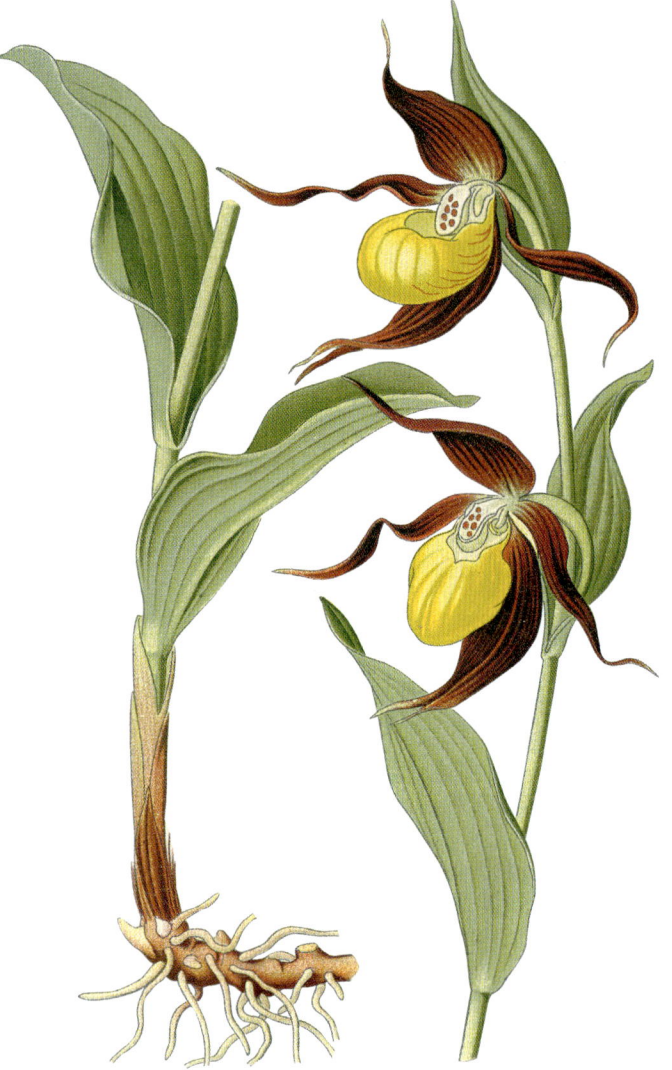

Above: The Eurasian lady's slipper orchid, *Cypripedium calceolus*, England's rarest plant, which was reduced in the twentieth century to a single plant. The Sainsbury Endangered Orchid Project at Kew has ensured that it is now re-established in 15 sites. This illustration was drawn for A. Masclef's *Atlas des Plantes de France*, 1893.

Cypripedium reginae **(as** ***Calceolus Marianus Canadensis*** **) in**
***Canadensium Plantarum Aliarumque Nondum Editarum Historia*, 1635**

This early illustration of *Cypripedium reginae* (as *Calceolus Marianus Canadensis*) was drawn for J. P. Cornut's *Canadensium Plantarum Aliarumque Nondum Editarum Historia*. Cornut's name was taken up by Linnaeus in his *Species Plantarum* in 1753. Linnaeus failed to realize that the names listed under his *C. calceolus* represented several species.

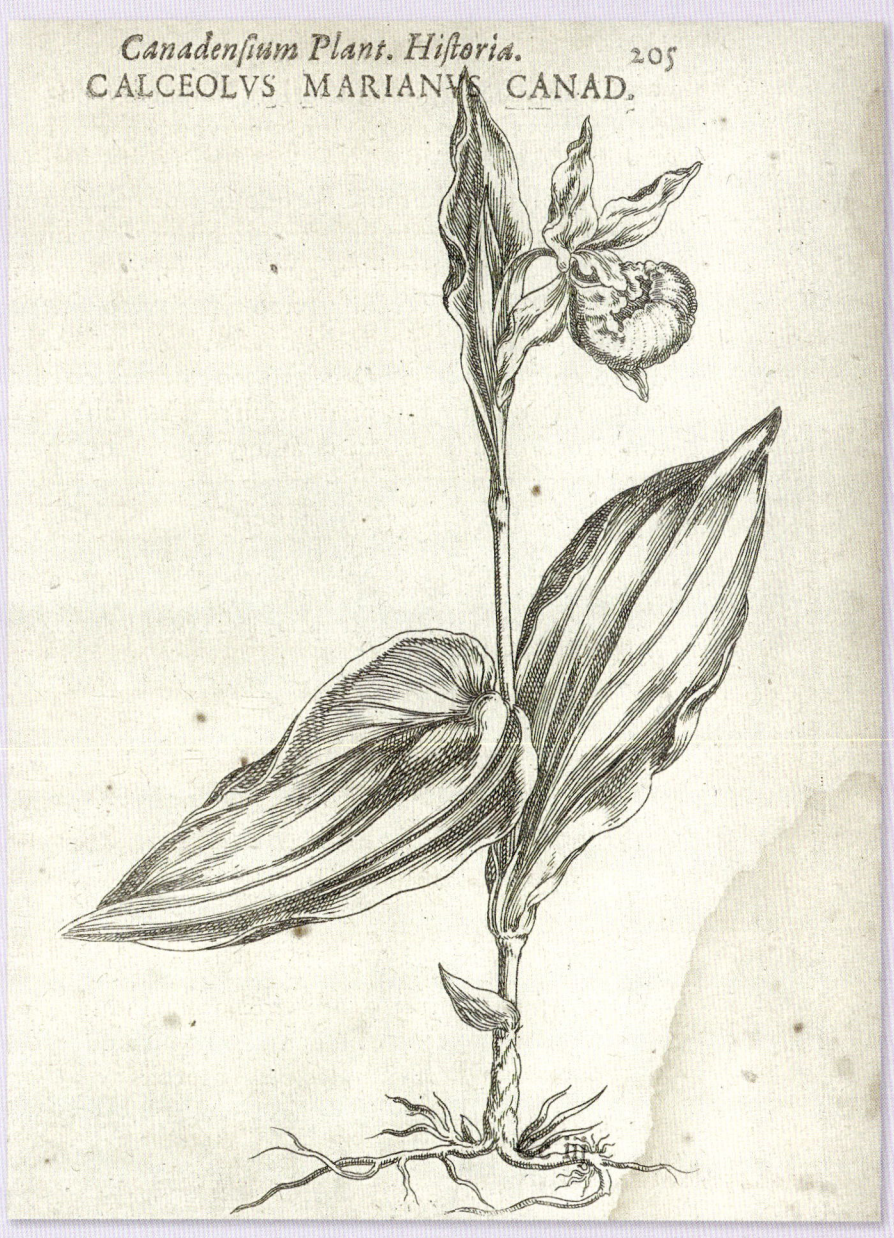

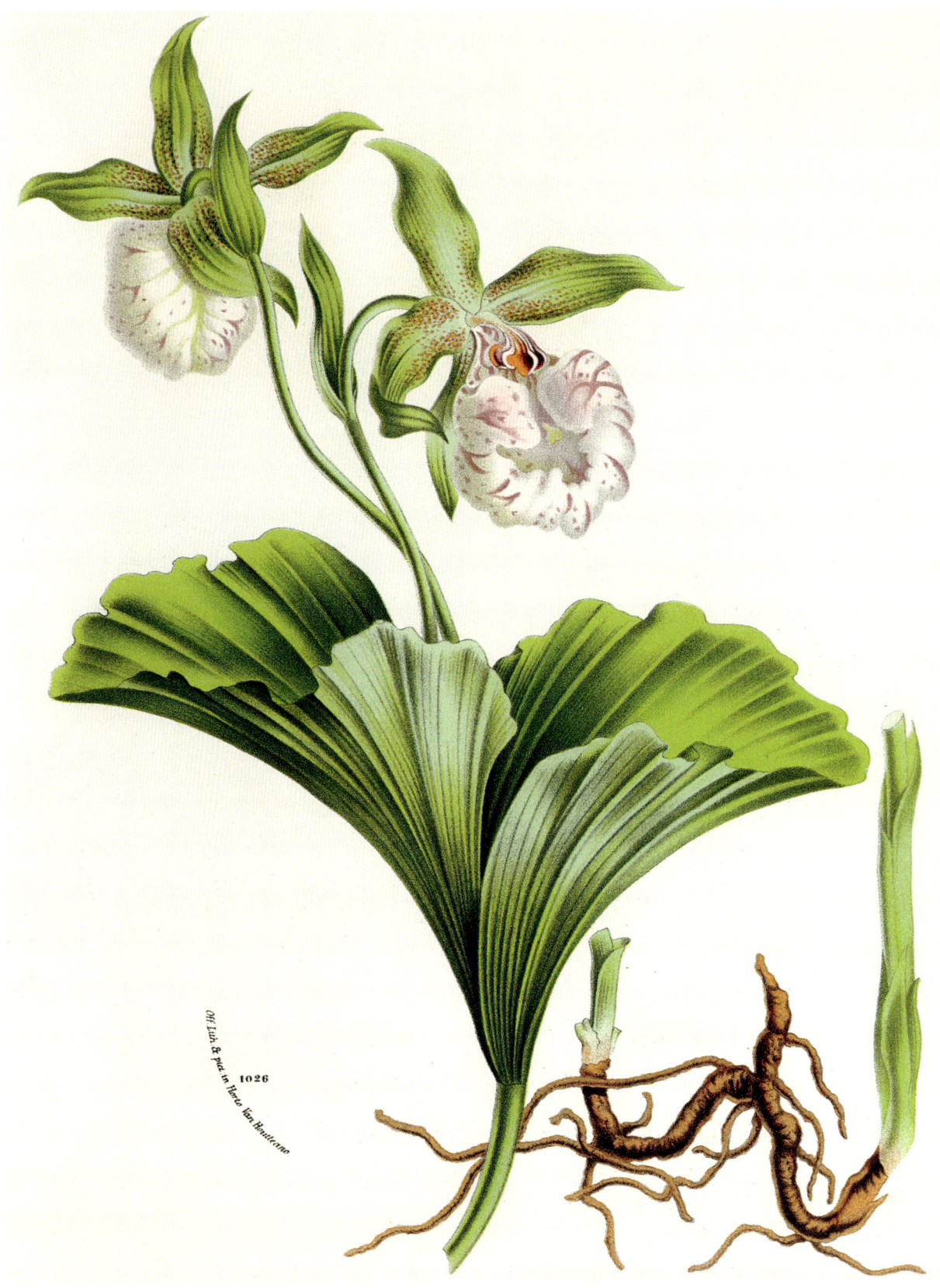

Ch. Lith. & pict in Horto Van Houtteano

1026

Mark Catesby in *The Natural History of Carolina, Florida and the Bahama Islands* (1754).

Philip Miller's *Gardeners Dictionary* (1731) included three hardy slipper orchids, namely *C. calceolus*, *C. parviflorum* and *C. reginae*. His coloured illustration of *C. calceolus* in his *Figures of the Most Beautiful, Useful and Uncommon Plants Described in the Gardeners Dictionary* (1758) is possibly the first depiction of a British plant.

Charles Darwin was intrigued by the slipper-shaped lip of *C. calceolus*, and correctly identified it as a trap for pollinating insects. Solitary bees are attracted to the glossy slippery staminode that lies above the lip, and then fall into the flower and can only escape after they have passed under the stamens and stigma and emerged out of the basal apertures.

The genus *Cypripedium* is circumboreal, but most members of the genus are found in China, where 30 species occur. Some of these orchids are remarkable plants. For example, *C. subtropicum* has stems 1 m (3 ft) tall, or more, and flowers with a lip that resembles a small rotting apple. *Cypripedium japonicum and C. formosanum* both have a long stem that bears paired, fan-shaped, pleated leaves, with large green and pink or pink flowers emerging between them. Several Chinese species, such as *C. lichiangense, C. margaritaceum* and *C. fargesii,* have a sessile, heavily spotted single leaf opposite an almost equally large leaf-like spotted bract, with a large, yellow or brown, heavily spotted flower lying between them. These species are pollinated by flies.

Left: *Cypripedium calceolus* from Otto Wilhelm Thomé, *Flora von Deutschland Österreich und der Schweiz*, 1885.

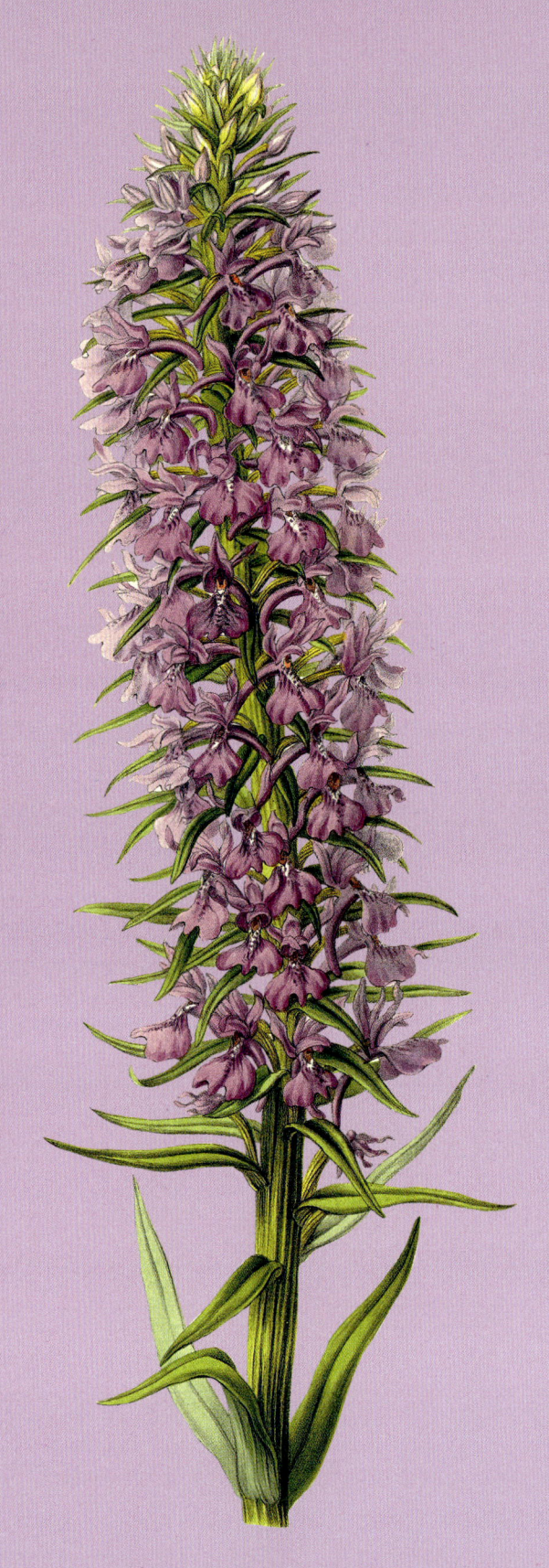

MADEIRAN ORCHID
DACTYLORHIZA FOLIOSA

The flora of the Atlantic islands of Madeira, the Azores and the Canary Islands, collectively known as Macronesia, is distinctive and different from that of Europe and the adjacent African coast. The flora of Madeira has obvious links to that of the other archipelagos, but the isolation and precipitous nature of the island have produced a distinctive number of endemics that are found exclusively in Madeira. One of these is the striking Madeiran orchid, *Dactylorhiza foliosa*. Its nearest relatives, found in Europe and north-west Africa, are usually referred to as marsh orchids or spotted orchids.

The Madeiran orchid has broad glossy green leaves that are unspotted or occasionally very finely spotted. From these rises a stout leafy inflorescence that bears a pyramidal to conical head of large rose-purple flowers, each subtended by a leafy green or purplish stained bract. This species grows in laurel forest, often in glades in the forest or along the margins of the "levadas" (the artificial streams that carry irrigation water around the island). Many endemic herbaceous plants, which are characteristically larger than their relatives in mainland Europe, grow in this unusual habitat, and *D. foliosa* is one of them.

Dactylorhiza differs little from *Orchis* in its habit and flowers, and this is undoubtedly an example of convergent evolution because these orchids attract similar pollinators. Indeed, *Dactylorhiza* species used to be included in a broadly defined genus *Orchis*, but were separated in the middle of the twentieth century when it was realized that their digitate tubers and long bracts more closely resembled those of the fragrant orchids (belonging to *Gymnadenia*, another European genus). This view is supported by recent DNA studies. The genus is widely distributed, with the majority of species being found in Europe, the Mediterranean and western Asia, but extending across temperate Asia into the Himalayas and across northern North America, where only two species, *D. aristata* and *D. viridis,* are found.

The taxonomy of *Dactylorhiza* in Europe is extremely complex because the species hybridize freely where they grow together, and many of the recognized species are of hybrid origin and polyploid – that is, they have double the usual number of chromosomes. However, this is not true of the Madeiran orchid, whose isolation has protected it from these complexities.

Unlike most marsh orchids, the Madeiran orchid is not quite hardy in the British Isles but will survive mild winters well. At Kew, a spectacularly large clump was grown in the old pyramidal Alpine House for many years, and a smaller clump now graces the new Alpine House. Orchids grown as *D. foliosa* in British gardens are usually misidentified plants of the southern European and north African species *D. elata*, or hybrids of various *D. majalis* subspecies.

In Europe and the Mediterranean, many species – often called marsh orchids – are found in bogs, marshes, dune slacks or wet grassland. The early marsh orchid, *D. incarnata*, and the alpine species *D. sambucina* are notable for being polymorphic. In the former, the typical variety has flesh-coloured flowers, but *D. incarnata* var. *coccinea* has red flowers and *D. incarnata* var. *ochroleuca* has pale yellow ones. In the latter, plants with flowers that are yellow, purple or purple with a yellowish flush, grow together in alpine meadows.

A number of species have (often heavily) spotted leaves. This is noticeable in a number of species, such as the common spotted orchid (*D. fuchsii*), the heath spotted orchid (*D. maculata* var. *ericetorum*) and the dark purple-flowered but very variable *D. majalis*, whose varieties include the southern marsh orchid (subsp. *integra*) and the northern marsh orchid (subsp. *purpurella*).

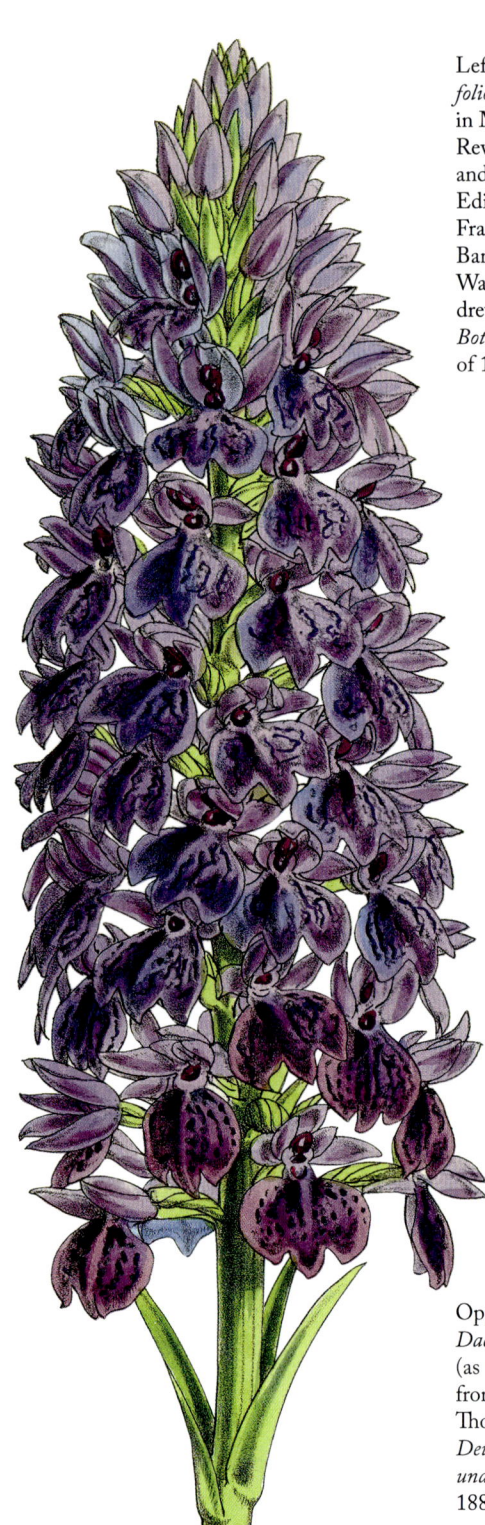

Left: *Dactylorhiza foliosa* collected in Madeira by the Rev. Richard Lowe and flowered in Edinburgh by Mr Fraser of the Comely Bank nursery in 1857. Walter Hood Fitch drew it for *Curtis's Botanical Magazine* of 1858.

Opposite: *Dactylorhiza maculata* (as *Orchis maculata*) from Otto Wilhelm Thomé, *Flora von Deutschland Österreich und der Schweiz*, of 1885.

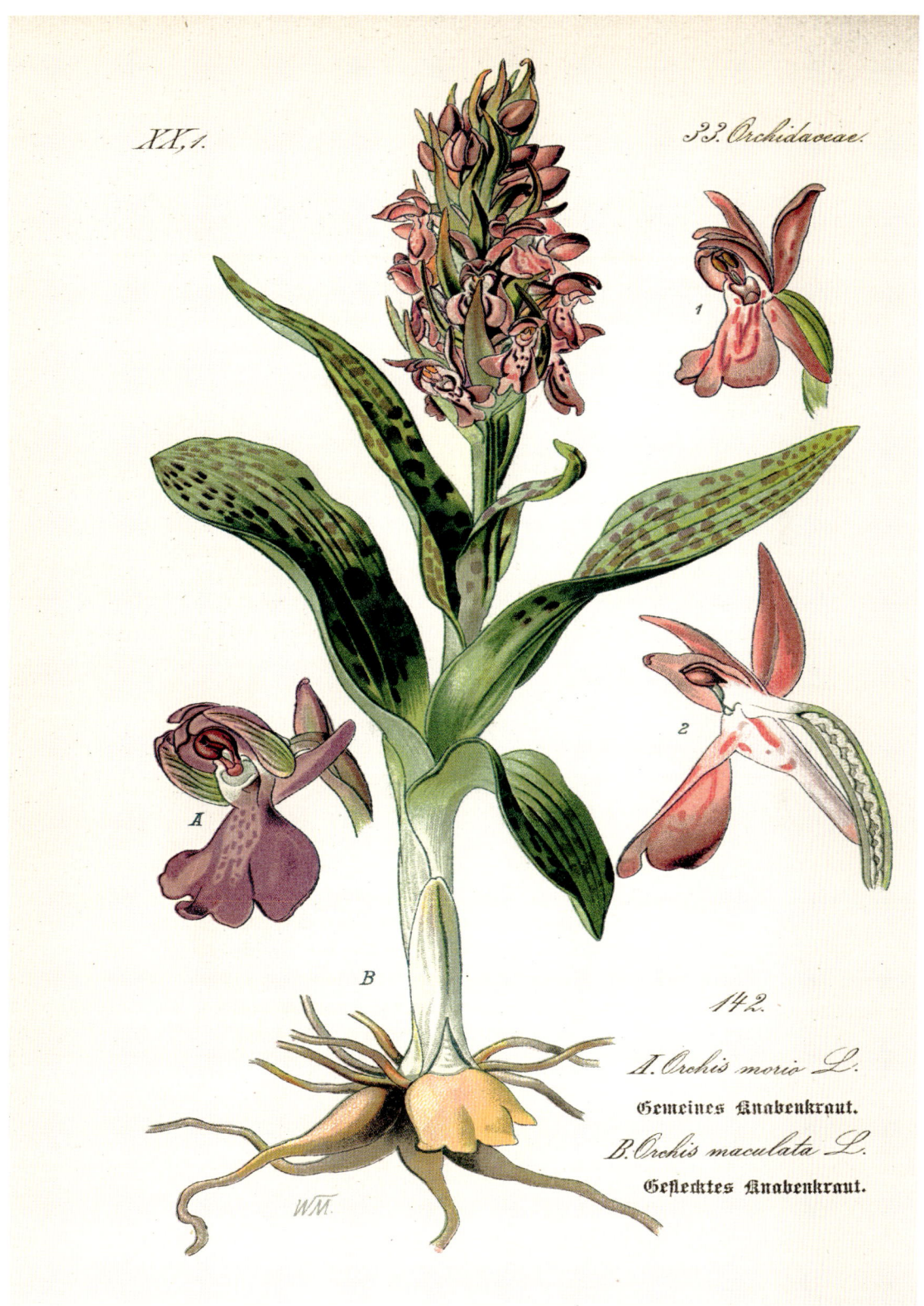

1

2

A

B

142.

A. Orchis morio L.
Gemeines Knabenkraut.
B. Orchis maculata L.
Geflecktes Knabenkraut.

WM.

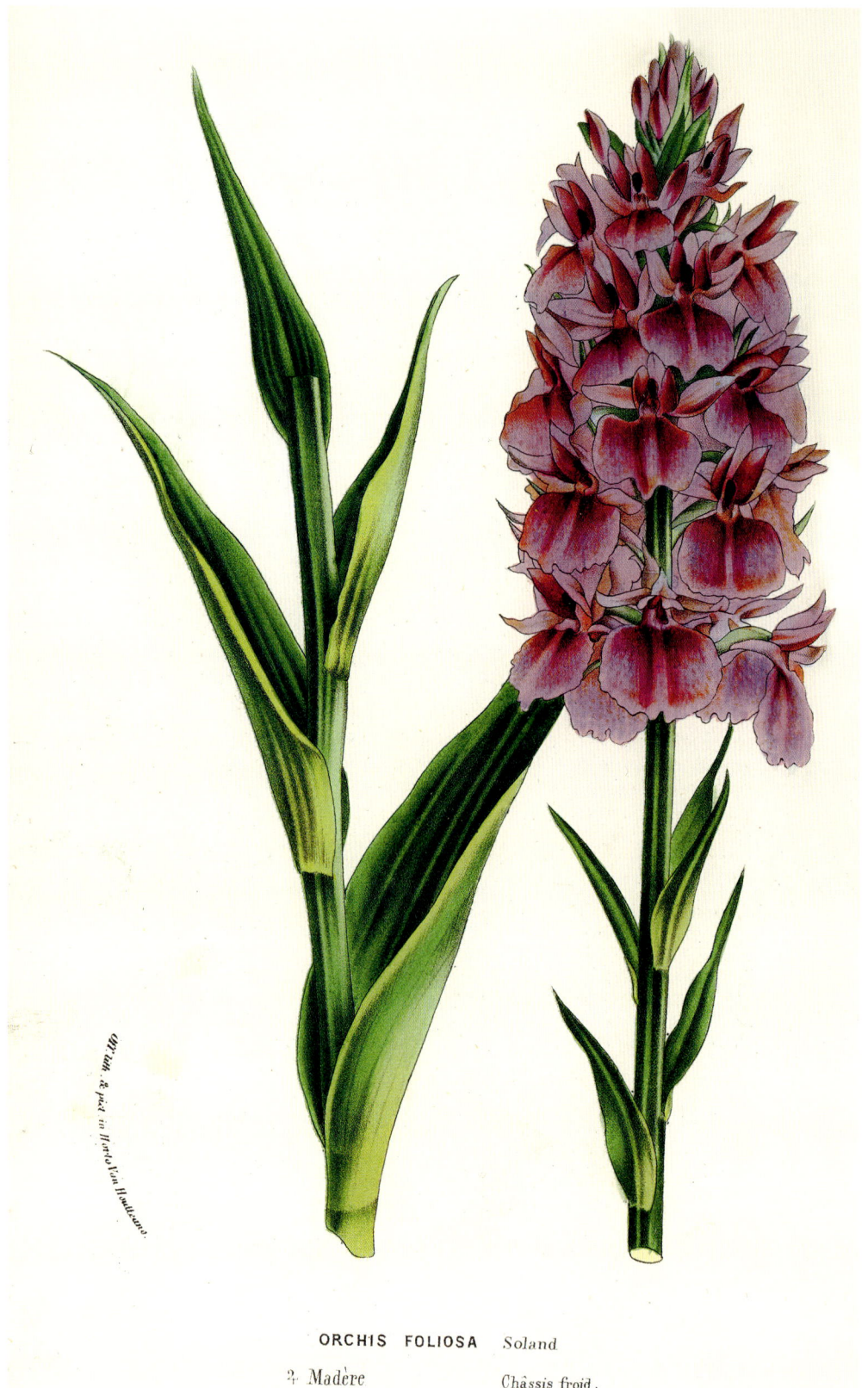

ORCHIS FOLIOSA *Soland*

♃ *Madère*   *Châssis froid.*
                                   276.

Herbarium sheet showing two specimens of *Dactylorhiza foliosa*

Two specimens of *Dactylorhiza foliosa* (as *Orchis foliosa*) from John Lindley's herbarium at Kew. The illustration of the left-hand plant is by Sarah Drake and was published in *Edwards' Botanical Register* in 1834.

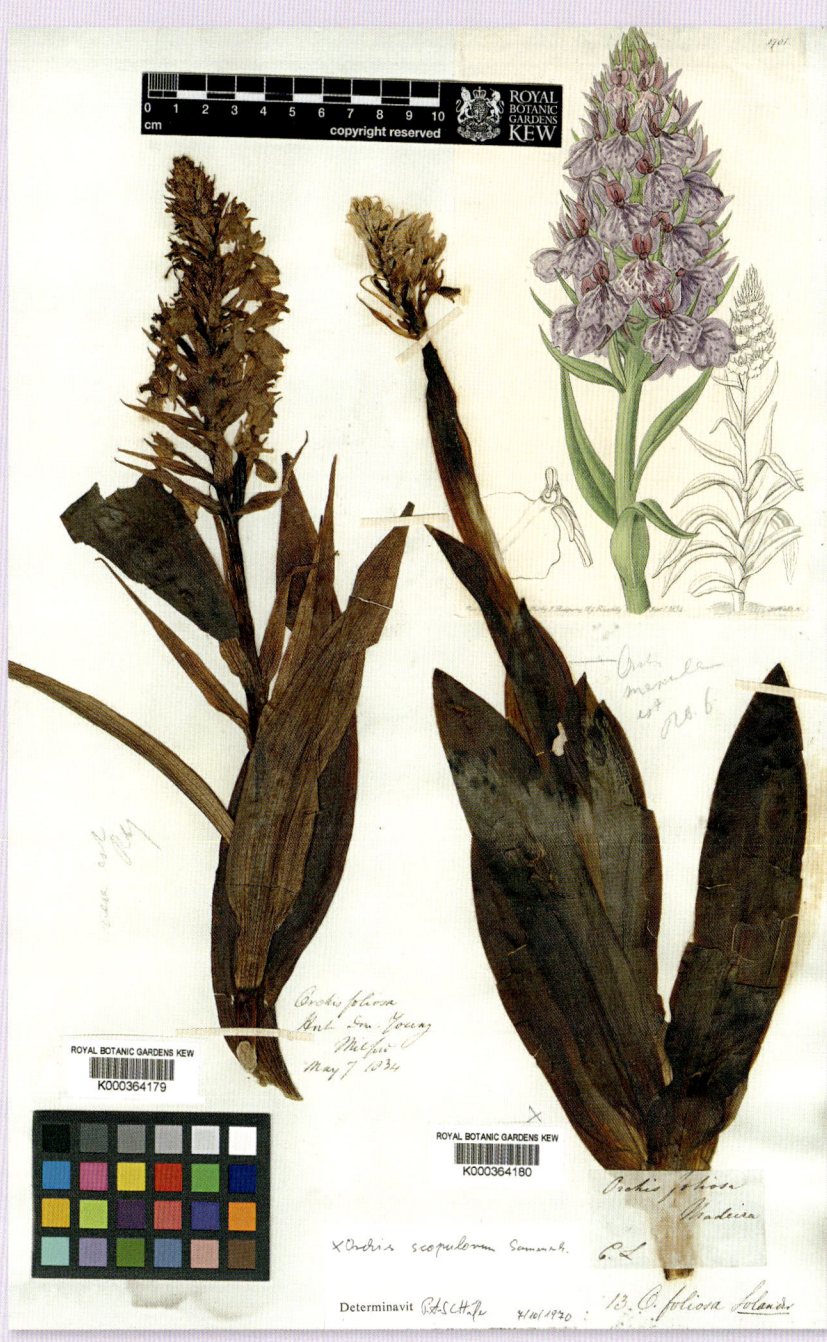

Opposite: *Dactylorhiza foliosa* from Louis van Houtte, *Flore des Serres et des Jardins de l'Europe*, 1877.

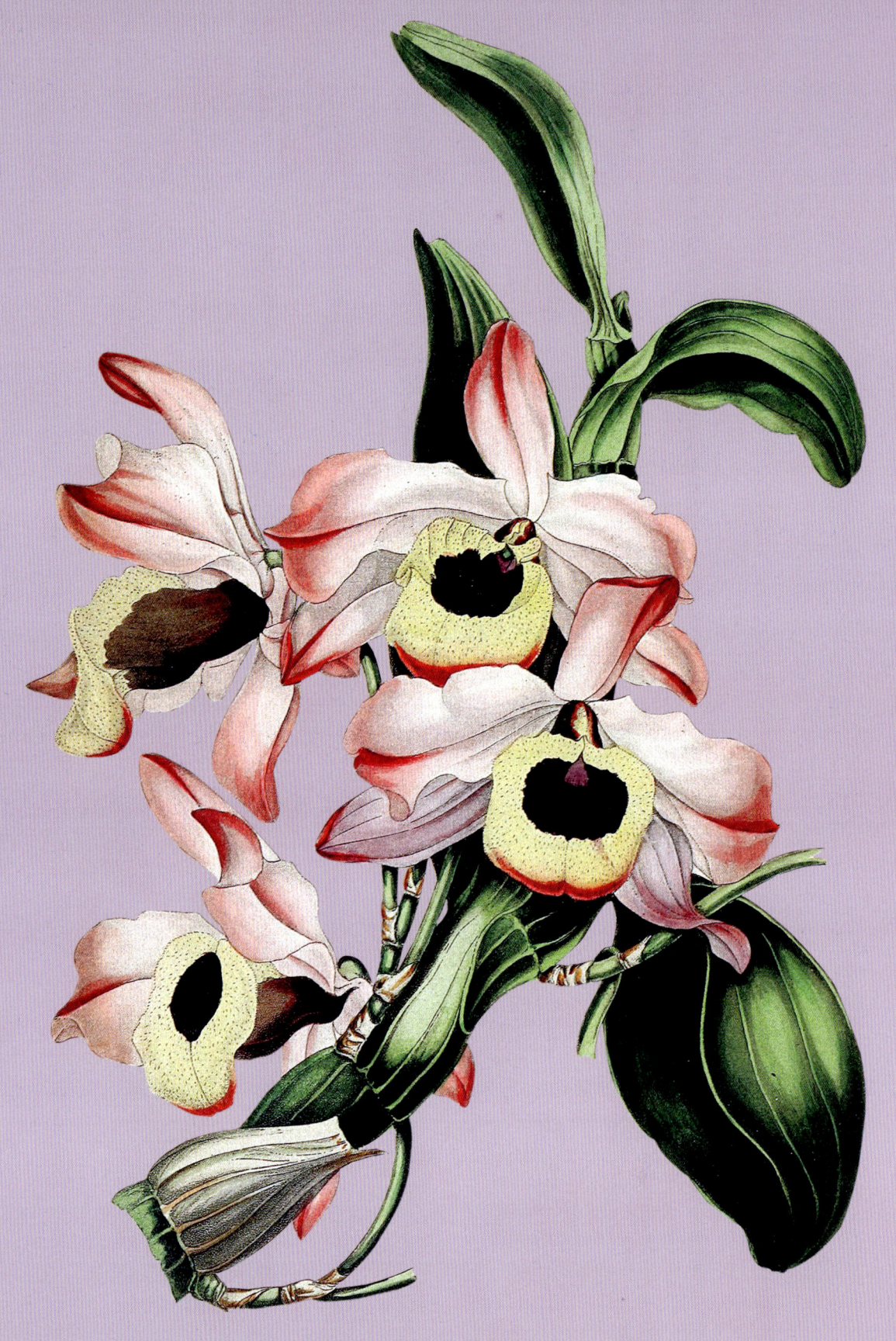

THE NOBLE ORCHID
DENDROBIUM NOBILE

Opposite:
Dendrobium nobile in
*Paxton's Magazine of
Botany and Register
of Flowering Plants*,
1839.

Right: *Dendrobium
nobile* (as *Dendrobium
nobile* var. *jaspidium*)
by C. de Brugne, in
*Lindenia: Iconographie
des Orchidées*, 1902.

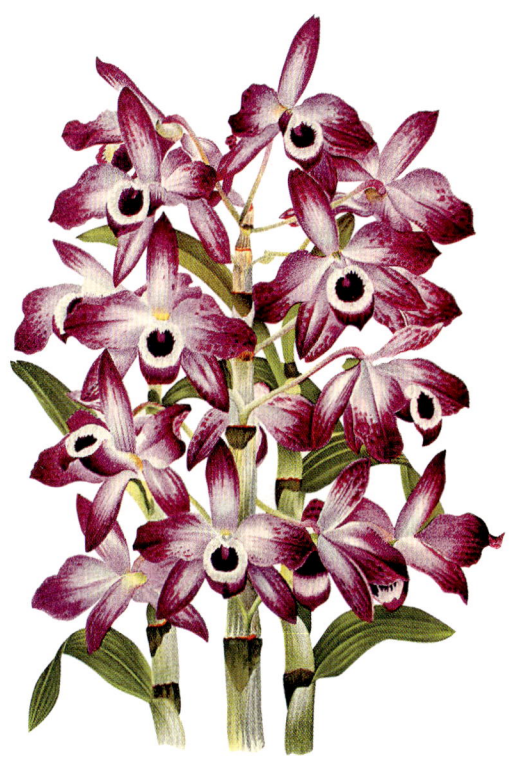

Beyond the flat plains of India and up through the foothills of the Himalayas is a tiny Indian state called Sikkim, tucked between Nepal, China and Bhutan. Here orchids thrive, relatively undisturbed by human activities, partly due to the extreme topography of the state, with winding single-track roads clinging to the edges of the steep mountains and hanging over deep valleys, and expanses of remaining vegetation, at a wide range of altitudes. This floral paradise contains over 500 different species of orchids, which were first documented by George King and Robert Pantling in 1898 in their monumental work *The Orchids of the Sikkim-Himalaya*, and more recently in 2007 by Sudhizong Lucksom in *The Orchids of Sikkim and North East Himalaya*.

One of the most striking and attractive of Sikkim's orchids is its state flower, *Dendrobium nobile*, the "noble orchid". Also found in southern China, Assam, Bangladesh, Bhutan, Nepal, Laos, Myanmar, Thailand and Vietnam, this plant has large purple-pink blooms 5–7 cm (2–2¾ in) across, with a distinctive velvety dark centre surrounded by a white border that makes the species easily recognizable. As they grow, many orchids in the genus *Dendrobium* produce "canes" – multiple long thin stems that have jointed sections from which the leaves emerge, with a new stem being produced each year. *Dendrobium nobile* is an example of a species with this vegetative growth form.

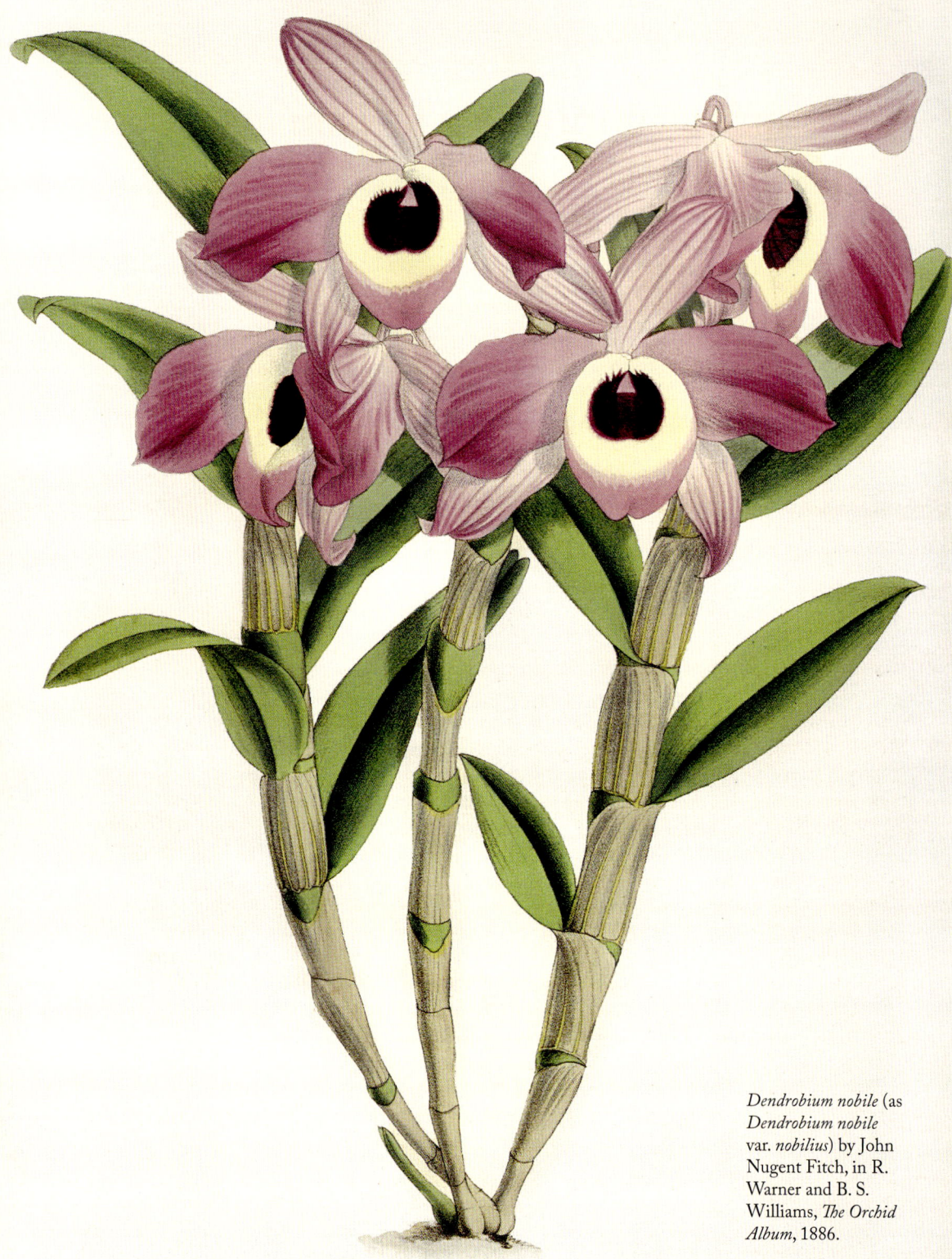

J.Nugent Fitch del et ith.

DENDROBIUM NOBILE NOBILIUS.

Dendrobium nobile (as *Dendrobium nobile* var. *nobilius*) by John Nugent Fitch, in R. Warner and B. S. Williams, *The Orchid Album*, 1886.

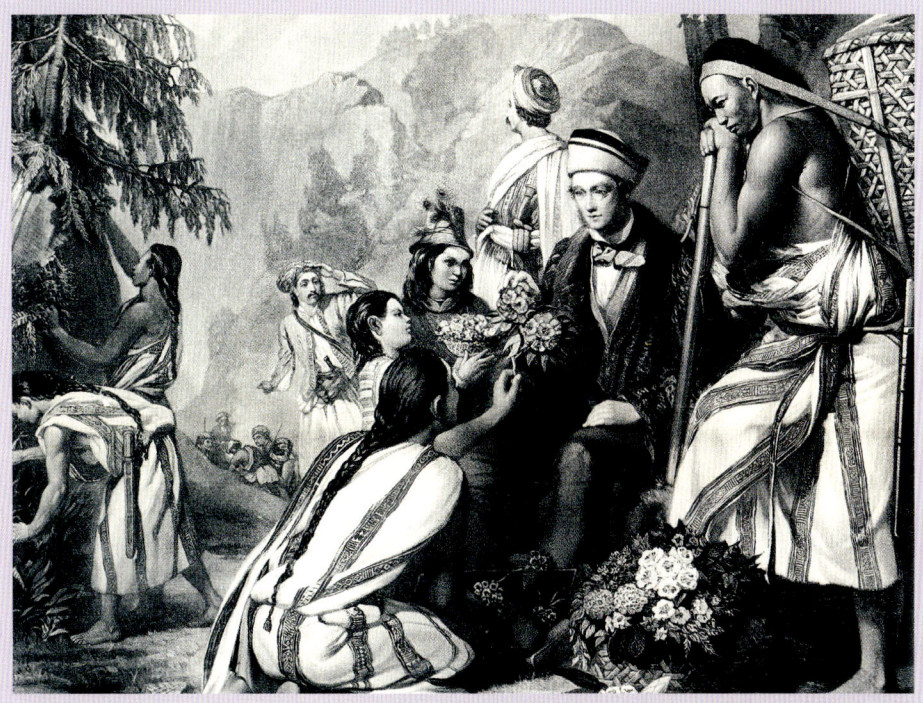

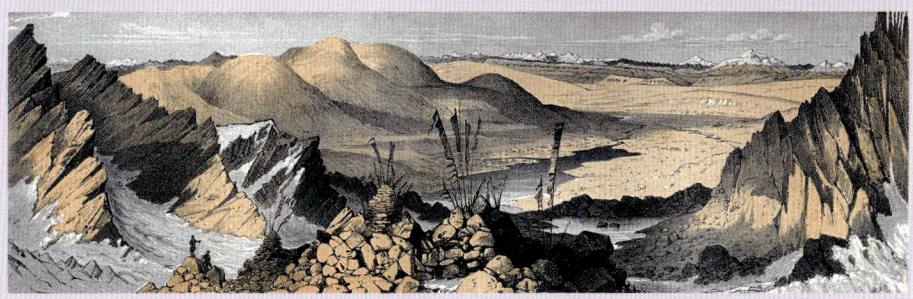

The Sikkim landscape by Walter Hood Fitch (above), based on an illustration in Joseph Dalton Hooker's *Himalayan Journals*, and *Portrait of Dr Hooker in Sikkim with Lepcha collectors around him* (top), mezzotint by William Walker after a painting by Frank Stone, 1854

Joseph Dalton Hooker's field notebooks included pencil illustrations of plants, vignettes of people, animals and mountain views, which he made as he travelled and documented his explorations. Many of these drawings were later used by the botanical artist Walter Hood Fitch to produce the images that illustrated the hugely popular published copies of Hooker's *Himalayan Journals*. This landscape depicts a glacial valley in northern Sikkim from the Donkia Pass, looking north west towards Tibet and Tso Lhamo (Cholamo) Lake.

The portrait of Hooker shows the botanist and explorer seated in the foothills of the Himalayas in Sikkim, with Mount Kanchenjunga in the background. Around him are the Lepcha plant collectors, Nepalese guards and Ghorkha sepoys who were accompanying him, wearing a range of local clothing, and bringing Hooker plants from the surrounding forests.

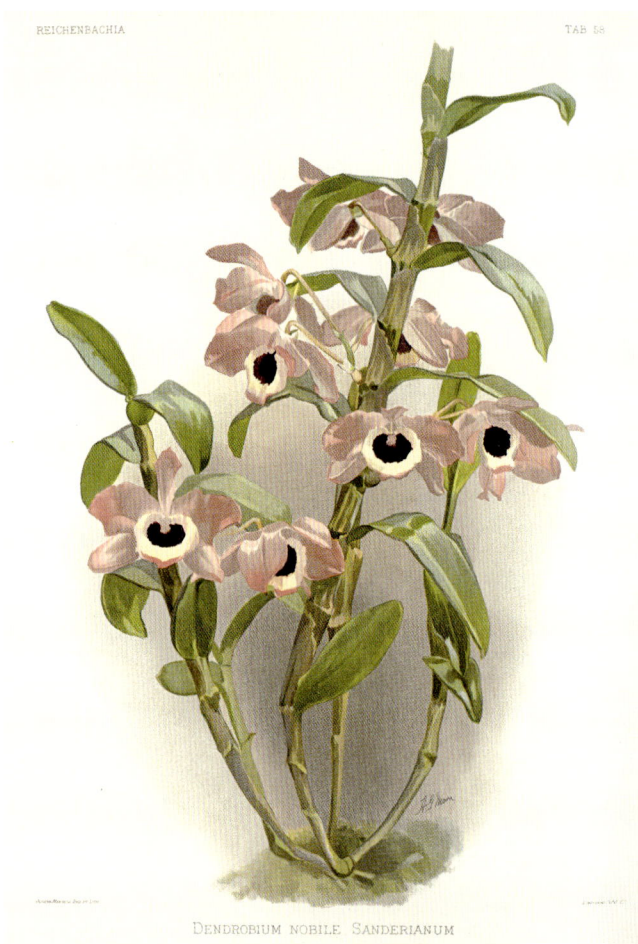

DENDROBIUM NOBILE SANDERIANUM

Above: *Dendrobium nobile* (as *Dendrobium nobile* var. *sanderianum*) by Joseph Mansell, in F. Sander *Reichenbachia: Orchids Illustrated and Described*, 1890.

Opposite: *Dendrobium nobile* by Sarah Drake, in John Lindley's *Sertum Orchidaceum*, 1838.

Joseph Dalton Hooker, who would later become the Director of the Royal Botanic Gardens, Kew, was probably the first European to see *Dendrobium nobile* growing in the wild, as he explored Sikkim in the mid-1800s with Archibald Campbell, the superintendent of Darjeeling. Tensions remained high after the 1814 Gurkha War between the British East India Company and Nepal, and borders continued to be changed in the region. British-ruled India regarded Sikkim as an ally against Nepal and an important part of the Silk Road across the Himalayas to China, but relations with the tiny self-ruled country were deteriorating. With so many difficult borders around them, the Dewan (prime minister) of Sikkim was suspicious of the two British men exploring the furthest reaches of his mountain kingdom and drawing maps of it as they went. When Hooker and Campbell directly contradicted his instructions not to cross the border with Tibet, the Dewan had them arrested and imprisoned at a monastery near the capital, Gangtok. Fortunately, negotiations with the British, including threats of military invasion, secured their release within weeks. Hooker made it out of Sikkim with his life and an extraordinary cargo of plants he had collected during his exploits, including many orchids new to science which he brought back to London for John Lindley, the orchid expert, to describe.

Hooker's travels in the Himalayas, the Antarctic and the Americas allowed him to record plants around the world and at different altitudes. It was to his close friend Hooker that Charles Darwin first confided his developing theory of evolution. Hooker was similarly fascinated by the underlying patterns that he saw in plants in the wild. His theories ultimately resulted in the birth of the field of biogeography and contributed to him becoming one of the most important botanists of the nineteenth century.

Pl. 3.

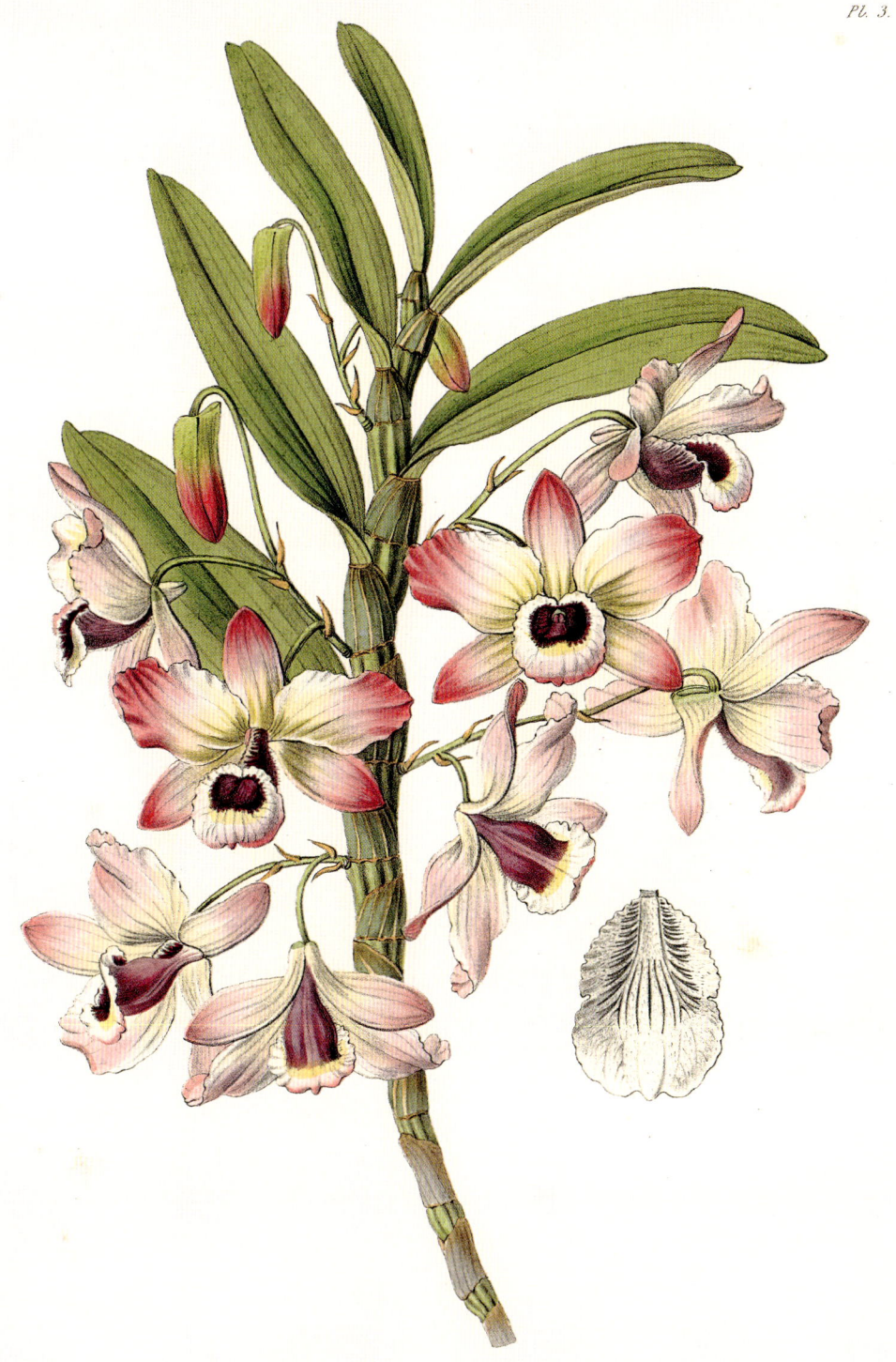

Dendrobium nobile.

Mrs Drake, delt.

On Stone by M. Gauci.

Pubd by J. Ridgway & Sons, 169, Piccadilly, Sepr 1 1837.

LOW'S VANDA
DIMORPHORCHIS LOWII

Opposite:
Dimorphorchis lowii
(as *Renanthera
lowii*) flowered by
Sigismund Rucker
of Wandsworth in
the autumn of 1862
and illustrated by
Walter Hood Fitch
for *Curtis's Botanical
Magazine*, 1864.

Below: John Day's
two-page watercolour
of *Dimorphorchis lowii*
(as *Renanthera lowii*),
which he drew in his
greenhouse in 1887.
He bought the plant
from Low & Co. Note
the distinctive basal
flowers.

The majority of orchids have only one type of flower in their inflorescence. However, a select few have two or even three types of flowers. One of these, *Dimorphorchis lowii*, which is a *Vanda* relative, is certainly one of the strangest and most spectacular of all Asiatic orchids. The genus is one of only two genera (the other being *Grammatophyllum*) in south-east Asia with inflorescences that bear two quite distinct types of flower, the basal two (yellow with a few fine red spots) being quite different in shape and

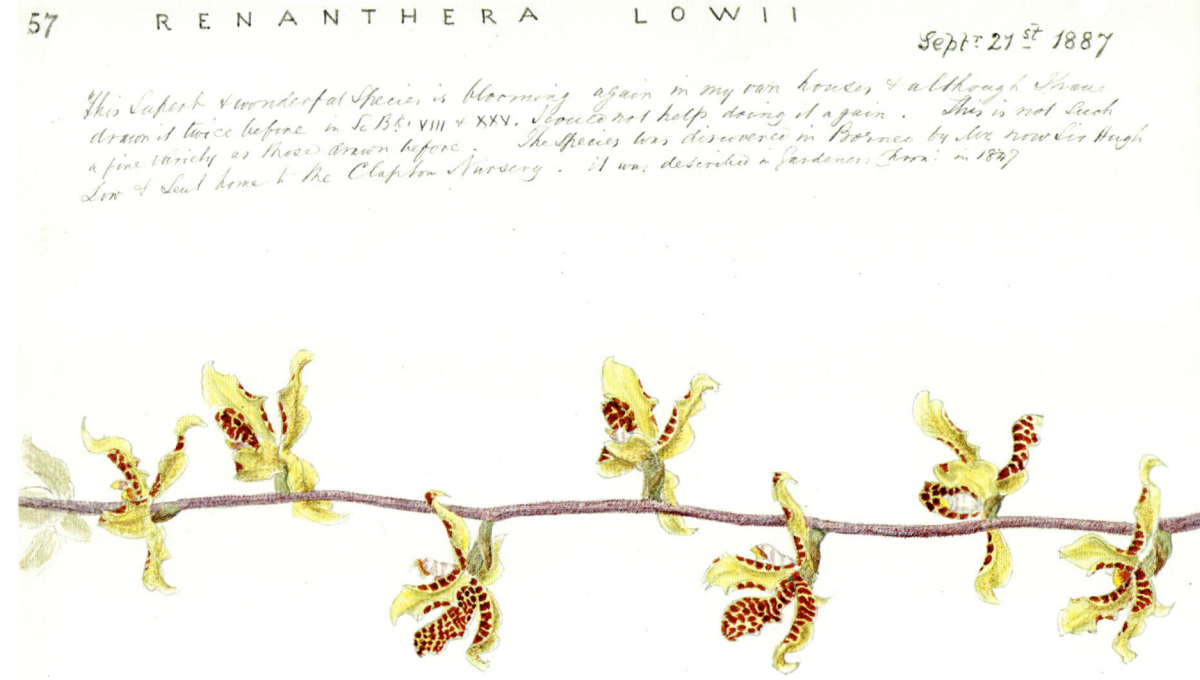

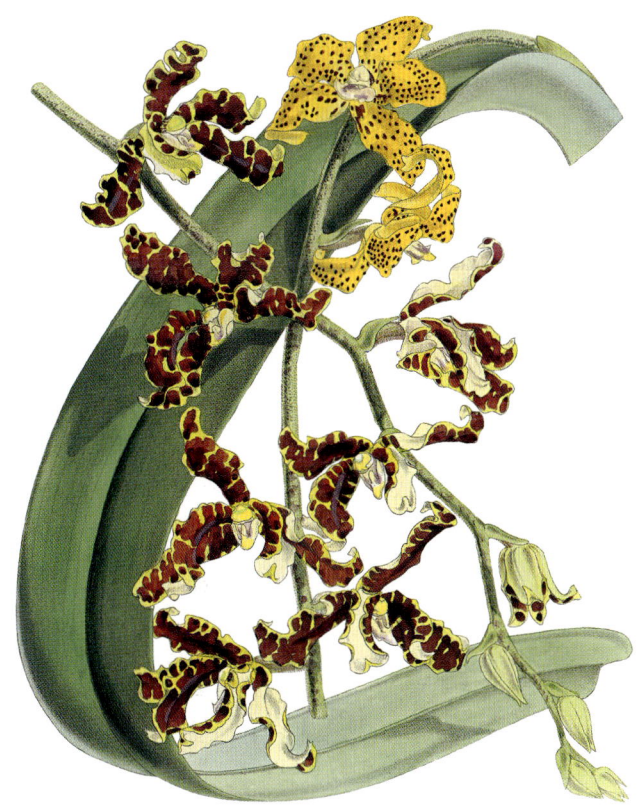

colour from the lower ones (very heavily blotched with red on a whitish base). Unlike *Catasetum* and its relatives in the tropical Americas, all of the flowers of *Dimorphorchis* are fertile, the basal ones being female and the apical ones being bisexual. *Dimorphorchis lowii* is found only on the island of Borneo, where it was discovered by Hugh Low, colonial treasurer on Labuan and a friend of Rajah James Brooke. He sent plants of the species to his family orchid nursery, Low & Co. of Upper Clapton, who introduced it into cultivation. In 1849, Mrs Lawrence of Ealing paid £21 for a plant at auction at Stevens's sales rooms in London.

The orchid grower and artist John Day illustrated the two types of flower of this orchid in his scrapbooks on 3 August 1864 from a plant of the original importation that had flowered

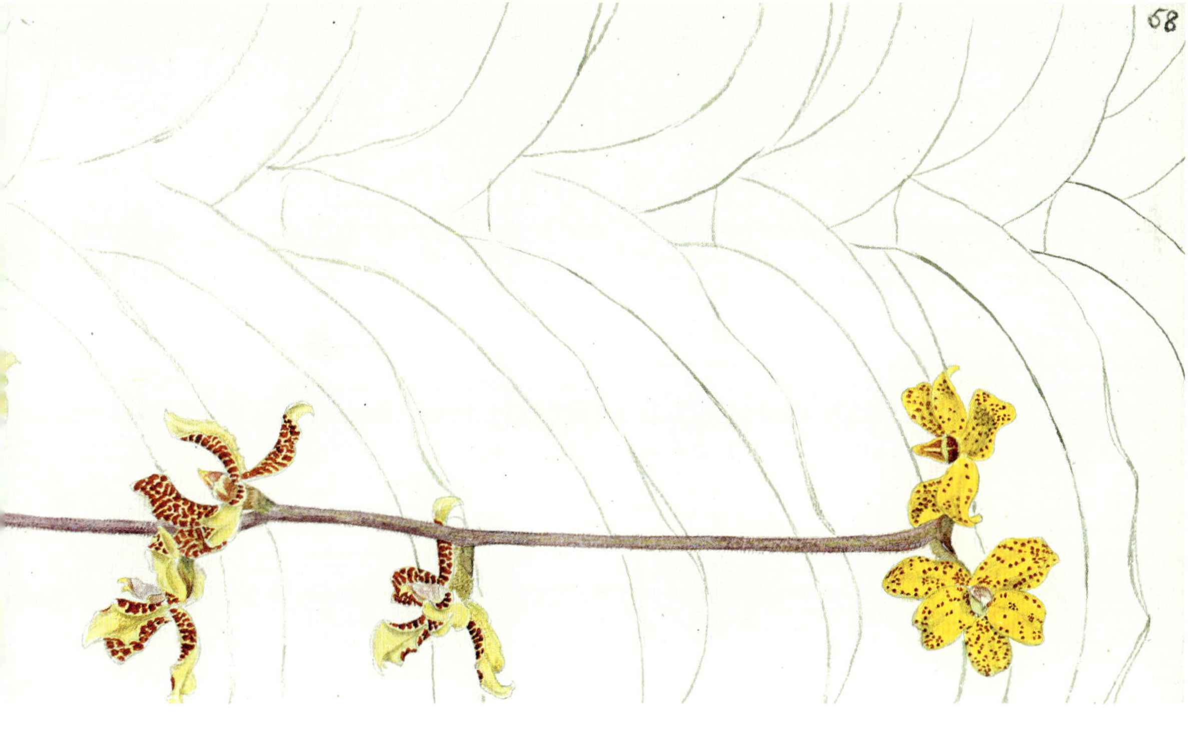

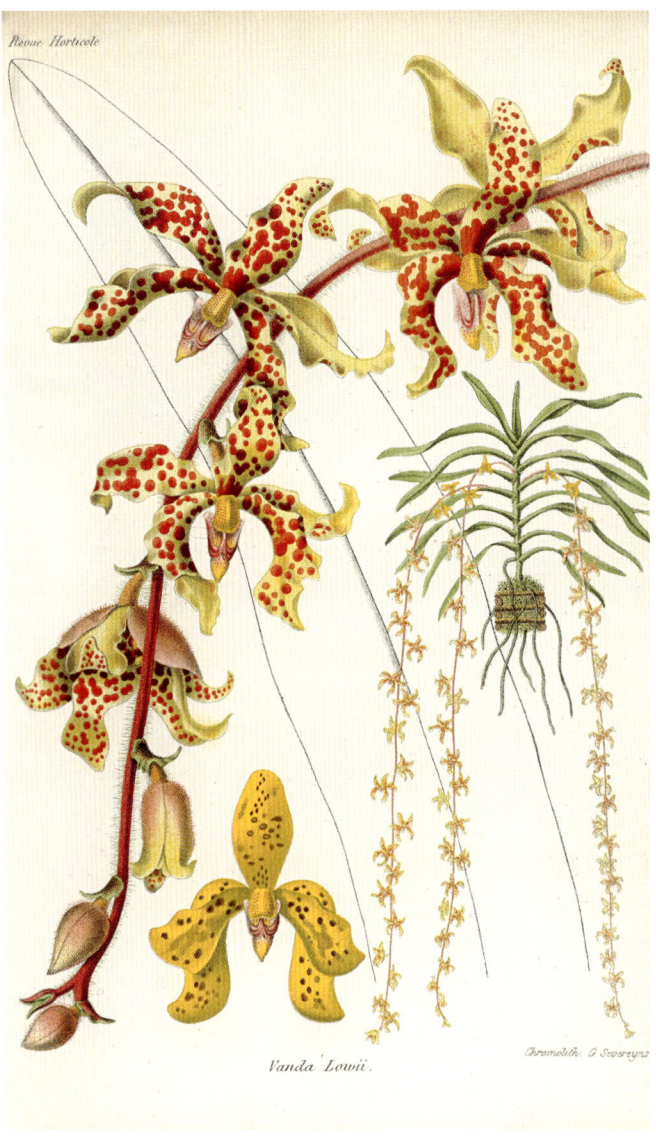

Revue Horticole

Vanda Lowii.

Chromolith. G Severeyns

from William Bull at Stevens's sale on 9 June 1873, and flowered two of them at Tottenham in August 1879 for the first time. He commented that the plant he had painted was "a much lighter coloured one than usual. I have another in bloom now which is much darker, being nearly all deep cinnamon red with few yellow bars and spots."

Day painted *Dimorphorchis lowii* again on 21 September 1887, towards the end of his life. This drawing is a fine double-page spread, and he noted that "this superb and wonderful species is blooming again in my own houses and although I have drawn it twice before in Scrap Book viii & xxv, I could not help doing it again." Day's painting is accompanied by a note that the "yellow flowers smell of cucumber".

John Day's watercolour of two flowers and floral dissections drawn three days beforehand on 18 September 1887 is of particular interest. Although also labelled as "*Renanthera lowii*" (a synonym of *D. lowii*), it is without doubt the first ever illustration of *Dimorphorchis tenomensis*, a closely allied species that was first described by Anthony Lamb in 1994 in the first volume of *Orchids of Borneo*. To date it is known only from southern Sabah in Borneo.

All of the *Dimorphorchis* species are epiphytes, growing on trees, usually by rivers, streams and swamps in Borneo. The inflorescences are pendent, and a large plant of *D. lowii*, the most common and widespread species, can bear several inflorescences, each growing up to 2 m (6½ ft) or more in length.

Above: *Dimorphorchis lowii* (as *Vanda lowii*) drawn for *Revue Horticole* in 1868.

for Sigismund Rucker of Wandsworth, London. By 1868, well-grown plants were fetching between £23 and £33 12s at auction. In 1883, William Bull paid £52 10s at auction for Lord Egerton of Tatton's plant. Day bought plants

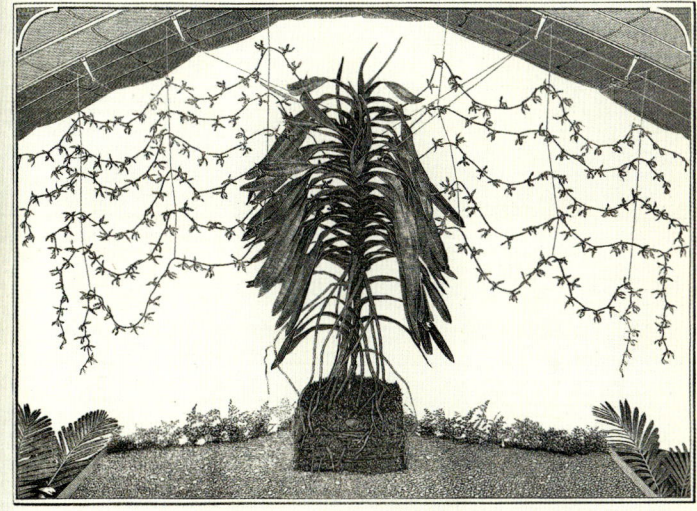

RENANTHERA LOWI.

OUR illustration (fig. 117), taken from a photograph kindly furnished us by Mr. Bergmann, the Director of Baron Rothschild's garden at Ferrières, shows the wonderful plant of Renanthera Lowi, grown by him and exhibited this spring at one of the meetings of the Central Horticultural Society of France. At the time the photograph was taken there were eleven flower-stalks, each over 3 yards in length, and bearing in the aggregate 280 flowers. In the original description of the plant by Dr. Lindley in our columns (1847, p. 239) it is stated that Mr. Low found the plant growing on trees in Borneo with 200 horizontally spreading branches, with pendulous flower-stalks, 10—12 feet in length, the individual flowers supported on mossy stalks, and each about 3 inches across, lemon-yellow in colour, and blotched

but planted with a mixture of Larch, Beech, Pine, Hazel, Birch, and Oak, will repay the expenses of planting, rent, and management, during the first ten or fifteen years, together with compound interest at 5 per cent. The profits of future falls will be as follows :—In thirteen years, or at twenty-three years' growth, £24 10s. per acre ; in the next thirteen years (thirty-six years' growth), £39 per acre ; and after that a triennial profit of £12 per acre, or £4 per annum, until the final felling of the Oak, as timber of the first class, worth from £200 to £250 per acre. We have known land in Kent planted with Chestnut for hoppoles, which paid a great deal more than in the case brought forward by Mr. Hunter, but its value to rent was four or five times more than the 5s. or 10s. per acre he mentions. So he may be right, and we all know that the forestry of Perthshire is unsurpassed—Mr. Hunter's book, in fact, is the more valuable from

1872. The next return was made in 1880, when the results of the recent progress of arboriculture, which must be manifest to all who know the country, had raised the area of its plantations, young and old, to 94,563 acres. Mr. Hunter does not perhaps over-estimate their value at £35 per acre, and as ornamental timber is planted and maintained for love and not for money, the commercial value of the timber of the enlarged plantations of Perthshire does not at all adequately represent the growth of wealth in that county.

Mr. Hunter enlarges with natural pride on the Perth Nurseries, laid out in 1766, and recognised as the immediate source and seed-bed of a great deal of the fine timber now growing in the surrounding country. He then takes his readers to Blair Athole and Dunkeld, and to the Ladywell Nursery, where the Duke's wood manager, Mr. M'Gregor, showed

FIG. 117.—RENANTHERA LOWI : FLOWERS LEMON-YELLOW WITH CINNAMON BLOTCHES.

with cinnamon. Renanthera Lowi is one of those species which bear dimorphic flowers—the difference in form not, as is generally the case, being connected with sexual differences in the flower, inasmuch as it is stated that the two flowers have been fertilised each by the other (*Gard. Chron.* 1867, p. 292).

Notices of Books.

The Woods, Forests, and Estates of Perthshire, *with Sketches of the Principal Families in the County.* By Thomas Hunter. (Perth : Henderson, Robertson & Hunter.)

Most beautiful are trees !—" sylvan scenery never palls "—and they are profitable too, in Perthshire at any rate. Mr. Hunter says, in the introduction to his scattered papers, which are now published, as we ventured to hope they would be, in the form of a useful and attractive volume, that the tree thinnings of an acre of land, worth, say, from 5s. to 10s. per acre,

its abundant information on the arboriculture of a county whose woods and forests, as he remarks, possess " exceptional interest."

There is no doubt that the ancient forests of Scotland had fallen into decay, and that Dr. Johnson's strictures on the scarcity of timber were not without foundation. It was useless to think of agricultural or other improvements till after the death of Rob Roy and the cattle lifters, but as soon as circumstances permitted, half a century or more after Cromwell's improved farming, and Sylva Evelyn's planting in the South, the spirit of improvement spread northwards.

In 1812, Scotland's woods, coppices, and plantations reached 913,695 acres. A vast quantity of planting had been accomplished in the eighteenth century, and a slight reaction appears to have then set in, or perhaps the demands for railways and other purposes thinned the woods, for in 1872 the area had been reduced to 734,490 acres. The woods of Perthshire must have been largely utilised, for their area diminished from 203,880 acres in 1812, to 83,525 in

him the management of seed and seedlings on a great estate. The story of the Larches is again repeated, and an excellent illustration is given of the " parent Larches " on the lawn at Dunkeld, figured in our columns, 1876, vol. v., p. 209. Glen Tilt is visited and illustrated, with the Pass of Killiecrankie, and then follows a very interesting sketch of the Athole family from early in the fourteenth century to the present time.

It may be remembered that so far as our space permitted, we gave a similar sketch in an account of Blair Athole in these columns. Mr. Hunter has adopted the same plan, and to his history of the woods he has added that of the estates and families connected with them, with many interesting details of the trees and their surroundings. The accounts of Menteith, Taymouth, Blair Drummond, the residence of the well-known improver, Lord Kaims ; of Drummond Castle and Scone, seem to us particularly interesting from the introduction of characteristic history. The Scottish aristocracy, and,

Engraving of *Dimorphorchis lowii* from *The Gardeners' Chronicle*, 24 November 1883

An engraving of an amazing plant of *Dimorphorchis lowii* (as *Renanthera lowii*) from *The Gardeners' Chronicle* of November 1883. Nowadays this is a rare plant in cultivation and to find a plant of this size is unheard of. The suspension of the inflorescences on wires speaks of the cheap labour available in the Victorian days. Every greenhouse in the larger collections employed a boy to open and close the vents, depending on weather conditions outside.

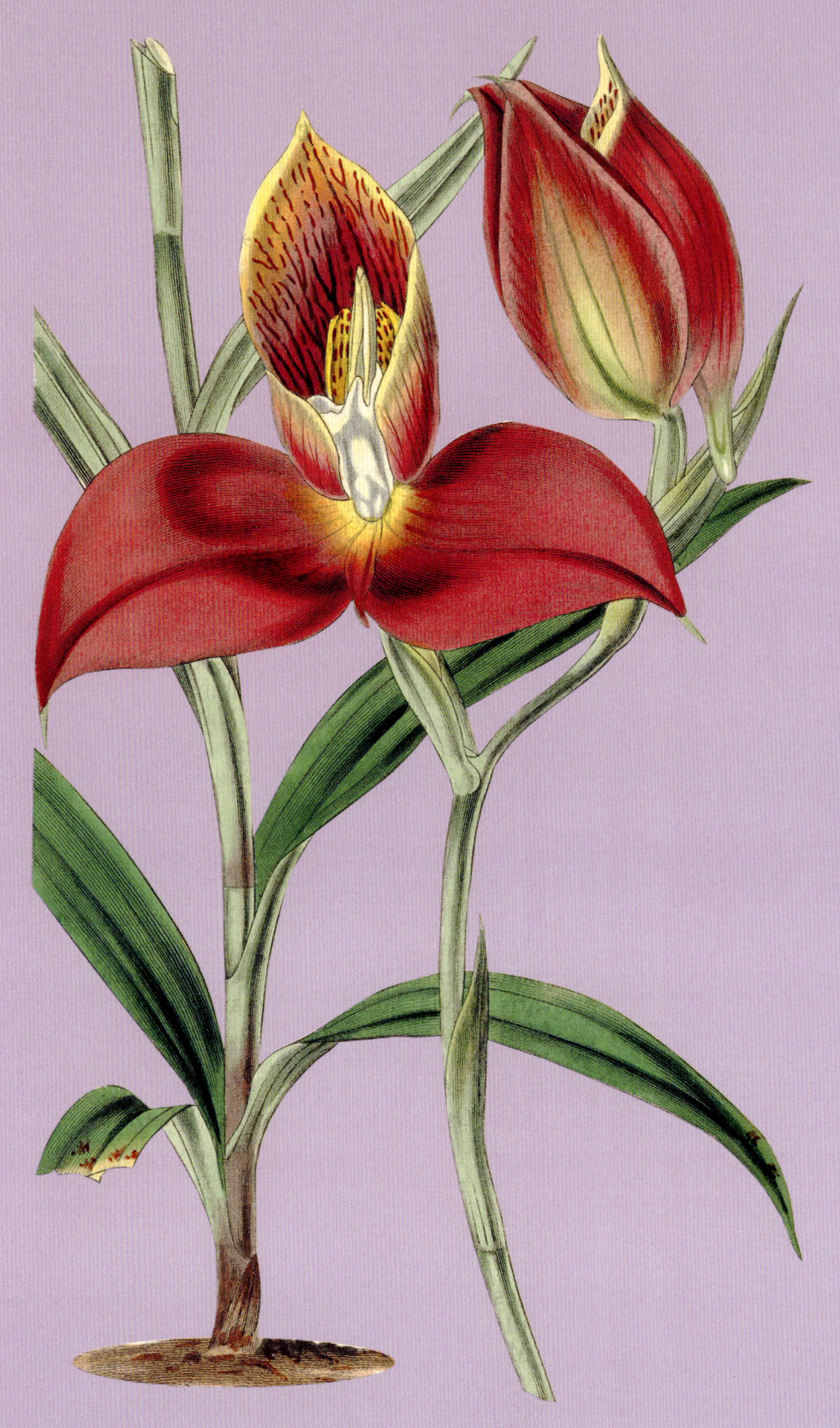

PRIDE OF TABLE MOUNTAIN

DISA UNIFLORA

Opposite: *Disa uniflora* (as *Disa grandiflora*) by Walter Hood Fitch, in *Curtis's Botanical Magazine*, 1844.

This species, the floral symbol of the Western Cape province of South Africa, is unmistakeable with its large ruby-red flowers, usually borne as a single bloom per plant. *Disa uniflora* used to be common on Table Mountain, but is now much less frequently seen, having attracted the attentions of unscrupulous orchid hunters.

The nomenclatural history of this species is studded with illustrious names. It is thought that John Ray, the great naturalist of the late seventeenth century, may have been referring to the species in his *Historia Plantarum Generalis* (1704) when he wrote of an "orchid Africana flore singulari herbaceo". The earliest known collection of this species, and indeed of any member of the genus *Disa*, is from nearly 50 years later, and was made by Jan Auge, Superintendent of the Cape Town garden of the Dutch East India Company. Specimens were sent to a number of botanists in Europe, as a result of which the Swedish botanist Peter Jonas Bergius came to obtain material in Stockholm and first published both the generic name, and *Disa uniflora* as its type species, in 1767. Bergius

used Carl Linnaeus's still relatively new binomial naming system (the botanical nomenclature system used today had been instigated by Linnaeus in 1753, the date of publication of his *Species Plantarum*). The Swedish naturalist Carl Peter Thunberg, known as the father of South African botany, sent specimens of the species to the son of Linnaeus, who was at that time Professor of Botany at Uppsala University. Considering the need for a more appropriate epithet than "uniflora" for a plant with such a large and striking flower, especially as it was now apparent that the plants did not always bear just one bloom, Linnaeus the Younger published the name *Disa grandiflora*, and the species was widely known by this name for many years. Unfortunately, under the strict *International Code of Nomenclature for algae, fungi, and plants*, it is not permissible to rename taxa for such reasons, and the name *Disa grandiflora* is technically illegitimate. The later name is superfluous as the species already had a valid name, *Disa uniflora*, and this is the name by which the species is correctly known.

Disa flowers may be red, pink or occasionally white or yellow, in colour, and they are pollinated by butterflies. The dorsal sepal of *Disa* species forms an inflated hood that encloses the central parts of the flower, with two large lateral sepals on either side which are quite similar to the dorsal sepal, although they may be of a different colour to it. The petals are much smaller and tucked inside the flower and may help the pollinator to guide its proboscis inside the spur to gather nectar. The labellum is normally small and has no obvious function – very unusually among orchids, where the labellum often plays an important role in attracting and enabling pollinators to visit flowers and picking up and depositing pollinia as they do so. The combination of the large hooded dorsal sepal and the spur, which may contain nectar and be up to 10 cm (4 in) long, or almost absent, distinguishes *Disa* species from other terrestrial orchids.

Disa species may have a reputation for being difficult to grow, but they thrive under cool damp conditions that mimic the environment near the streams and waterfalls of their natural habitats.

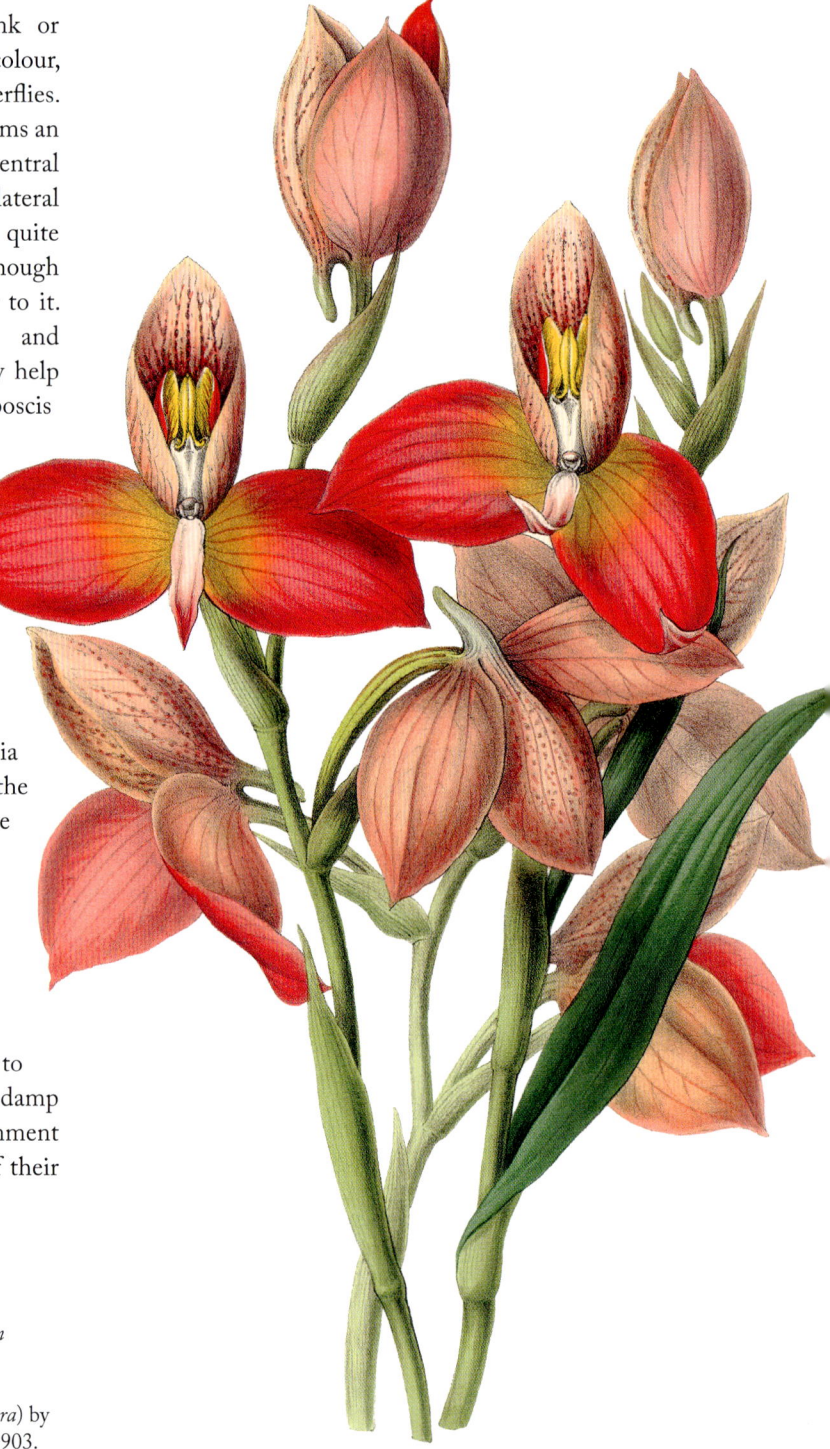

Right: *Disa uniflora* (as *Disa grandiflora*) by Sarah Drake, in John Lindley's *Sertum Orchidaceum*, 1838.

Opposite: *Disa uniflora* (as *Disa grandiflora*) by J. R. Guillot, in *Revue Horticole*, serié 4, 1903.

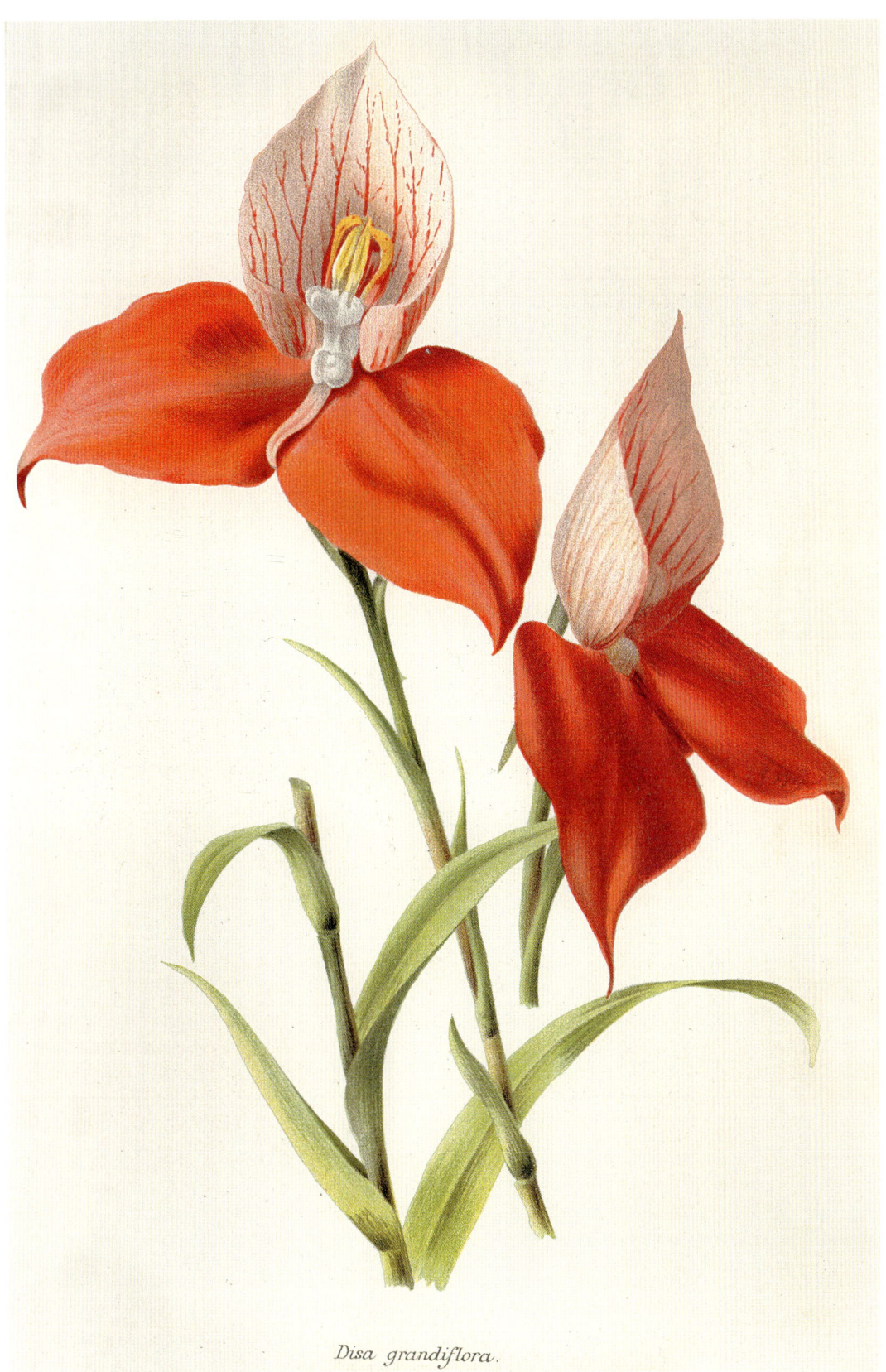

Disa grandiflora.

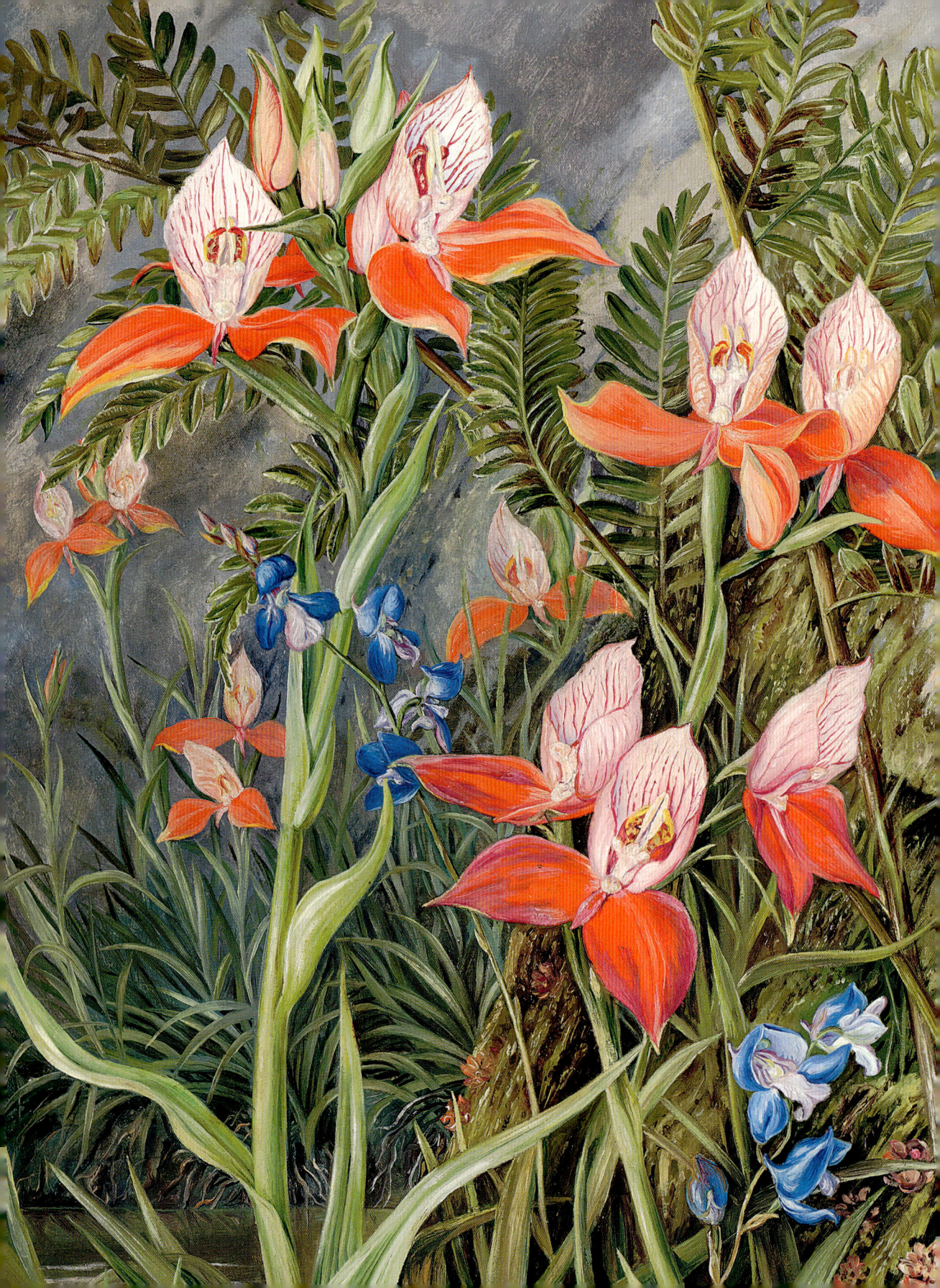

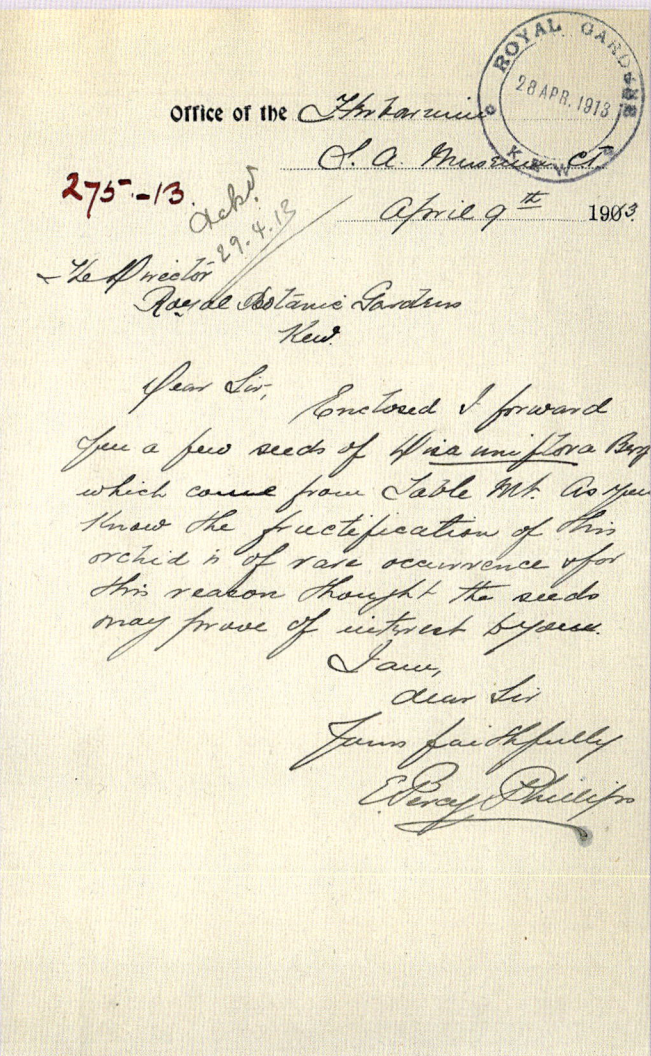

Office of the *Herbarium*
S.A. Museum Ct.
April 9ᵗʰ 1903

The Director
Royal Botanic Gardens
Kew

Dear Sir,
Enclosed I forward
you a few seeds of *Disa uniflora* Berg.
which come from Table Mt. As you
know the fructification of this
orchid is of rare occurrence & for
this reason thought the seeds
may prove of interest to you.
I am,
dear Sir
Yours faithfully
E. Percy Phillips

Letter from E. Percy Phillips to Sir David Prain, from Cape Town, 9 April 1913

The Directors' Correspondence in the Archives of the Royal Botanic Gardens, Kew contains thousands of communications between the directors and botanists and others all over the world, over the last two and a half centuries. Many letters discuss the accompanying specimens, plants and/or seeds being sent from one collection to another, as gifts or on request.

In this letter, from just before the First World War, Percy Phillips, the Curator of the Herbarium of the South African Museum and author of *The Genera of South African Flowering Plants* (1926), writes to David Prain, Director of the Royal Botanic Gardens, Kew, sending a packet of *Disa uniflora* seed – and comments on how, since fruiting of the plant is rare, the seed might be of particular interest.

Director between 1905 and 1922, Prain had previously been Director of the Royal Botanic Gardens, Calcutta and also of the Botanical Survey of India before returning to the UK.

Opposite: *Disa uniflora* in *The Glory of Table Mountain, Cape of Good Hope*, by Marianne North, 1882.

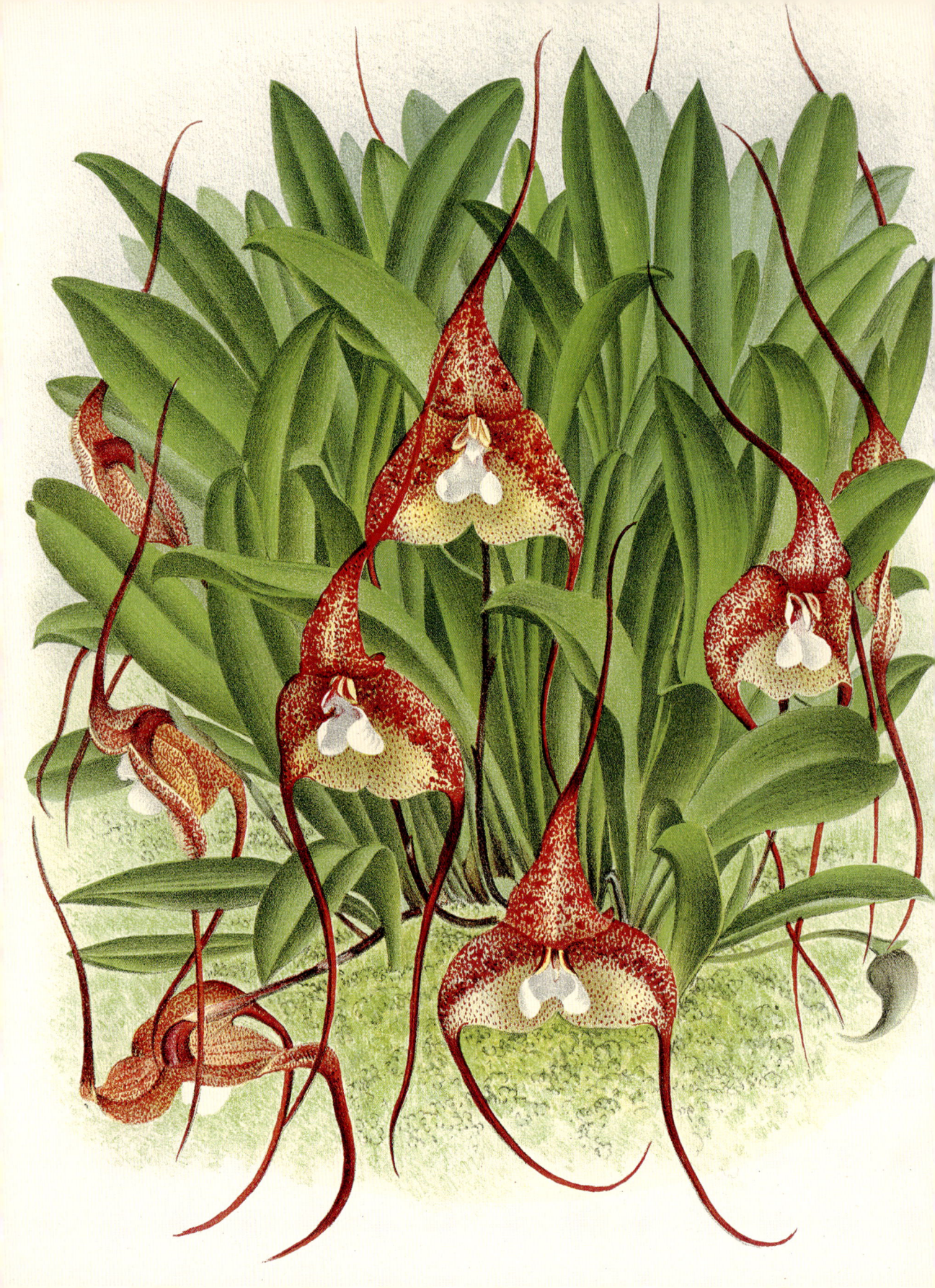

BLACK CHIMAERA OR VAMPIRE ORCHID

DRACULA VAMPIRA

"little dragon" is the actual meaning of the orchid genus name *Dracula*, deriving from the Latin word *draco*, rather than a reference to the famous fictional Count from Transylvania. Either interpretation of the name fits rather well though with the sinister, intricate, often black-purple flowers of this species.

The American botanist Carlyle Luer erected the genus in 1978 as a distinct group from the extremely speciose tropical American genus *Masdevallia*. Basing his decision on the differences in the leaves and flowers between the two genera, and particularly the presence of the mushroom-like labellum in *Dracula*, Luer moved approximately 60 species into his new genus, changing their names from *Masdevallia* species in the process.

Luer had recently described the species *Masdevallia vampira* before he moved it to the newly created genus *Dracula*, to become *Dracula vampira*. Only known from a single mountain in Ecuador, the species epithet was chosen for the resemblance of the orchid's flowers to bats, specifically the bat genus *Vampirus*,

and also in homage to the old middle European word *vampir*.

Dracula vampira was known in cultivation for around 15 years before it was first described, and was probably originally collected by the German botanist Friedrich Carl Lehmann, who collected plants – especially orchids – widely in Ecuador and Colombia for nearly 30 years in the late 1800s and early 1900s. Lehmann sent plants to the great Victorian orchid nurseries of Low and Sander in England, and the main collection of his herbarium specimens and botanical paintings is held at the Royal Botanic Gardens, Kew, with many duplicates at major herbaria in Europe and North America.

Found in the cool, high-altitude cloud forests of Mexico, Central America and the South American Andes, *Dracula* species have no pseudobulbs in which to store water and will dry out quickly if not in cool, moist conditions. The large flowers of *Dracula vampira*, unlike those of many other *Dracula* species, do not have hairs or warts, and are covered in thin purple-black veins. These striations are so numerous and so closely spaced

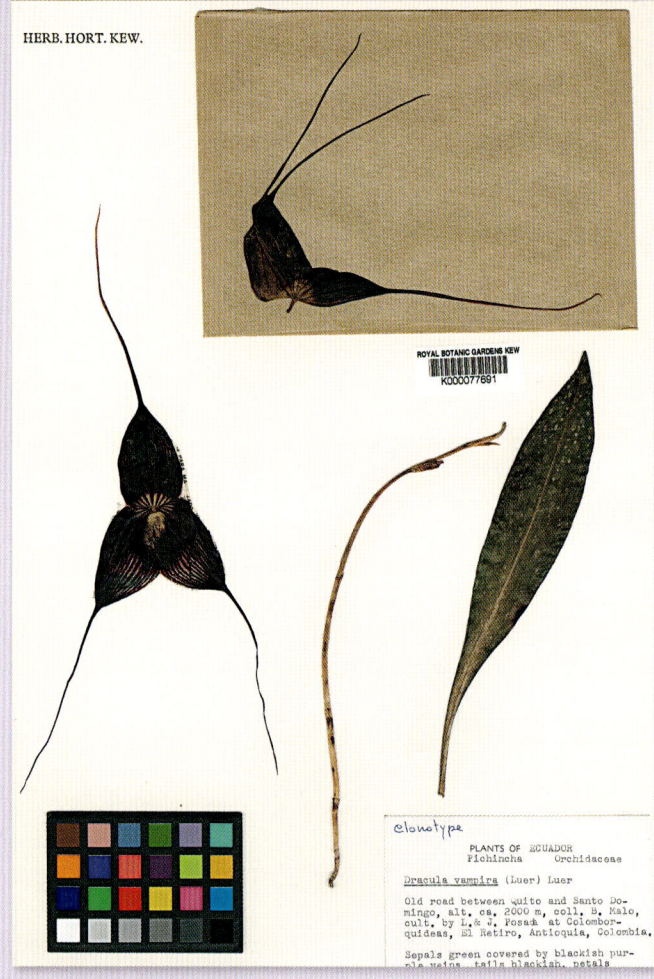

Herbarium sheet from the Royal Botanic Gardens, Kew, of *Dracula vampira* (Luer) Luer

The Herbarium of the Royal Botanic Gardens, Kew, contains approximately 7 million specimens of dried pressed plants from across the entire plant kingdom, collected from around the world over the last 300 years.

Specimens are crucial reference points for plant naming and classification, and baseline information on records of plants in cultivation, the range of natural variation found in the wild and the extent of the species' distribution. Throughout the history of botanical illustration, including in modern times, dried specimens have often been the only material of a particular plant that the artist capturing it has ever seen.

This *Dracula vampira* specimen is an example that is particularly well-pressed. Orchids are notorious for making bad pressed specimens because their usually very three-dimensional flowers tend to distort or deteriorate in the process. Further, the colours and scents of flowers tend to be lost, but with detailed notes recorded on the specimen label, as here, this specimen captures the most important information known about this rare species.

that the flower may appear completely black even though the sepals behind are actually green in colour, and each sepal has a long thin black "tail" extending from its apex.

The white ridged labellum with pinkish veins at the centre of the *Dracula* flower is particularly intriguing and looks – and even smells – like the cap of a small gilled mushroom. The flowers are known to attract small flies called fungus gnats, and chemical analysis has shown that the scents emitted by some *Dracula* species are typical of those produced by mushrooms. Seeking ideal locations in which to lay their eggs, the fungus gnats are attracted to what they think is their preferred fungal host, and during their efforts inside the orchid's flowers they transfer the bundles of pollen, called pollinia, from one plant to another.

Many *Dracula* species, including *Dracula vampira*, are found only in very restricted geographical locations, and many are collected for the horticultural trade. All of the species are extremely sensitive to changes in temperature and humidity. In combination with their reliance on fungus gnats and the gnats' own reliance on the presence of their usual fungal host in the habitat, the threats of climate change and encroaching human development are disturbing their natural habitat and threatening the survival of *Dracula* species in the wild. *Dracula vampira* itself is considered to be critically endangered in its native habitat.

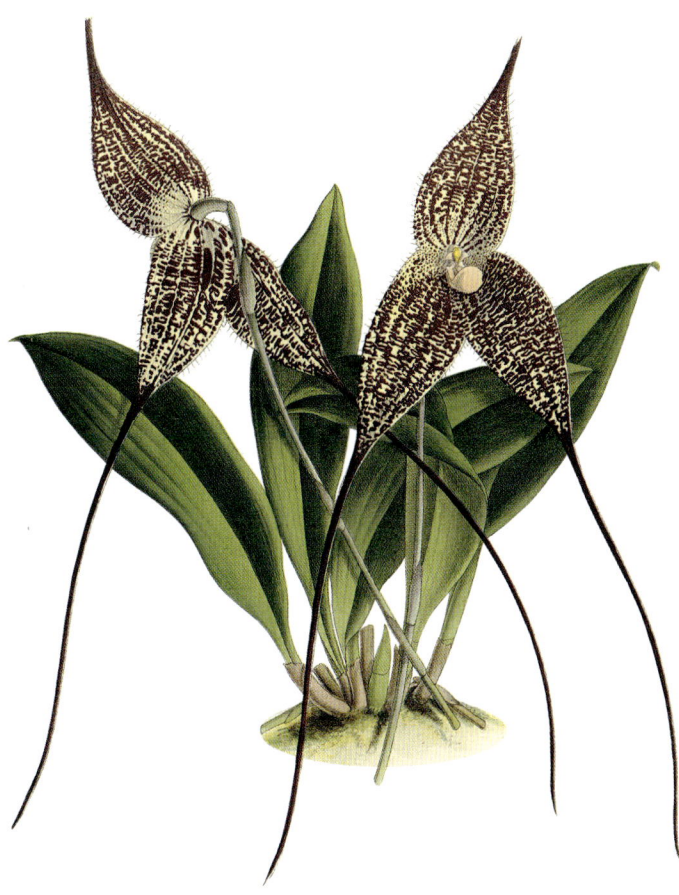

Black chimaera or vampire orchid   *Dracula vampira*

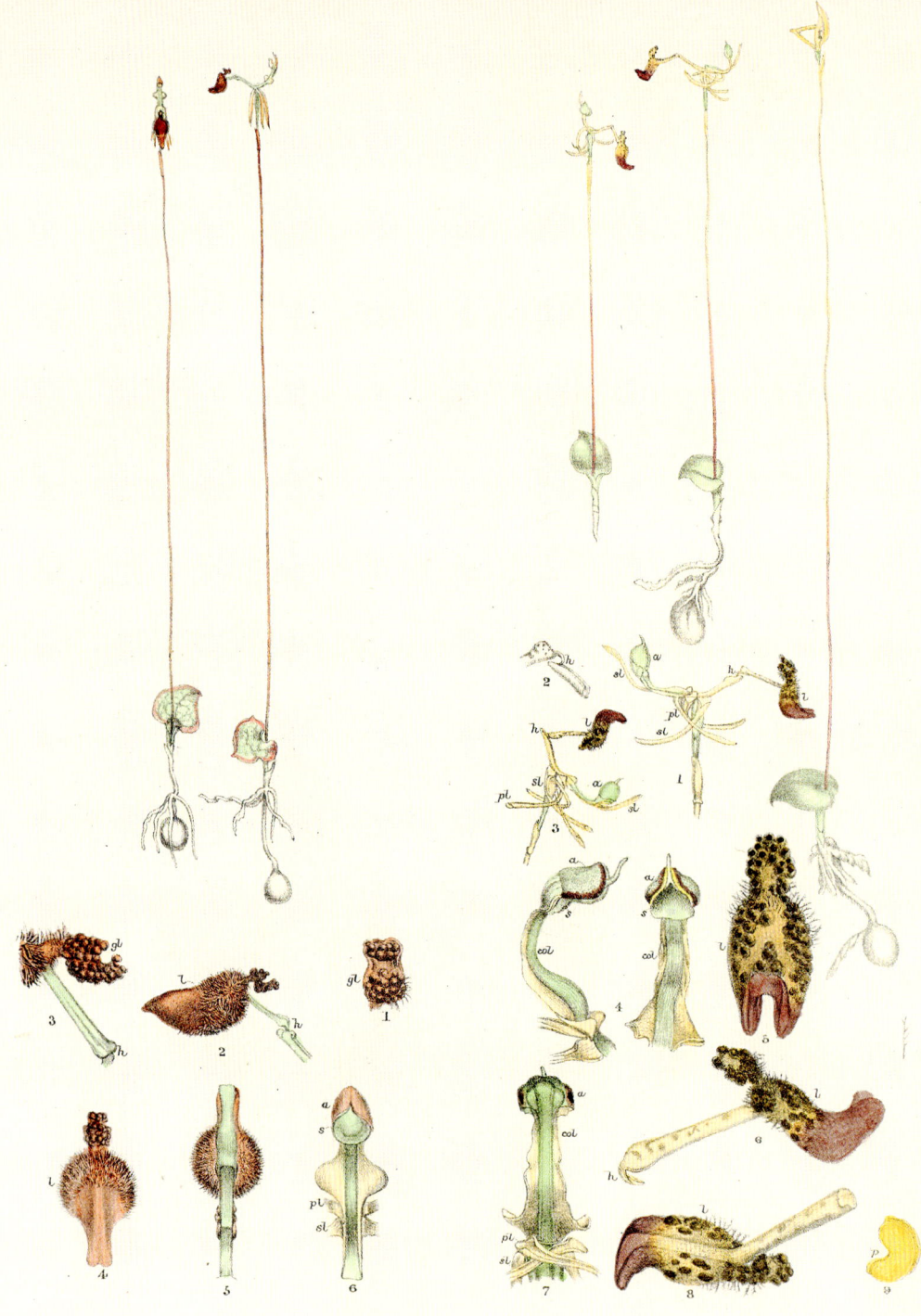

From Nature by R.D.Fitzgerald.F.L.S

On Stone by Arthur J. Stopps

DRAKÆA

Glyptodon   Elastica

Printed at the Surveyor General's Office Sydney N S W

May 1883.

GLOSSY-LEAVED HAMMER ORCHID
DRAKAEA ELASTICA

Opposite: *Drakaea elastica* by Robert David Fitzgerald, in *Australian Orchids*, 1875–82.

Right: *Caleana major* by W. Archer and Walter Hood Fitch, in *The Botany of the Antarctic Voyage of H. M. Discovery Ships* Erebus *and* Terror *in the Years 1839–1843*, 1860.

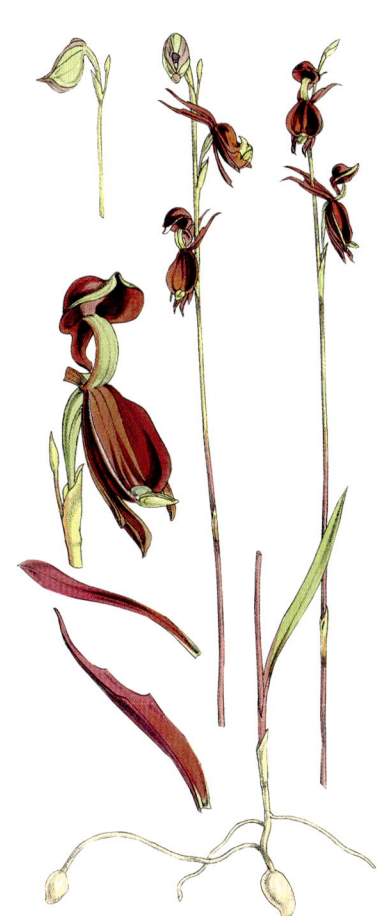

Australia has a huge diversity of orchid species, most of which are endemic to the country – that is, they are species that are found only in Australia and nowhere else. Many are terrestrial species, growing in the ground rather than being epiphytes, growing in trees. The genus *Drakaea* was described by the English botanist John Lindley in his article "A sketch of the vegetation of the Swan River Colony", which was published in three parts in *Edwards' Botanical Register* between 1839 and 1840. Working on material sent to him from Australia by the botanist James Drummond, an early settler in the region, Lindley described many orchid species new to science in this work, including species in "two curious new irritable genera" – one of these being *Drakaea elastica*, the first species to be described in the genus.

Lindley wrote:

> … a single flower placed at the end of a slender smooth erect scape, from twelve to eighteen inches high, and its labellum, which is hammer-headed, and placed on a long arm with a moveable elbow joint in the middle, is stated by Mr Drummond to resemble an insect suspended in the air, and moving with every breeze.

Lindley and Drummond had accurately surmised the mimicry employed by the species in order to achieve pollination. *Drakaea* species are nowadays regarded as excellent examples of sexual deception in plants, tricking male thynnid wasps into mistaking the labellum of each flower for a female wasp of the same species. Female thynnid wasps are wingless and climb to the tip of a straight blade of grass, where they begin to release chemical pheromones when they are ready to mate.

Not only do *Drakaea* species mimic their appearance, with their wasp-like flower on top of a wiry stem emerging from the grassland, but the pheromones produced by the flower emulate those released by the female wasp. The fooled male wasp grasps the labellum and tries to fly away and mate with it. In the process of the insect's exertions, the hinged labellum swings the wasp against the fertile column at the centre of the flower. The somewhat confused wasp eventually releases its grip on the "female", and leaves with the orchid's pollinia attached to its thorax and/or having deposited pollinia from another flower which had previously successfully deceived it. With a hinged labellum that swings their pollinating partners against the column, it is not surprising that these orchids have become commonly known as "hammer orchids".

Caleana is a terrestrial genus from Australia and New Zealand which employs a similar mode of pollination by sexual deception of insects. Known as the "flying duck orchids", the flowers have the rather extraordinary appearance of cartoon-like ducks in flight, with swept back lateral sepals like wings, and a hinged, curled labellum like a duck's head and bill. As in the *Drakaea* species, the labellum of a *Caleana* flower mimics and attracts insect pollinators in search of a mate, but in this case the orchid attracts sawflies rather than thynnid wasps. Rather than repeatedly swinging the deceived fly against the column, the *Caleana* labellum swiftly hinges the flower closed, trapping the fly against the column until the labellum returns to its original position and the insect is able to escape.

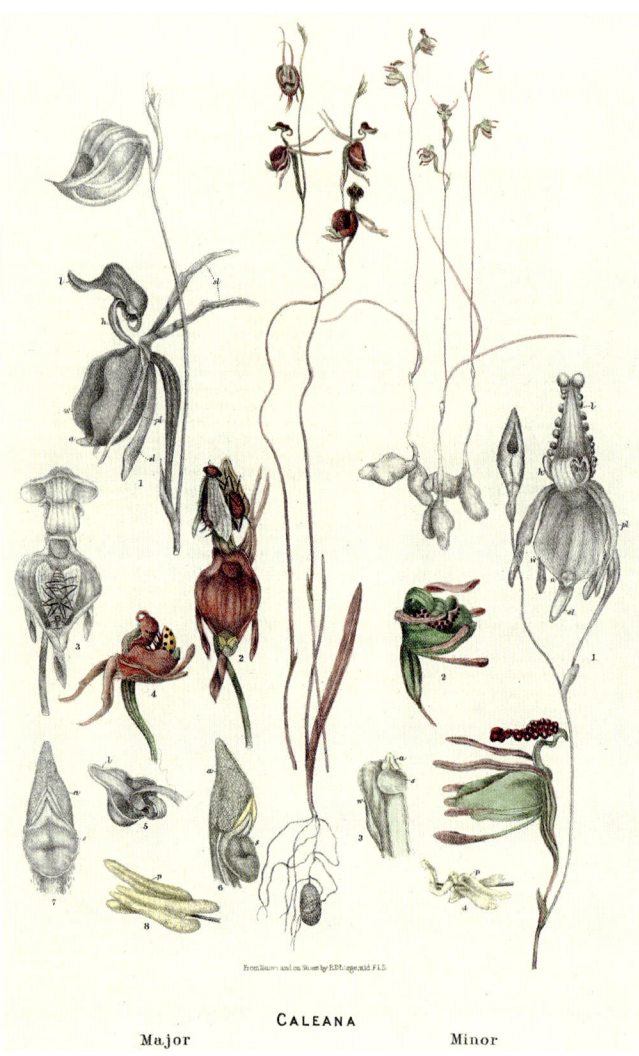

From Nature and on Stone by R.D. Fitzgerald, F.L.S.

CALEANA

Major   Minor

its position. This plant is rare, and where it does grow is not easily found, its whole appearance being that of charcoal, among which it usually springs up.

Besides these the Colony yields two curious new irritable genera of the Arethusean division of this order; both however small-flowered, and apparently dull-coloured. Of these

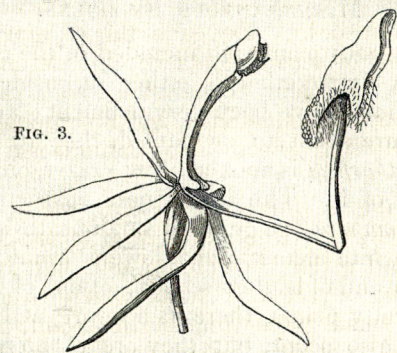

Fig. 3.

Drakæa elastica[263] has a single flower placed at the end of a slender smooth erect scape, from twelve to eighteen inches high, and its labellum, which is hammer-headed, and placed on a long arm with a moveable elbow joint in the middle, is stated by Mr. Drummond to resemble an insect suspended in the air, and moving with every breeze. The other plant

"A sketch of the vegetation of the Swan River Colony", John Lindley (1839), Part Three of *Appendix to the first twenty three volumes of Edwards' Botanical Register*

John Lindley and his contemporaries often annotated herbarium specimens with illustrations and dissections of flowers and complex or tiny characters – many miniature pieces of art in their own right as well as being scientifically valuable and instructive. Some of these illustrations were so useful they appear in the published species descriptions or later works, as here, in Lindley's publication about the botanical discoveries from Swan River. The full Latin diagnosis of the new species, *Drakaea elastica*, is on the page that followed, but the text describes the construction of the flower and its moveable and insect-like lip – and the line drawing illustrating the text is that originally drawn by Lindley on the herbarium specimen, itself the "type" specimen for the species.

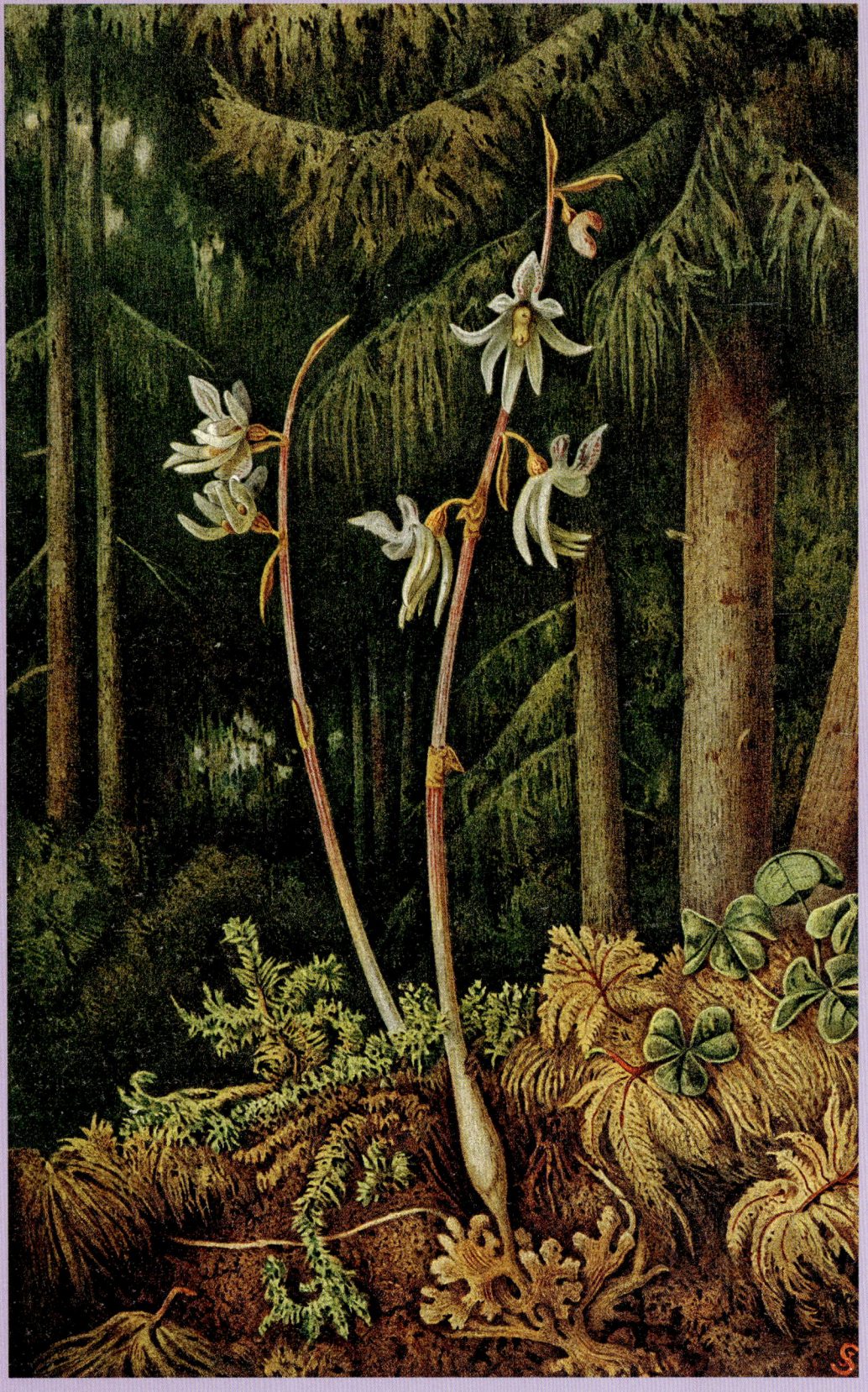

GHOST ORCHID

EPIPOGIUM APHYLLUM

Opposite: *Epipogium aphyllum* in *Ohnblatt im Moder des fichtenwaldes* by J. Seelos, in Anton Kerner von Marilaun *Pflanzenleben*, 1913–16.

Right: *Epipogium aphyllum* by Max Schulze in *Die Orchidaceen Deutschlands, Deutsch-Oesterreichs und der Schweiz*, 1894.

The curious, enigmatic terrestrial orchid *Epipogium aphyllum* was first described in Britain in 1854, but was only intermittently seen subsequently, and was actually thought to be extinct in the UK for over 20 years until a single flowering plant was rediscovered in 2009. Completely lacking chlorophyll, this leafless plant cannot manufacture its own carbohydrates via photosynthesis, and so is entirely dependent on a mycoheterotrophic relationship with a fungus found in the soil where the plant is growing.

Growing in the shade of oak and beech woodland in the Chiltern Hills of Buckinghamshire and Oxfordshire in south-east England, and in the Welsh borders of Herefordshire and Shropshire, the species is at the westernmost limit of its distribution across temperate Eurasia, from Japan to the UK. One of the main difficulties in finding the species in the wild is due to the fact that it emerges above ground only when it reproduces. Each inflorescence, usually only one per plant, grows to a height of up to 20 cm (8 in) above the woodland leaf litter. The labellum of the flower may be quite

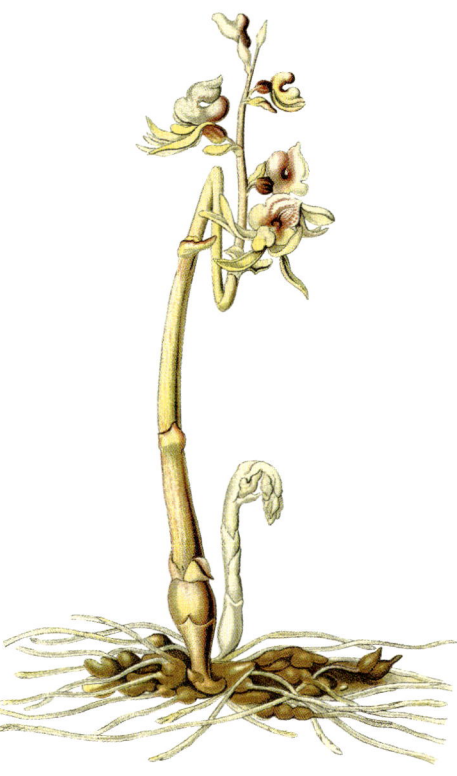

variable, but usually has at least some purple-pink colouration.

Saprophytic plants obtain their nutrients from decaying organic matter, whereas mycoheterotrophic species derive their nutrition via a fungal partner.

Tab. 4821.

EPIPOGON Gmelini.

Gmelin's Epipogon.

Nat. Ord. ORCHIDEÆ.—GYNANDRIA MONANDRIA.

Gen. Char. Flores resupinati, pedunculis brevibus non contortis sed bracteatis insidentes. *Perianthii laciniæ* exteriores subæquales, patentes; duæ interiores exterioribus similes. *Labellum* erectum (superum) trilobum, lobis lateralibus parvis patentibus, lobo terminali maximo, integerrimo, concavo et punctis elevatis notato, basi in calcar inflatum et adscendens desinens. *Gynostemium* oblongum, rectum, supra stigma in androclinium magnum, profundum et apice truncatim dilatatum. *Anthera* stipitata sed androclinio inserta, subrotunda, gibba, antice mucronulata, bilocularis, loculis longitudinaliter dehiscentibus. *Pollinaria* duo, oblonga, caudiculata, caudiculis supra basin pollinariis affixis, basi junctis, sub anthesi reflexis et proscollæ solutæ adglutinatis. *Pollen* sectile. *Staminodia* obsoleta. *Proscolla* magna cordata, emarginaturæ androclinii supra stigma adhærens. *Stigma* valde prominens, transversim ellipticum. *Germen* non contortum, ovatum, uniloculare, multiovulatum, ovulis spermophoris tribus parietalibus affixis. *Fred. Nees.*

EPIPOGON Gmelini. *Ledeb. Fl. Ross. v. 4. p. 77.*

EPIPOGUM Gmelini. *"L. C. Richard, de Orchid. Europ. Annot. p. 36."*

EPIPOGIUM Gmelini. *Lindl. Gen. et Sp. Orchid. p. 383. Fred. Nees, Gen. Plant. Germ. cum Ic.*

EPIPOGIUM aphyllum. *Reichenb. Fl. Excurs. p. 135.*

LIMODORUM Epipogium. *Sw. Nov. Act. Ups. v. 6. p. 80.*

SATYRIUM Epipogium. *Linn. Syst. Veget. p. 676. Jacq. Fl. Austr. t. 84.*

EPIPOGUM. *Gmel. Fl. Sib. v. 1. p. 22. tab. 2. f. 2.*

Even upon the continent of Europe, Dr. Fred. Nees calls this a "planta rarissima;" and it is singularly gratifying to us that the first figure of it published in this country, should be from a specimen, an undoubted native of England. It was discovered on the 9th of September of this year (1854), as related in the 'Journal of Botany' for October, by Mrs. Anderton Smith, the lady of the Rev. Anderton Smith, at Tedstone Delamere, Herefordshire. "All the specimens were found at the foot of a very steep woody bank, close to a brook; the soil very wet and stiff."

DECEMBER 1ST, 1854.

That it has remained so long undiscovered in this country, and that it is still considered so rare on the Continent, is due to the fact of its having no foliage and no conspicuous colours to attract attention ; or it may have been passed by for some of our other colourless and aphyllous plants. Once known to be a native of Britain, other stations may be expected to be soon detected. Various localities are given in the middle and north of Europe, from Switzerland, Austria, the Caucasian Provinces, to Sweden, and westward as far as Lake Baikal, and the River Irkut, Province of Tunka. It was first known as a Siberian plant, and admirably described and figured by Gmelin (*l. c.*) under the name of "*Epipogum**," a little more than a century ago. Linnæus referred the plant to *Limodorum*, and called the species Epipogium,—quoting the synonym of Gmelin also incorrectly as *Epipogium*. This spelling of the word has by authors been adopted, till Richard, in his 'Annotations,' as quoted by Lindley, named the plant "*Epipogum Gmelini*." At length Ledebour gave the generic name the usual termination, "*Epipogon ;*" but he refers to authors whom I have not the means of consulting " Patze, Meyer et Elkan Flora d. Provinz Preussen, p. 93," in justification of the change. I have adopted the same as the most correct, and quite in accordance with that of the original author. Mr. Brown however, in his Prodromus Nov. Holl. p. 330, under *Gastrodium*, is the first of the later botanists (1810) to allude to *Epipogium* as a genus : " Affinitatem haud levem habet cum *Epipogio* (quod Limodorum Epipogium, *Sw.*), præsertim anthera decidua cum polline e particulis elastice cohærentibus, necnon stigmate ad basin columnæ elongatæ sito."— Lindley indeed places it in his Division GASTRODIEÆ of his fifth Tribe ARETHUSEÆ.

It is observed by M. Schlauter, in Fred. Nees' 'Flora Europæa,' that the plant does not appear annually in the same spot, but every two years : the swollen branches of the root eventually becoming new flower-stems, and requiring two years to be perfected.

DESCR. Parasitic? *Root* a mass of thick, branching, fleshy fibres, very much resembling that of *Corallorhiza innata*, the apices of the branches often swollen (said to be incipient flower-stems). *Stems* a span or more high, arising from a thickened branch, or portion of the root, swollen a little above the base, and there articulated ; the rest of the stem is erect, terete, of a pale reddish or tawny colour, speckled with red, of a fleshy or almost waxy texture, and sheathed with three or four membranaceous, inconspicuous scales, terminating in an erect *raceme*

* "*Epipogum* dixi, quia barba (by which he means the labellum) hujus floris inverso ordine disposita est." *Gmel.*

of four to five or six moderately-sized *flowers*. *Pedicels* short, not longer than the small fleshy *bracts*. *Sepals* and *petals* all directed downwards, but curved forwards, narrow-lanceolate, nearly equal, pale sulphur-yellow. *Lip* superior ; it may be described as ovate in general form, of a thick and fleshy texture, the ground-colour white, three-lobed ; the lateral lobes small, ovate, obtuse, moderately spreading, the middle lobe large, suddenly reflexed, acute, having a cavity (and externally a tubercle corresponding with it a little below the apex) ; the whole upper surface studded with soredia, or small rough prominences, arranged in lines, and of a rose-colour ; the base beneath is prolonged into a large pouch or blunt *spur*, as long as the ovary ; this is white, tinged with purple. *Column* rather short, terete, and somewhat gibbous below, apterous above, flattened in front, and bearing the *stigma*. *Anther-case* terminal, subhemispherical, erect, two-celled. *Pollen-masses* two, tapering into slender stalks, which are attached to a white triangular gland. *Ovary* straight, not twisted, short, three-lobed, nearly turbinate, yellowish, streaked with pale red.

Fig. 1. Front view of a flower. 2. Side view of a labellum, with the spur.
3. Column and anther. 4. Pollen-masses :—*magnified.*

Description of *Epipogium aphyllum* synonym in *Curtis's Botanical Magazine*, 1854

Plants often have multiple botanical names, for a range of reasons. Often synonyms are the result of changing ideas of what a species is – what one botanist considers to be different variants of a single species may each be considered separate species by another. A species found in many places could be named multiple times by different people. There are strict nomenclatural rules about naming, and unravelling which is the most "correct" name can be difficult.

Epipogium aphyllum has at least 10 synonyms, several of which were never properly published and so cannot be used. One synonym is *Epipogium gmelini* (shown here when it was used later in another publication), originally but invalidly published in 1817. Not all of the requirements to publish a new name were fulfilled in the publication, so the name is considered *nomen nudum* – it is an invalid unusable name. Now the species is considered to be the same as *Epipogium aphyllum*, which was published in 1814, and because the earliest name automatically takes priority.

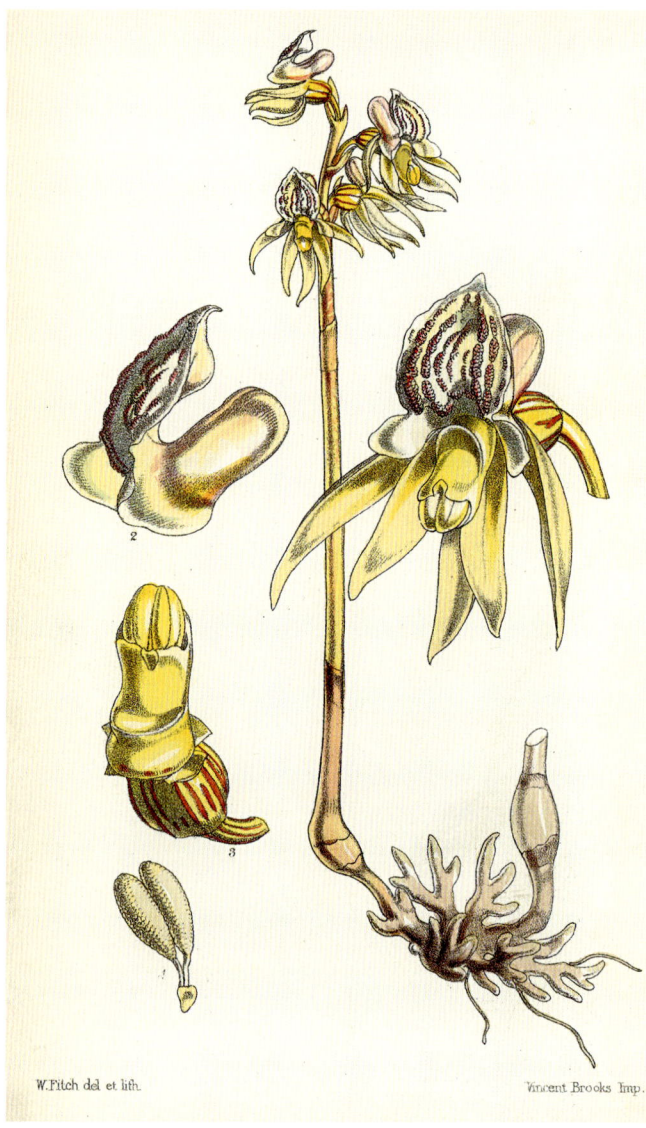

the orchid and different strains of fungus, making their co-occurrence even less likely to be encountered. If the "correct" fungus is not present, or dies out in a particular location, the orchid will not be able to survive.

The British plants of this orchid seem to be considerably less robust than their continental relatives, producing no more than two inflorescences per plant, each bearing no more than four flowers. Outside of the British Isles it is reported that individuals of the species may produce as many as 30 flower spikes, each of which may grow up to 30 cm (1 ft) in height and bear up to seven flowers.

The ghostly colouration, or rather lack of colouration, combined with this orchid's elusive nature, disappearing from records for decades and spending most of its life cycle underground, have led to the very appropriate common name for this species – the ghost orchid.

The American "ghost orchid", *Dendrophylax lindenii*, is a completely different, distantly related species, and although it too has no leaves, it has a very different life history, growing as an epiphytic subtropical species in Florida, Cuba and the Bahamas. Unlike *Epipogium aphyllum*, which has no chlorophyll, the roots of *Dendrophylax lindenii*, which form a tangled mass and attach the plant to its host tree in swampy areas, are green due to the presence of chlorophyll, and are able to photosynthesize and produce carbohydrates to enable the plant to grow. The large white flowers of *Dendrophylax lindenii* appear to be suspended in front of the host tree, with two long, gently twisted tendrils hanging from the labellum.

Above: *Epipogium aphyllum* by Walter Hood Fitch, in *Curtis's Botanical Magazine*, 1854.

Opposite: *Epipogium aphyllum* by Otto Wilhelm Thomé, in *Flora von Deutschland Österreich und der Schweiz*, 1885.

Orchid–fungus relationships may be very specific, and only one fungus, or a restricted range of fungi, can form associations with the orchid. In other cases the relationship is much broader, and a wide range of fungi can fulfil this crucial role. In rare and restricted range species, such as *Epipogium aphyllum*, it is thought that the partnership is probably quite specific, even with distinct forms of

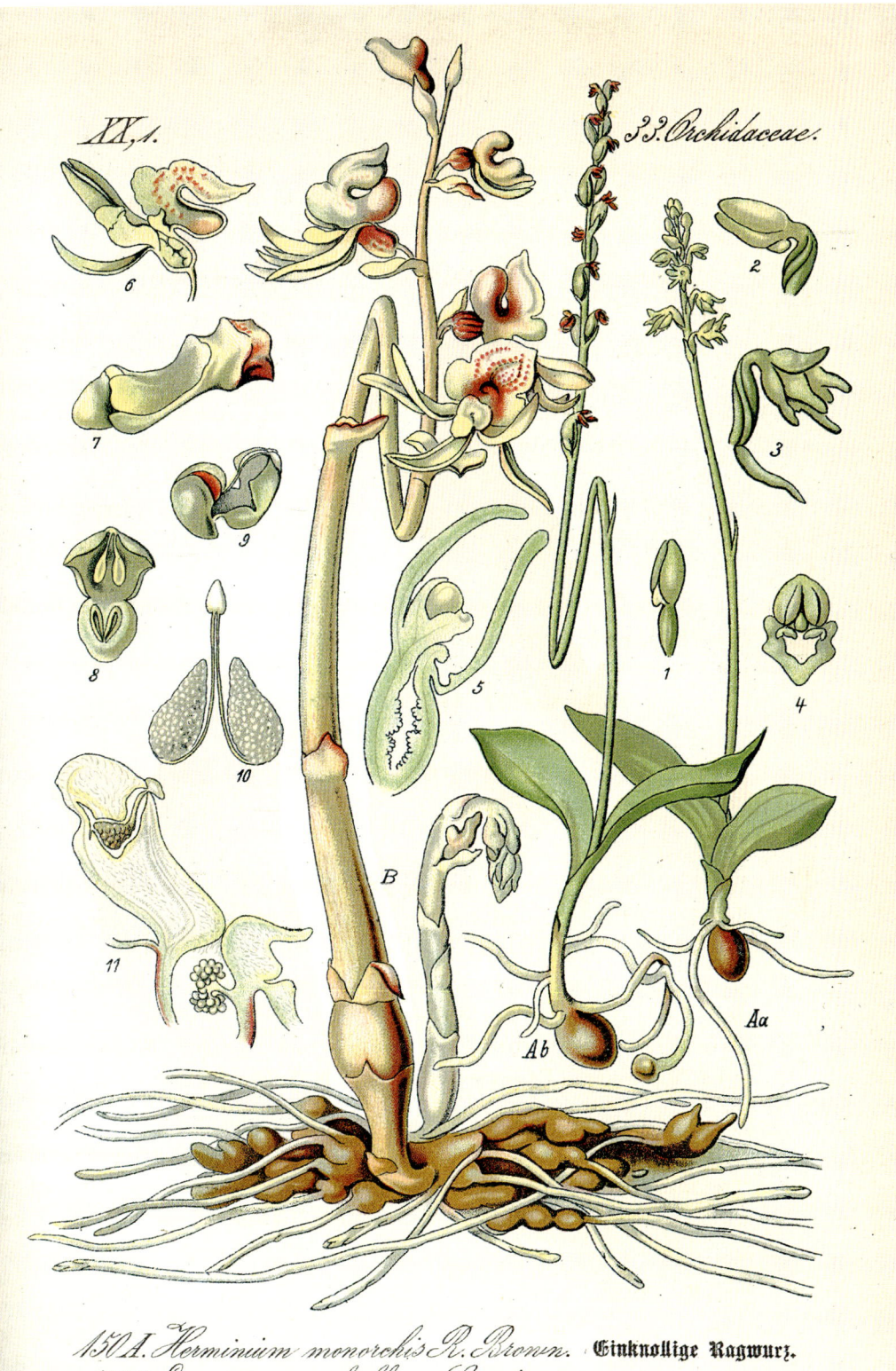

150 A. Herminium monorchis R. Brown. Einknollige Ragwurz.
150 B. Epipogium aphyllum Swartz. Blattloser Bartständel.

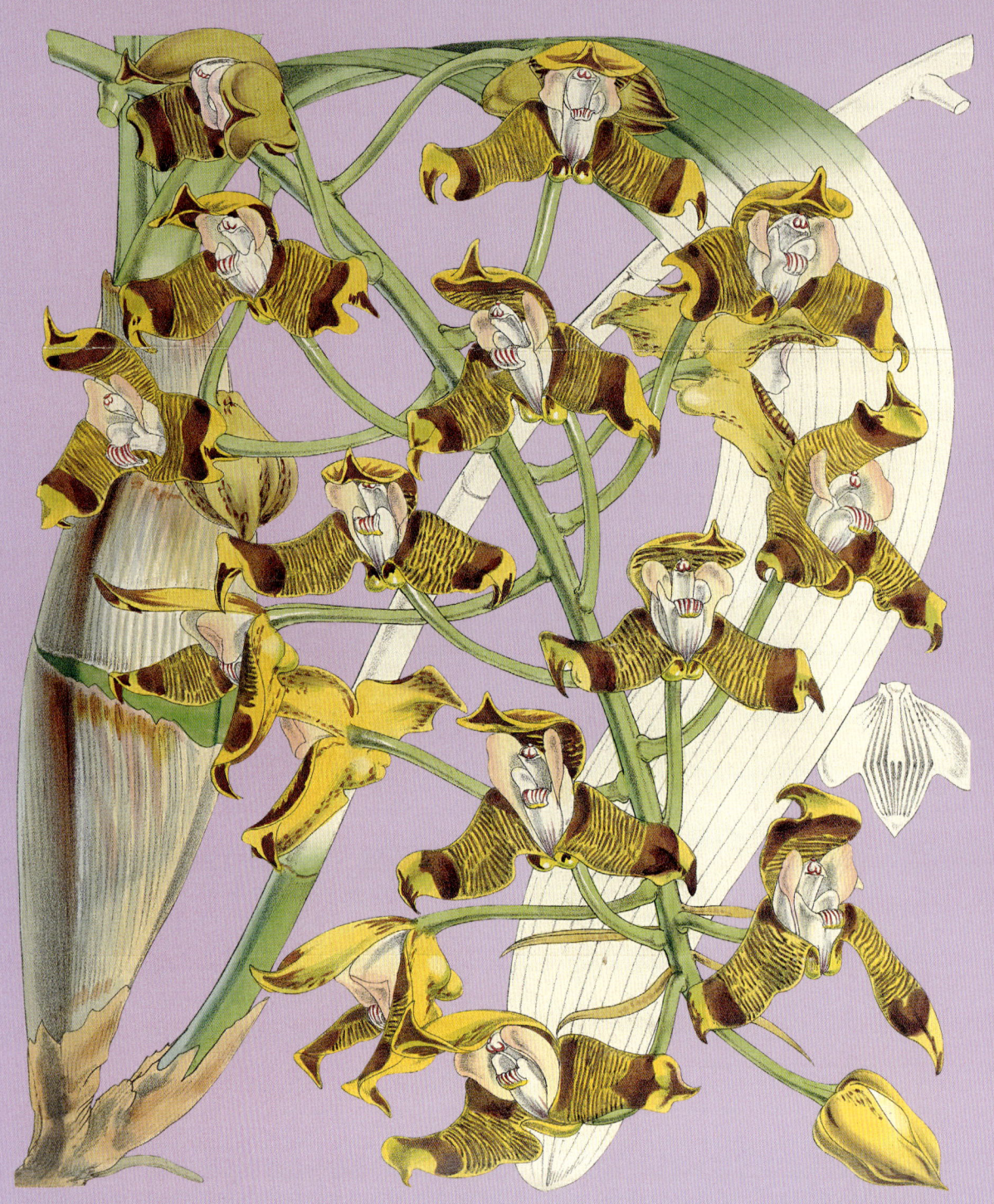

ELLIS'S GRAMMANGIS

GRAMMANGIS ELLISII

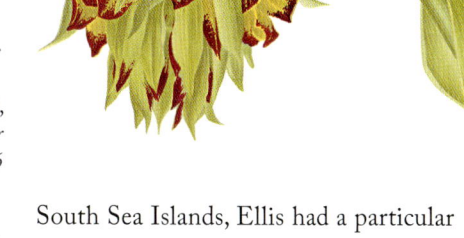

But my greatest treasure was a large bulbed plant, of quite a new species; and as it is now growing well, and showing flowers, I hope it may be added to the already rich collections of orchids cultivated in our country. It had a large flower-stalk, a seed-pod the size of an orange, and the natives said the flower was scarlet and purple.

Rev. William Ellis (1858),
in *Three Visits to Madagascar
During the Years 1853-1854-1856*

The Reverend William Ellis travelled to Madagascar several times between the late 1850s and the late 1860s for the London Missionary Society, seeking to convert the Malagasy people to Christianity. However, during this time he devoted a considerable proportion of his energies to discovering and documenting the people of this little-explored tropical island and their culture and ethnography, as well as the island's geology, flora and fauna. Having originally trained as a gardener before becoming an ordained missionary and travelling in South Africa and the South Sea Islands, Ellis had a particular interest in orchids.

The showy sprays of large waxy flowers and the unusual four-sided spindle-shaped pseudobulbs of *Grammangis ellisii* were documented by Ellis, on his travels in the humid forests of eastern Madagascar. This plant is one of nearly 1,000 orchid species that grow on the island, the majority of which are found only there (described as "endemic" species).

On his return to England, after his last and longest stay in Madagascar, for a period of four years, Ellis continued to grow many of the species he had brought back with him in a specially built stove-house at his home in Rose Hill, in the then rural area of Hoddesdon, north of London. The greenish-brown to almost bronze-coloured tepals of the *Grammangis ellisii* flower contrast with the yellow and red striped labellum, and the waxy long-lived blooms have a striking glossy sheen. These characteristics have resulted in this species being regarded as one of Ellis's most spectacular contributions to orchid cultivation in Europe. Ellis's exotic collection became well known and was visited by botanical luminaries of the day, including John Lindley, of the Royal Horticultural Society, and William Hooker, then Director of the Royal Botanic Gardens, Kew.

One of only two species in the genus, the sister species to Reverend Ellis's discovery was published only in 1969, over a hundred years later. *Grammangis spectabilis* is one of the rarest species in Madagascar (and indeed in the whole world), with just nine plants known in the wild, and only very few in cultivation. The French botanists Jean Marie Bosser and Philippe Morat observed the species in south-west Madagascar, in the Sakaraha area just beyond the Zombitse National Park. Bosser and Morat realized that the plants they had found represented a distinct species on account of the smaller tepals, and the more ornate labellum with thorn-like appendages instead of keel-like structures. In view of the spectacular display of flowers borne by the few plants they had found, on inflorescences up to 60 cm (2 ft) long, they gave it the epithet *spectabilis*.

Right *Grammangis ellisii* by John Day, 1880.

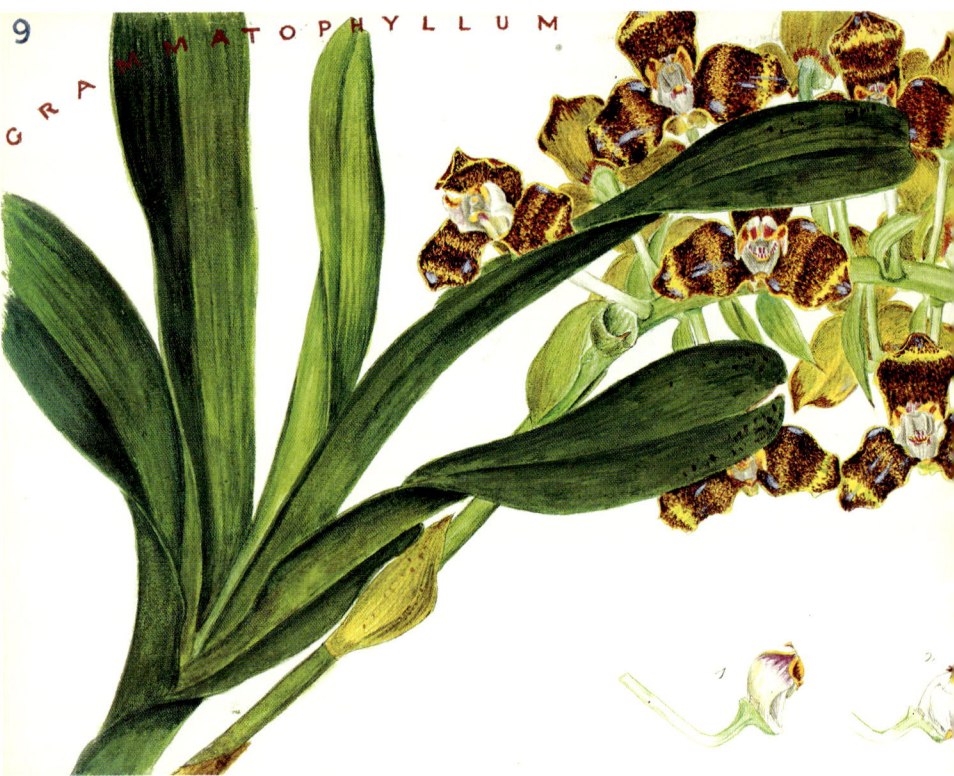

The species is so rare and the location where it grows is so inaccessible to botanists searching for it that it was not until the mid-1990s that another specimen was collected, from the same locality, and more recently, in 2015, a few more plants were located inside the National Park. Local people call the species *sariakondro*, from the Malagasy words *sary*, meaning "looks like", and *akondro*, meaning "banana", referring to the thick, slightly curved pseudobulbs the orchid produces.

It is thought that a combination of over-collection of orchids by plant hunters, especially in the past, and ongoing habitat loss caused by felling of trees for timber and charcoal, and often opportunistic mining for gemstones, have led to the extremely precarious likelihood of this species' survival in the future.

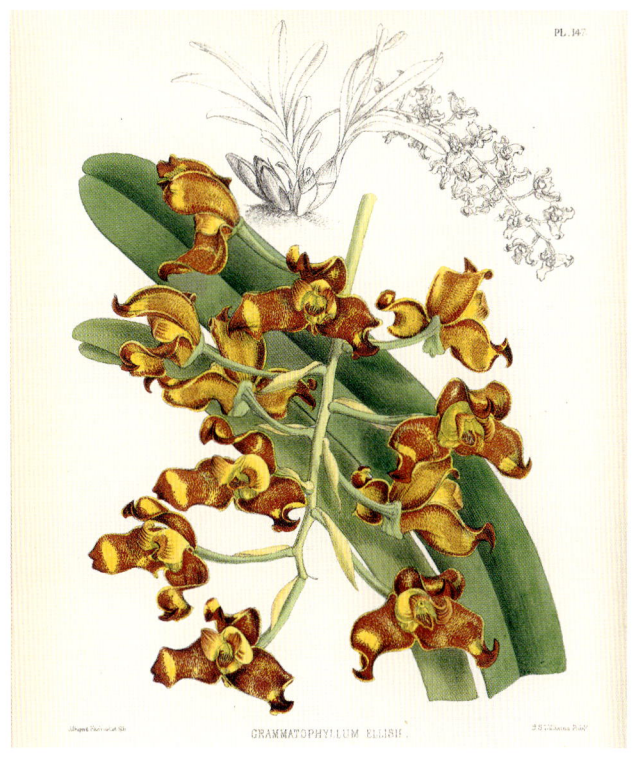

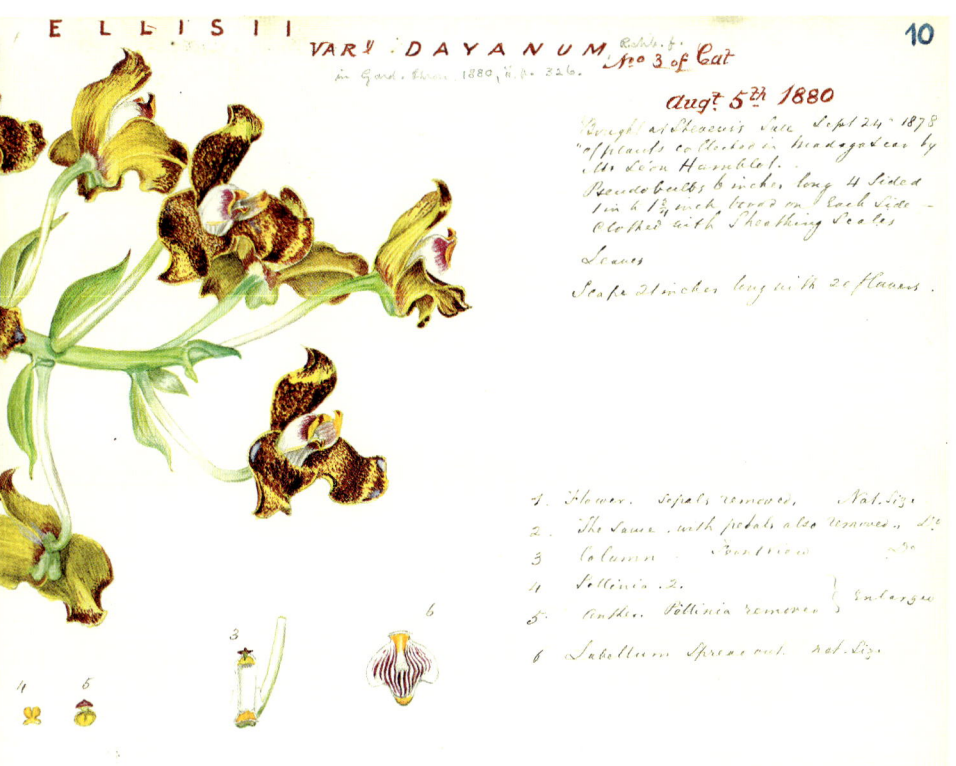

Above: *Grammangis ellisii* (as *Grammatophyllum ellisii*) by John Nugent Fitch, in R. Warner and B. S. Williams, *The Orchid Album*, 1885.

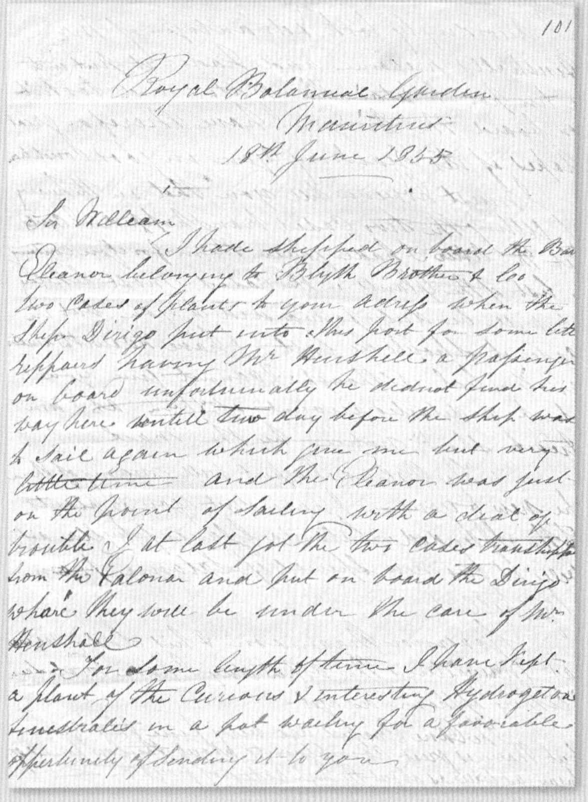

Letter from James Duncan to Sir William Jackson Hooker, from Mauritius, 18 June 1855

James Duncan was a British horticulturalist who was charged with restoring what are now known as the Sir Seewoosagur Ramgoolam Botanical Gardens, in Mauritius in the mid-1800s when the island was under British colonial rule. The gardens had originally been founded by the French Governor Mahé de la Bourdonnais and then the first director Pierre Poivre in the mid-to-late 1700s, initially as vegetable gardens and then for the introduction of spices, before later falling into disrepair.

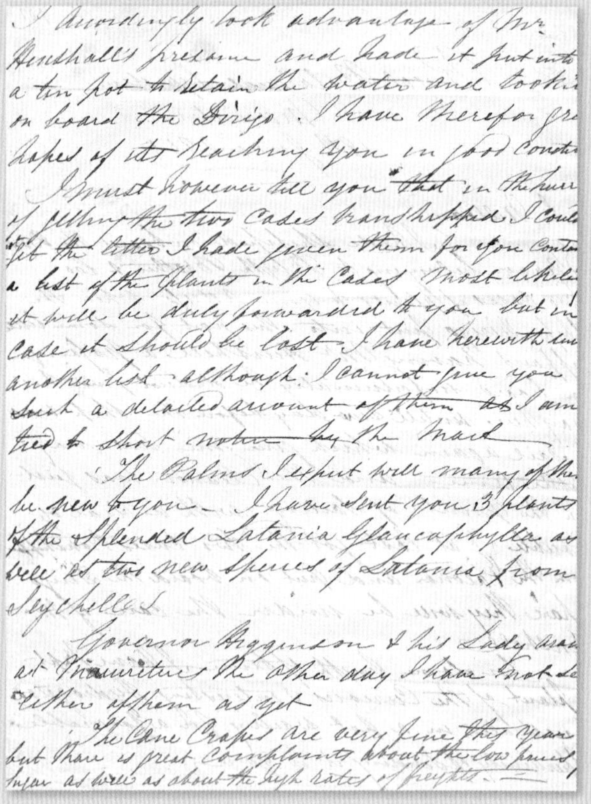

101A

[Handwritten letter to Sir W. J. Hooker — partially legible]

If permission could be got for the Queen of Madagascar to allow Mr. Henshell to explore that Island I make no doubt but a great number of fine new plants would be got from there — I have often tried to get the Capt of the Ships that buys Bullocks here to bring seeds or plants but have not succeeded as they are not allowed at pres.t to bring away anything but Bullocks, Poultry & Rice I should however think those restrictions will soon be relaxed or not enforced as they are at present

The Rev.d W. Ellis a Gentleman connected with the Missionary Society of London visited Madagascar last year he applied for leave to visit the Court which is held in the interior of the island his application was favourably renewed and granted but unfortunately the Cholera broke out in Mauritius at the very time and after Mr Ellis had proceeded on his journey about 40 Miles he was stop.t and told that in consequence of the Cholera being at Mauritius he could not proceed any further

he was therefore obliged to turn back Mr Ellis brought some splendid plants of Angræcum Superbum & a Sesquipidale Hydrogeton fenestratus and some other kinds of Orchidea but he appears to so much attached to Orchaceous plants as not to care for any other — I furnished him with some Cases and made favour of a very few kinds which were all but dead confined on Home some of them are however going to grow

The last time I heard from him he was at the Cape whither he had been able to get his plants home alive I have not heard I end this hurried letter

Your Most Obedient Humble Servant
James Duncan

P.S. The Brige Sailed on the 15th

To Sir W. J. Hooker

Like many other correspondents around the world, Duncan would periodically send new plants from the region to Sir William Jackson Hooker by ship, and in this letter he mentions several cases of plants he is sending and that he expects many will be new to Hooker. Interestingly he mentions the Reverend William Ellis, who would soon observe the species *Grammangis ellisii* in Madagascar (or perhaps already had) and who was making his way back to England with his own "splendid" orchid collections.

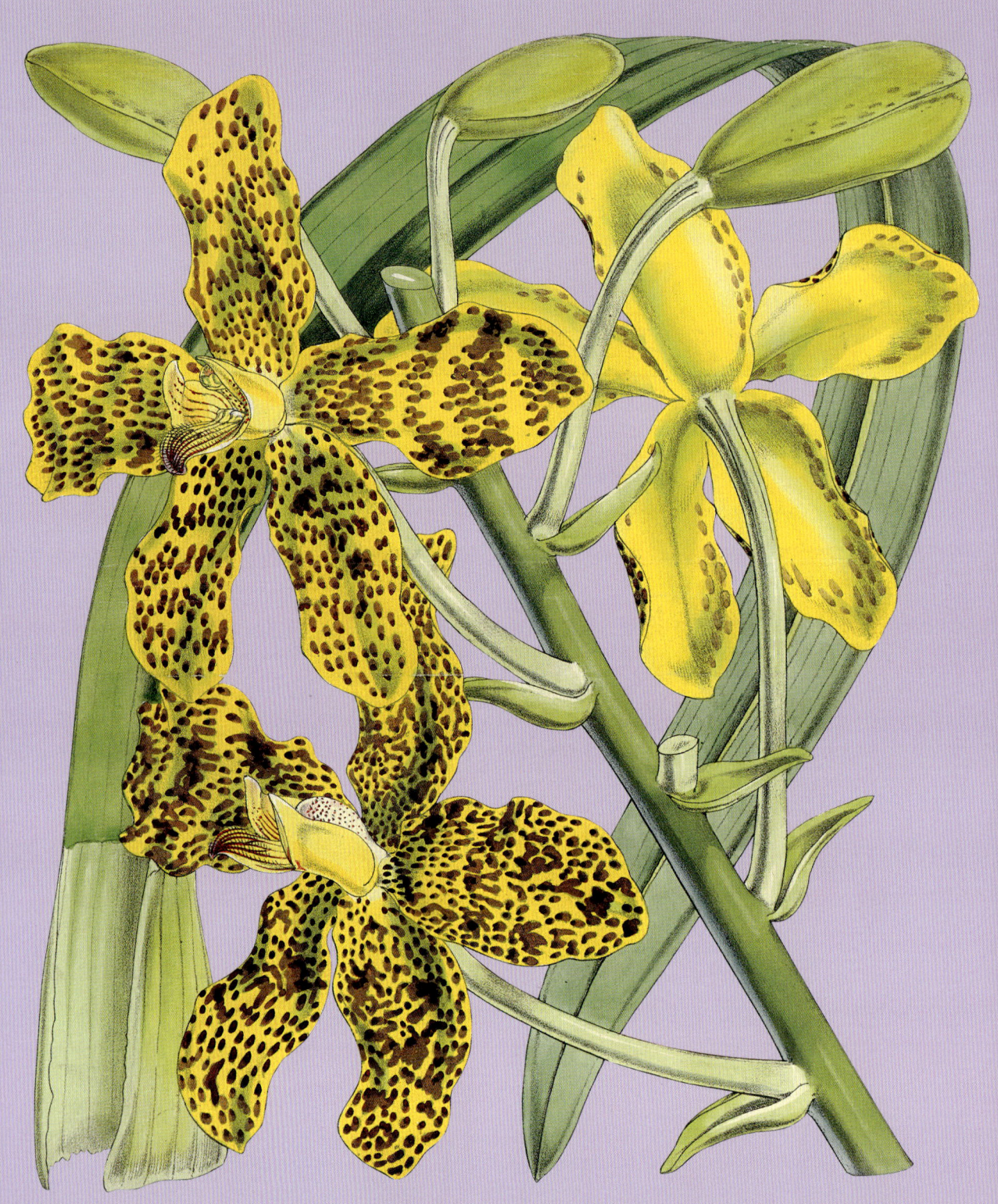

TIGER ORCHID
GRAMMATOPHYLLUM SPECIOSUM

Opposite: Walter Hood Fitch's illustration of *Grammatophyllum speciosum* from *Curtis's Botanical Magazine* of 1860 was drawn for a magnificent specimen flowered by Mr Carson, gardener to W. G. Farmer of Nonsuch Park, Ewell, Surrey, in October 1859.

Right: Walter Hood Fitch's illustration of *Grammatophyllum stapeliiflorum* from *Curtis's Botanical Magazine* of 1867. Its name reflects the stapelia-like colouration of its flowers.

The tiger orchid, *Grammatophyllum speciosum*, is a spectacular tropical epiphytic orchid from south-east Asia. It produces many long cylindrical stems, up to 3 m (10 ft) or longer, bearing many long leaves in their apical half, and large trusses of flat yellow flowers heavily spotted with dark brownish purple on their sepals and petals. It is found in lowland rainforests, commonly growing on large trees along river banks, and can form a massive plant, often becoming so heavy that it damages or even kills the tree on which it is growing. A large specimen, reported to weigh 2 tons (probably because it was attached to a tree branch or part of a tree trunk), caused a sensation when it was exhibited at the Great Exhibition in London in 1851. Another specimen cultivated on a lawn at the Singapore Botanic Garden may well be over 100 years old and is several metres in circumference. Large plants like this can bear over 7,000 flowers. The tiger orchid has peculiar roots of two types – normal spreading roots and

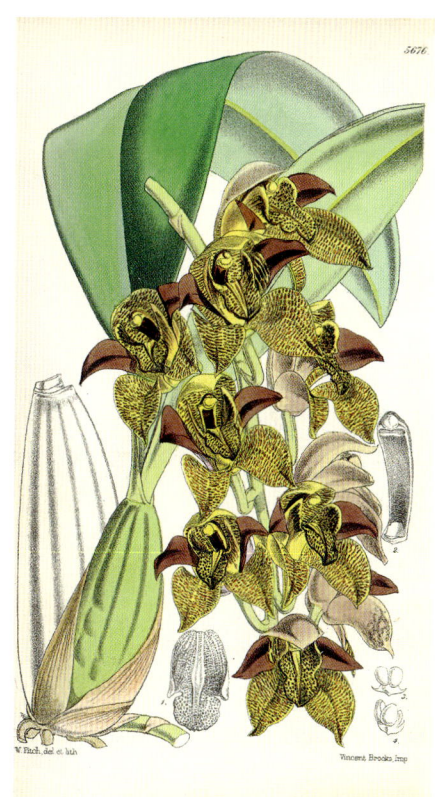

erect spiky tapering ones that act as traps for leaf litter. The latter type is likely to collect nutrients as the trapped leaves decay, which is a useful attribute in the nutrient-poor epiphytic environment.

65

GRAMMATOPHYLLUM multiflorum.

Many-flowered Letter-leaf.

GYNANDRIA MONANDRIA.

Nat. ord. ORCHIDACEÆ, § VANDEÆ.

GRAMMATOPHYLLUM *Blume; Perianthium* explanatum, patens, sepalis petalisque subæqualibus. *Labellum* cum columnâ articulatum, nanum, trilobum, cucullatum. *Columna* arcuata, erecta, semiteres, basi callosa. *Anthera* subbilocularis. *Pollinia* 2, globosa, basi sulcata, in extremitatibus glandulæ arcuatæ sessilia.——Herba *epiphyta, caulescens. Caules simplices, incrassati. Folia linearia, disticha, striata.* Pedunculi *radicales, longissimi, (v. terminales?) multiflori. Flores speciosissimi.* Gen. et Sp. Orch. p. 173.

G. multiflorum; racemo erecto longissimo multifloro, bracteis ovato-oblongis obtusis squamiformibus dorso convexis, sepalis oblongis obtusiusculis planis, petalis acutis subconformibus angustioribus, labelli trilobi pubescentis medio hirsuti lobo intermedio plano oblongo rotundato lateralibus erectis subfalcatis, jugo in medio carnoso elevato ad basin lobi intermedii interrupto in lamellas 4 simplices cis apicem evanescentes producto, columnæ margine supra basin elevato flexuoso incurvo foveam altam obconicam circumdante. *Botanical Register, 1835, misc. no. 80.*

For this noble Orchidaceous plant now figured we are indebted to the exertions of Mr. Hugh Cuming, who discovered it in Manilla, and sent it to his customers in England. I am not aware of its having flowered anywhere except with Mr. Bateman, who sent me in May, 1838, the specimen, of which the annexed plate represents the upper part; the whole raceme was upwards of two feet long, and bore forty-eight flowers, each about an inch and half in diameter.

The plant has very much the aspect of a gigantic *Cymbidium,* with long coriaceous leaves, distichous at the base, and in fact there is not much to separate Grammatophyllum

* From γραμμα a letter, and φυλλον a leaf, in allusion to the marking of the leaves of the flower.

December, 1839.   2 A

from that genus; the principal mark of distinction yet remarked consists in the gland of the pollen-masses, which in Cymbidium is triangular, and in the present genus is crescent-shaped, with one pollen-mass on each extremity of the crescent. I observe however that the base of the column is rolled up so as to form a fistular cavity, or cuniculus, near the base of the labellum; but I am uncertain whether to regard this as a generic character or not.

It was hoped, when this plant was imported, that it would prove the famous Letter-plant of Amboyna, Java, and the neighbouring coast, so called because its flowers are marked with deep brown stains arranged upon a pale ground so as to resemble grotesque characters. In this however we have been disappointed, as, notwithstanding the noble appearance of this, it is very inferior to the Letter-plant. Of that I have before me a single flower from Dr. Wallich's Herbarium, gathered at Pulo Dinding, in Cochin China, by Mr. Finlayson, which must have been four inches from the tip of one sepal to that of the opposite petal, or a foot in circumference!

As the species is in this natural order among the easiest to cultivate, it is well worth possession, even in a small collection, notwithstanding that the flowers want richness of colour: it is probable however that they will improve in this respect.

Grammatophyllum multiflorum described in *Edwards' Botanical Register*, 1839

Grammatophyllum multiflorum was introduced from Manila in the Philippines by Hugh Cuming, who sold a plant to James Bateman of Knypersley Hall, Staffordshire, who flowered it for the first time in May 1838. John Lindley described and named it in *Edwards' Botanical Register* of 1839 and his account is accompanied by Sarah Drake's illustration of the inflorescence. It is closely related to the widespread *G. scriptum* whose distribution ranges from central Indonesia to the Solomon Islands. Some authors consider the island forms conspecific, although a recent account of the orchid flora of the Philippines distinguishes them at specific rank. Bateman, the author of the monumental *The Orchidaceae of Mexico and Guatemala* and *A Monograph of Odontoglossum*, was one of the leading orchid growers in Victorian England and developed a remarkable garden at Biddulph Grange.

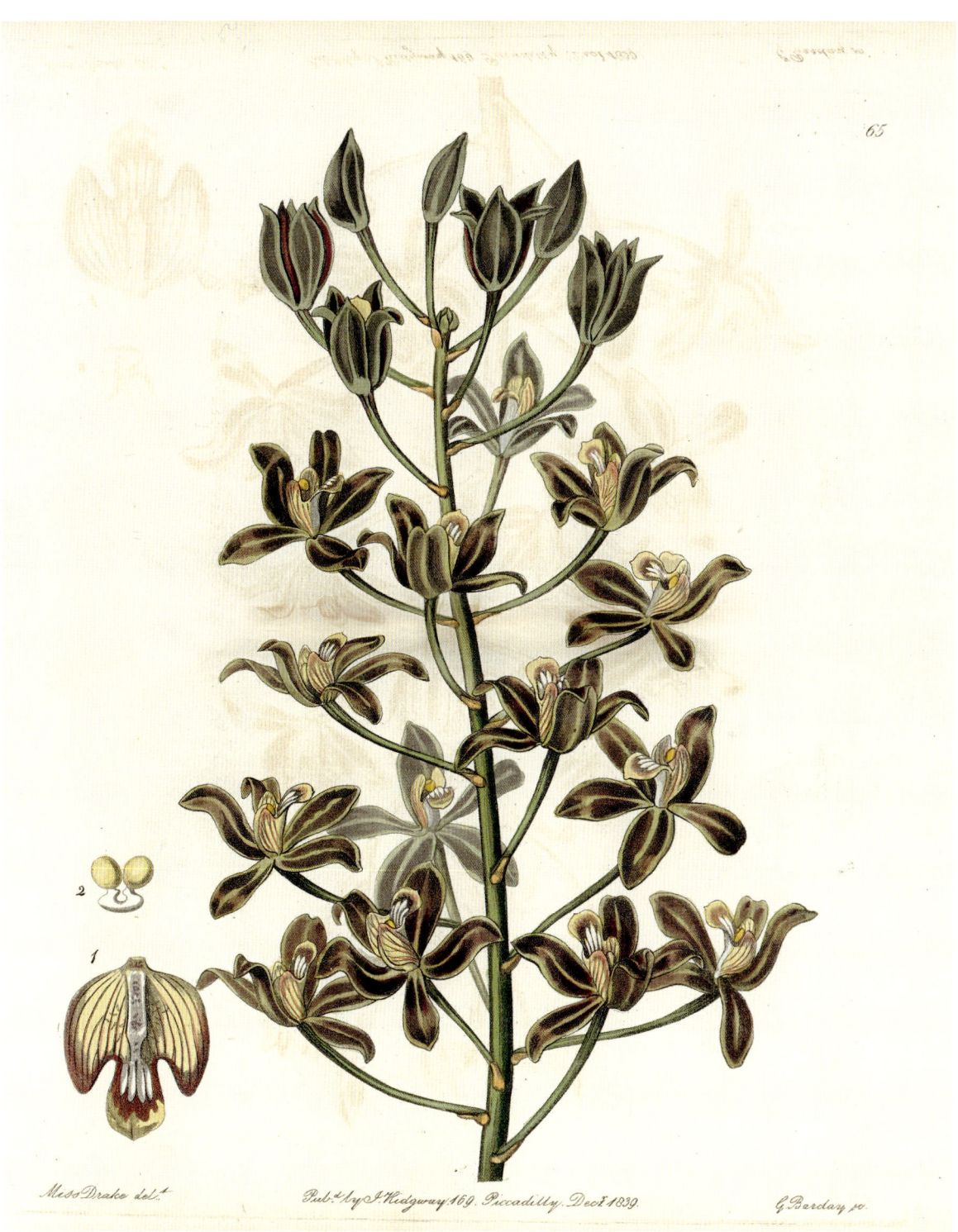

Mess Drake delt.   Publd. by J. Ridgway 169. Piccadilly. Decr 1839.   G. Barclay, sc.

Tiger orchid   *Grammatophyllum speciosum*   **129**

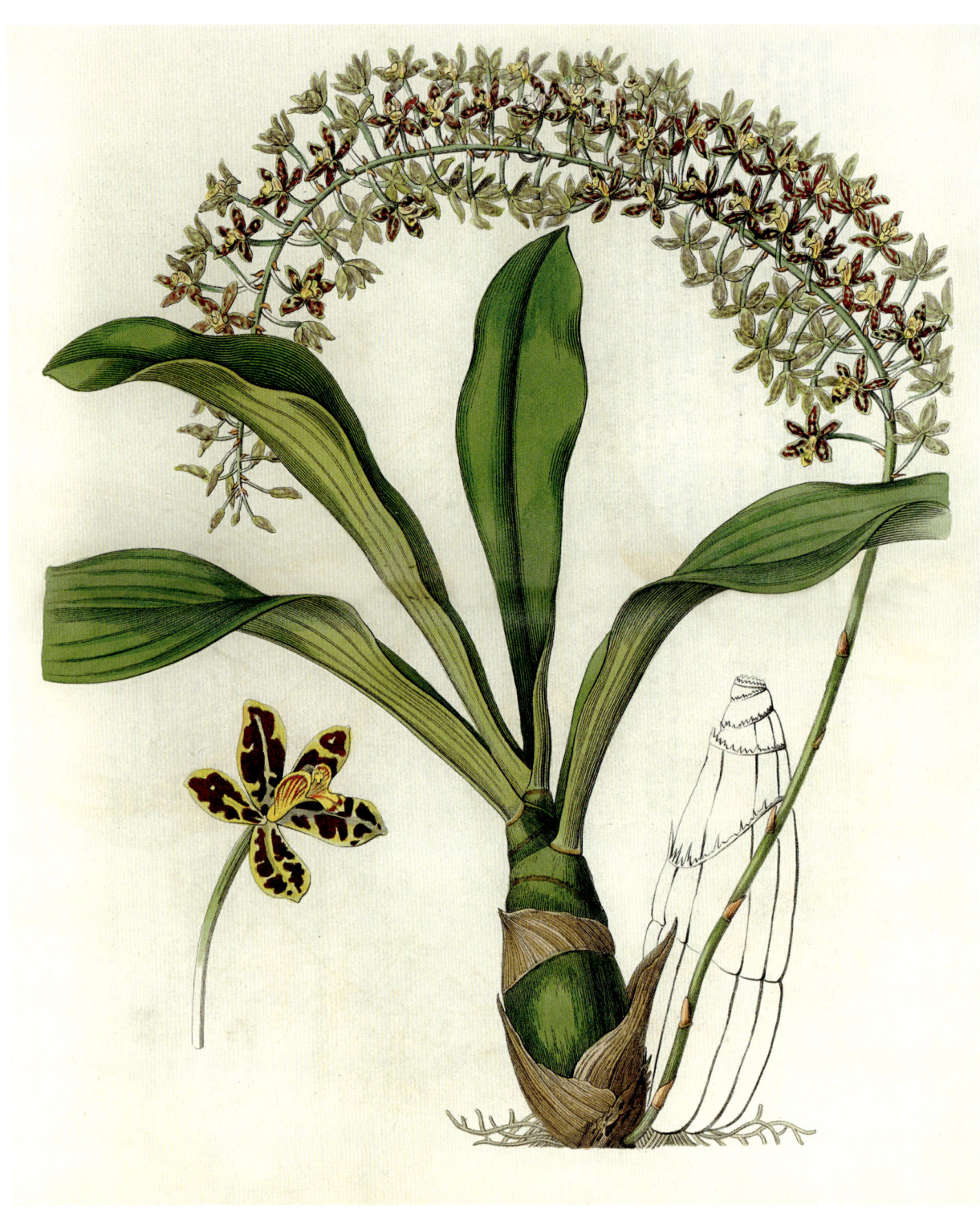

130 Tiger orchid *Grammatophyllum speciosum*

This orchid was described in Java in the early nineteenth century, by the German botanist Carl Blume, then Director of the Buitenzorg Botanic Gardens in western Java. However, it is in fact quite widespread, ranging from Burma, Thailand and the Malay Peninsula throughout the Malay Archipelago. In the Philippines the similar but slightly smaller species *G. wallisii* can be found; it also differs from *G. speciosum* in having flowers with a base colour of white or cream.

Grammatophyllum is a small genus of about 12 species related to the well-known genus *Cymbidium*. The greatest diversity in the genus is found in the Philippines, where seven species occur. However, Georg Everard Rumphius, the "blind seer of Ambon", was the first to illustrate a *Grammatophyllum* plant (*G. scriptum* as *Angraecum scriptum*) in the sixth volume of his posthumously published *Herbarium Amboinense* (1751). *G. scriptum* and *G. mulitflorum* are large *Cymbidium*-like plants with yellowish flowers spotted to a greater or lesser degree with brown or dull purple. They are often found growing on trees by the ocean. Sarah Drake's beautiful illustration of *G. multiflorum* for *Edwards' Botanical Register* shows a plant from the Philippines collected by Hugh Cuming, one of the first professional orchid collectors who sent plants back to Loddiges nursery in Hackney, London.

Grammatophyllum stapeliiflorum, from Peninsular Malaysia and the western and central Malay Archipelago, is the most aberrant species in the genus, with cupped dark blackish-purple flowers that have a peculiar unpleasant odour. This probably serves to attract flies as pollinators, whereas the other species in the genus attract large bees.

Grammatophyllum is replaced in tropical Africa by the similar *Ansellia africana*, another species that has both spreading and erect roots and yellow flowers spotted with dark purplish brown. This plant is commonly found growing on doum palms by the Kenya coast, but also occurs in a variety of vegetation types across Africa. Throughout its wide range this species is variable with regard to flower size and colour, usually bearing more or less heavily spotted sepals and petals, but sometimes having unspotted yellow flowers. Walter Hood Fitch illustrated a South African specimen from Natal, under the name *A. gigantea*, in *Curtis's Botanical Magazine*. East African plants were illustrated by Helen Faulkner near Tanga in Tanzania and by Marjorie Tweedie on Mount Elgon, both of whom were long-term and resident collectors for the Kew Herbarium. One of the most interesting sketches in the Kew archives is that of a flower by Dr John Kirk, a British resident in Zanzibar and the medical officer and botanist on David Livingstone's ill-fated Zambesi expedition.

In Madagascar, *Grammangis ellisii* replaces *Ansellia*. Walter Hood Fitch's illustration of it for *Curtis's Botanical Magazine* may well be one of the Reverend William Ellis's collections from eastern Madagascar.

All of these plants are collected for horticulture for their attractive flowers, but *Ansellia* is also collected for use in traditional medicine in many locations across Africa.

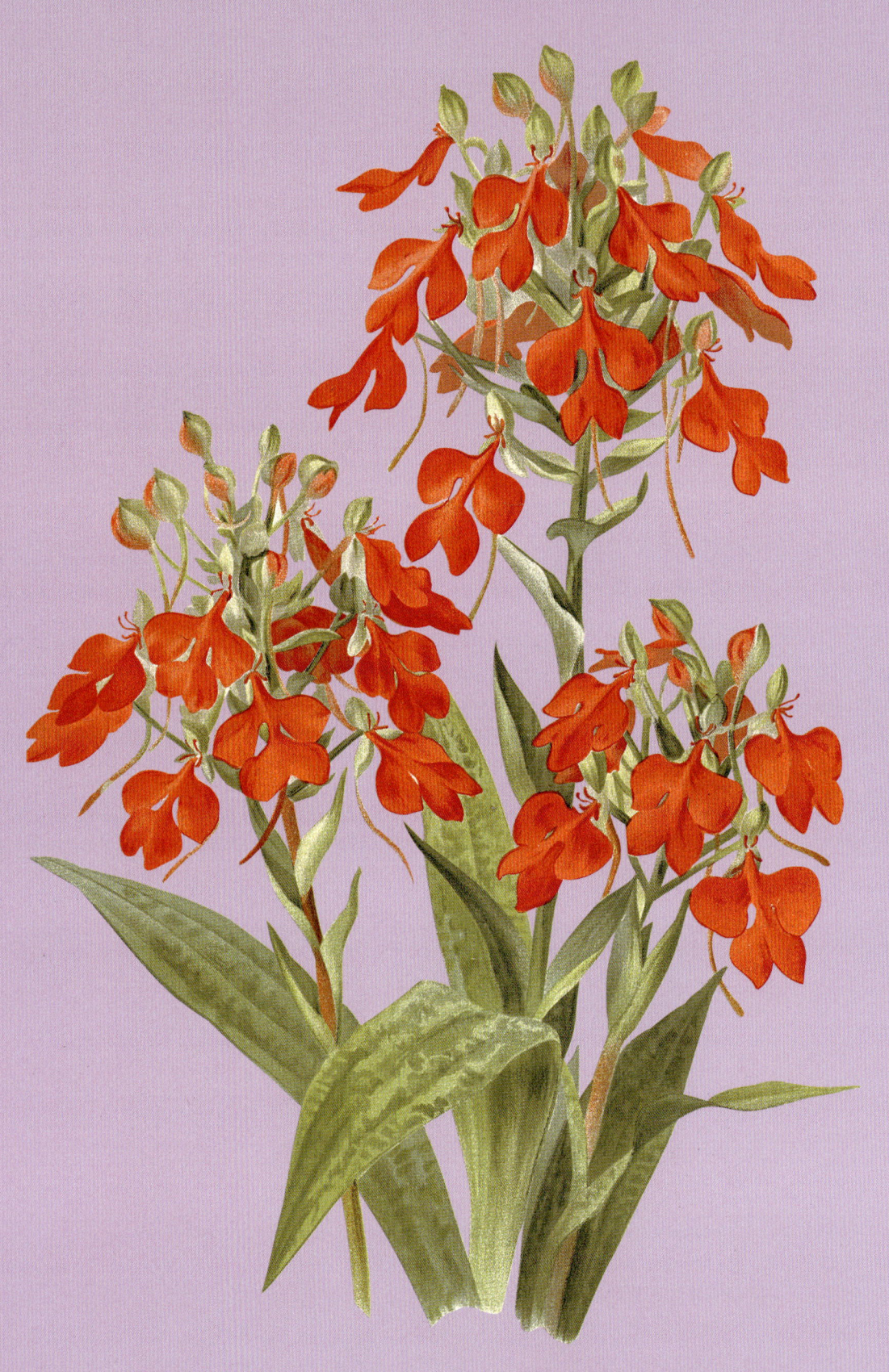

LITTLE DRAGON ORCHID

OR RED DRAGON ORCHID

HABENARIA RHODOCHEILA

Henry Fletcher Hance (1827–1886) arrived as a 17-year-old in Hong Kong in 1844, shortly after it became subject to British rule after the First Opium War with China. He rapidly became Hong Kong's first locally based plant hunter and botanist. *Habenaria rhodocheila* was described by him in 1866 based upon a specimen collected by Dr Sampson on the banks of the North River in Guangzhou (Canton) in southern China. The name refers to the red lip of the flower. This delightful ground orchid is known in the region as the "little dragon orchid" or "red dragon orchid" because its flower somewhat resembles a Chinese dragon, with the hood representing the head and the brightly coloured lip representing the body.

It is not a large plant, reaching a height of only about 25 cm (10 in), but it is one of the most beautiful of all ground orchids. The flower colour varies from pillar-box red through orange-red to yellow. For many years it was better known as *Habenaria militaris*, a name coined by the eminent German botanist and orchid expert Heinrich Gustav Reichenbach because the flowers reminded him of red-coated soldiers.

This orchid is found across southern and eastern China, south-east Asia and the Philippines, flowering in late summer and early autumn. In Hong Kong it is found on the hills at 200–900 m (660–2,950 ft) above sea level, growing along watercourses, banks and footpaths, and in crevices in rocks.

Habenaria is the largest genus of terrestrial orchids, and has a cosmopolitan distribution. It is best represented in tropical Africa and Asia, but also has well over 100 species in the tropical Americas. No representatives of the genus are found in Europe, although a single species, *Habenaria tridactylites*, is found in the Canary Islands. *Habenaria* flowers are complex, and at first sight appear to have too many parts. They are

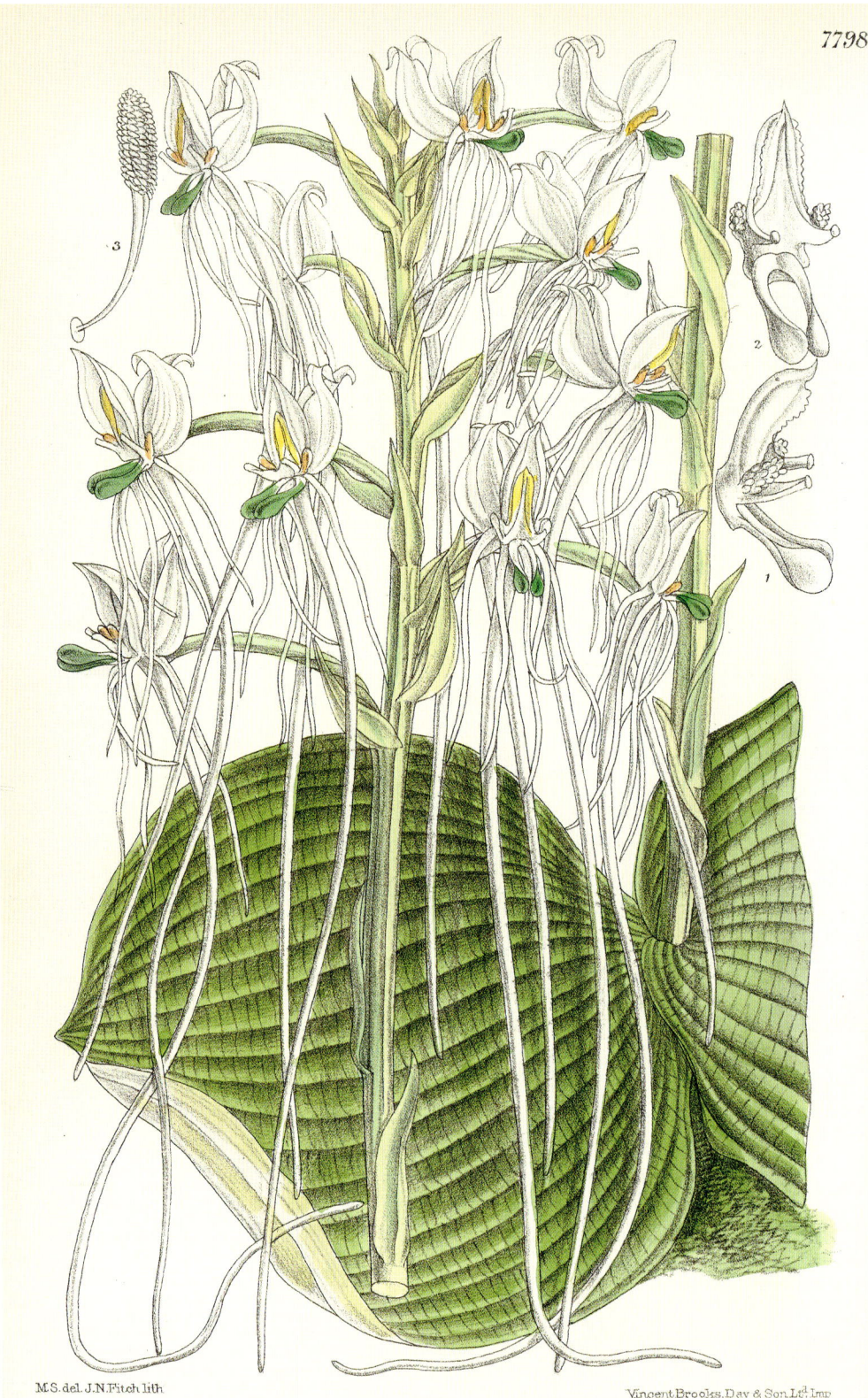

M.S.del. J.N.Fitch lith.

Vincent Brooks,Day & Son Lth Imp

L Reeve & Cº London

usually dominated by a large lowermost three-lobed lip. The side lobes of the lip of several species have comb-like outer margins. In addition, the petals are often divided to the base. The lip has a nectar-filled spur at the base. Above the lip lies the column with two anther loculi that bear the pollen masses, and above that lies a hood formed from the dorsal sepal and petals.

Habenaria carnea is closely related to *H. rhodocheila*, but differs in that it has a fuller flower with a broader flesh-coloured lip. It has been successfully crossed with *H. rhodocheila* to produce a series of attractive, easily cultivated hybrids. Some of the African and Asian species with comb-like side lobes to the lip are particularly fine, with large white, or green and white flowers and long

slender spurs. *Habenaria davidii* is a magnificent species from western China.

Tropical Africa has the greatest diversity of *Habenaria* species, with many large-flowered representatives. *Habenaria splendens* and *H. praestans*, both of which have large green and white flowers, live up to their names but are rarely if ever seen in cultivation. *Habenaria tentaculigera* has remarkable flowers in which the sepals and posterior petal lobe form a deeply concave helmet over the column, the anterior slender petal points upwards, the three-lobed lip points downwards, and the spur has a knee-like bend at its base and is then sigmoid above with a bulbous tip. Another group has either one or two prostrate oval leaves at the base, and a long, many-flowered inflorescence above. *Habenaria armatissima*, a widespread species in tropical and South African woodlands, which is often found on termite mounds, has flowers with a pendent narrowly cylindrical spur up to 21.5 cm (8½ in) long. *Habenaria walleri*, a wet grassland species, has a similar habit but has white flowers with broad segments and a pendent spur 13–17 cm (5–6¾ in) long. Both are undoubtedly pollinated by hawkmoths. A large number of African species have flowers resembling gnats, mosquitoes or flies. *Habenaria schimperiana* and *H. genuflexa* are two of the more common and widespread species with such flowers.

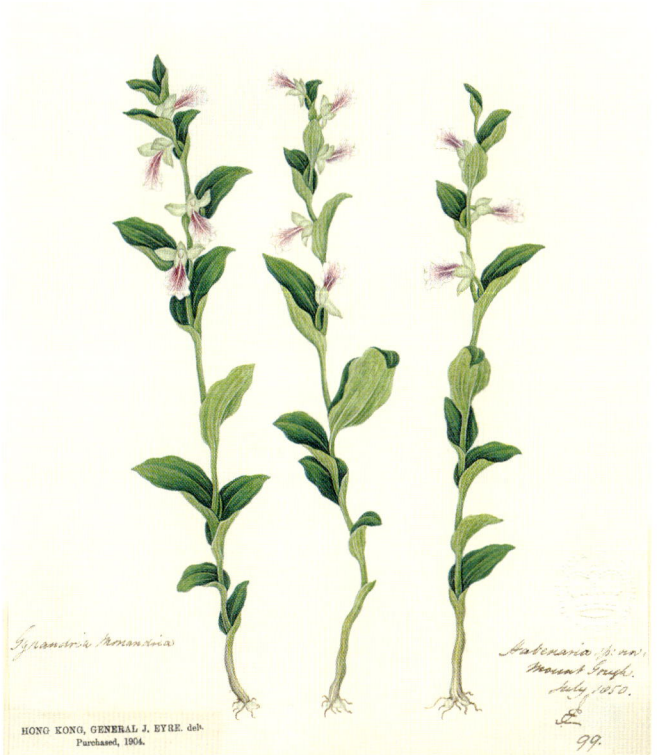

HONG KONG, GENERAL J. EYRE. del.
Purchased, 1904.

Left: *Brachycorythis galeandra* (mistakenly as *Habenaria* sp. nov.) grows with *Habenaria rhodocheila* in Hong Kong where it was illustrated by Capt. John Eyre, a soldier stationed in Hong Kong during the early years of British rule.

Whampoa, 18. Nov. 1872.

My dear Hooker,

Your letter of 19. Sept. reached me a few days ago only. Of course, I saw in the papers the shameful persecution to which you have been subjected by that vulgar-minded animal Ayrton, & read all the correspondence; and I shd. have written to express my deep sympathy with you under this disgraceful attack, had I not myself, on the 12th. September, been stricken by the heaviest blow which can fall on a man in this world. My beloved wife, the playmate of my childhood, who had borne me eight children, and from whom I had never been separated since our marriage, twenty years ago, died in my arms of apoplexy, supervening with extreme rapidity on hemiplegia, only four hours having elapsed from the time of the paralytic stroke to her last breath. Half an hour previous to the attack, I was laughing, & kissing, and playing with her! To add to my agony, there was no medical man, nor even a lady, at the time at Whampoa; so that, amidst all my sorrow, I was obliged to keep a clear judicial mind, as all the treatment and attendance devolved on me. I am quite prostrated & heartbroken; and, though more than two months have elapsed, I feel at times as if my mind would give way, & as if I could not long survive this blow. I trust strength will be given me to do so, for she has left me with six motherless children, the youngest not yet seven. Though her husband, I must say she was the sweetest, gentlest, tenderest & most unselfish woman I ever saw; and I do not believe a more perfect type of pure womanhood ever existed. If I could but apply my mind to botanical

Letter from Henry Fletcher Hance to Sir Joseph Dalton Hooker, from Whampoa, 18 November 1872

Henry Hance was the first resident botanist to work on the flora of Hong Kong. He wrote this sad letter that records the death of his wife to Joseph Hooker from Whampoa in Guangdong province, China. Hance joined the civil service in Hong Kong in 1854. In 1861 he became vice-consul be for the best, and distract me somewhat from the painful thoughts which now fill my mind to overflowing; but, since my loss, I have been quite powerless to do a single thing! and I cannot tell if I shall be able for a very long time. Kew Gardens will for ever have a very sad, though sweet & sacred interest for me; for it was in the long walk opposite the palm-house, by the lake, and leading towards the ornamental chimney, that my lost angel consented to be my wife, on the 31. December 1851. In the little leisure her devotion to her family allowed her, she assisted me in work; & you have a good many labels in her handwriting at Kew. I dedicated one or two species (a Camellia, an Aganosma) to her. This is a very sad letter; but you, who have a dear wife to cheer you, amidst the torments & annoyances to which you have been subjected, will understand, and, I am sure, sympathise with my deep grief, at the sudden rupture of

confidence of which no shadow ever fell across. I know, from all I have seen around me, for years, that there are very few marriages such as ours.

Pray remember me most kindly to Mr. Bentham. I know nothing of any fern being used in the manufacture of Porcelain. I presume the ashes are merely employed for their alkaline salts — & if so, it is likely that the commonest hill sorts — Gleichenia dichotoma, & Pteris aquilina, would furnish them.

I am,
My dear Hooker,
Yours very sincerely
H. F. Hance

in Whampoa, near Canton, and, in 1886, consul in Amoy. He devoted his spare time to botany and was the author of the supplement to George Bentham's *Flora Hongkongensis* (1872). His collections are housed in the Kew Herbarium.

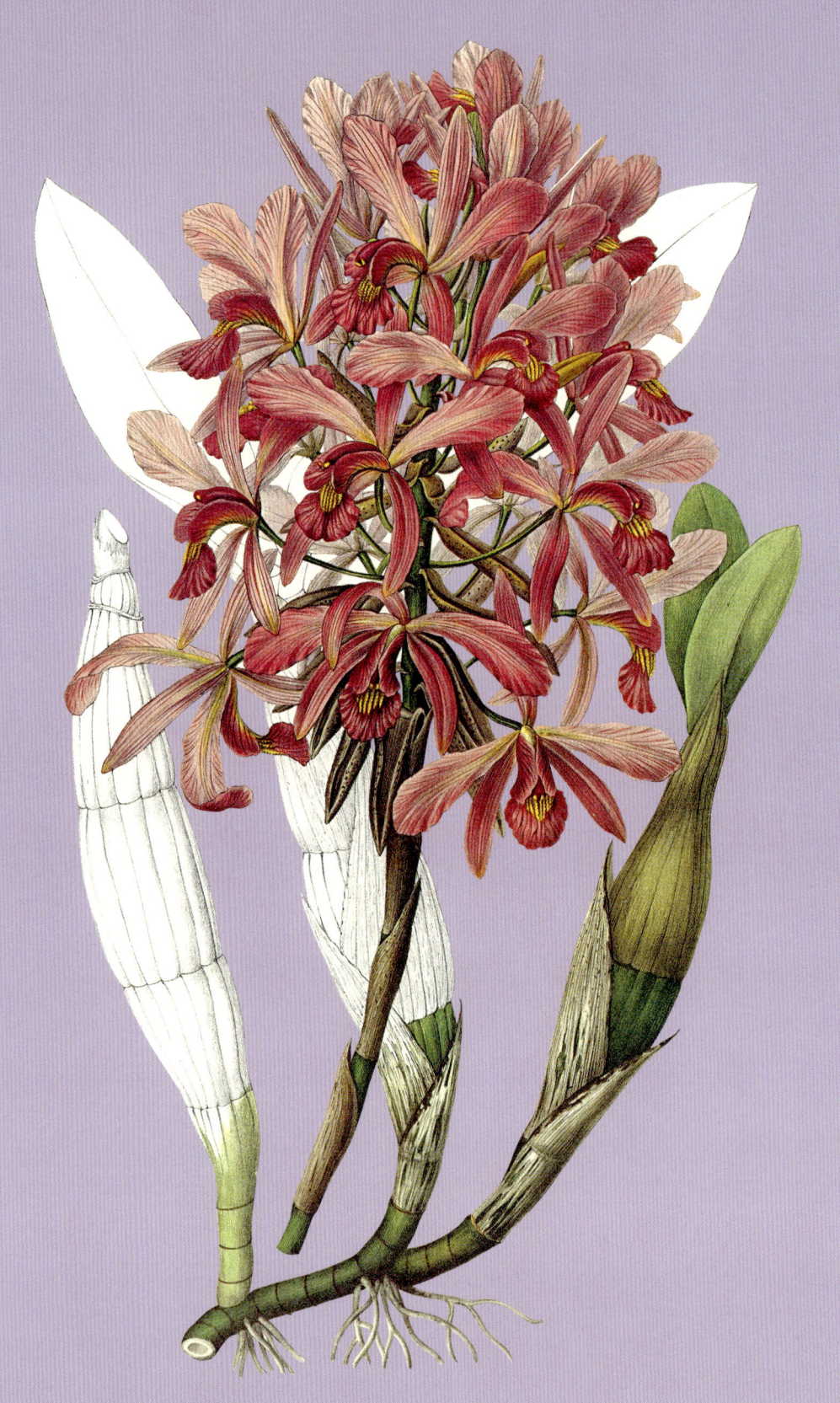

SUPERB LAELIA

LAELIA SUPERBIENS

The genus *Laelia*, which was established by John Lindley in 1831, was distinguished from the allied genus *Cattleya* by having eight, rather than four, pollen masses. However, this character is not now considered diagnostic and, after several incarnations, the genus has been pared down recently with most of the Brazilian species being transferred to *Cattleya*. *Laelia* is now confined to a group of Mexican and Central American epiphytic species. The derivation of the name is obscure but is thought to refer to a Roman family.

Laelia superbiens is by far the most spectacular species in the genus, as is suggested by its name. Its inflorescences, which reach a height of 1.7 m (5½ ft), have a stalk 1.2 m (4 ft) long clothed in papery sheaths, and bear in their apical part up to 20 large rose-pink flowers with a dark purple lip and golden callus. The plant has large fleshy pseudobulbous stems that bear two or three leathery spreading dark green leaves towards their apex. John Lindley described this orchid in 1840 based upon collections by George Ure Skinner (1804–1867) and Theodore Hartweg (1812–1871), both of whom were prolific orchid collectors. Skinner commented: "Saw you ever anything like this!!", and Hartweg wrote, "I have found it most rarely and evidently planted by the Indians before their doors, in 'Acatenango,' from whence I brought the specimen now sent, and in 'Sumpango.'"

Laelia superbiens is found in southern Mexico, Guatemala, Honduras and Nicaragua, growing epiphytically in oak woodland and forest at 1,400–2,200 m (4,600–7,000 ft) above sea level. It is usually found growing in small colonies in exposed windy places. Nowadays, however, it is rare and exploited. In Chiapas in southern Mexico, this species and the pink-flowered orchid *Guarianthe skinneri* are called "candelarias" and are used for decoration during the Candelmas festival on 2 February and the feast day of St Sebastian on 25 February. Consequently, these plants are often found growing on trees in local towns and villages.

Several other *Laelia* species are also regarded as sacred flowers, and feature in festivals such as the Day of the Dead in Mexico. The white-flowered form of *Laelia anceps* var. *dawsonii* has been cultivated for generations in southern Oaxaca and is used on 12 December

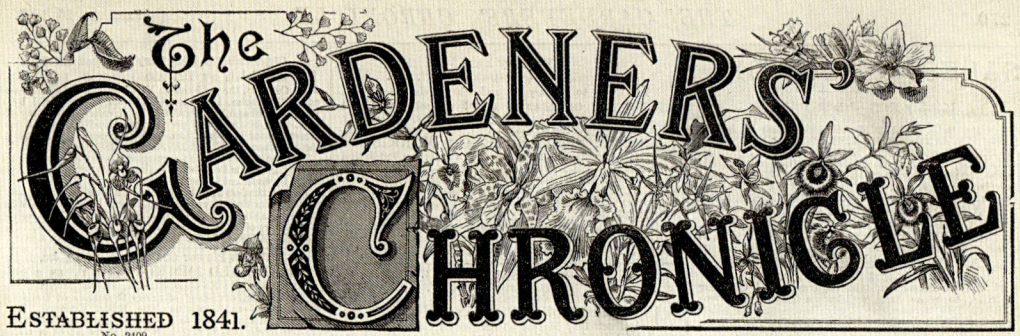

The GARDENERS' CHRONICLE

Established 1841.
No. 2409.

No. 9.—Vol. I. {Third Series.}   SATURDAY, FEBRUARY 26, 1887.   {Regt. as a Newspaper. / With Supplement.} Price 3d. Post-free, 3½d.

CONTENTS.

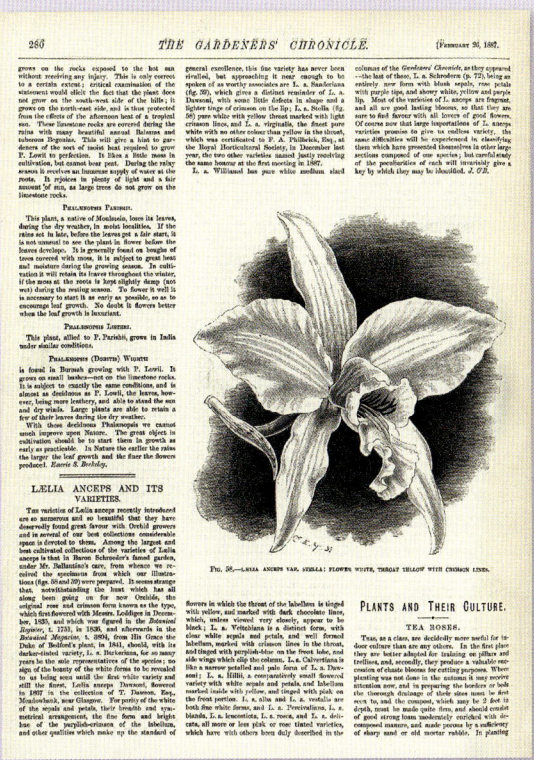
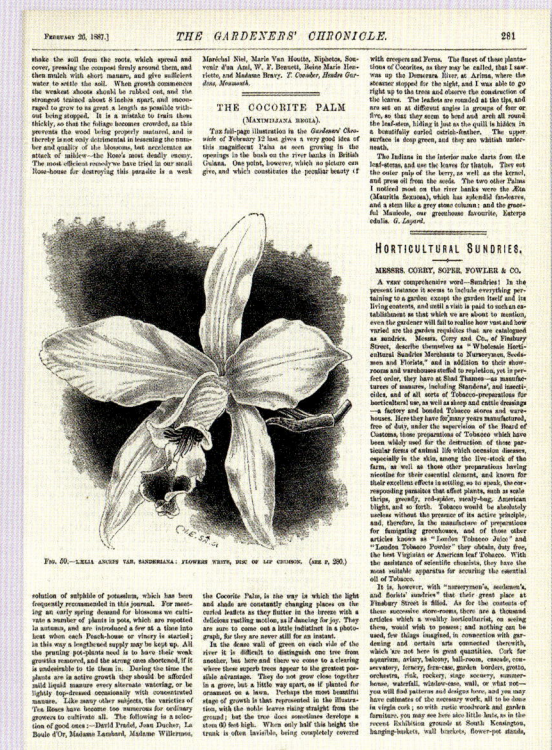

Laelia anceps and its varieties described in *The Gardeners' Chronicle*,
26 February 1887

The German orchid specialist Heinrich Gustav Reichenbach used *The Gardeners' Chronicle* as a vehicle for the rapid publication of his newly described orchids. Each month his descriptions of new species appeared with succinct descriptions and acknowledgements of where he had obtained the specimens, which were usually sent to him by English orchid growers, such as John Day, and nurseries, notably those of Sander and Veitch.

Reichenbach was the man who took over the mantle of pre-eminent orchid specialist after the death of John Lindley in 1865. Under the terms of Reichenbach's will, his orchid herbarium remained inaccessible for 25 years following his death, but is now available in the Natural History Museum in Vienna. He was a frequent visitor to Kew and his spidery annotations can be found on many Kew specimens.

each year in the festival of the Virgin of Juquila, one of the most venerated Catholic sanctuaries in southern Mexico. The tombs and crosses in the cemetery of Chilapa in Guerrero are decorated with inflorescences of this orchid, the pink orchid *Barkeria scandens* and *Tagetes* flowers every year on 2 November. *Laelia autumnalis* is used to decorate churches in Michoacan, Morelos, Ocuilan and Amecameca on All Saints' Day. The "flower of May", *Laelia speciosa*, is used to garland yokes during the fiesta of St Isidore, the patron saint of farmers, on 15 May to celebrate the start of the rainy season in Mexico. In Oaxaca, the inflorescences of *Laelia furfuracea* and *L. albida* are used as ornaments on tombs, altars and nativities. All of these traditions undoubtedly predate the arrival of the Spanish.

Nowadays, the most widely cultivated species is *Laelia anceps*, which is also the most variable species with regard to its flower colour. Its flowers are typically rose-purple with a dark purple lip adorned with a golden callus, but forms with white, pink and bluish flowers are widely available.

Right: Marianne North visited Brazil in 1872 and 1873 where she painted the fine native *Cattleya purpurata* (as *Laelia purpurata*).

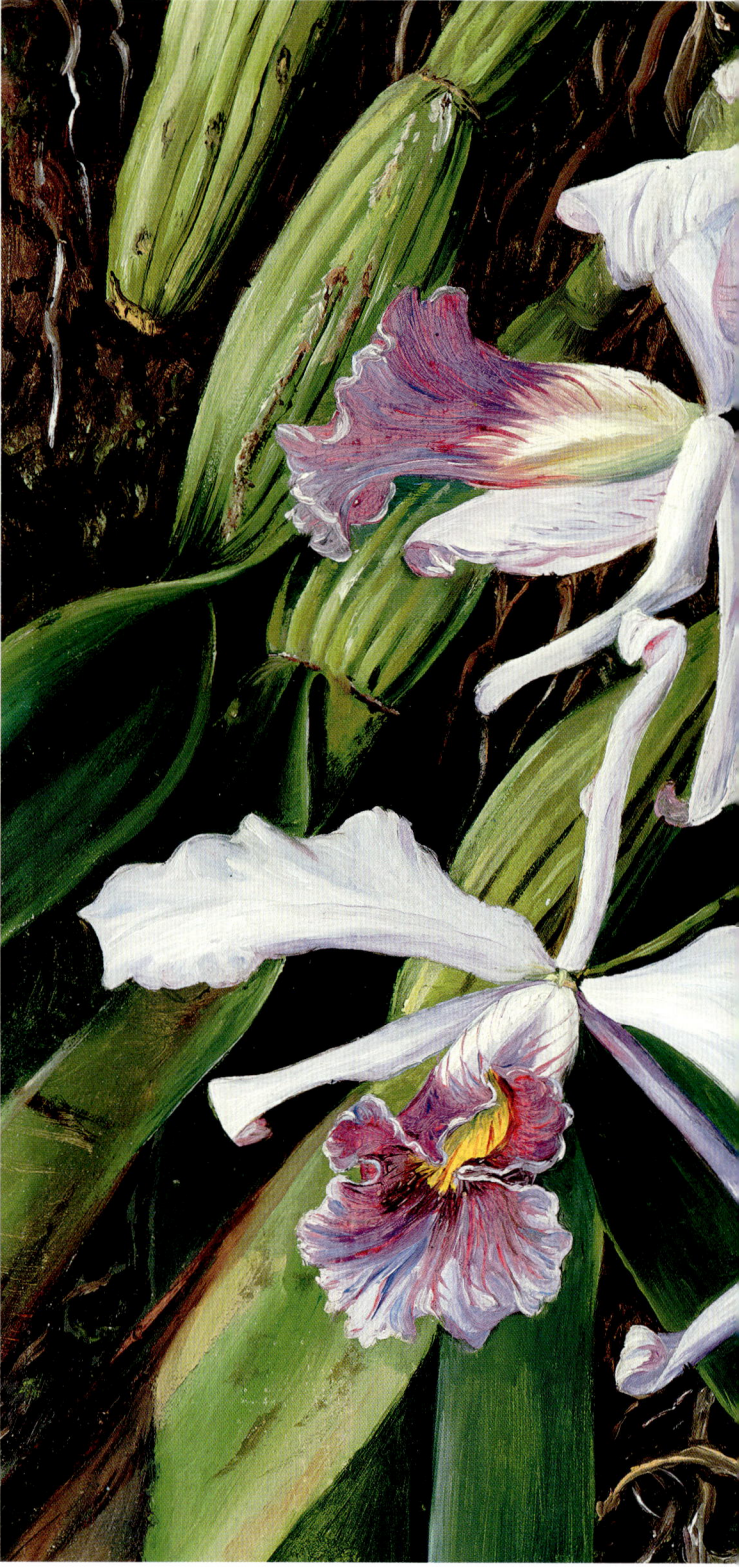

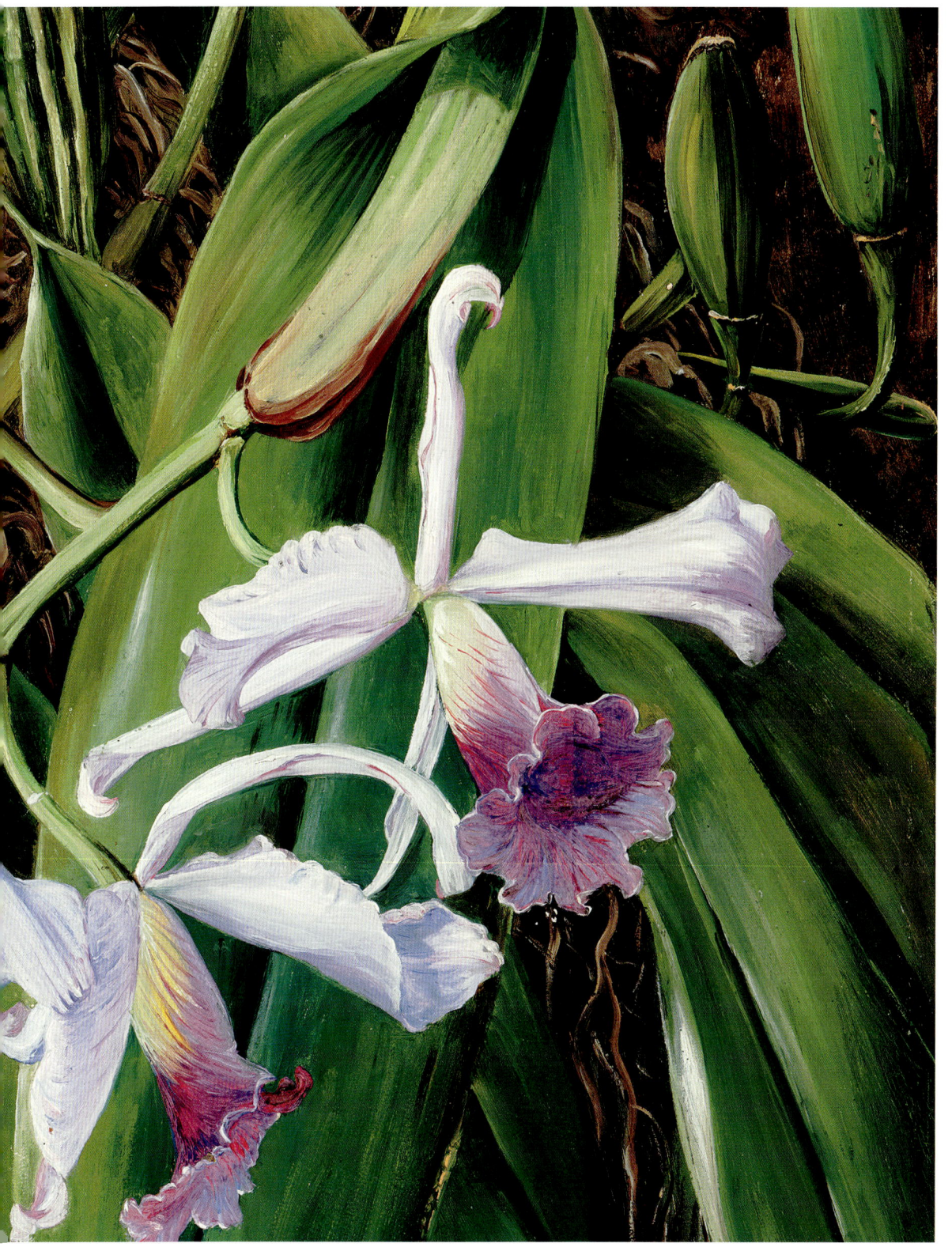

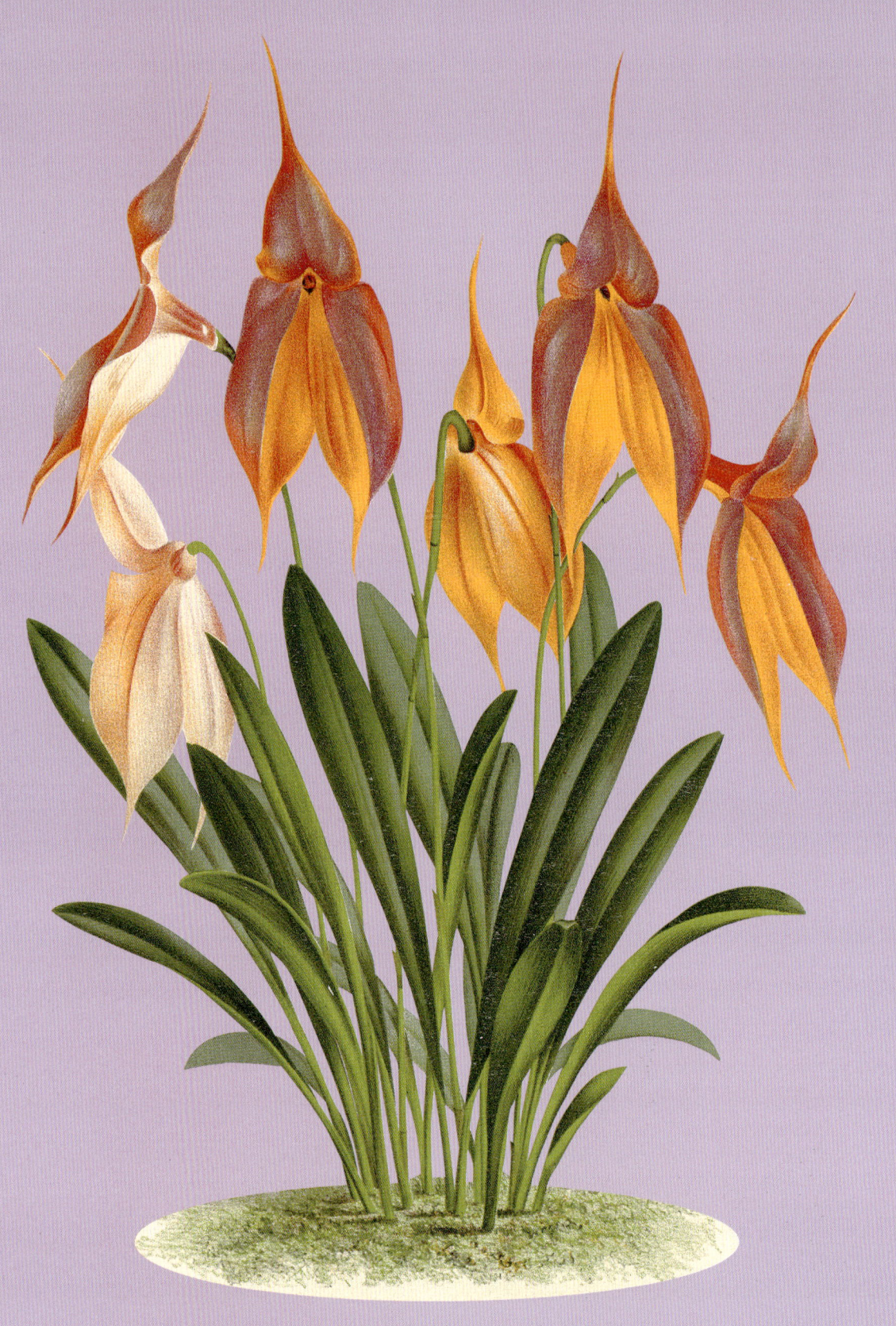

VEITCH'S MARVEL
MASDEVALLIA VEITCHIANA

The orchid *Masdevallia veitchiana* is a highlight of many visitors' experience at Machu Picchu, the ancient Inca site in the Peruvian Andes. It is particularly common on Wayna Picchu, the mountain peak that overlooks the ruins of the Inca town, and can also occasionally be seen on the Inca trail approaching the site. Its scarlet triangular flowers are remarkable in that the function of the petals is taken over completely by the sepals, which are fused into a short tube at the base, but then flare into a triangular lamina with each angle bearing a slender red tail. The petals, lip and column are all found within the sepal tube and are tiny in comparison with the sepals.

This species is certainly the most stunning of all the masdevallias. It was described by Heinrich Gustav Reichenbach in *The Gardeners' Chronicle* in 1868, based on a plant imported from Peru by James Veitch & Sons, after whom it is named. It was collected for them by Walter Davis, probably in the vicinity of Machu Picchu, where it can still be found growing on rocks at an altitude of 3,400–4,000 m (11,150–13,000 ft), high on the summits around the Inca ruins. It holds its brilliant scarlet flowers high above the leaves, and the flowers have a purple sheen produced by the layer of small purple papillae that cover the lower sepals.

John Day found this feature immensely difficult to capture on paper, and made several attempts throughout his life to do so, but was unhappy with the results. On 24 November 1871 he painted the orchid for the first time, using a plant that he had purchased at the sale of Sigismund

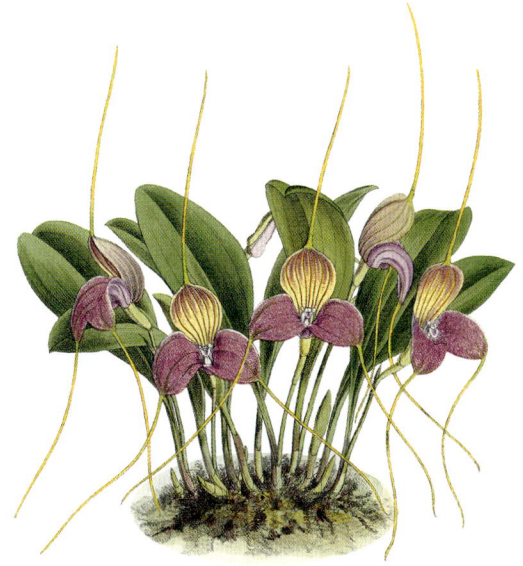

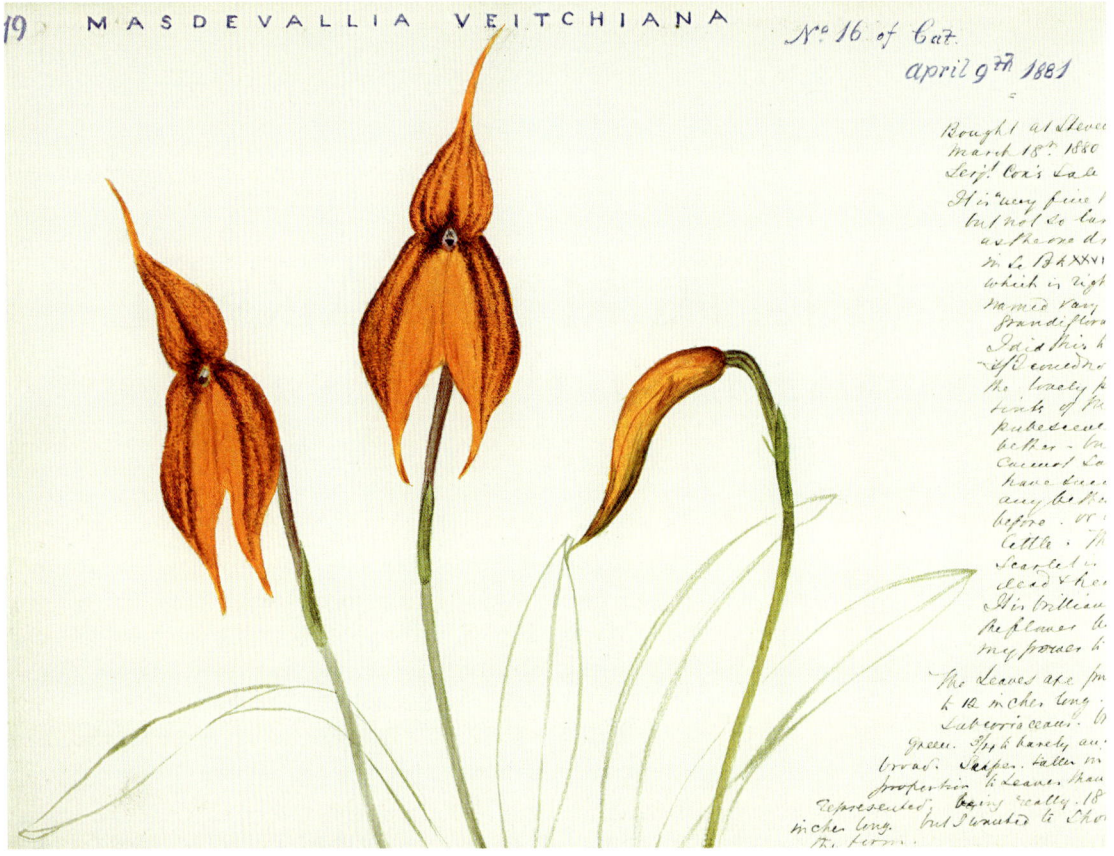

N.º 16 of Cat.
april 9th 1881

Bought at Steve...
March 18th 1880
Serj! Cox's Sale
It is very fine...
but not so lar...
as the one d...
n.º 13 XXVI
which is rig...
named var...
grandiflora
I did this b...
if I could...
the lovely p...
tints of th...
pubescence...
better. On...
cannot se...
have bee...
any bett...
before. o...
little. Th...
Scarlet...
dead & he...
It is brillia...
the flower h...
my power t...
The Leaves are fro...
to 12 inches long...
Subcoriaceous. b...
green. Apply barely an...
broad. Scapes fallen in...
proportion to Leaves than...
represented, being really 18...
inches long. but I wanted to sho...
th. form.

Above: John Day's portrait of *Masdevallia veitchiana* flowered by him at Tottenham in 1881 and drawn for his scrapbooks.

Rucker's plants at Stevens's sales rooms in August of that year. He thought it:

> … a lovely thing of the most exquisite and brilliant colour which I have found past my skill to do justice to or even to give a notion of. The ground colour is brilliant scarlet-orange, and it has a short close velvety pubescence in lines down the sepals of the most lovely magenta-violet colour possible.

On 30 April 1880 he painted *Masdevallia veitchiana* var. *grandiflora*, which he had bought from Benjamin Williams, who had named it. Day thought it a splendid variety and described the flower as "the largest I have ever saw, measuring 6½ inches long by 2½ inches broad." He tried again the following year, when on 9 April he drew a plant he had purchased at Sergeant Cox's sale at Stevens's sale rooms on 18 March 1880. He noted that it was very fine, but not as large as var. *grandiflora*.

Masdevallia veitchiana hybridizes in nature with the yellow-flowered *M. davisii*. It has also been used to produce artificial hybrids, such as *Masdevallia* Chelsonii (*M. veitchiana* × *M. amabilis*), the first artificial hybrid in the genus, which was raised by John Seden for the orchid nursery of Veitch & Sons of Chelsea, and first flowered for them in 1880. John Day drew it on 5 November 1881.

Masdevallia veitchiana belongs to a very large genus that is common throughout the Andes, and whose range extends into Central America and the mountains of southern Mexico. Many other *Masdevallia* species have showy or unusual flowers and are widely cultivated today. Examples include *M. harryana* from the northern Andes (which can have white, pink or purple flowers equal in size to those of *M. veitchiana*), *M. coccinea* (which has orange-red flowers, but borne in a short pendent inflorescence) and the Venezuelan species *M. tovarensis* (which has large pure white flowers). Many *Masdevallia* species have dark purple or dark purple spotted flowers and are pollinated by flies.

Victorian botanists and gardeners had a much broader concept of the genus *Masdevallia* than we do today. One of the most collectable of all Victorian orchid books, Florence Woolward's *The Genus Masdevallia*, commissioned by the Marquis of Lothian, is generally considered to be responsible for the initial surge in interest in the genus. The work of the American botanist Carlyle Luer over the past 30 years has transformed our knowledge of *Masdevallia* and its allies. In doing so it has also resurrected horticultural interest in these strange plants, most of which have very reduced habits with erect wiry stems bearing a solitary leaf, and terminal flowers with large, often showy sepals and small petals and a small lip. Most of the *Masdevallia* species of Victorian times are now classified within either the genus *Masdevallia* or the genus *Dracula* (see page 94), the latter having been established by Luer in 1978 (in the journal *Selbyana*) for those species of *Masdevallia* that have a pendent flower with a lip which mimics a fungus. Even in its modern sense, the genus *Masdevallia* is large, containing about 300 species, and is widespread in Central and South America, especially in montane habitats. There are about 100 species of *Dracula*, most of which have flowers that are spotted or streaked with blackish maroon or dark purple. They are found in the Andes of South America and in the mountains of Central America. Other genera that have been removed from *Masdevallia* since Victorian times are *Dryadella*, *Porroglossum* and *Zootrophion*.

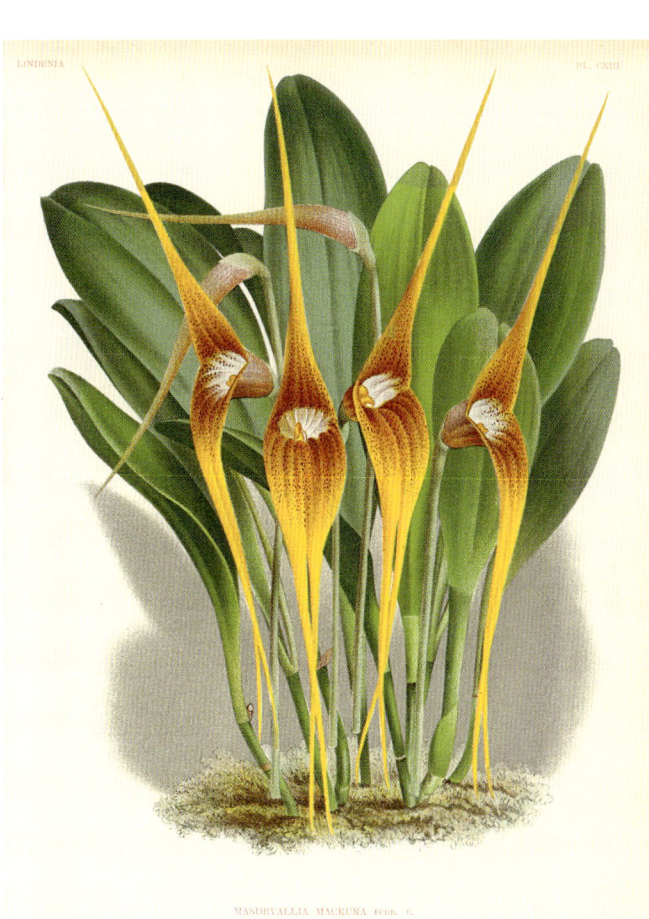

MASDEVALLIA MACRURA ROOR. F.

Pl. XXXIV.

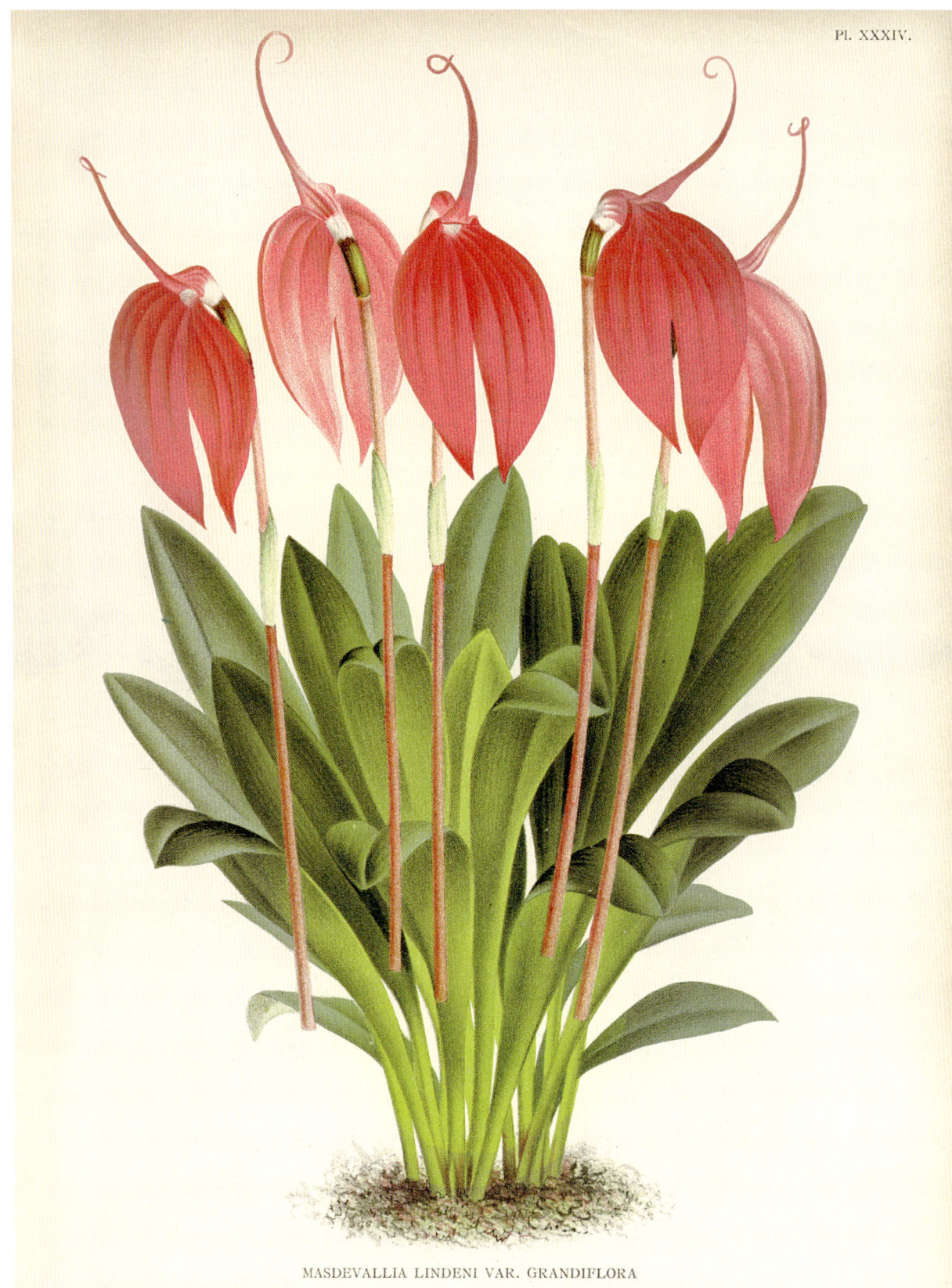

MASDEVALLIA LINDENI VAR. GRANDIFLORA

Opposite:
Masdevallia harryana (as *Masdevallia lindenii* var. *grandiflora*) drawn for J. J. Linden, *Lindenia: Iconographie des Orchidées* of 1885. The famous orchid collector and nurseryman Jean Linden introduced it in 1867.

Descriptions of *Masdevallia eduardii* and *Masdevallia roezlii* in *The Gardeners' Chronicle*, 18 December 1880

The German orchid specialist Heinrich Gustav Reichenbach's descriptions of *Masdevallia* (now *Porroglossum*) *eduardii* and *Masdevallia* (now *Dracula*) *roezlii* in *The Gardeners' Chronicle* of 1880. At this period, *Masdevallia*, which then included genera such as *Dracula*, *Dryadella* and *Porroglossum*, were becoming increasingly popular because of the many novelties that were being introduced and described. The possibility of flowering a new species was a major attraction for orchid growers who dreamed of having a new species named after them. Many succeeded as the pages of *The Gardeners' Chronicle* can testify. The Marquis of Lothian was particularly fond of masdevallias and commissioned Florence Woolward to illustrate those that flowered in his collection at Newbattle Abbey in Scotland. Florence's magnificent *The Genus Masdevallia* was published in 1896 and is a highly sought-after volume today.

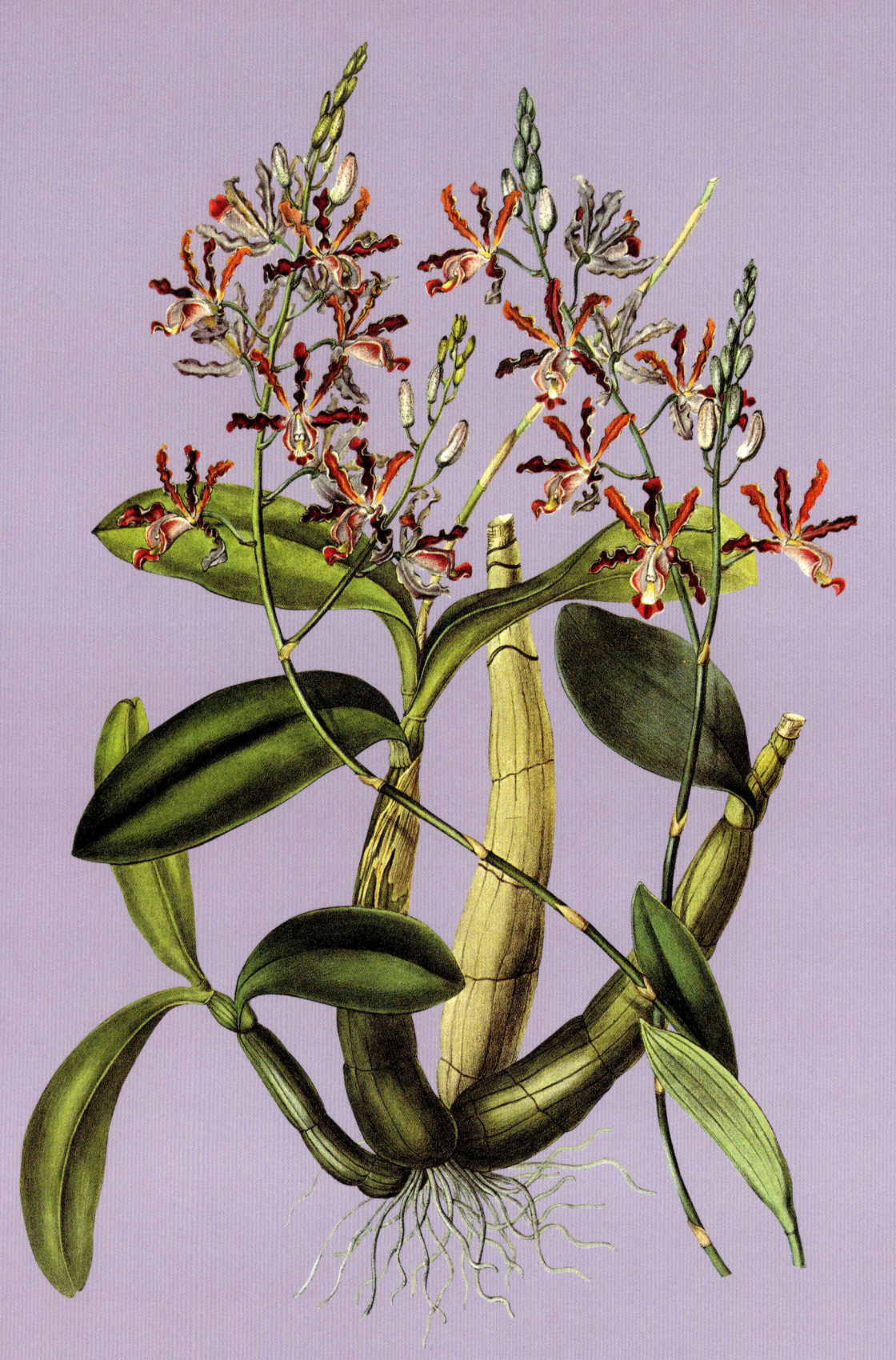

TRUMPET ORCHID OR COW'S HORN ORCHID
MYRMECOPHILA TIBICINIS

Opposite:
Myrmecophila tibicinis
(as *Schomburgkia
tibicinis*) by Sarah
Drake, in *The
Orchidaceae of Mexico
and Guatemala*, 1841.

In the low coastal forests of Central and South America, any attempt to collect an orchid from the genus *Myrmecophila* will quickly explain the name of this genus, from the Latin words *myrmex* meaning "ant" and *philos* meaning "friend" or "lover", as hordes of hissing ants swarm out from inside the plant and attack the invader. *Myrmecophila* species have evolved to form mutualistic partnerships with ants, with an alternative and rather unusual use for a proportion of their large stem storage structures known as pseudobulbs.

Unlike true bulbs, which are the underground stems formed from many overlapping leaf bases, pseudobulbs are swollen above-ground stems, which are usually used as storage organs. Many epiphytic orchids have pseudobulbs, and usually a new one develops each year with new leaves and/or inflorescences emerging from it. The older pseudobulbs will lose their leaves and flowers but may continue to support the plant for many years, before gradually shrivelling up and detaching from the plant. Pseudobulbs may be of all shapes and sizes, from the small rounded egg-shaped balls that are common in the genus *Bulbophyllum*, to the large, angled structures of *Grammangis* species, and the long thin multi-segment "canes" that are seen in the genus *Dendrobium*.

Some *Myrmecophila* pseudobulbs act as permanent (or occasionally seasonal) homes for multiple species of ants. These "domatia" have a hole at one end that enables the ants to enter and leave the hollow, conical structure. The ants feed on nectar from the orchid's flowers and pack the pseudobulbs with debris from the surroundings, a combination of dead or dying plant material, dead insects and sand. The domatia themselves are not dead, and by using organic debris to furnish their homes inside living plant organs, the ants are providing the orchid with a ready source of nutrients that the plant slowly absorbs as the material decays. Carbon isotope studies have shown that carbon from the materials added by the ants becomes absorbed by the plant, in a similar manner to the results obtained from such studies of the nutrient exchange between orchids, their mycorrhizal fungi and their host plants.

The ants provide another benefit to the

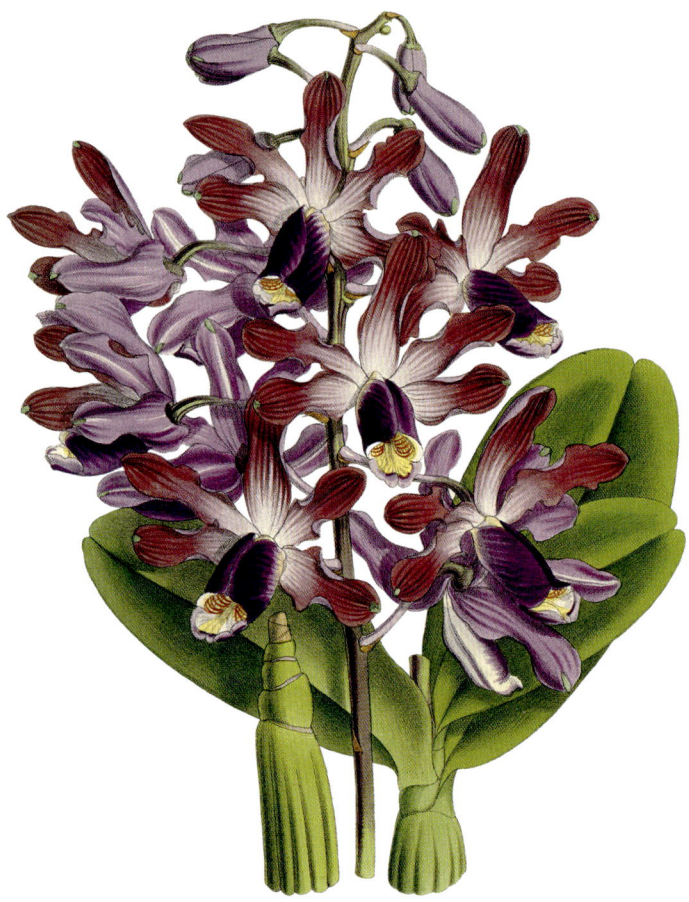

The ants aggressively defend the plant from any kind of disturbance or damage, and swarm out of their domatia whenever an intruder is detected. Protecting the young leaves, root tips and developing flower buds, as well as feeding the plant in what is otherwise a nutrient-poor environment up in the branches of a tree, the mutualism between this orchid and ants is another example of the ingenuity of orchid and animal co-evolution.

Myrmecophila used to be known by the name *Schomburgkia*, named for Robert Hermann Schomburgk, the German-born botanist, surveyor and geographer who worked in South America and the West Indies. Among many other accomplishments, Schomburgk also observed the enormous waterlily *Victoria amazonica*, and in his military capacity was responsible for drawing up the provisional border between Venezuela and British Guiana, the Schomburgk Line, in the 1840s. In 1917, the English orchidologist Robert Rolfe moved all of the species of *Schomburgkia* which have ant domatia into a new genus, *Myrmecophila*, and the rest of the species into the genera *Laelia* and *Pseudolaelia*. The genus *Schomburgkia* was no longer accepted, and the name is gradually falling out of use. With its huge inflorescences, up to 4 m (12 ft) in length and bearing approximately 20 flowers each, *Myrmecophila tibicinis* is perhaps the most spectacular species in the genus.

Above: *Myrmecophila tibicinis* (as *Schomburgkia tibicinis*) by John Nugent Fitch, in R. Warner and B. S. Williams, *The Orchid Album*, 1886.

Opposite: Herbarium specimen of *Myrmecophila tibicinis* (as *Schomburgkia tibicinis*), held at the Royal Botanic Gardens, Kew.

orchid in return for their lodgings and nectar. James Bateman wrote of George Ure Skinner's collection of *Myrmecophila tibicinis* in the wild in Guatemala that:

its original discoverer was not permitted to obtain quiet possession of his prize, as swarms of fiery ants, to which the hollow stems afford a snug retreat, issued forth in thousands to repel the spoiler, and inflicted pangs which none but the most ardent naturalist would have braved.

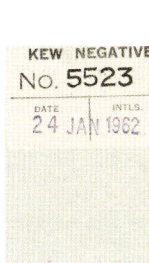

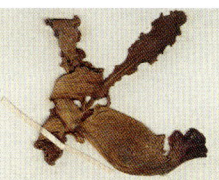

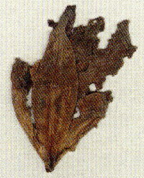

Epidendrum titicinis Bateman.

30

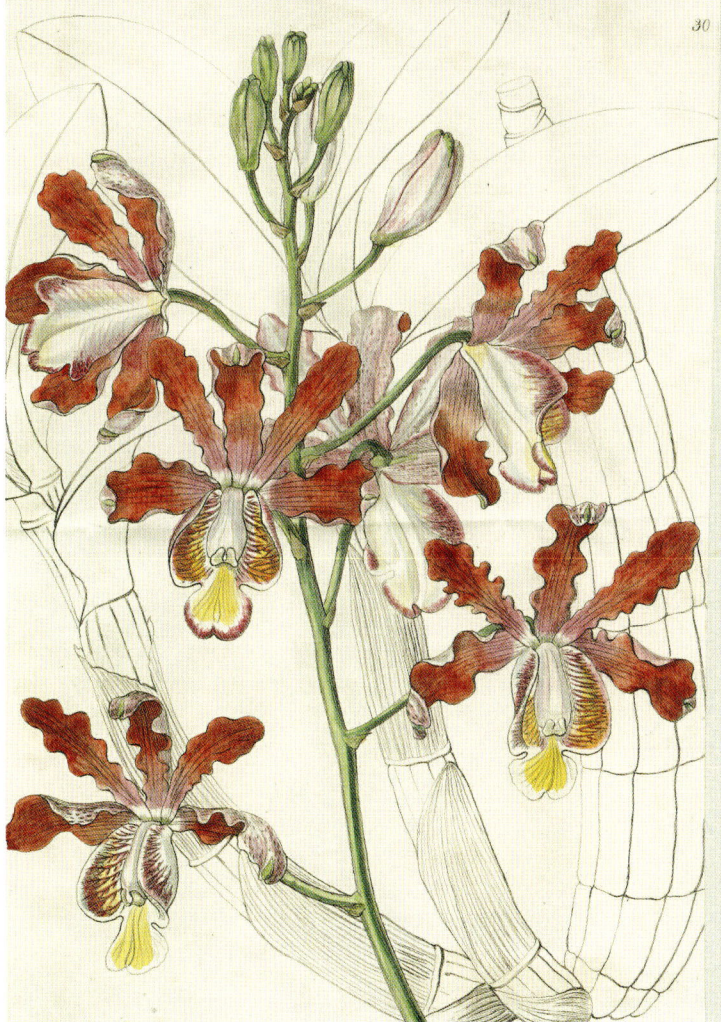

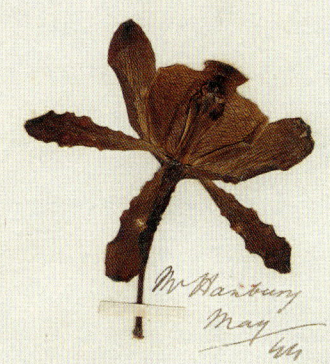

Mr Bantury
May 41

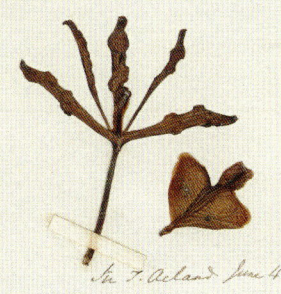

Sir T. Acland June 41

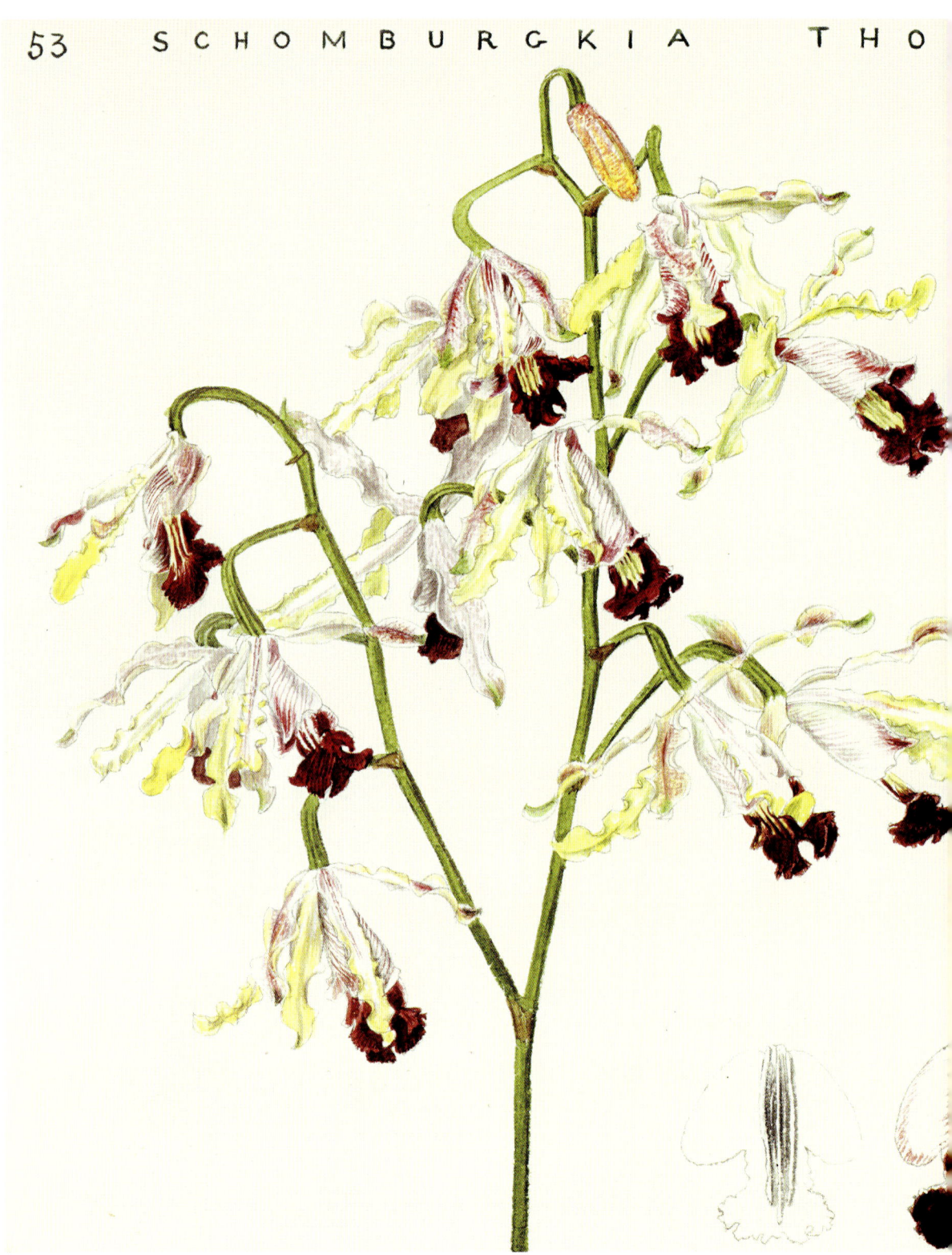

154 Trumpet orchid or cow's horn orchid *Myrmecophila tibicinis*

H.G. Reich

June 5th 1887

This beautiful species
was first seen at the
Royal Horticultural
Society's Exhibition at
Liverpool in June 1886
where it was greatly
admired. It was
exhibited by Mr.
Thomson of St. Helens
Lancashire who
promised me a spike
of flower when it bloomed
again which promise
he most kindly
fulfilled. After
drawing it I sent it on
to Profr. Reichenbach
suggesting that if new
he should name it
after Mr Thomson which
he has done

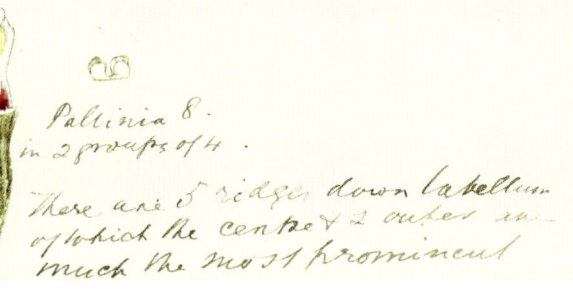

Pollinia 8.
in 2 groups of 4.

There are 5 ridges down labellum
of which the centre & 2 outer are
much the most prominent

Left: *Myrmecophila
thomsoniana* (as *Schomburgkia
thomsoniana*) by John Day,
1887.

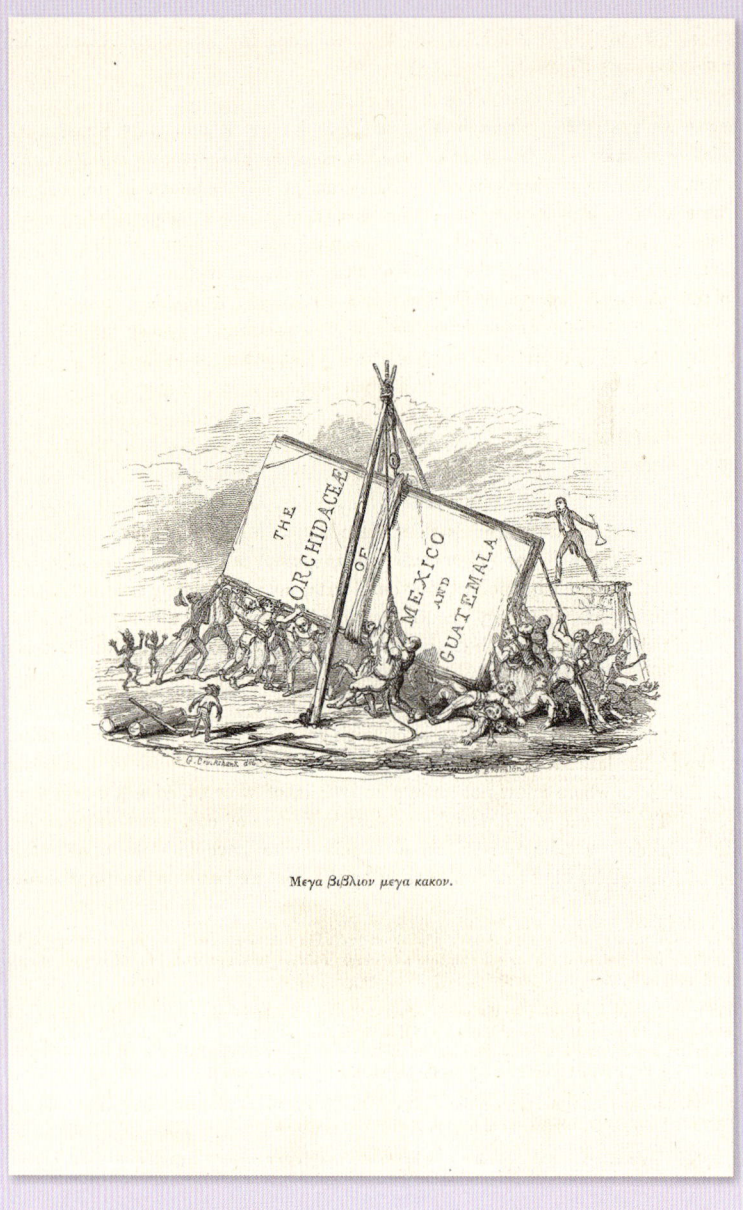

Μεγα βιβλιον μεγα κακον.

**Extracts from *The Orchidaceae of Mexico and Guatemala*
by James Bateman (1843)**

James Bateman's monolithic tome *The Orchidaceae of Mexico and Guatemala*
has the distinction of being one of the largest and most sought-after
botanical volumes ever published. It comprised 40 "giant folio" format
lithographic plates, bound into a single volume with descriptions of each of
the exotic species presented, and 38 wood-engraved "vignettes" by George
Cruikshank, and only 125 copies were produced. Measuring 531 × 726 mm

The original specimen reached Knypersley as early as 1836, but made no attempt to flower until the spring of 1840, when the spike, after attaining the length of several feet, was unluckily broken off. Sir THOMAS ACLAND was more fortunate, and in the ensuing summer had the satisfaction of flowering the species in high perfection in his garden at Killerton. The spike then produced was exhibited at a meeting of the Horticultural Society, from whence it passed into the hands of the artist, who has furnished a most characteristic representation. The species is less bright in its colouring than was expected, but no doubt many varieties exist, and perhaps some of these may as far surpass the subject of the plate as others certainly fall short of it; among the latter may be ranked one that flowered at Knypersley last year (1841), the blossoms of which were much paler, and in all respects inferior to those of the figure.

In cultivation this is the most manageable species of the untractable genus to which it belongs. Suspension on a block of wood, in a hot and damp situation, appears to be the condition most congenial to its growth, but a season of rest is necessary to induce it to flower. Yet even in the collections where it succeeds the best, it lacks the vigour exhibited in imported specimens.

The ants of Honduras, as it has been already shown, turn to good account the long hollow stems of this singular plant; another purpose to which they are applied may be gathered from the Vignette, where an Indian child is seen sounding with all his might "an echoing horn," formed by merely cutting off the extremities. His companions emulate his musical ardour, but in their attempts to possess the *matèriel* are interrupted by a catastrophe.

In such request are these vegetable trumpets among the wild urchins of Honduras, that the plant yielding them is called "the trumpet-plant,"—an epithet that has suggested its specific name.

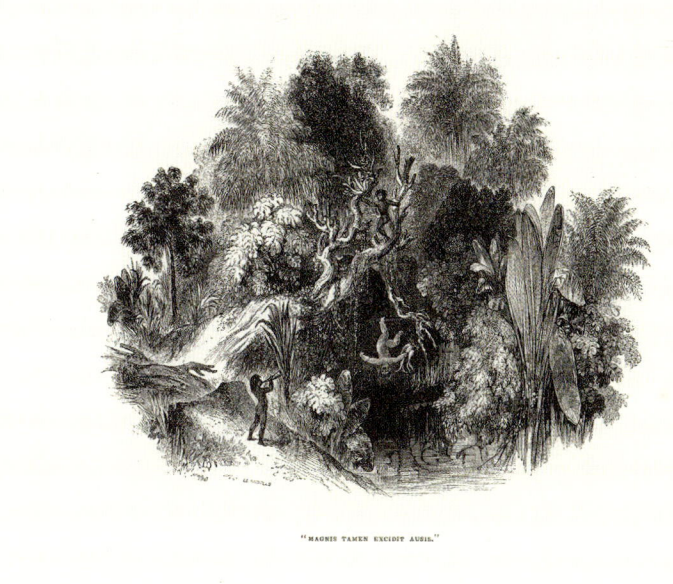

"MAGNIS TAMEN EXCIDIT AUSIS."

(27 × 15 inches), many of the original illustrations were by Sarah Drake who worked for John Lindley and illustrated some 1,500 plants over her career. The lithographs were produced by a master of the technique from Malta, Maxim Gauci, who converted the original paintings onto stone and then print, before they were hand coloured in each separate volume. In the entry for *Myrmecophila tibicinis*, Bateman describes and illustrates the use of the hollow pseudobulbs as "vegetable trumpets" by children in Honduras. One of Cruikshank's vignettes lampoons the vast size of the volume with a horde of Lilliputian workers using pulleys to try to manoeuvre the huge tome.

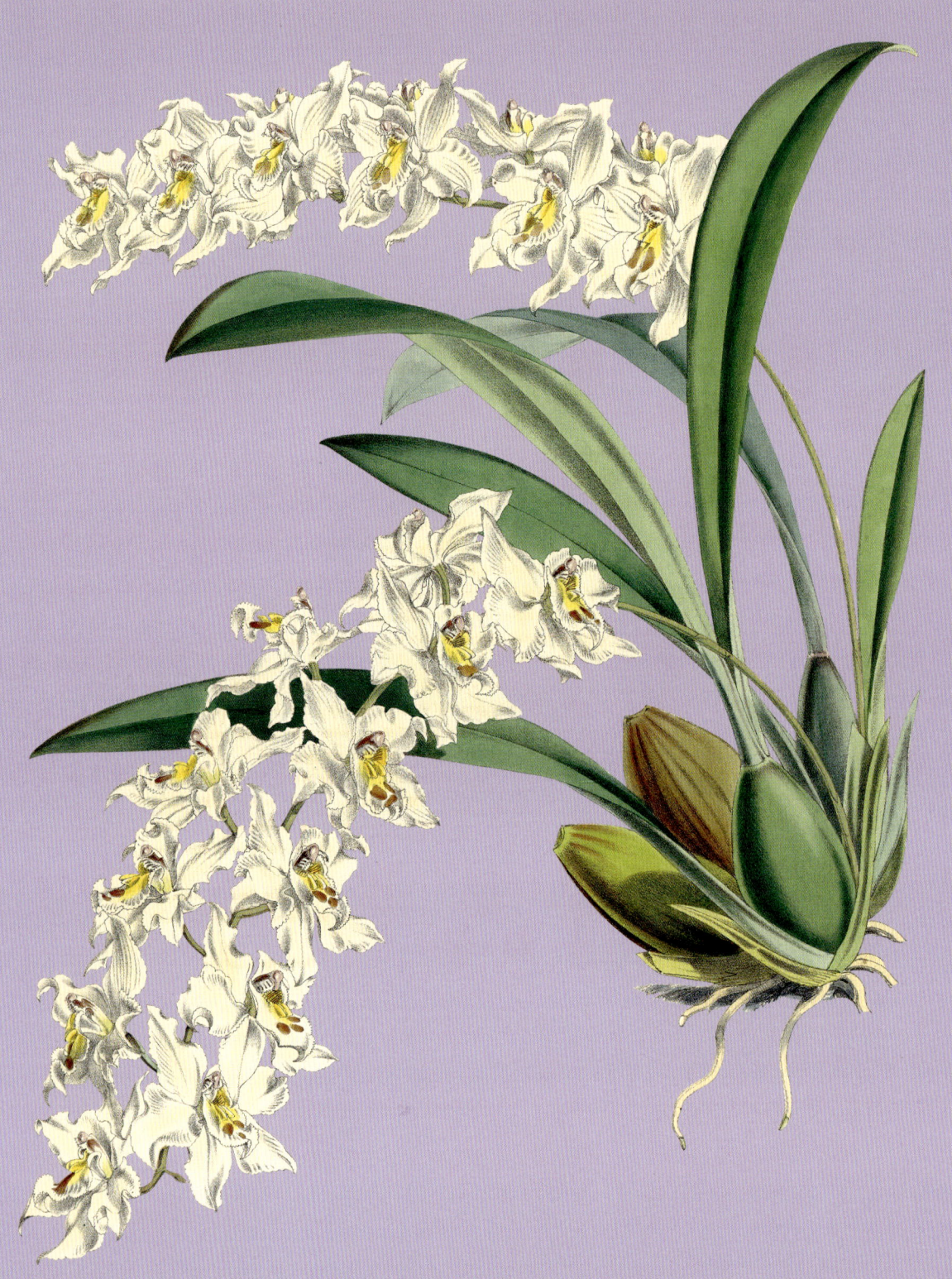

PRINCESS ALEXANDRA'S ODONTOGLOSSUM

ONCIDIUM ALEXANDRAE

Opposite: *Oncidium alexandrae* (as *Odontoglossum crispum*) drawn for James Bateman's *A Monograph of Odontoglossum*, 1874, an account which popularized the genus to the point that odontoglossums became the most expensive orchids of the late Victorian period.

Right: *Oncidium alexandrae* (as *Odontoglossum alexandrae* var. *guttatum*) flowered by W. W. Saunders of Reigate in August 1867 and drawn by Walter Hood Fitch for *Curtis's Botanical Magazine* in 1868.

The publication by James Bateman of *A Monograph of Odontoglossum* (1864–74) introduced orchid growers to a group of sensational epiphytic orchids with elegant sprays of attractive star-shaped flowers. An initial trickle of species in the mid-nineteenth century turned within a few years into a flood. The subsequent rise in the popularity of odontoglossums during late Victorian times can be traced through the pages of journals such as *The Gardeners' Chronicle*, where new introductions and discoveries were regularly illustrated, described and advertised for sale by orchid nurseries. These great sales were held regularly at Stevens and Protheroe & Morris in London.

Until recently, naming of the species in this group was relatively uncomplicated. However, a better understanding of the evolution of orchids, aided by DNA analysis, has led to the disappearance of the genus *Odontoglossum*, mostly subsumed in the large genus *Oncidium*. Thus the orchids described and beautifully illustrated in James Bateman's monograph are now distributed in genera such as *Cuitlauzina*, *Cyrtochilum*,

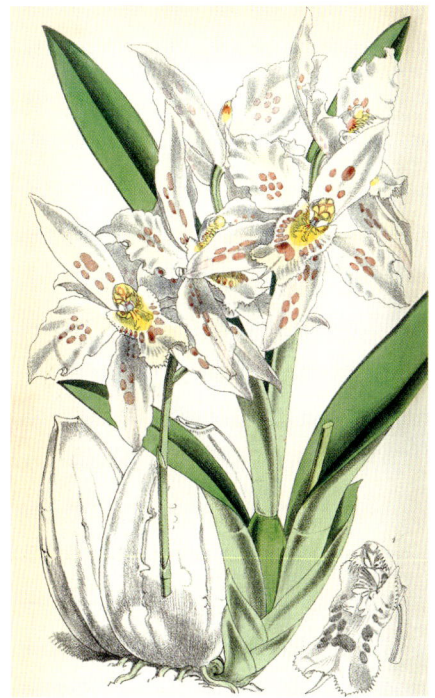

Oncidium, *Miltoniopsis*, *Rhynchostele*, *Rossioglossum* and *Ticoglossum*. Nevertheless, many orchid growers still use the name *Odontoglossum* for the Andean species and their many hybrids.

At the Royal Botanic Gardens, Kew, the archives hold a unique collection of orchid paintings of these plants by John

Day, a well-known orchid grower and accomplished artist, based at Tottenham, just north of the City of London. He catalogued, illustrated and commented upon orchids as they were introduced and flowered in London from 1863 until 1885, a period when orchid growing assumed a dimension which almost matched that of "tulip mania" in the Netherlands.

Following the publication of Bateman's monograph, odontoglossums became increasing popular and sought after in cultivation. John Day documented the best of the novelties introduced from the Andes, illustrating (often many times) at least 22 species and 13 natural hybrids. The latter sparked an interest among plant breeders, and by the turn of the century attention had moved to artificial hybrids as growers realized that they could grow them from seed. With a broad palette of species, growers were inspired to create novelties only hinted at and not seen in the wild.

The Andean species *Odontoglossum crispum* (now *Oncidium alexandrae*) was probably the most sought-after orchid of Victorian times. It is native to the Andes of central and southern Colombia, having been collected in 1841 or 1842 by Theodore Hartweg, who was collecting for the Horticultural Society of London, between Zipaquira and Pacho in the Colombian Andes. John Lindley named it in 1845.

Living plants did not reach Europe until 1865, when William Blunt, for the nursery of Low & Co. of Upper Clapton, John Weir, for the Horticultural Society of London, and F. Schlim, for the nursery of Jean Linden of Brussels, sent collections of it back from Colombia. Considered distinct from *O. crispum* at the time, Weir's plants were called

O. alexandrae by James Bateman, and this epithet was the accepted one when it was transferred to *Oncidium*, because "*crispum*" had already been used in *Oncidium* for a different Brazilian species.

It soon became apparent that the variation of this orchid was remarkable, and Day was driven to comment that "to attempt to name every variety of this most variable species would be endless". It was this very diversity, particularly in flower colour and form, which ensured the growing popularity of this species – a popularity that led to cult status and the highest prices for the best clones at auction. Thus, Baron Schroeder paid the amazing price of 165 guineas (equivalent to about £10,000 today) at Protheroe & Morris's sales room in Cheapside for a small plant of *O. alexandrae* var. *schroederi* that bore three flowers, while Sir Trevor Lawrence paid 155 guineas on 9 June 1886 to Mr Walter Cobb for another plant at a Protheroe & Morris sale.

Day painted var. *macrospilum* at the nursery of B. S. Williams in Holloway, which he described as "a very grand variety of this splendid and very variable species… [which] he bought home from Belgium … last week, exhibited it on Tuesday last at the Royal Horticultural Society" on 29 March 1884. On 26 June of the same year Veitch persuaded Day to draw their var. *veitchianum*, a plant that was subsequently exhibited by Baron Schroeder at the Royal Horticultural Society. John Day's final watercolour of this, and one of his best, depicts var. *wolstenholmiae*, named after his sister, a plant that flowered at Tottenham High Cross out of a batch that he had purchased from the nursery of Low & Co. the previous month, and Day noted, "I have never seen anything like it."

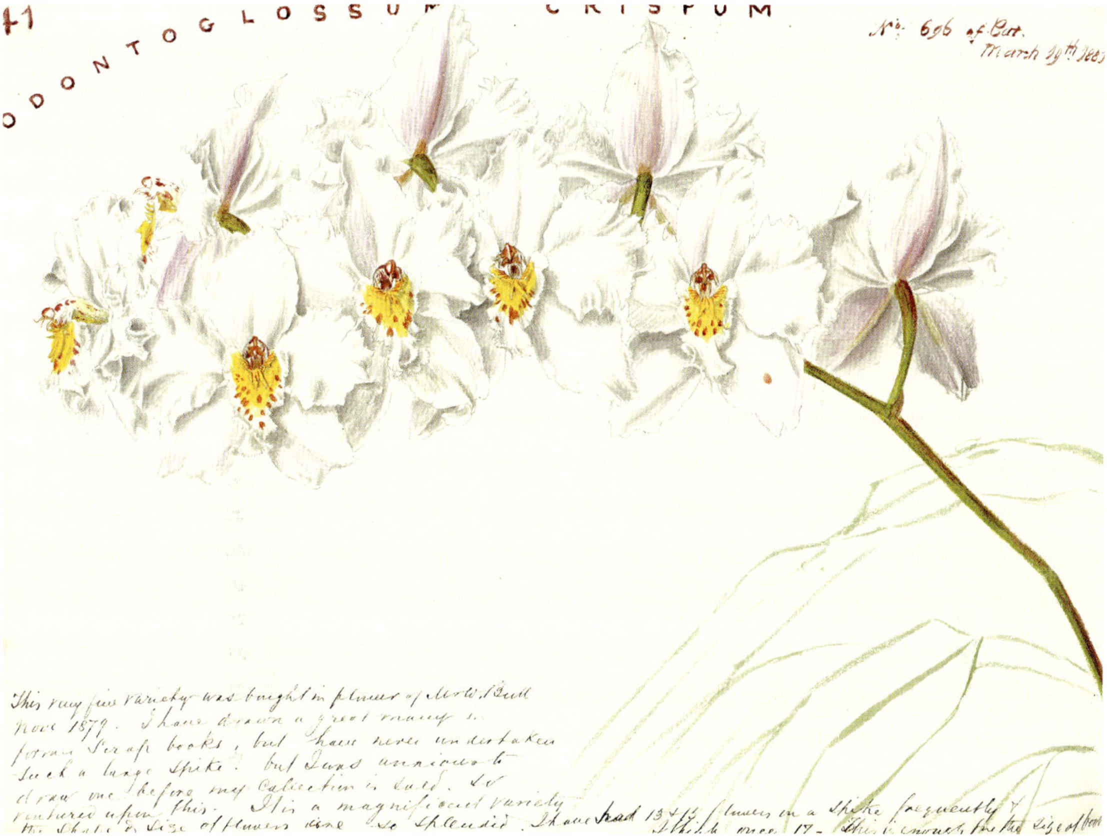

This rare fine variety was bought in flower of M.r W. Bull
Nov.r 1879. I have drawn a great many in
former Scrap books, but have never undertaken
such a large Spike, but I was unwilling to
draw one before my Collection is laid. So
ventured upon this. It is a magnificent variety
the Shape & Size of flowers are so splendid. I have heard 13 & 14 flowers on a Spike frequently &
I think more 17 — These enquies the full Size of bloom

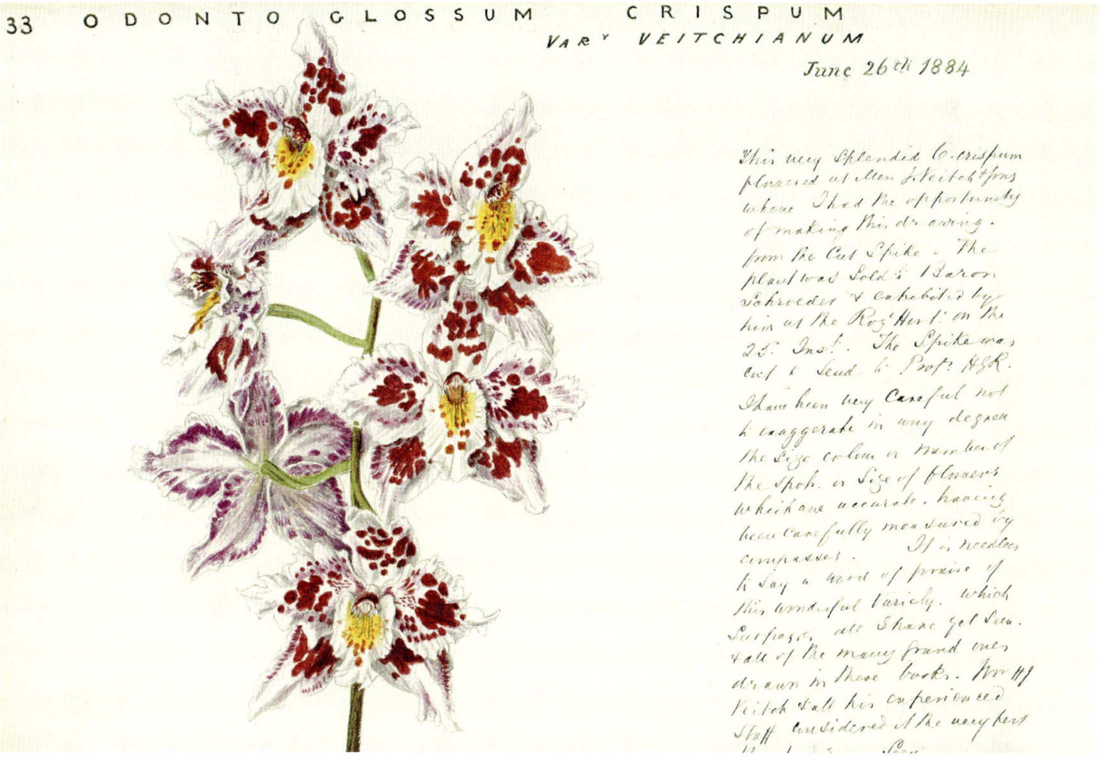

June 26th 1884

This very Splended O. crispum
flowered at Messrs S. Veitch & Sons
where I had the opportunity
of making this drawing.
from the Cut Spike — The
plant was Sold & Baron
Schroeder & exhibited by
him at the Roy. Hort.l on the
25.th Inst.t The Spike was
cut & sent to Prof.r H.G.R.
I have been very careful not
to exaggerate in any degree
the Size colour or number of
the Spots, or Size of flowers
which are accurate, having
been carefully measured by
compasses.   It is needless
to say a word of praise of
this wonderful variety. which
Surpasses all I have yet seen.
& all of the many grand ones
drawn in these books. M.r H.J
Veitch & all his experienced
Staff considered it the very best

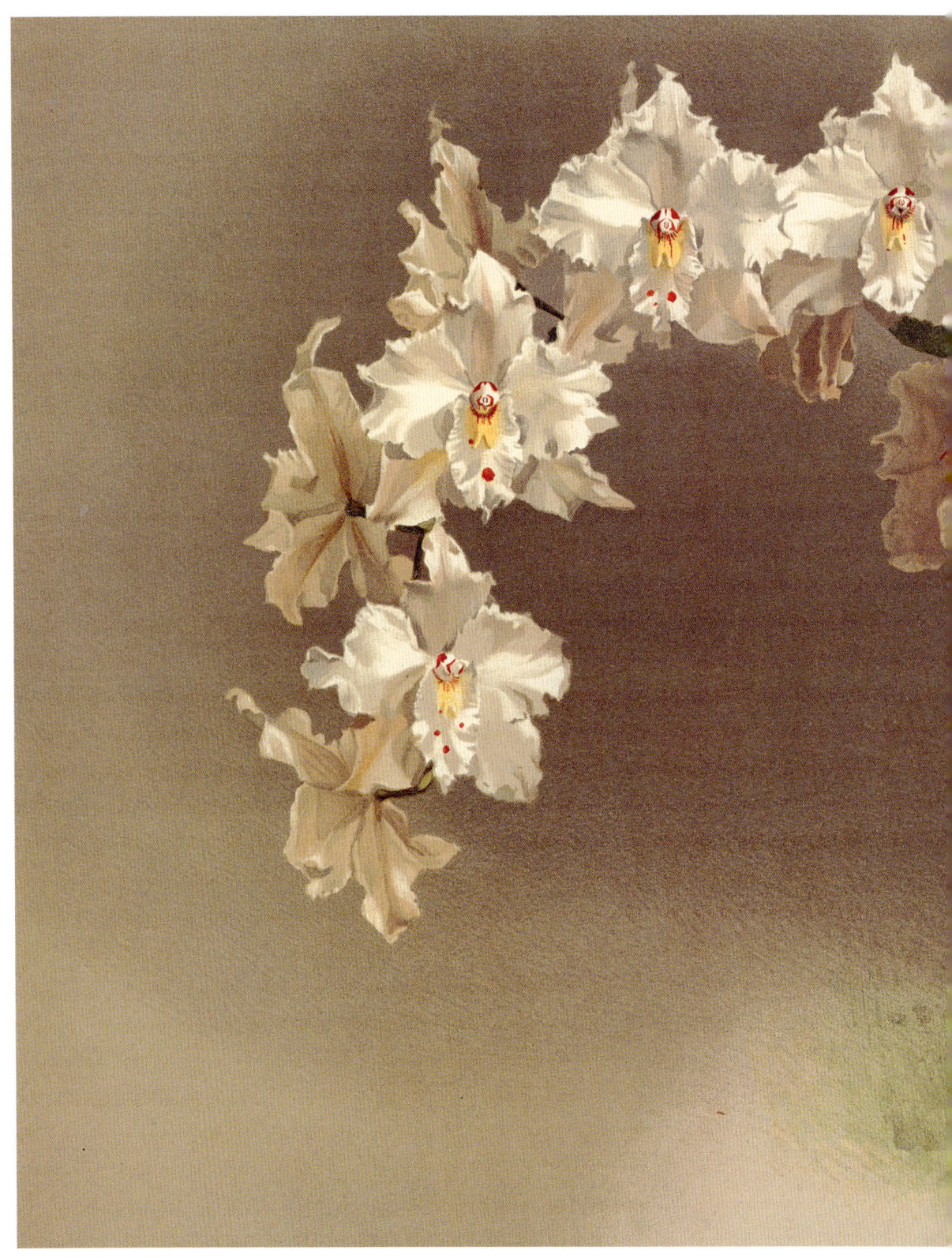

162 Princess Alexandra's odontoglossum *Oncidium alexandrae*

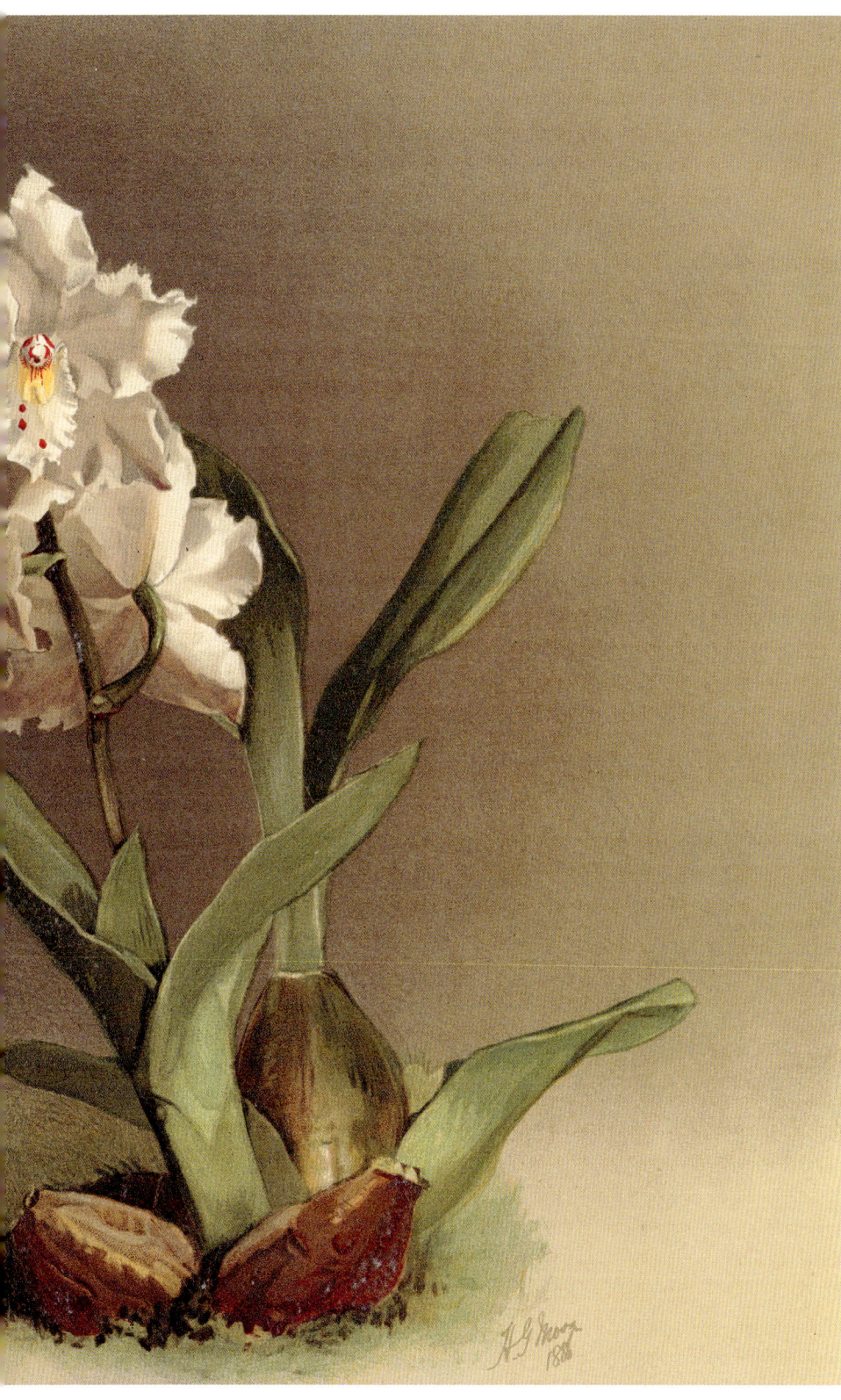

Left: *Oncidium alexandrae* (as *Odontoglossum crispum* var. *veitchianum*) drawn by Henry Moon for Frederick Sander's *Reichenbachia* of 1896. Moon was Sander's son-in-law.

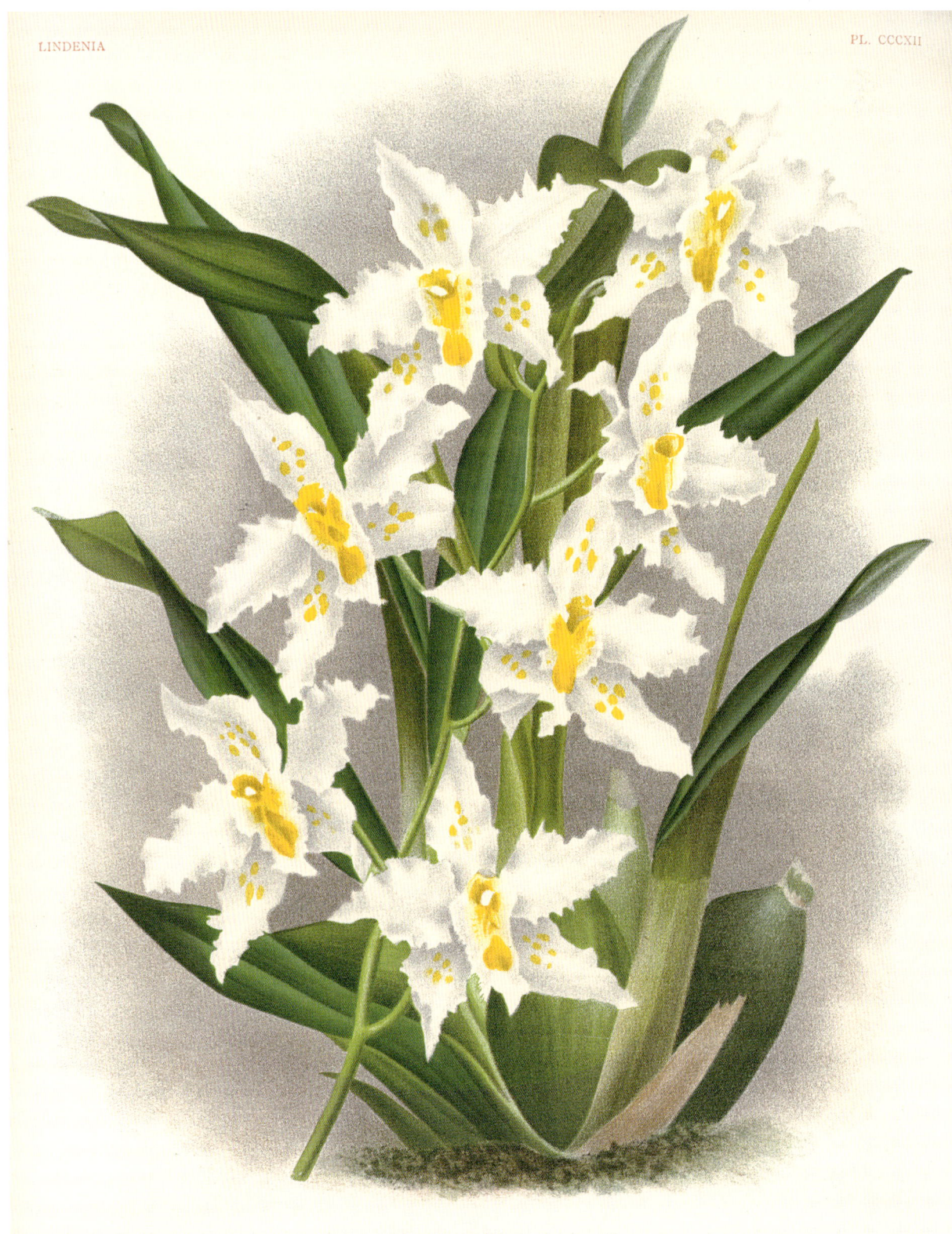

ODONTOGLOSSUM·CRISPUM LINDL. var. XANTHOTES HORT.

Opposite: *Oncidium alexandrae* (as *Odontoglossum crispum* var. *xanthotes*) flowered by Baron Schroeder of The Dell, Egham, drawn for J. J. Linden, *Lindenia: Iconographie des Orchidées*, 1885. This variety lacks the purple spots found in the typical variety.

INTRODUCTION.

At the time (1864) when this Monograph was commenced, the successful application of the system of cool treatment to Orchids accustomed to a moderate temperature in their native haunts gave a fresh impulse to the cultivation of that charming tribe of plants. By its means, what might almost be regarded as a new Orchid-world, teeming with interest and beauty, was suddenly brought within our reach. A fresh field was opened to the enterprise of collectors, the spirits of cultivators revived, and the hopes of botanists mounted high. Foremost among the spoils that we sought to secure, stood the various members of the genus Odontoglossum, which from the days of Humboldt[*] and Lexarza, was known to abound in species pre-eminent for the loveliness and delicacy of their flowers but which had hitherto mocked the utmost efforts of our most skilful growers. For although (thanks to the labours of Warczewitz and Lobb) the Horticultural Society and Messrs. Veitch had more than once received large consignments of Orchids —among which were many *Odontoglossa*—from the mountain ranges of New Grenada and Peru, they had invariably succumbed under the stifling atmosphere to which, in common with the denizens of India, Guiana, or Madagascar, they were remorselessly consigned. Here and there, indeed, an accidental success was achieved in a greenhouse, but the hint was turned to no account, and as a rule—notwithstanding the repeated warnings and remonstrances of Mr. Skinner, Warczewitz, and others—for thirty years we persisted in the incredible folly of growing "cool" Orchids in "hot" stoves; so deeply rooted in the minds of horticulturists was the original prejudice! But it yielded at last, and no sooner had a few houses—constructed and managed on the cool-culture system—made it clear that the Orchids of temperate regions were prepared to submit to the skill of the cultivator, than a general raid was made upon the more accessible countries in which they were known to abound—more especially certain districts in Mexico and New Grenada. To the latter country, collectors were simultaneously sent off by the Horticultural Society, who despatched Mr. Weir; by Mr. Linden, of Brussels; and by Messrs. Low, of the Clapton Nursery; and all these rival envoys, much to their own mortification and chagrin, found themselves sailing for the same destination in the same steamer on the same errand!

It was now that the idea occurred to me of devoting a work of adequate dimensions to the illustration of the particular genus, which from the dried specimens in our herbaria, the plates in *Pescatorea*, the figures of Humboldt, and the descriptions of travellers was evidently destined to hold the first place among all the numerous company of cool Orchids; and thus began the

[*] The mention of the illustrious traveller's name reminds me of the obligations under which he laid me when I first visited Berlin, in the spring of 1836; for, young as I was, he deigned to pour into my delighted ears all the stores of Orchid-lore collected during his memorable wanderings among the Andes of New Grenada and Peru. Here, he said, the greatest store of beauteous Orchids was to be found, and we are now beginning to realize the truth of his remark.

Introduction to *A Monograph of Odontoglossum*, by James Bateman, 1874

James Bateman's classic *A Monograph of Odontoglossum* was dedicated to Princess Alexandra, the Princess of Wales, to whom *Oncidium alexandrae* was also dedicated. The link between orchid growing and royalty was particularly strong during this period, with various members of the royal family and of the nobility being keen orchid growers. Bateman's book was instrumental in increasing the popularity of the genus *Odontoglossum*, now subsumed into *Oncidium*. Even then, he quotes John Lindley: "The more we build the partition walls between *Odontoglossum*, *Oncidium*, etc., the more the species break them down."

Bateman was an influential orchid grower and garden designer. His Biddulph Grange garden, made up of many small gardens, each with a distinct theme, has recently been resurrected and is open to the public.

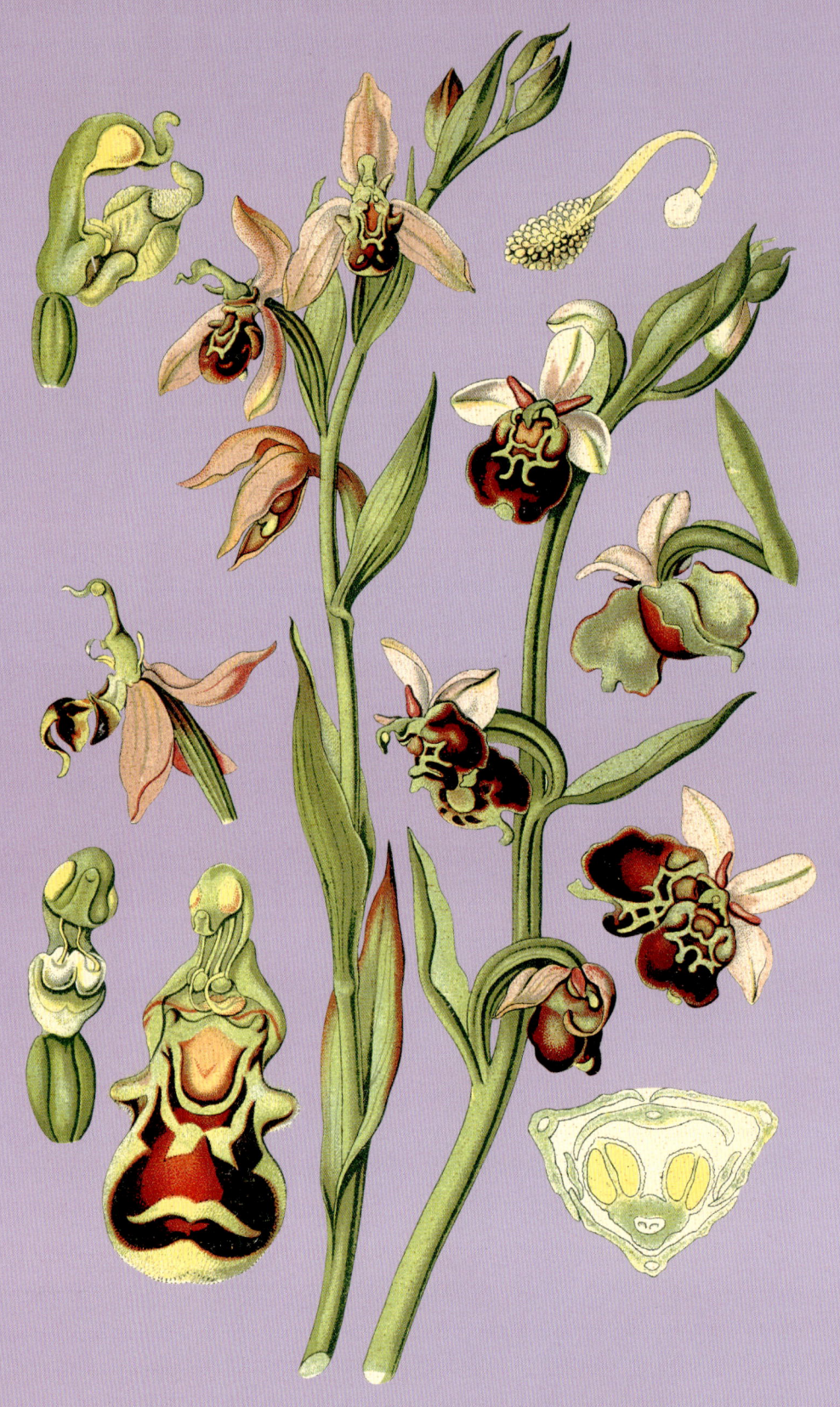

BEE ORCHID
OPHRYS APIFERA

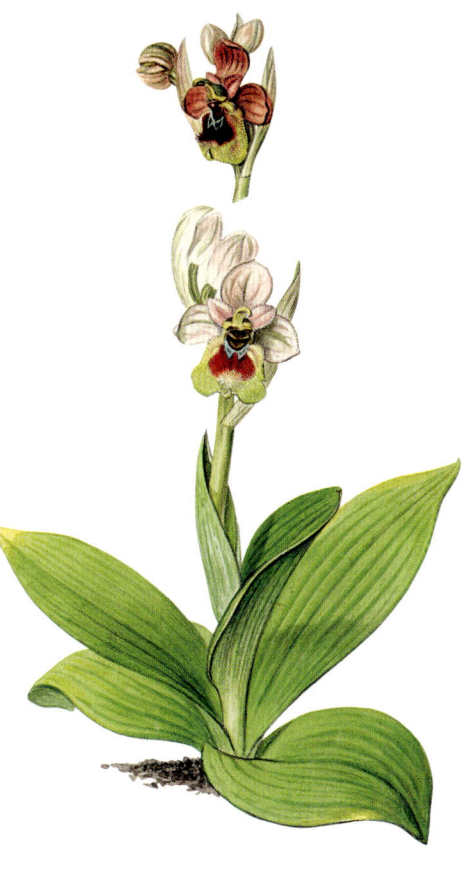

Deception, mimicry and sexual frustration – these are probably not the first words that most people would associate with the diminutive bee orchid, *Ophrys apifera*, when seeing it in the wild, but this species has evolved to become an expert in all of these in order to reproduce. The strategy is known as "pseudocopulation" and is seen in many orchids, particularly terrestrial species found in temperate climates. The result of the gradual co-evolution of a plant species with its pollinator, the labellum of the flower (a modified petal) changes very gradually over many generations, evolving to more closely resemble the body of the female bee. Male bees are attracted to this mimic and attempt to mate with the "female". During the ensuing struggle to mate, the pollen of the orchid – packaged into small parcels, called pollinia, in almost all orchids – is deposited on the frustrated male bee. When the insect finally gives up its attempt to mate, it flies off with the pollinia firmly attached to its body, ready to be deposited on the next bee orchid flower for which it accidentally falls.

Unlike many other flowers, species that are pollinated by pseudocopulation do not "reward" their pollinator with a nectar meal in return for transferring their pollen to another flower so that seed can be produced. The pseudocopulatory relationship is entirely based on the mimicry of the flower deceiving the insect into visiting it, and then tricking the insect into making the same mistake again, so that the pollen reaches another flower of the same species. It is thought that because the insect is frustrated by the orchid and does not receive any compensatory reward, it will move further away from the first plant and be deceived next by a more distant – and thus more likely genetically distinct – plant, rather than

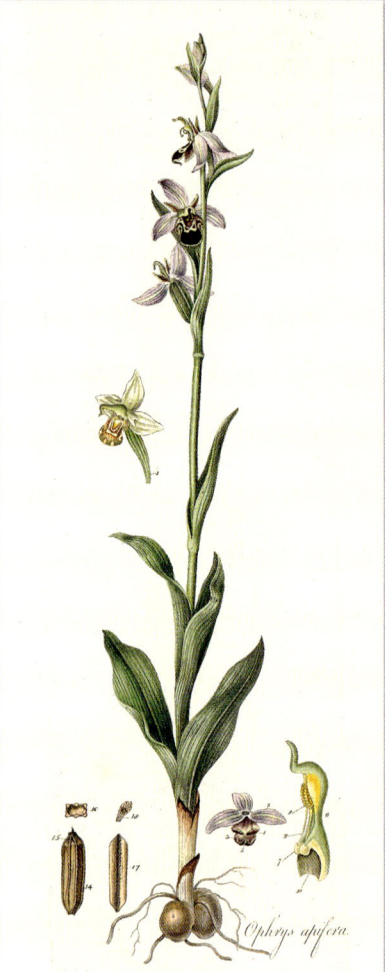

OPHRYS APIFERA. BEE OPHRYS.

OPHRYS *apifera*, labello trilobo, lobo medio majore semitrifido : lacinia media longiore subulata deflexa. *Br. in Hort. Kew. ed. 2. vol. 5. p. 195.*
OPHRYS apifera. *Huds. Angl. p. 391. With. Bot. Arr. ed. 3. vol. 2. p. 38. Hull Br. Bot. p. 196. Relh. Cant. p. 339. Smith Fl. Brit. vol. 3. p. 938. Curt. Fl. Lond. ed. 1. Engl. Bot. t. 383. Willd. Sp. Pl. vol. 4. p. 66. Swartz Gen. et Sp. Orchid. p. 46. Pers. Syn. Pl. vol. 2. p. 510. Desfongch. Fl. Gall. p. 612.*
ORCHIS *fucifora galea et alis purpurascentibus. Raii Syn. p. 379.*
ORCHIS fucum referens, galea et alis purpurascentibus. *Vaill. Bot. Par. tab. 30. f. 9.*
ORCHIS fucum referens major, foliolis superioribus candidis et purpurascentibus. *Bauh. Pin. p. 83.*
Germ. *Die Bienenblume. Hummelblume.* Span. *Hierba de la Abeja.*

CLASS AND ORDER. GYNANDRIA MONANDRIA.

(Div. 1. *Anthera adnata, terminalis, persistens. Pollinis massae e lobulis angulatis elastice cohaerentibus, basi affixae. Br.*)

[Natural Order. ORCHIDEÆ, *Juss. Br. Decandolle.*]

GEN. CHAR. *Corolla subpatens. Labellum ecalcaratum. Glandulae pollinia cucullis distinctis inclusae. Br. in Hort. Kew.*

RADIX bulbi duo, subrotundi, inaequales, radiculis longis vix fibrosis supra instructi.	ROOT two roundish unequal bulbs, furnished at top with a few small longish fibres, but little branched
CAULIS semipedalis aut pedalis, teres, foliosus.	STALK from half a foot to a foot high, round, leafy.
FOLIA vaginantia, ovato-lanceolata, subtus subargentea, lineata, saepe mutilata et fusca.	LEAVES embracing the stalk, of an ovate pointed shape, underneath silvery, with linear fibres, frequently imperfect, and of a brown colour.
BRACTEÆ magnæ, vaginantes, virides, longitudine floris.	FLORAL-LEAVES large, in the form of a sheath, green, and of equal length with the flowers.
FLORES a tribus ad sex, spicati.	FLOWERS from three to six, growing in a spike.
PERIANTHIUM superum, sexdivisum ; foliola tria exteriora ovata, concava, reflexa, purpurascentia, serioribus pallidioribus, subcarinata, carina viridi, *fig. 2* ; tria interiora valde inaequalia ; horum duo lateralia exterioribus quadruplo minora sunt, angusta, hirsuta, viridia, postice canaliculata, ad basin latiora, antrorsum exsertia ; tertium vel labellum amplum, dependens, leniter convexum, suborbiculatum, fusco-sericeum, maculis flavis frequenter variegatum, trilobum, *fig. 3*, lobis lateralibus subtriangularibus, hirsutis, reflexis, *fig. 4* ; medio majore semitrifido, *fig. 5*, laciniis reflexis, glabris, media longiore subulata.	PERIANTH above six-partite ; the three exterior leaflets ovate, concave, turning back, purplish, somewhat keel-shaped, the keel green, *fig. 2* ; the latter flowering palest ; the three interior very unequal ; of them the two lateral ones are four times smaller than the others, narrow, hairy, green, hollow behind, broadest at bottom, and projecting forward ; the third or labellum is large, hanging down, somewhat convex, roundish, of a silky brown colour, frequently variegated with yellow spots, having three lobes, *fig. 3* ; the lateral lobes somewhat triangular, hairy, reflexed, *fig. 4* ; the middle one large semitrifid, *fig. 5*, the lacinia reflexed, smooth, with the middle one longer and subulate.
ANTHERA, *fig. 6*, terminalis, viridis, elongata, claviformis, apice incurvato et sursum recurvato-acuminato, bilocularis, loculis per totam longitudinem distinctis, et basi ad pollinis pedunculum recipiendum saccatis, *fig. 7.*	ANTHER, *fig. 6*, terminal, green, elongated, club-shaped, at the apex incurved and then recurvato-acuminate, two-celled, with the cells distinct throughout the whole length, and saccate at the base, *fig. 7*, for the reception of the footstalk of the pollen.
POLLEN triangulare, flavum, in massam ovatam, pedunculatam, *fig. 8*, congestum ; pedunculo longo, gelatinoso, pellucido, basi in glandulam disciformem dilatato.	POLLEN triangular, yellow, collected into an ovate pedunculated mass, *fig. 8* ; the footstalk long, gelatinous, pellucid, *fig. 9*, dilated at the base into a disciform glandule.
OVARIUM oblongum, hexangulare, angulis obtusis rectis ; Stigma concavum, *fig. 10*, melleo liquore obductum, cui particulae antherarum frequenter adhaerent.	OVARY oblong, having six angles, the angles obtuse, not twisted ; the Stigma concave, *fig. 10*, covered with a viscid substance like honey, to which small particles of the anthers frequently adhere.
PERICARPIUM : Capsula oblonga, fusca, uncialis, *fig. 14*, unilocularis, *fig. 16*, trivalvis, valvis carinatis, *fig. 15.*	SEED-VESSEL : a Capsule about an inch in length, oblong, brown, *fig. 14*, of one cavity, *fig. 16*, and three valves, the valves keel-shaped, *fig. 15.*
SEMINA plurima, minuta, arillata, oblongo arillo, membranaceo, pellucido, reticulato, *fig. 18*, *lente aucta*, interiori parti carinae longitudinaliter affixa, *fig. 17.*	SEEDS numerous, small, arillate, with the aril oblong, membranaceous, transparent, and reticulated, *fig. 18*, *magnified*, affixed lengthwise to the inside of the keel of each valve, *fig. 17.*

Flowers in the months of June and July : the seed is ripe the latter end of August.
The Bee Ophrys grows generally on chalky ground near woods, and sometimes in meadows, in various parts of this kingdom, but is become more rare than formerly in the vicinity of London. In chalky places about Dartford and Bexley, Kent ; in meadows and common fields near Merton, Croydon, Banstead, on Box-Hill, Surrey, and many other places at a distance from town, it is one of the most common of the tribe. When treated in the manner recommended for the *O. aranifera*, it grows readily and flowers more freely in the garden than either of the other species of Ophrys. *G.*
The root appears to possess the same virtues with those of the Orchis from which salep is made, but being much smaller, is not worth cultivating on that account. The great resemblance which the flower bears to a bee, makes it much sought after by Florists, whose curiosity indeed often prompts them to exceed the bounds of moderation, root-

Ophrys apifera

Description and illustration of *Ophrys apifera* in *Flora Londinensis*, by William Curtis, 1777

William Curtis, of the Chelsea Physic Garden, published *Flora Londinensis* in six volumes between 1777 and 1798. Documenting the native flora found growing in and around the London area, Curtis employed artists such as James Sowerby and Sydenham Edwards (who later founded *Edwards' Botanical Register* in 1815) to illustrate each of the 12 issues in a volume with hand-coloured copper plate engravings.

The original watercolour painting of *Ophrys apifera* by William Kilburn was used by Curtis to produce a copperplate engraving for the plate in the hand-coloured copies distributed to subscribers. Fewer than 300 copies were produced, and the last volume was published only after the launch of *The Botanical Magazine* (later known as *Curtis's Botanical Magazine*) by Curtis in 1787. This periodical focused on plants of horticultural interest, especially exotic plants being introduced from around the world, and was much more financially successful than *Flora Londinensis*, which, nevertheless, had been lauded and well received. As Curtis later said of the two series, "One brought me pudding, the other praise".

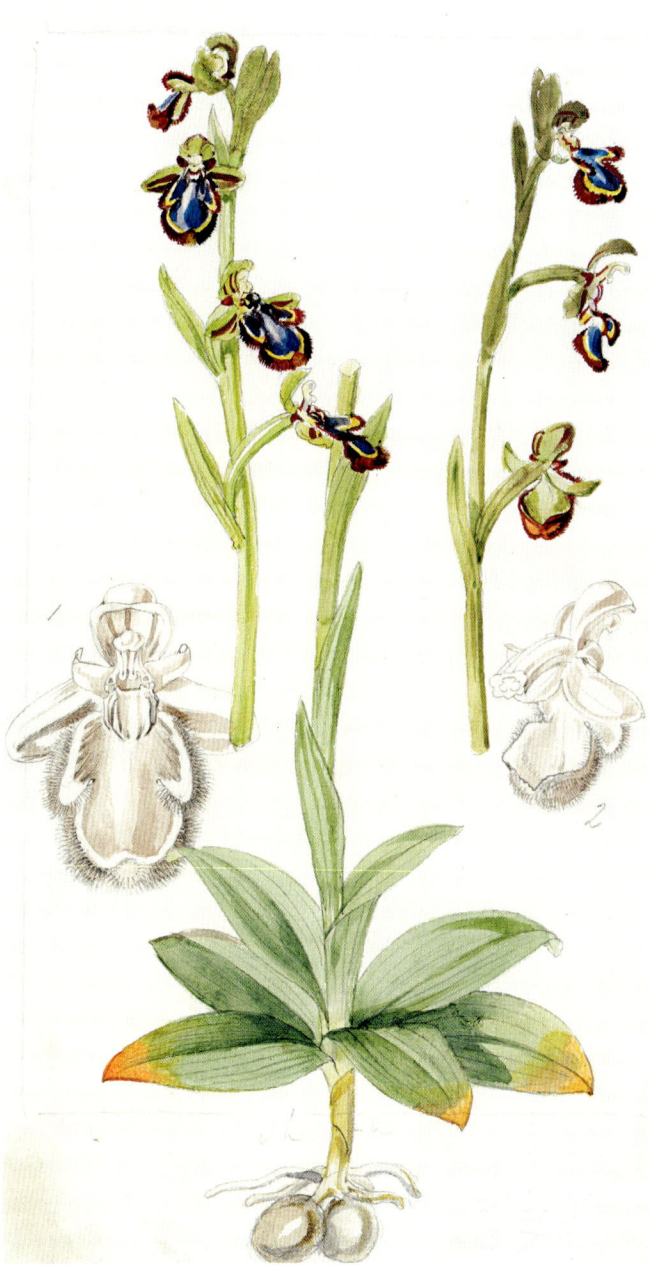

continuing to forage on flowers on the same or neighbouring plants, which are likely to be less genetically diverse. Seed produced from genetically diverse parent plants will tend to produce healthier and more vigorous offspring compared with the potential effects of inbreeding between flowers on the same plant or close neighbours. Pseudocopulation not only results in the pollination of the orchid's flowers, but also increases the fitness of the offspring produced.

Ophrys apifera has many relatives in the same genus which mimic different pollinating insects, ranging from flies to wasps and spiders, but many other species in the Orchidaceae family deceive their pollinators in a range of ways. For example, as seen elsewhere in this volume, members of the genus *Drakaea* (see page 112) in Australia mimic female flies, deceiving the male fly which inadvertently triggers the hinged labellum to throw it violently against the pollinia.

With a large natural range, *Ophrys apifera* is found in the wild from the UK, Ireland and the Mediterranean to the Caucasus in the east, across Turkey to northern Iran, the Middle East and North Africa. In the UK, this species is found in the south and the south-east, growing on chalk grasslands. Interestingly, there does not seem to be a natural pollinator for the species in the UK, where it is almost always an obligate self-pollinator.

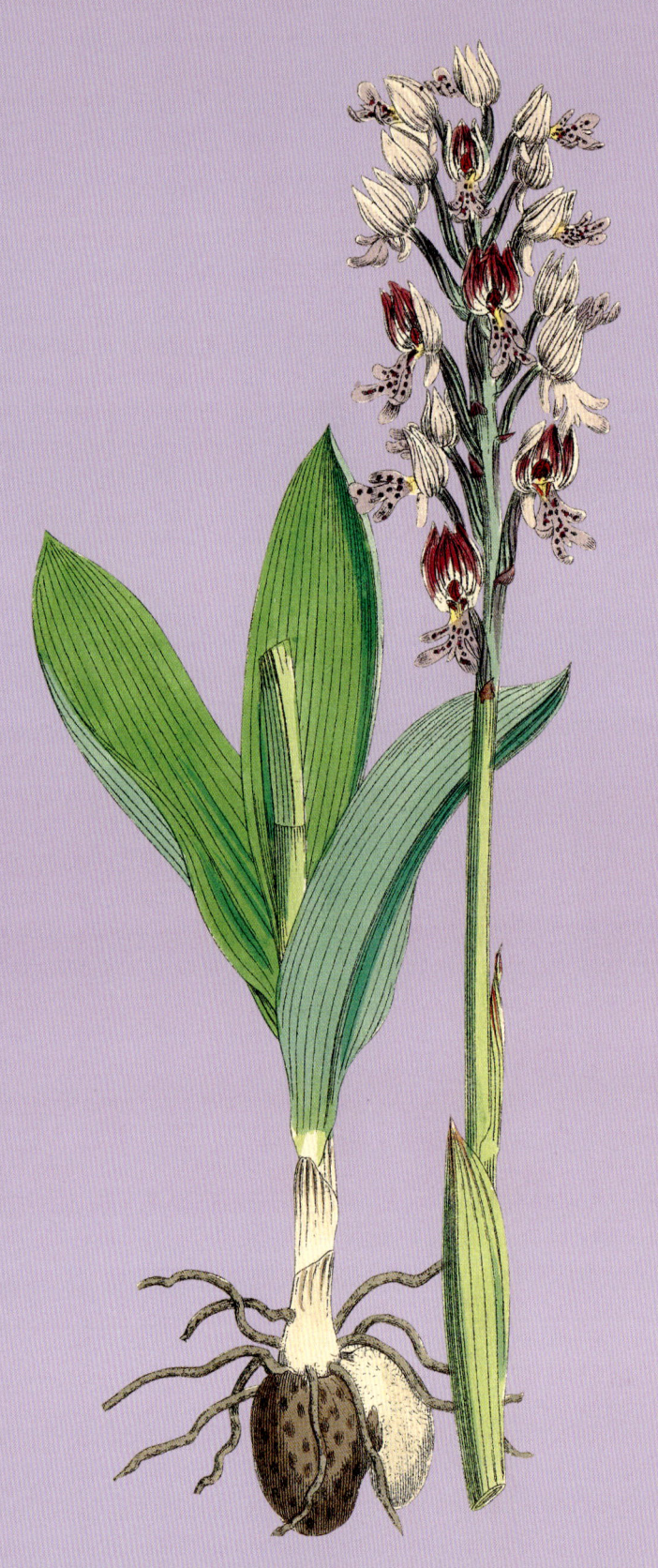

MILITARY ORCHID
ORCHIS MILITARIS

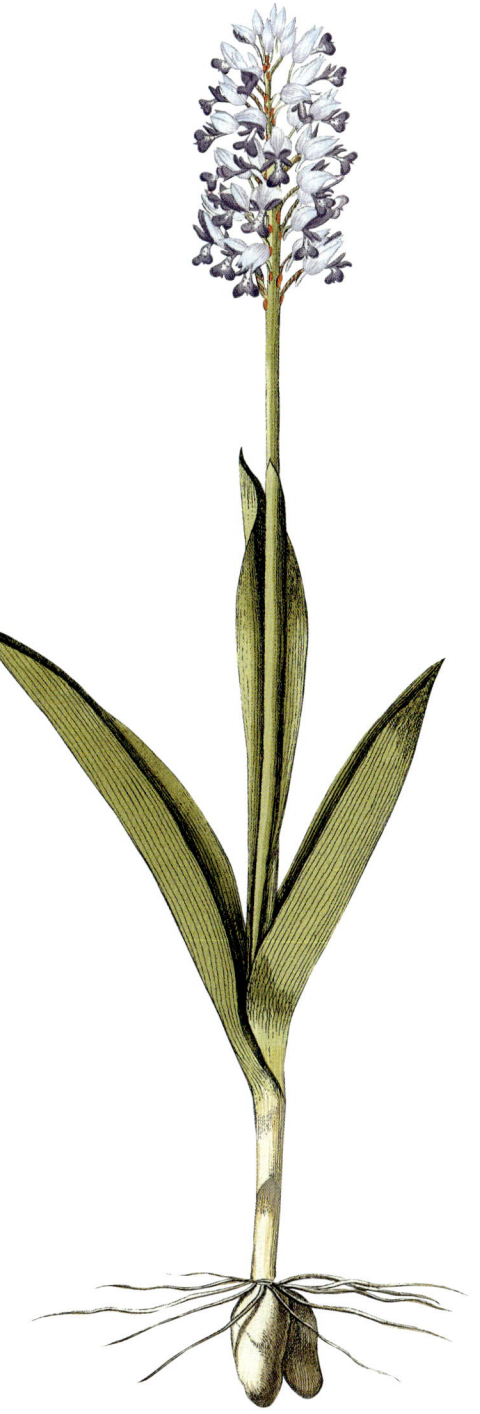

Opposite: *Orchis militaris* from J. E. Sowerby's *English Botany*. Sowerby's illustrated series was the first fully illustrated account of English flora, originally published 1790–1814, with the third edition published 1863–86.

Right: Nikolaus Jacquin's magnificent *Icones Plantarum Rariorum*, one of the finest illustrated plant monographs, dealt with rare plants flowering in the collection of the Habsburg emperor in Vienna. This illustration of *Orchis militaris* appeared in the third volume published 1786–93.

The military orchid, *Orchis militaris*, has the honour of being the type species of the genus *Orchis*, due to its having been described by Carl Linnaeus in the first edition of his *Species Plantarum* (1753). This volume is fundamental to the naming of all plants because it was the first to use consistently the binomial Latin (scientific) naming system and is accepted as the starting point for all modern botanical nomenclature.

The vernacular name of this species refers to the lip, which is a modified petal that hangs below the other floral segments, acting as a landing platform for potential pollinators. The lip has four long lobes and thus is said to resemble a soldier in the same way that other common European orchids are said to resemble bees (*Ophrys apifera*), flies (*Ophrys insectifera*), ladies (*Orchis purpurea*), lizards (*Himantoglossum hircinum*) and monkeys (*Orchis simia*).

Naturally, such distinctive plants were known long before Linnaeus was born and had been given vernacular names centuries earlier in Ancient Greece and the Roman Empire. They appear in the old herbals of the Renaissance where they were given names in the form of descriptive Latin phrases. Thus, *Orchis militaris* was known to the German herbalist Leonhart Fuchs (of *Fuchsia* fame) as "*Orchis morio latifolia*" (*De Historia Stirpium Commentarii Insignes*, 1542), and to the Swiss botanist Caspar Bauhin as "*Cynosorchis latifolia, hiante cucullo, major*" (*Pinax Theatri Botanici*, 1620). The utility of Linnaeus's binomial names was quickly appreciated, and they were widely adopted in the following years. The ancients were particularly intrigued by the tubers of the military orchid and similar species. These were ellipsoid or spherical in shape and paired (one old tuber and one new one) at the base of the plant. They strongly resembled the human testicles, and

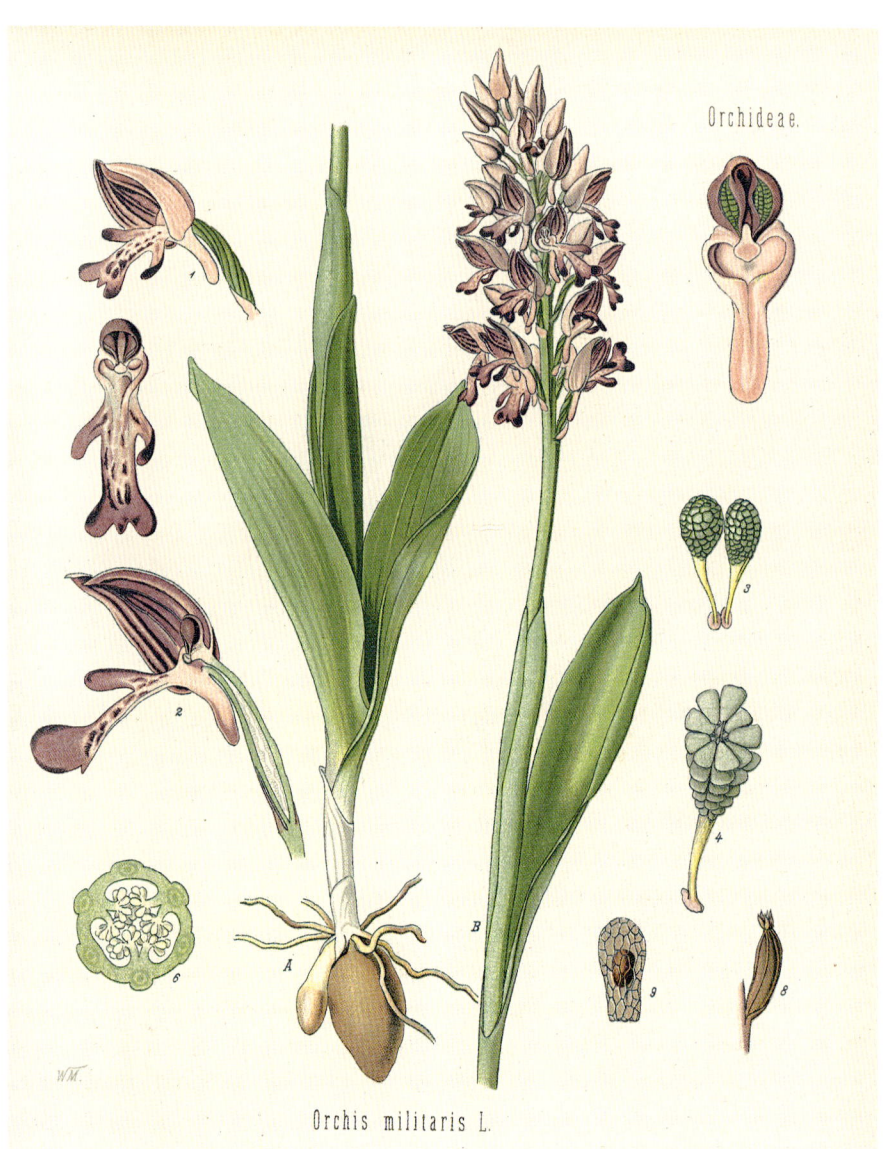

Orchideae.

Orchis militaris L.

Opposite: *Orchis purpurea* (mistakenly identified as *O. militaris*) from a composition drawn by G. Severeyns for *La Belgique Horticole*, 1852.

Left: *Orchis militaris* drawn by W. Müller, for F. E. Köhler's *Medizinal Pflanzen*, a German herbal of 1887.

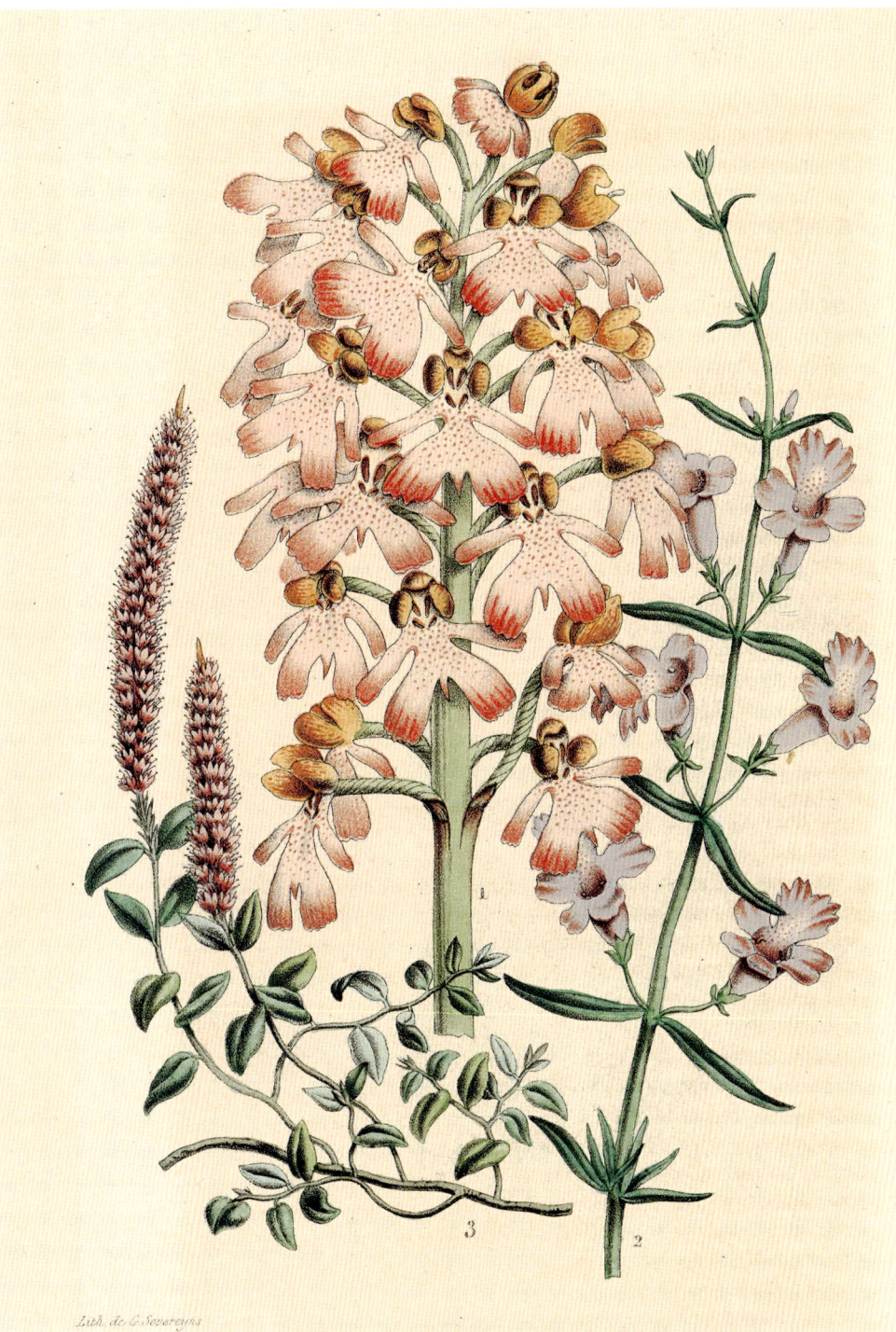

1. Orchis militaris var: iodocranus.
2. Hemiandra pungens. 3. Polygonum vaccinii folium.

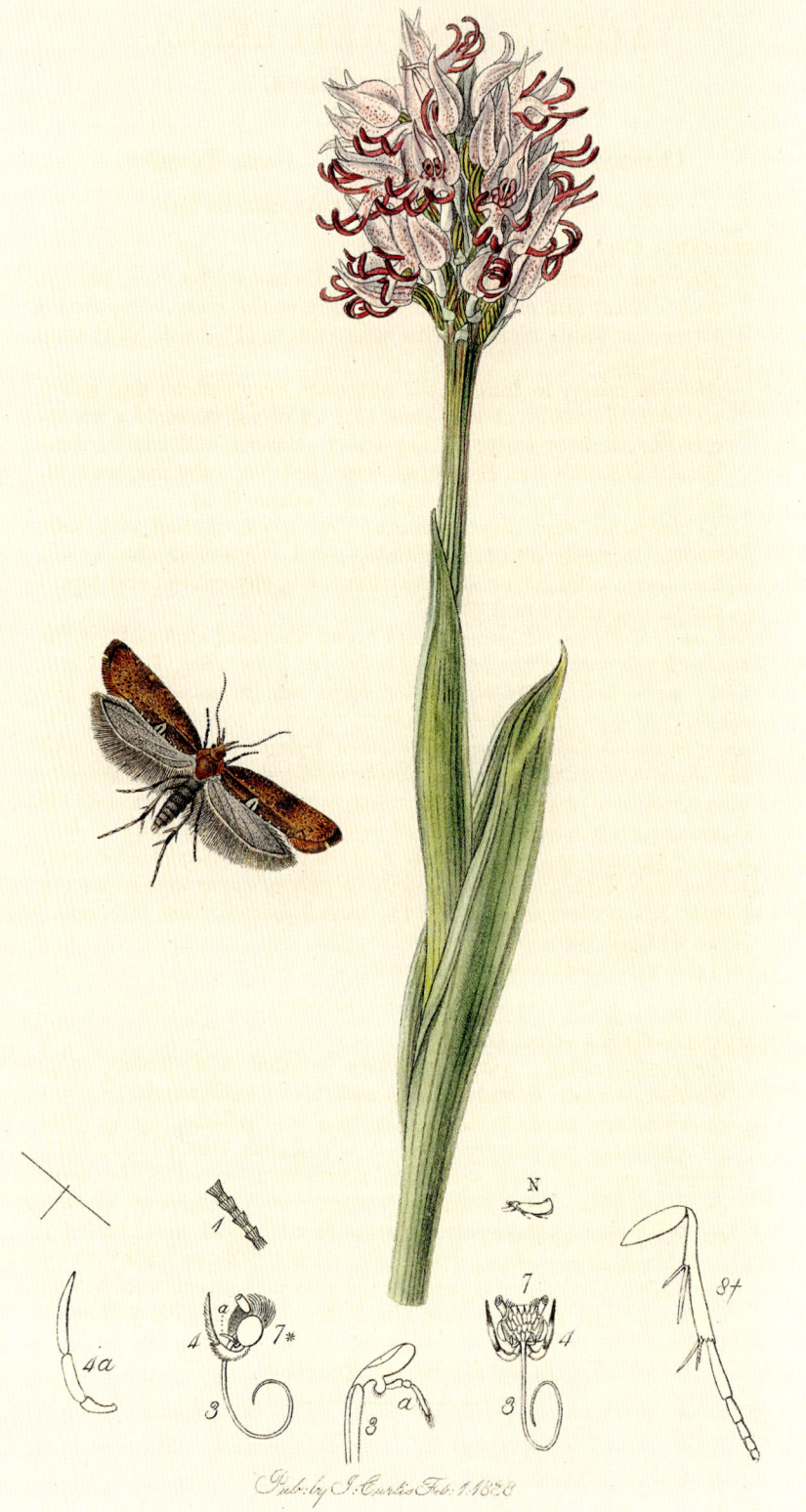

Pub. by J. Curtis Feb. 1. 1828

were widely used as an aphrodisiac from ancient times in the Middle East and the eastern Mediterranean. They were dug by women, cleaned, dried and sold in strings as "salep", a practice that continues to the present day in Turkey, Greece and adjacent countries. It is no coincidence that the name *orchis*, meaning a testicle, is derived from the Ancient Greek. The earliest reference to the purported aphrodisiac properties of orchid tubers can be traced to the Greek herbalist Theophrastus in his *Enquiry into Plants* (*c.* 285 BC), where he mentioned that orchid tubers reportedly had the ability both to promote erections and to cause impotence. Pliny the Elder, who was aware of Theophrastus's work, gave it a wider audience in his *Natural History* (77–79 AD), and repeated his claims that the larger, firmer tuber "taken in water, is provocative of lust; while the smaller or, in other words, the softer one, taken in goat's milk, acts as an anti-aphrodisiac".

John Parkinson summed it up when he wrote in his *Theatrum Botanicum* (1640):

> Pliny also writeth the same words out of Dioscorides, yet it is generally held, but almost all now adayes, that the firm roote onely is effectual for that purpose, and the loose or soft spongy roote to be either of no force or to hinder that effect.

This rather contradicts his earlier view expressed in his *Paradisi in Sole Paradisus Terrestris* (1629), that,

> for force of Venereous quality I cannot say, either from my selfe, not having eaten many, or from any other, on whom I have bestowed thee ….

> It would seem that Dioscorides doth attribute a great Venereous faculty to the seede, whereof I know not any hath made any especiall experiment with us as yet.

Although *Orchis militaris* is a rare and endangered plant in the British Isles, being confined to a few localities in the Chilterns and East Anglia, it is more widespread across northern and central Europe, and extends its range eastward to Mongolia. It grows in sparse calcareous grassland and in light shade in open woods, usually on chalk or limestone.

This orchid is predominantly pollinated by queen bumble bees (e.g. *Bombus lapidarius*, *B. pratorum*, *B. vestalis*) and honey bees. Efforts are being made in England to protect it and improve its chances of survival by habitat restoration and the reintroduction of appropriately sourced plants to sites where it used to grow.

Its closest relatives are the lady orchid (*O. purpurea*) and the monkey orchid (*O. simia*). Both of these species are rare and endangered in England, occurring in the south-east on chalk but at the north-western limits of their European distributions. Both occasionally hybridize with the military orchid, and the hybrids can cause confusion because they are morphologically intermediate between the parents. However, the lady orchid prefers woodland to the more open habitats of *O. militaris*, whereas the monkey orchid has a more Mediterranean range in very open habitats. Thus their ecology and, to a lesser extent, their flowering time and pollinator preferences do tend to keep them apart.

DE HISTORIA STIR-

PIVM COMMENTARII INSIGNES, MA XIMIS IMPENSIS ET VIGILIIS ELA BORATI, ADIECTIS EARVNDEM VIVIS PLVSQVAM

quingentis imaginibus, nunquam antea ad naturæ imitationem artificiosius effi-
ctis & expressis, LEONHARTO FVCHSIO medico hac
nostra ætate longè clarissimo, autore.

Regiones peregrinas pleriq, alij alias, sumptu ingenti, studio indefesso, nec sine discrimine uitæ non-
nunquam, adierunt, ut simplicium materiæ cognoscendæ facultatem compararent sibi:
eam tibi materiam uniuersam summo & impensarum & temporis compendio,
procul discrimine omni, tanquam in uiuo iucundissimoq uiridario,
magna cum uoluptate, hinc cognoscere licebit.

Accessit ijs succincta admodum uocum difficilium & obscurarum
passim in hoc opere occurrentium explicatio.

Vnà cum quadruplici Indice, quorum primus quidem stirpium nomencla-
turas græcas, alter latinas, tertius officinis seplasiariorum &
herbarijs usitatas, quartus germanicas continebit.

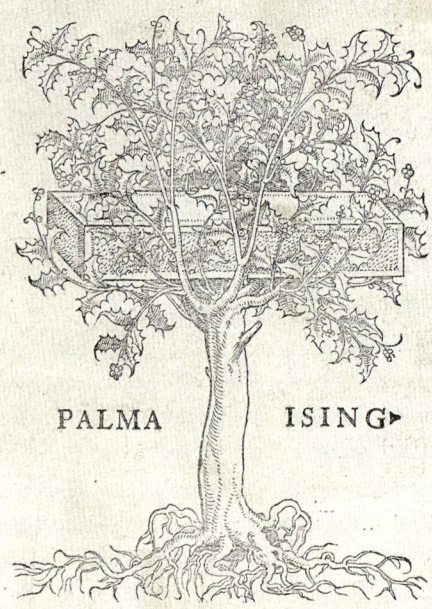

PALMA   ISING

Cautum præterea est inuictissimi CAROLI Imperatoris decreto, ne quis
alius impunè usquam locorum hos de stirpium historia com-
mentarios excudat, iuxta tenorem priuilegij
antè à nobis euulgati.

BASILEAE, IN OFFICINA ISINGRINIANA,
ANNO CHRISTI M. D. XLII.

Viro Nobilissimo, clarissimo, Experientissimo, Dño LVDOVICO KEPPLERO
philosoph. et Medic. Doctori &c. Genero suo animitùs dilecto, dono dedit
M. Matthæus Reimerus, in Academia patria profess. publ. et Senat. prid. Calend.
Martii, Anno M. DC. XL.

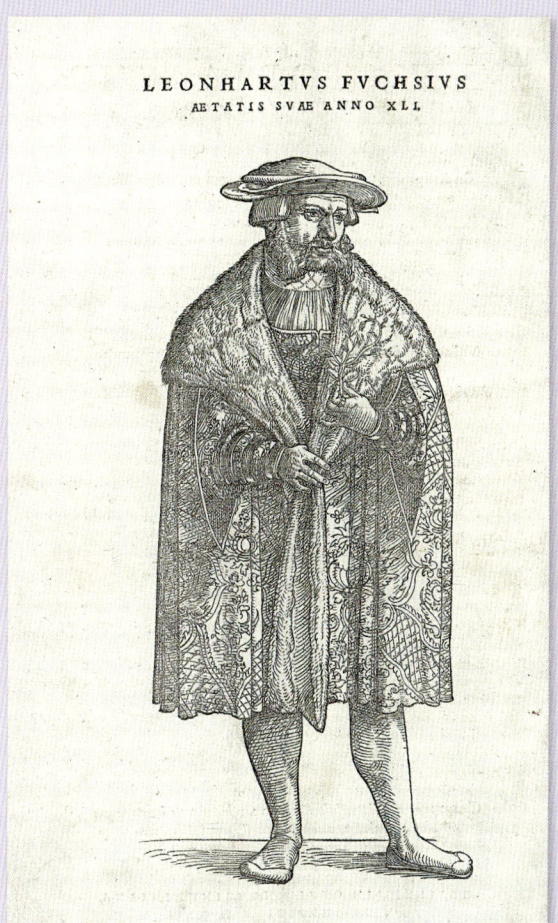

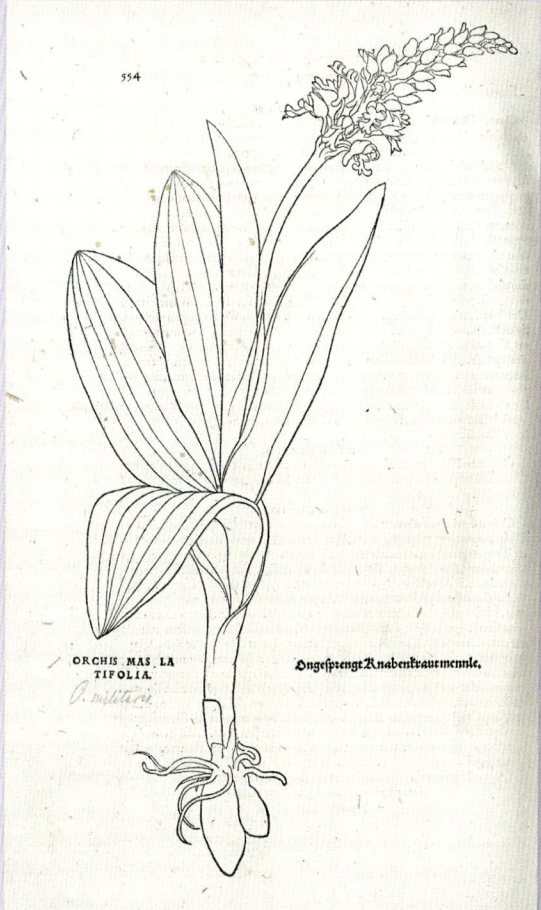

Pages from *De Historia Stirpium Commentarii Insignes*, published in 1542

Leonhart Fuchs' *De Historia Stirpium* of 1542 was illustrated with the finest woodcuts yet to appear in a herbal. They were drawn by Hans Weiditz, a pupil of Albrecht Dürer. His original watercolours survive in the sixteenth-century herbarium of Felix Platter, now housed in the city museum in Bern, Switzerland. The ornamental shrub genus *Fuchsia* is named in his honour.

Fuchs' herbal set a precedent for returning to nature to re-examine plants and better understand them. This was particularly important because the classical herbals of Dioscorides and Theophrastus dealt with Mediterranean species, many of which did not occur further north where interest in medicinal plants was growing rapidly. In England, the first herbal to take this approach was written by William Turner (*A New Herball*, 1551), but the later work by John Gerard (*Herball*, 1594) is better known today.

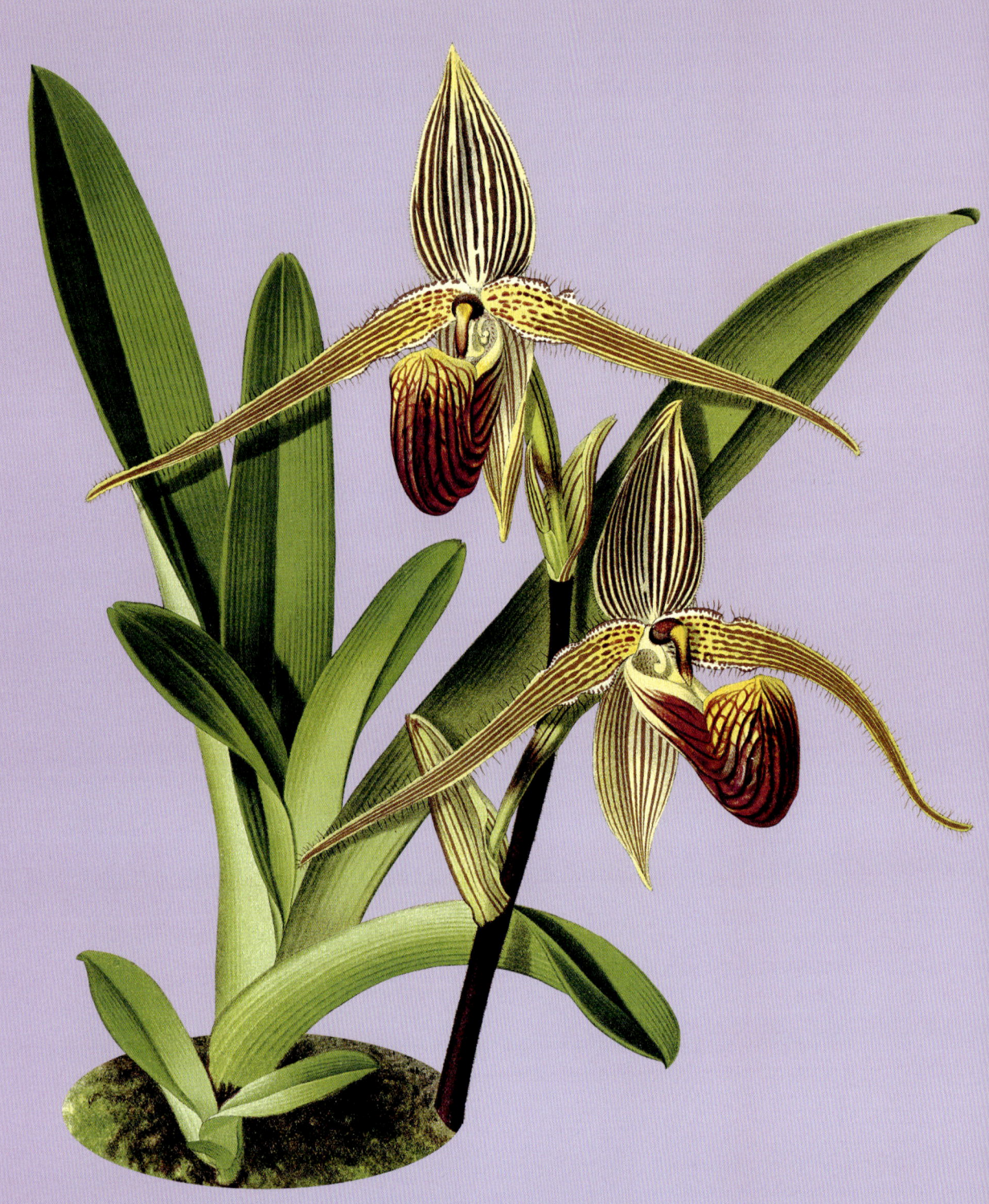

ROTHSCHILD'S SLIPPER ORCHID
PAPHIOPEDILUM ROTHSCHILDIANUM

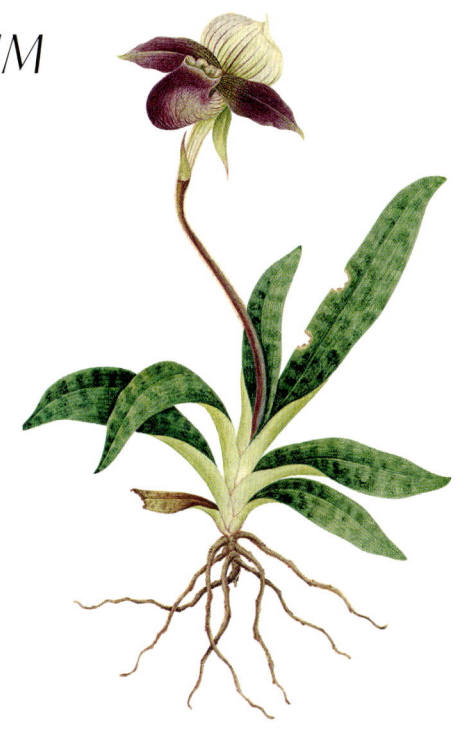

Opposite:
Paphiopedilum rothschildianum (as *Cypripedium elliottianum*) drawn by John Nugent Fitch, for R. Warner and B. S. Williams, *The Orchid Album*, 1891.

Right: *Paphiopedilum purpuratum* is one of Hong Kong's rarest native plants, collected almost to extinction for horticulture and for the aquarium trade. When John Eyre painted it in Hong Kong in 1848 he noted that it was not rare: "I have found it in many other places, and in particular abundance on the marshy patches in the second ravine E of the Albany Barracks, one of the most prolific parts of the Island in orchids".

One kind of the beautiful genus Cypripedium, or Ladies' Slipper, so named for its curious form of the labellum, far surpasses in beauty any of its tribe from other countries.

Hugh Low, in *Sarawak* (1848)

Baron Ferdinand de Rothschild, the eminent Victorian orchid grower, has the distinction of having the most spectacular orchid in the genus *Paphiopedilum* named after him. *Paphiopedilum rothschildianum* was introduced into cultivation by Jean Linden in May 1887, and early the following year by Sander & Sons of St Albans, England. Heinrich Gustav Reichenbach based his original description (as *Cypripedium rothschildianum*) on a flower sent to him by Frederick Sander, the self-proclaimed Orchid King, and it was said to have come from New Guinea. This appears to have been a deliberate attempt to mislead Sander's competitors, because we now know that the orchid is endemic to Mount Kinabalu and its environs in north-east Borneo.

Paphiopedilum rothschildianum, which many people consider to be the finest of all wild orchids, was collected in 1885 by a collector from the Belgian nursery of Jean Linden. It was collected again on 19 February 1886 by John Whitehead, a British zoologist who was surveying the fauna of Mount Kinabalu. In his account he described finding "a very fine *Cypripedium* … growing amongst the piles of loose rock on top of the hills. This species, of which I made a sketch, I am told is *C. rothschildianum*, the same species as is found in New Guinea: this seems to me too improbable." He was

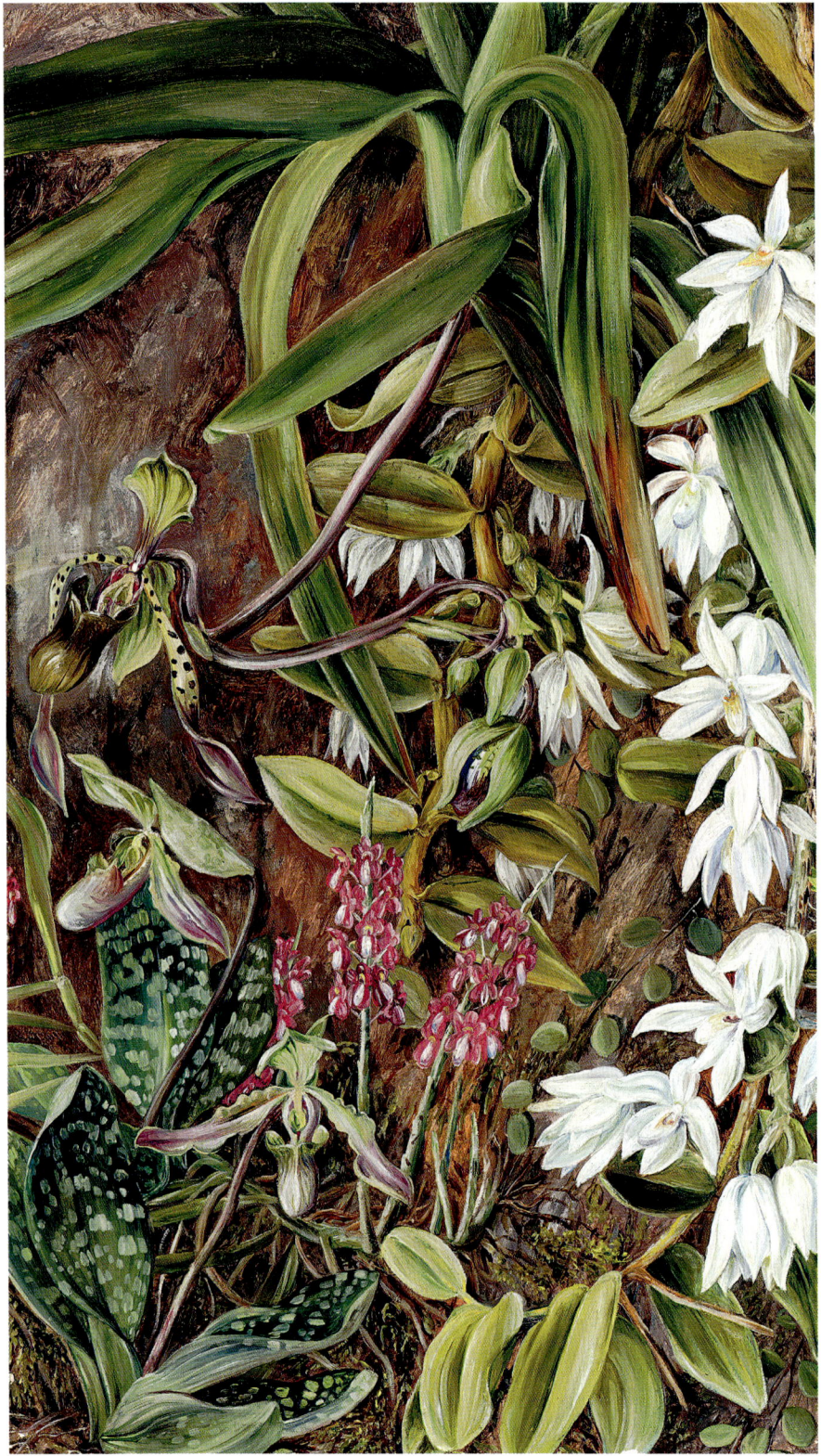

Left: Marianne North visited Kuching, Sarawak in 1876 as guest of the second Rajah Brooke and his wife Margaret. This painting includes two slipper orchids, *Paphiopedilum lowii*, and *Paphiopedilum bullenianum*, the pink-flowered *Dyakia hendersoniana* and the white-flowered pigeon orchid, *Dendrobium crumentatum*.

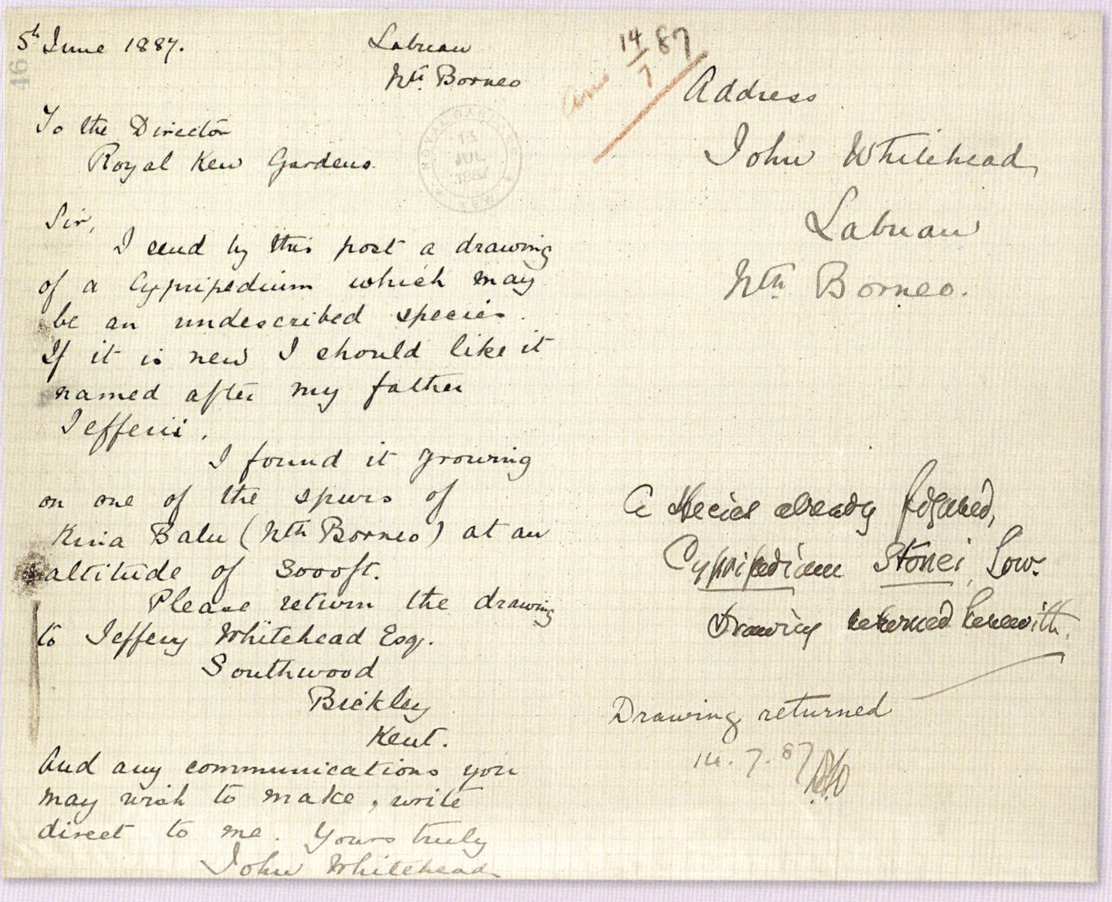

Letter from John Whitehead to Sir William Thiselton-Dyer, from Labuan,
North Borneo, 5 June 1887

John Whitehead (1862–1899), an ornithologist and zoological collector, discovered *Paphiopedilum rothschildianum* on the slopes of Mount Kinabalu in Borneo in 1886. This letter, written while on an expedition that took in peninsular Malaysia, Java, Borneo and Palawan, from 1885 to 1888, records his observation of the orchid. Unfortunately, his request to have it named for his father was usurped by Heinrich Gustav Reichenbach, who named it for Ferdinand de Rothschild, one of the best customers of the Sander nursery.

Whitehead made a second expedition to the Philippines between 1893 and 1895, but died from fever in Hainan at the start of his third expedition.

correct, and this misleading information had probably been given him by Sander, to whom he sent plants.

The lure of spectacular novelties tempted other nurseries to join in the search for orchids and other plants in Borneo. Frederick Sander sent J. Förstermann to Borneo and was rewarded by seeing the strangest of all slipper orchids, namely the bizarre *P. sanderianum,* which has pendent petals that reach 1 m (3 ft) or more in length. This orchid survived in cultivation until the turn of the century, but then disappeared. It was rediscovered by an expedition from the Royal Geographical Society in the early 1980s on a survey of the limestone region of Gunung Mulu in northern Sarawak.

The news of *P. sanderianum* and *P. rothschildianum* led to a positive "feeding frenzy" among the European orchid nurseries, each of which sent out collectors to scour the island for these and other novelties. An idea of the scale of collecting can be gauged from the letters of the Swedish plant collector Ericsson to Frederick Sander between April 1887 and November 1894. Ericsson sent 4,500 slipper orchids to Sander from Sarawak on 4 April 1887. He collected 4,000 plants of *P. rothschildianum* in September 1888 and noted that Ravensway's collector was also gathering them. Despite writing in October 1888 that "I think after this trip we give up Borneo altogether for here everybody is collecting Orchis, a perfect nuisance", he continued to send more orchids, including 1,300 plants of *P. sanderianum* in November 1889, six cases each of *P. hookerae* and *P. rothschildianum* in July 1890, and 3,000 plants collected by Waterstradt in May 1895.

Borneo is one of the hotspots for slipper orchids. Hugh Low (later Sir Hugh Low), Rajah Brooke's colonial treasurer for Sarawak, collected a slipper orchid in Sarawak in Borneo in 1846, and it was named (as *Cypripedium lowii*) in his honour by John Lindley. Low collected five other Bornean slipper orchids, namely *P. dayanum* (1856), *P. javanicum* var. *virens* (1862), *P. stonei* (1862), *P. hookerae* (1863) and *P. bullenianum* (1865), the first two on the slopes of Mount Kinabalu during his historic ascent of the mountain. Surprisingly, he missed *P. rothschildianum,* which grows with *P. dayanum* in some localities. Low sent the plants back to the family nursery, Low of Clapton, one of the pioneering orchid nurseries in Victorian England.

Of all the species in the genus, *P. rothschildianum* must be one of the rarest in nature. Despite extensive searching over a period of 130 years, the typical variety has been located in only three sites on the lower slopes around Mount Kinabalu, in one of which it is certainly now extinct, and in another locality nearby where it has been collected to extinction. These are the very places that are under greatest threat from destruction of their habitat by logging, mining and shifting agriculture. The strange staminode of *P. rothschildianum* attracts hoverflies, as its glandular hairs mimic an aphid colony, the normal brood site of the hoverfly larvae. The female flies deposit their eggs on its surface but sometimes fall into the lip. Their only possible exit is through the gap between the base of the lip and the column, so the flies pass beneath the stigma and pollinia. A visit to a second flower followed by a similar scenario will therefore effect pollination.

Opposite
Paphiopedilum rothschildianum var. *platytaenium* flowered at the Linden nursery in Ghent and drawn for J. J. Linden, *Lindenia: Iconographie des Orchidées* in 1898.

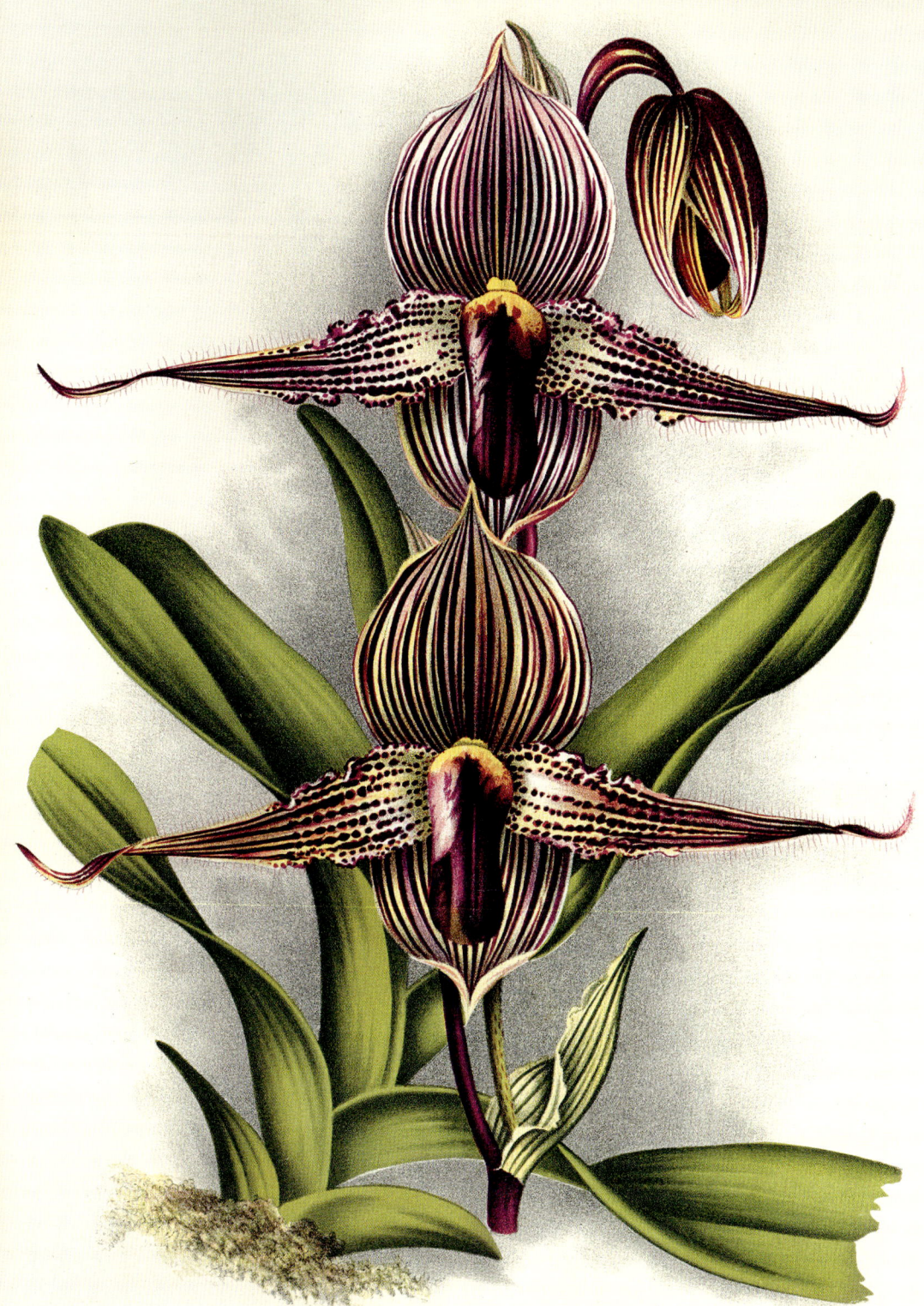

G. Putzys pinx.

CYPRIPEDIUM ROTHSCHILDIANUM RCHB. F. var. PLATYTOENIUM L. LIND.

P. De Pannemaeker chrom.

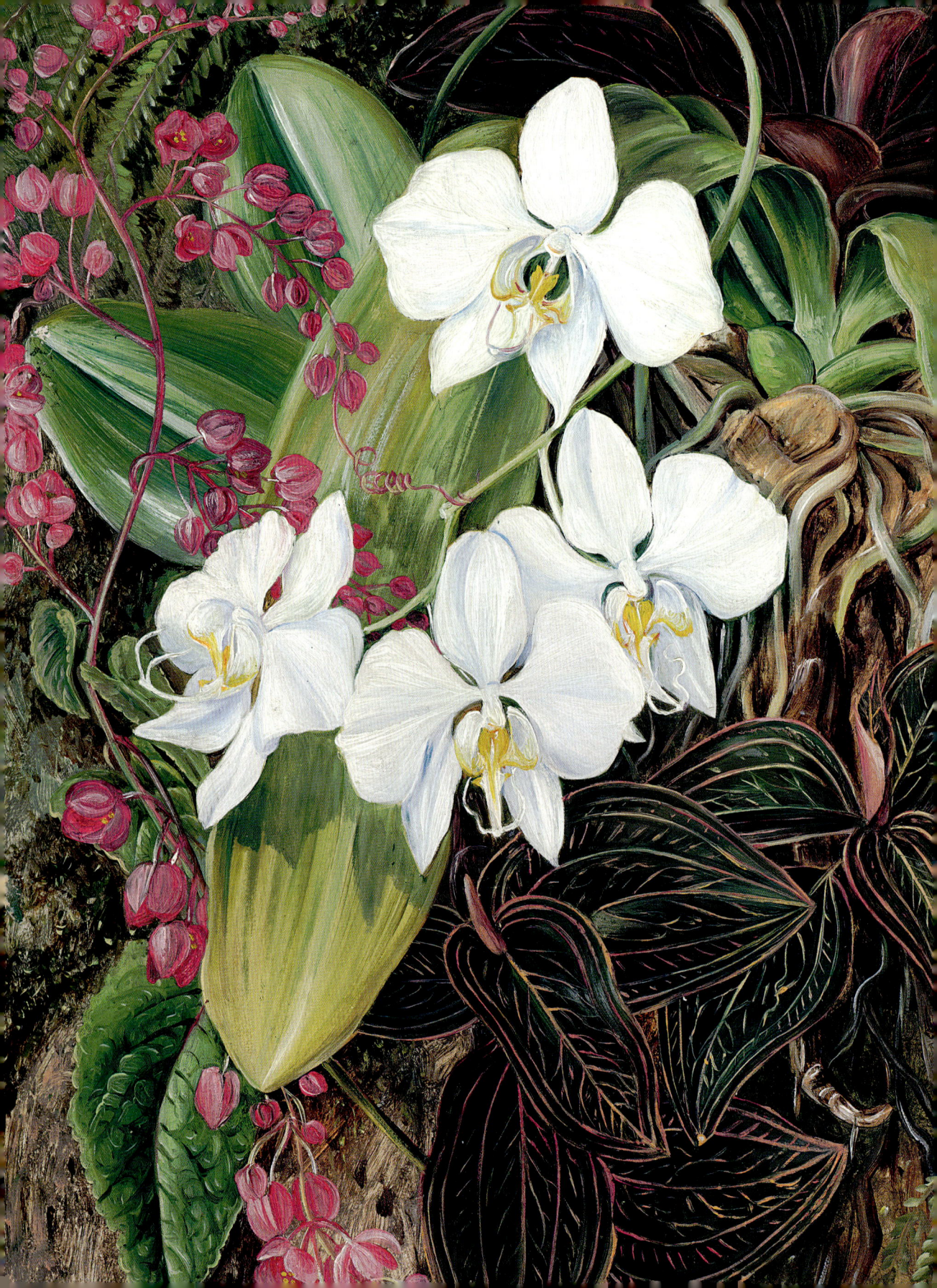

WHITE MOTH ORCHID
PHALAENOPSIS AMABILIS

The moth orchid genus *Phalaenopsis* has become the most widely cultivated orchid genus in modern times. These orchids are compact plants with a few large leathery basal leaves borne on a short stem, and they produce graceful arching spikes with many large showy flat flowers. There are three main reasons for their popularity: the flowers last for up to 3 months or more; they occur in a wide range of colours, from white to pink, purple or yellow with a plain, spotted or candy-striped pattern; and they can be mass produced in the laboratory and grown like carnations in heated glasshouses, thus allowing fast and uniform production at low cost. The genus comprises about 60 species distributed from northern India across south-east Asia into the Malay

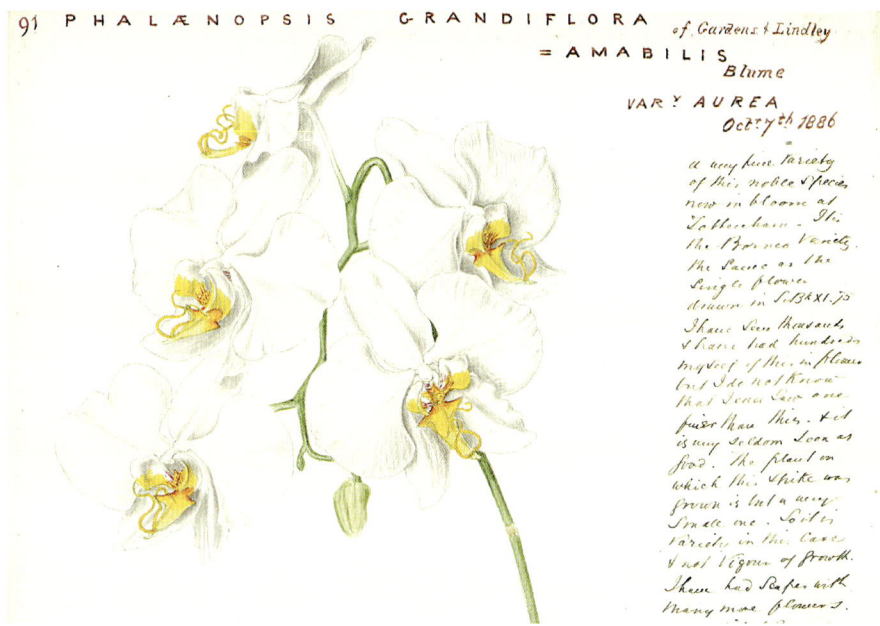

Archipelago across to the Philippines, New Guinea and Northern Australia. Five species have had a particularly influential role in plant breeding, namely the white-flowered *Phalaenopsis amabilis* from the Malay Archipelago, *P. aphrodite* and *P. stuartiana* from the Philippines, and the pink-flowered *P. sanderiana* and *P. schilleriana*, both from the Philippines.

Georg Everard Rumphius, the "blind seer of Ambon", described and illustrated the white-flowered moth orchid, *Phalaenopsis amabilis*, which was among the first tropical Asiatic orchids to be described and illustrated, in his posthumously published *Herbarium Amboinense*. Moth orchids have always been popular and have consistently been sold for good prices at auction. As early as 1847, *P. amabilis* fetched 15 guineas (equivalent to about £1,000 today) at a sale at Stevens's Soho sales rooms.

In 1862, Heinrich Gustav Reichenbach described a second white-flowered species, *P. aphrodite*, from the Philippines. It generally has finer flowers than *P. amabilis*, reflected in the high prices that good plants fetched at auction. In 1856, Sir Trevor Lawrence paid £68 5s at Stevens's sales rooms for a plant collected in Luzon for the Horticultural Society of London.

John Day painted this orchid several times, his best-known painting being that of 20 December 1880, in relation to which he noted that "this plant is one of a fine lot collected in the Philippine Islands and brought home to Messrs Hugh Low & Co. by their traveller Mr Boxall last summer." A painting of the same spectacular plant appeared in Warner and Williams' *The Orchid Album* the following year.

The Philippino species *P. schilleriana*

and *P. sanderiana* are among the loveliest of all orchids, with arching branching sprays of delicate, rose-pink flowers that seem to float in the air above the attractively silver-mottled, dark green leaves. *P. schilleriana*, was described by Reichenbach, the German orchid specialist, in 1860 based upon a plant from Consul Schiller's large orchid collection in Hamburg. Good prices were paid for this beautiful orchid; for example, in 1875 Sir Trevor Lawrence paid £33 12s at auction for a plant from the collection of John Russell of Mayfield, Falkirk. John Day made several paintings of *P. schilleriana*. His remarkable plate of 22 March 1877 shows 15 lips over two pages. The plants were selected from:

> a quantity now in flower (and) will serve to illustrate the great variability of form which this lovely plant indulges – hardly two are exactly alike, some are dark and some spotted, some white, some narrow, some broad – and every variety of shape, particularly of the lamina with its bifid apex, straight, curved, blunt, slender, clumsy or almost abortive. I might draw pages without exhausting them all.

Plants of *P. schilleriana* continued to flow into the auction rooms, and Day produced a beautiful painting of a plant from a later Low importation in February 1884.

P. sanderiana, which has large pink flowers similar in colour if not in intensity to those of *P. schilleriana*, has proved to be one of the most important parents in hybridizing because of its attractive flowers and foliage, and also because it

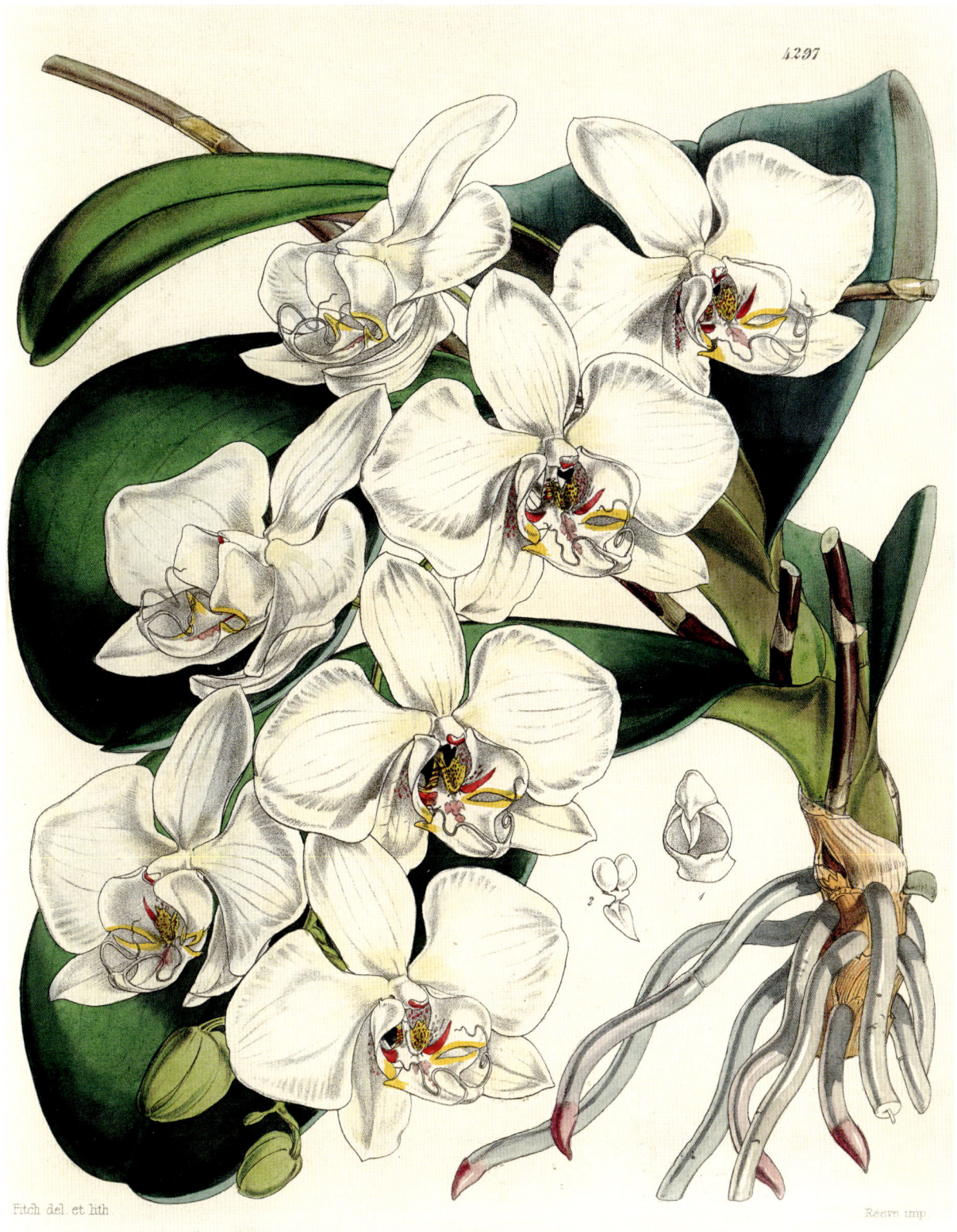

4297

Fitch del. et lith

Reeve imp.

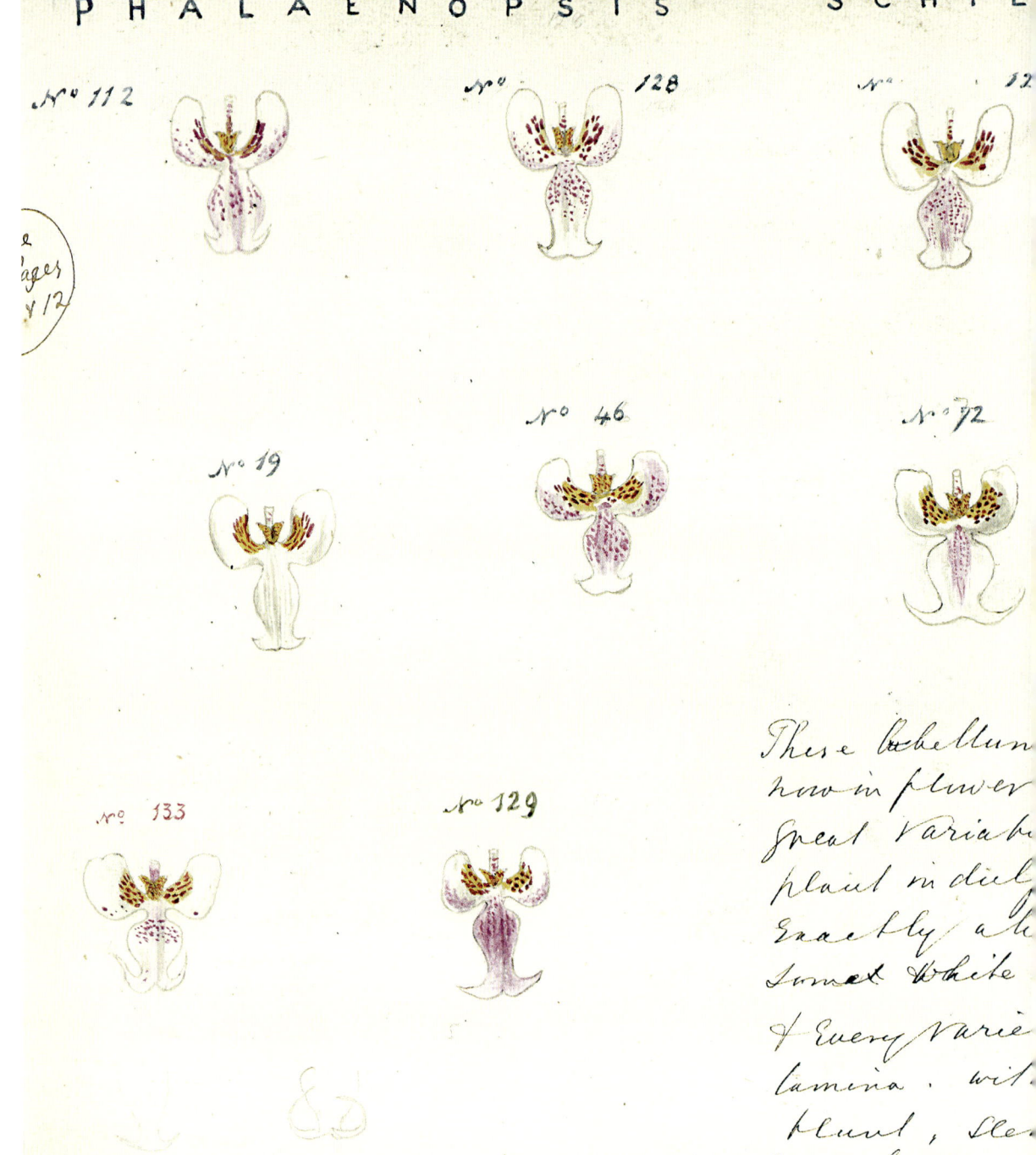

Above: John Day's illustration of the variation found in the floral lip of plants of the Philippine *Phalaenopsis schilleriana*, grown by him at Tottenham and drawn in 1877.

March 22nd 1877

Nº 125

Nº 118

...lected from a quantity
Serve to illustrate the
...of form in which this lovely
hardly any two are
Some are dark & some spotted
...narrow some broad —
...shape, particularly of the
...bifid apex. straight, curved
..., clumsy or almost abortive
...without exhausting them all.

flowers in late summer and autumn rather than in the spring. It was described in 1882 by Reichenbach, who named it for Frederick Sander, the eminent orchid nurseryman, who introduced it into cultivation with his own special flourish, calling it "the red Phalaenopsis". His collector, Carl Roebelen, observed it on Mindanao in the Philippines, and collected 21,000 plants for shipment back to England. Unfortunately, a hurricane struck the Philippines on 28 June and swept all the plants away. Sander's only comment by telegram was "Return. Recollect", which Roebelen duly did, although the second consignment was considerably smaller. On 30 October 1883, John Day first illustrated a plant he saw at the nursery of Low & Co., who had received a small consignment from William Boxall in the Philippines shortly after Roebelen's consignment had arrived.

Deep purple has been introduced into hybrid moth orchids from the Malayan species *P. violacea* and *P. bellina* from the western Malay Archipelago, and spots and coloured stripes have been introduced from the Philippine species such as *P. lueddemanniana* and its allies. The latter have very fleshy and long-lasting flowers, but they are usually borne on short stalks.

Following their success with the artificial hybridization of other orchids, Veitch's nursery on the King's Road, Chelsea, turned its attention to *Phalaenopsis*. John Seden, their talented grower, crossed *P. amabilis* (as *P. grandiflora*) with *P. violacea* in 1881, sowed the seed in January 1882 and flowered the result in May 1887. John Day painted this orchid on 21 May at Veitch's nursery in Chelsea.

White moth orchid   *Phalaenopsis amabilis*   **189**

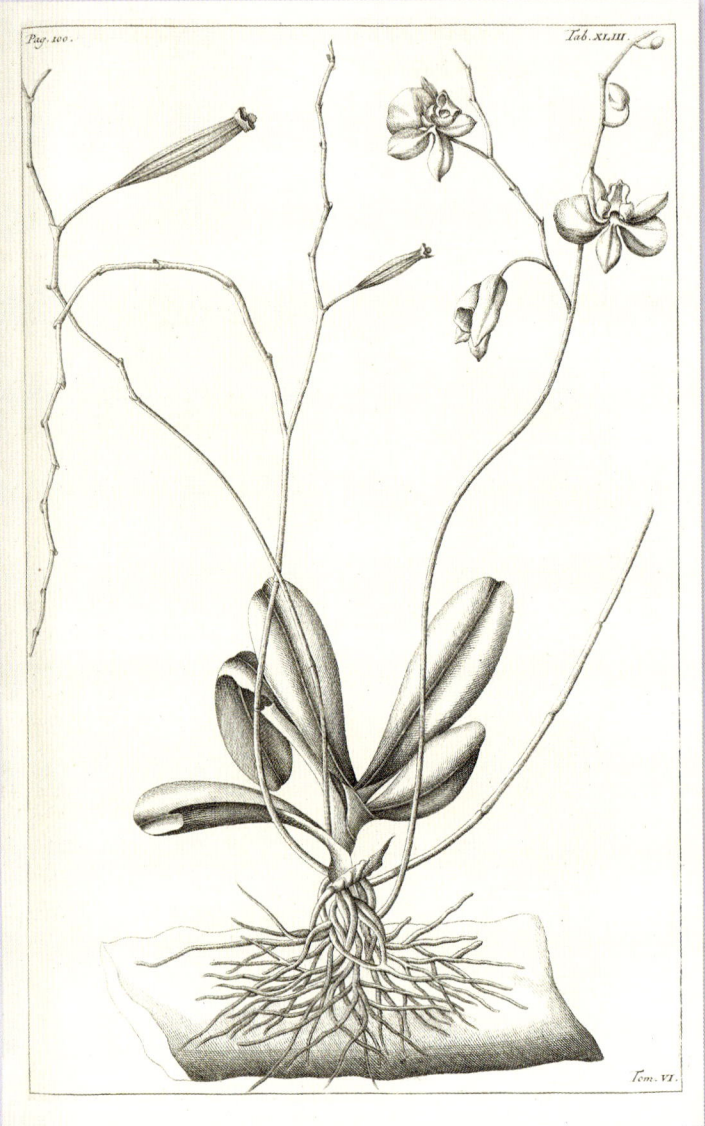

Pag. 100.

Tab. XLIII.

Tom. VI.

Angraecum album duplex described in *Herbarium Amboinense* by Rumphius, 1741

The original description and illustration of *Phalaenopsis amabilis* (under the pre-Linnaean name *Angraecum album duplex*) was published by Georg Everard Rumphius from his posthumously published *Herbarium Amboinense* (1741).

Rumphius's life saw many tragedies. In Ambon, his wife and daughter perished in an earthquake, his library, collections and manuscripts were destroyed in a fire, and the first copy of his *Herbarium Amboinense* was lost in a shipwreck on its way back to the Netherlands, where he was employed by the Dutch East India Company. Following this, he lost his sight to glaucoma while working on his *magnum opus*. In consequence, he is known to posterity as "the blind seer of Ambon".

CAPUT SECUNDUM.

Angræcum album duplex. Angrec pœti.

Secunda & tertia Angræci species est alba major & minor, utræque a præcedenti quoad flores maxime differentes.

Primo. *Angræcum album majus*, convolvulacea fere planta est, primo enim multis & longis radicibus sese circumvolvit circa arborum truncos, tanquam chordulæ essent, quæ exterius sordide albent, interne virent & lento nervo gaudent, sub planta intricatam formantes congeriem, quæ aliquando laxe dependet, & tam incompta est quam in ulla planta, folia fasciculata tria quatuorve simul proveniunt sine bursis, excepto quod inferior caulis parum ventricosus sit & striatus.

Exterius seu maximum folium duodecim ac sexdecim pollices longum est, tres quatuorve digitos latum, crassum, ac firmum, ac fere nervis destitutum, excepto quod in medio sulcatum sit, superius rotunde desinens, sique adcurate adtendatur, superior apex semper bifidus est, cujus unus angulus longior est, qui character est cunctorum Angræcorum, sed in prima specie non adeo notabilis quam in cunctis subsequentibus, ubi clarior est. Ex intricata radicum congerie juxta folia peculiaris excrescit caulis, obscure fuscis lineis notatus, crassitie pennæ, rotundus, lignosus, ac foliis destitutus, superius in quosdam laterales ramulos sese dividens, qui in amplos articulos distincti sunt, & in quorum summa parte flores progerminant, multo rariores numero, & majores quam in prima specie, peculiarem quoque habent formam, quæ difficilis descriptu & difficilior delineatu est, ac vicissim supra sese invicem locantur, quivis peculiari alba basi.

Compositus autem hic flos est ex quinque exterioribus petalis, flaccidis, & penitus albis, quorum bina lateralia maxima sunt, intra hæc altera conspicitur congeries trium minorum petalorum itidem alborum, formam habentes cochleæ seu calceoli, bina enim inferiora convoluta sunt in circulo.

Supremum petalum paulo magis sese elevat, & ad oras binas longas gerit barbas instar mystacum inflexas. In centro hujus circuli alterum crassum adparet petalum, quod pistillum est bisidum, ex luteo & purpureo colore distinctum, sic quoque circulus iste non directe in centro locatur floris, sed ad unam inclinat partem, in ipso autem floris centro album locatur germen, ex quo circulus oritur, in illo bina flava inveniuntur grana semen mentiëntia.

Lutea ista granula per album istud germen transparent & binos referunt oculos, ac caput repræsentant, Cicadæ, flos porro inodorus est.

Fructus est ex rotundo striata siliqua, ultra tres pollices longa, ac digitum crassa, sex protuberantibus costis donata, in quibusdam vero plantis hi fructus magis trigoni sunt quam hexagoni, & in tres quoque dehiscunt partes, quarum quævis pollicem lata est, prope apicem connexa. Interna farina pallide flava est, & decidit, sed filamentis lateralibus adhærent granula quædam alba, quæ si comprimantur, lympham emittunt. Octobri ac subsequentibus conspiciuntur mensibus.

Hæc species varietatem quandam habet, cujus flos eandem quidem habet formam, interne albus, sed externe ex læte purpureo colore splendens. Altera etiam ejus est varietas, cujus flos quinque expansa gerit petala, quorum bina lateralia latissima sunt, alba penitus, excepto quod internum germen sit luteum.

Nomen. Latine *Angræcum album majus*; Malaice *Angrec pœti besaar*, & Bombo terbang; Belgice *Vliegende Duive*; Baleyice *Angrec colan*, h. e. *Mas*, quum præcedens femina habetur, Amboinensibus nullum huc usque obtinuit nomen, sed in Lœhœa vocatur *Wanlecu*.

Locus. In crassis itidem sed curtis crescit arboribus, quæ musco obductæ sunt, uti in Kinar & Mangis, quas tanquam funis adscendit, & e quibus intricate dependit. Nullus ejus huc usque innotuit usus.

Secundo. *Angræcum album minus* caules quoque gerit quatuor & quinque pedes longos, quorum multi ex una oriuntur radice, quæ muscosa est, & tanquam emplastrum vetustis incumbit arboribus, multisque fibrillis circa eas nectitur.   Cau-

---

TWEEDE HOOFDSTUK.

Het dubbelvoudige witte Angrek.

DE tweede en derde zoorte van Angrec zyn de witte, bestaande in groot en klein, beide van 't voorgaande in bloemen merkelyk verschillende.

I. Angræcum album majus *is schier het zelfde gewas, want het slingert vooreerst met veele en lange wortelen, als chordelen rondom de stammen der bomen, buiten vuil-wit, binnen groen, met een taaje zenuwe, onder de planten een verwerden klomp makende, die zomtyds los hangt, en zoo wild als ik aan geen andere plante gezien heb, de bladeren komen ook drie in vier in bosjes by malkander, zonder beurzen, behalven den ondersten steel, die wat buikagtig, en gestreept is.*

Het buitenste of grootste blad is twaalf en sestien duimen lang, drie en vier vingeren breed, mede dik, en styf, schier zonder zenuwen, behalven in de midden gegeut, van vooren lopen ze rond toe, en als men 'er nauw op let, zoo is de voorste spits altyd in tweën gekloven, waar van de eene boek langer is, een kenteeken van alles Angreks. Aan de eerste zoorte zoo kennelyk niet, maar aan alle de volgende klaar te zien, uit den verwerden klomp der wortelen bezyden de bladeren komt ook een byzonderen steel op, met donkerbruine linien gespikkelt, in de dikte van een schaft, rond, boutagtig, en mede ongeblad, die zig boven in eenige zydetakken verdeelt, alle met wyde leden, aan wiens uiterste de bloemen voortkomen, veel weiniger in 't getal, en grooter dan aan de eerste zoorte, zy hebben ook een vreemd fatzoen, dat moeilyk te beschryven, en nog moeielyker af te teekenen is, zy staan egter met beurten boven malkander, ieder op een byzondere witte voet.

De bloem is gemaakt van vyf uitwendige bladeren, slap, en spier-wit, waar van de twee ter zyden de grootste zyn, binnen deze ziet men een andere vergadering van drie mede witte blaadjes, de gedaante van een Zeehoorn, of van een Schoenke eenigzints uitmakende, want de twee onderste zyn t'zamen gebogen in een cirkel.

Het bovenste blaadje verheft zig wat meer, en heeft aan zyn einden twee lange baarden, die gekruld staan als knevels. In de midden van deze cirkel ziet men een ander dik blaadje, als een pilaartje zig in twee hoofdekens verdelende, met geel en purper geschildert, zoo staat ook den cirkel niet regt in de midden van de bloem, maar helt na de eene zyde, regt in de midden van de bloem staat een wit heuvelke, waar uit den cirkel ontspringt, in 't zelve vindt men twee geele korrels, als of het zaad wilde zyn.

Deze geele korrels schynen door dat witte heuvelije als twee oogen, en verbeelden het hoofd van een Sprinkhaan, voorts is ze zonder reuk.

De vrugt is een uit den ronden gestreepte bouwen, ruim drie duimen lang, en een vinger dik, met ses uitsteekende ribben, dog aan zommige werden deze vrugten meer driekantig, dan seskantig, en splyten ook in drie deelen open, ieder een duim breed, by de spits aan malkanderen hangende. Het binnenste meel is bleek-geel, en valt daar uit, maar aan de zydedraden blyven eenige witte korrels hangen, en als men ze drukt, komt 'er water uit. Men vindt ze in October en de volgende maanden.

Deze zoorte heeft nog een verandering, daar de bloem wel van dezelve fatzoen is, binnen wit, maar buiten met een ligten purper schynende. Item nog een ander verandering, waar aan de bloem uit vyf uitgespreide blaadjes bestaat, waar van de twee aan de zyde zeer breed zyn, allegaar wit, behalven dat het binnenste heuveltje geel is.

Naam. *In 't Latyn* Angræcum album majus; *in 't Maleits* Angrec Poeti besaar; *en* Bombo terbang; *in 't Duits* vliegende Duive; *in 't Baleits* Angrec colan; *dat is het manneken; om dat ze het voor 't wyfken houden, by de Amboinesen heeft het nog geen naam, maar op Loehoe hiet het Wanlecu.*

Plaats. *Het wast mede op dikke dog korte bomen, en die mosagtig zyn, gelyk aan Kinar en Mangas-bomen, daar het als een zeel op loopt, en zeer verwert, geen gebruik hier van is tot nog toe bekent.*

II. Angræcum album minus *heeft ook steelen, vier en vyf voeten lang, waar van veele uit eene wortel staan, dewelke mosagtig is, en als een pleister tegens de oude bomen aanzit, en met veele vazelingen daarom slingert.*   Den

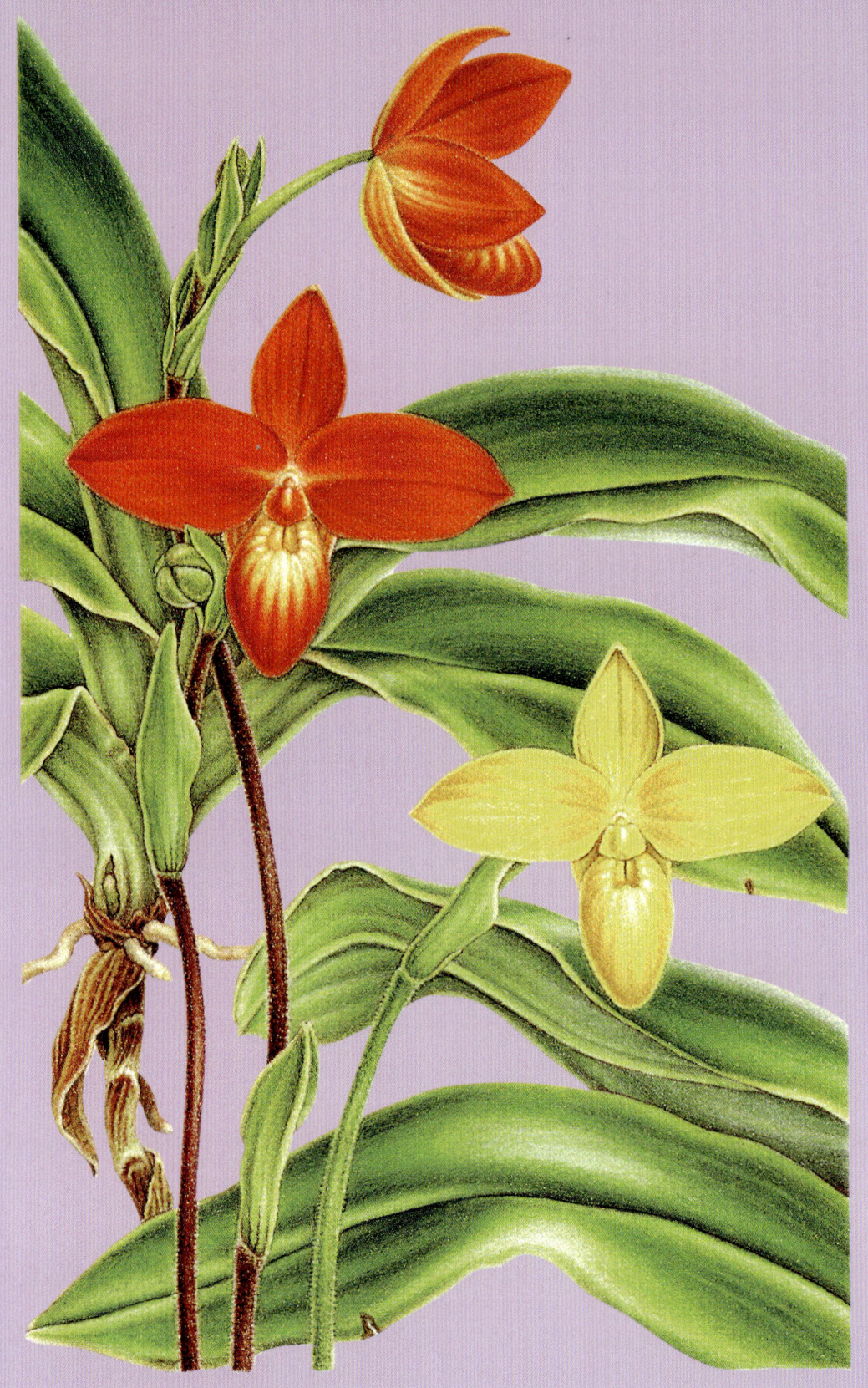

SCARLET SLIPPER ORCHID
PHRAGMIPEDIUM BESSEAE

Perhaps once in every decade an orchid new to science astounds the experts. *Phragmipedium besseae* certainly made a breathtaking impact when it was first shown at horticultural shows in the USA and Europe in the early 1980s. In a genus dominated by green, purple, brown or pale pink flowers, its brilliant pillar-box red blooms were surprisingly different.

Phragmipedium besseae was collected in northern Peru by J. Halton and Libbe Besse in 1979, and was named by Calaway Dodson and Lee Kuhn in Besse's honour in 1981 in *The Bulletin of the American Orchid Society*. This news surprised the orchid world, and when plants first flowered in cultivation they caused a sensation. Several clones received First Class Certificates and Awards of Merit from the American Orchid Society, the Royal Horticultural Society and others.

This orchid grows on steep cliffs in the deep valleys of the eastern flank of the Andes in northern Peru and southern Ecuador, where other red-flowered plants, such as begonias and fuchsias, are often found. Despite speculation

that its bright red flowers served to attract hummingbirds as pollinators, the small opening of the trap-like lip suggests that this orchid is pollinated by a small bee.

The sensation of *P. besseae* in the early 1980s started a passion for growing tropical American hard-leaved slipper orchid species and their hybrids which has continued unabated

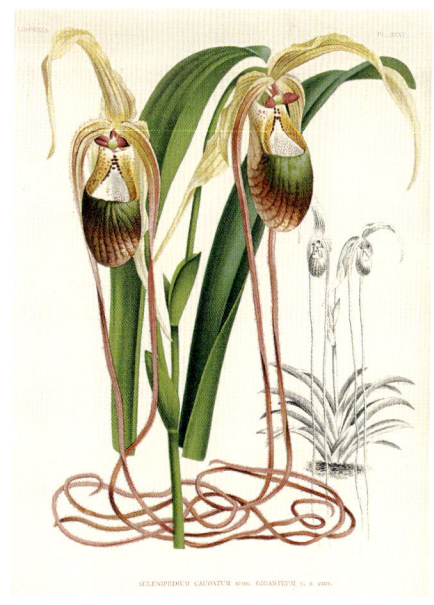

in orchid-growing circles. Its brilliant colour, relative ease of culture and propensity to hybridize freely with other *Phragmipedium* species ensured that it became the most significant species in the genus, particularly after Don Wimber, at the Eric Young Orchid Foundation in Jersey, used colchicine to double the chromosome number of its hybrid progeny to produce some spectacular red-flowered hybrids, the substantial flowers of which lasted for much longer than earlier diploid hybrids.

Despite massive over-collection in all of its known localities, several populations survive in Ecuador where, despite initial over-collection, they seem to have recovered well.

The similar species *P. dalessandroi*, sometimes considered to be a variety of *P. besseae*, was described by Calaway Dodson and Olof Gruss in 1996 based on a specimen collected by Dennis D'Alessandro at 900–1,300 m (3,000–4,260 ft) above sea level in the Cordillera del Condor on the upper Rio Bombuscaro in Zamora-Chinchipe Province in southern Ecuador. It has a more compact non-climbing habit, and a branching hairier inflorescence that bears many orange-red flowers with narrow, drooping petals and a rhombic staminode.

The tropical American slipper orchids have been known for over two centuries since Carlos III of Spain commissioned the Spanish botanists Hipolito Ruiz Lopez (1754–1816) and José Pavon Jimenez (1754–1840) to undertake the botanical exploration of Peru and Chile between 1777 and 1788. They collected and had illustrated two species, now known as *P. caudatum* and *P. boissierianum*, in Peru. Both paintings,

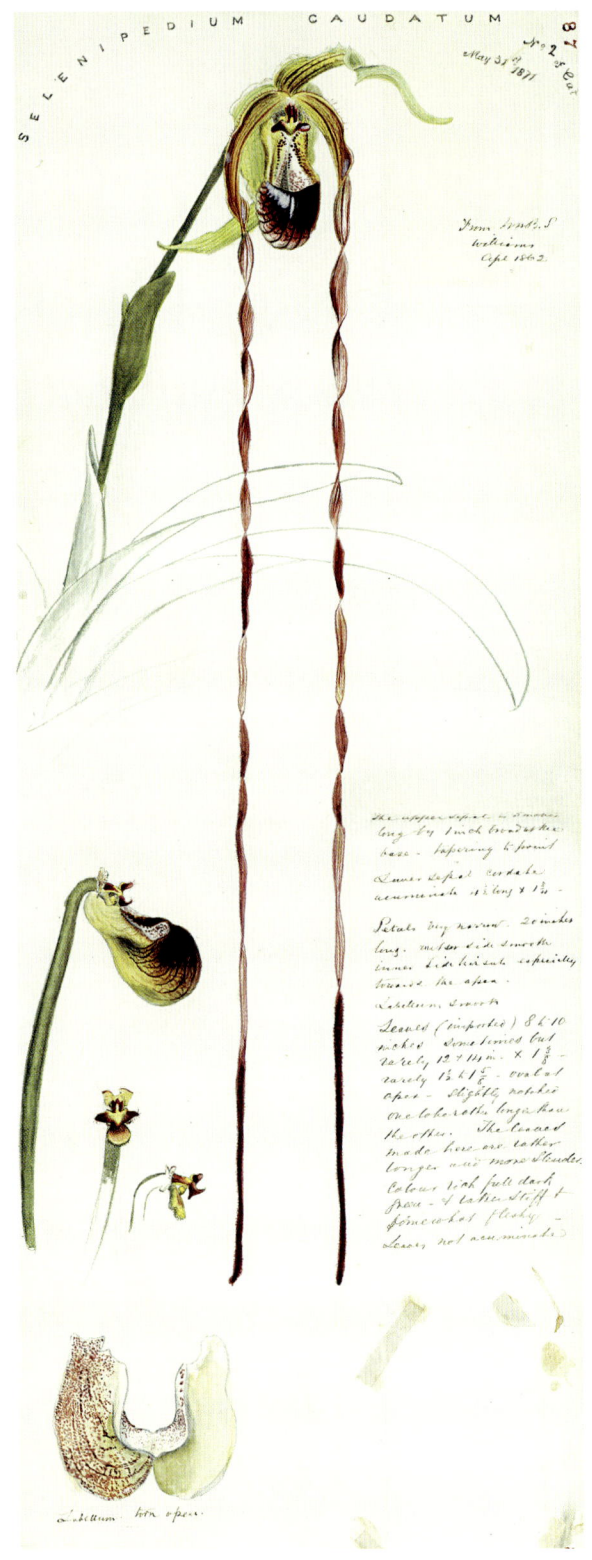

Opposite:
Phragmipedium humboldtii (as *Selenipedium caudatum*) drawn by John Day in 1871.

Right: The Colombian *Phragmipedium schlimii* (as *Selenipedium schlimii*) drawn by Walter Hood Fitch for *Curtis's Botanical Magazine* of 1866. Many of the early hybridizers used this species to produce white- and pink-flowered progeny.

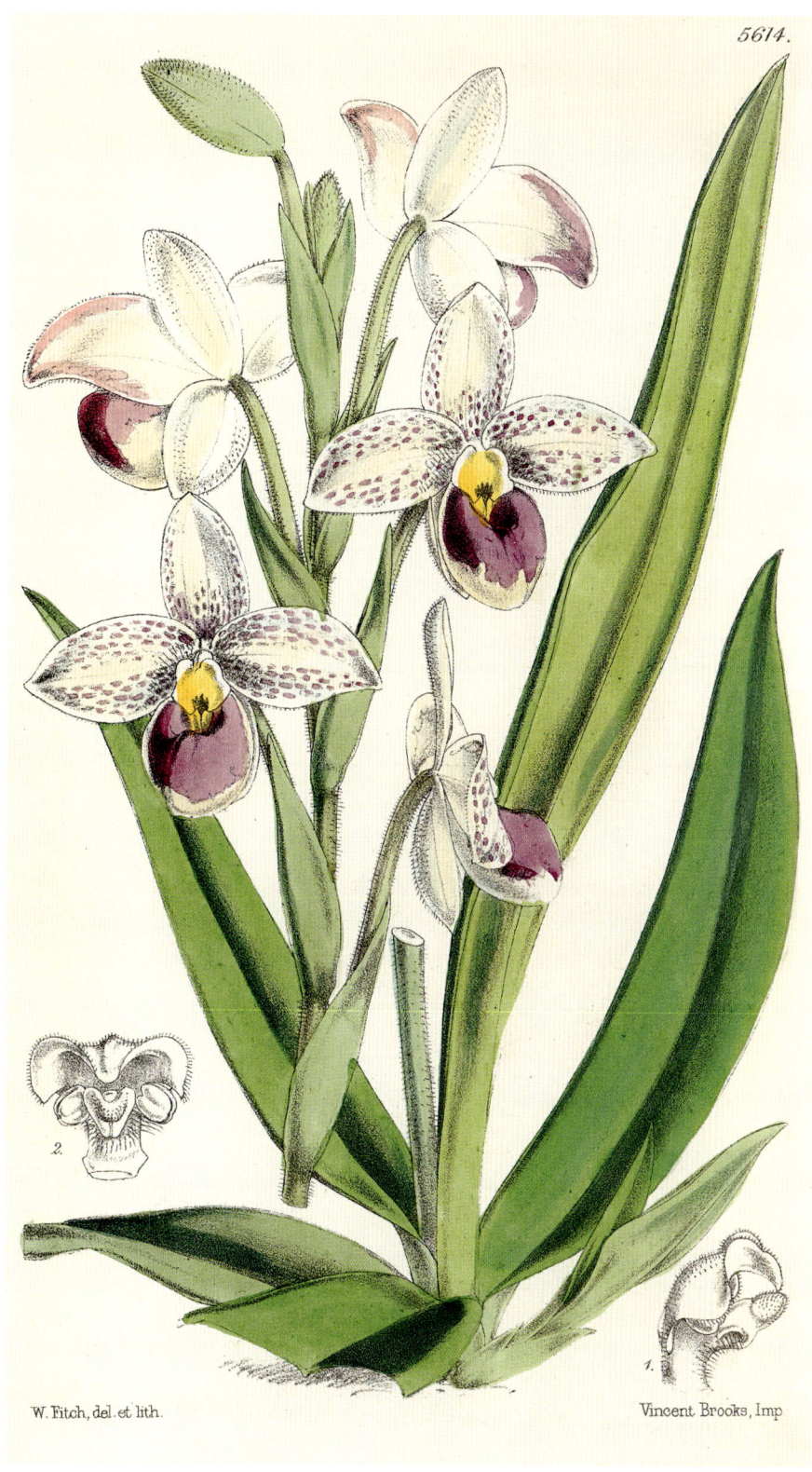

5614.

W. Fitch, del. et lith.

Vincent Brooks, Imp

Scarlet slipper orchid   *Phragmipedium besseae*   **195**

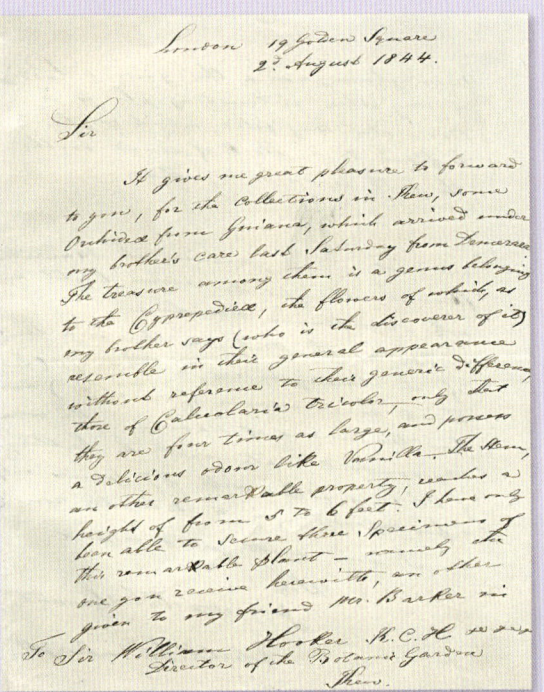

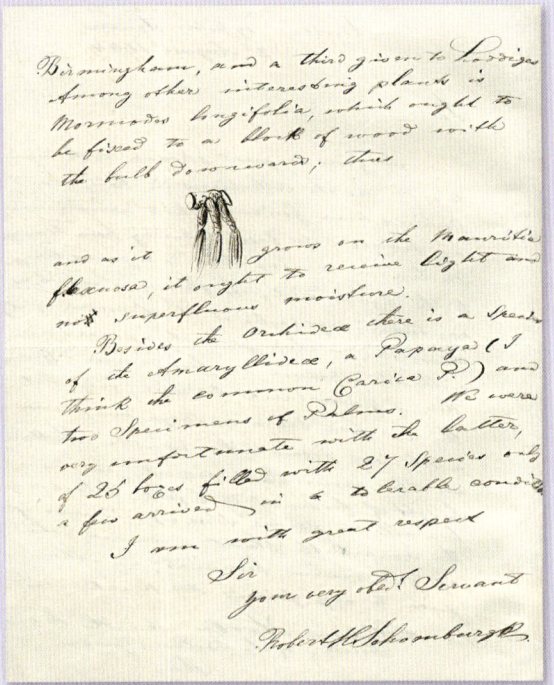

Letter from Robert Hermann Schomburgk to Sir William Jackson Hooker, from 19 Golden Square, London, 2 August 1844

Robert Schomburgk's letter of 2 August 1844 to Sir William Hooker at the Royal Botanic Gardens, Kew, reports sending to Kew a batch of Guyanan orchids collected there by his brother Moritz Richard, including the vanilla-scented *Selenipedium palmifolium*. Sir Robert (1804–1865) was a German-born explorer, botanist and geographer who led the Anglo-Prussian expeditions to British Guyana and Brazil in 1839 and 1841–44. On the

second expedition he mapped the border between British Guyana and Venezuela and Surinam. His discoveries included the waterlily *Victoria amazonica* and *Phragmipedium lindleyanum*.

His younger brother, Moritz (1811–1891), accompanied him on the second expedition. He emigrated to Australia in 1845 and, in 1865, he became Curator of the Adelaide Botanic Garden.

by the expedition's artists Brunete and Pulvar, are now deposited in the archives of the Jardín Botaníco de Madrid.

John Lindley described one from the Ruiz and Pavon collection, still in Lima, by Andrew Matthews (1801–1841) for Sir William Hooker as *Cypripedium caudatum*, but the second flower proved to be too badly preserved to be described. This species has remarkable hanging ribbon-like petals that can reach 1 m (3 ft) in length. At the same time he also described *Cypripedium lindleyanum* based on a specimen collected and named by Robert Schomburgk which had been collected by him on Mount Roraima in Guyana. Lindley commented at the time that "I unwillingly consent, at the particular instance of Mr Schomburgk, to allow this plant to bear my name, who [sic] have no title to the compliment". Schomburgk's original watercolour illustration is now held in Lindley's herbarium at the Royal Botanic Gardens, Kew.

In 1896, the Kew botanist Robert Rolfe was the first to recognize *Phragmipedium* as a genus distinct from the genera *Cypripedium* and *Selenipedium*, in which the slipper orchids had previously been placed, based upon its short stem, its fan of hard conduplicate leaves and its trilocular ovary.

Until *P. besseae* was described, *P. schlimii* was the most distinctive *Phragmipedium* species. It is a small plant with a very short stem and leaves and small pink flowers. It was observed by Louis Schlim while he was collecting for Jean Linden near Ocaña in Colombia. This was the first species to be described which did not have greenish, yellowish or brown flowers, and it became significant as a parent in early *Phragmipedium* breeding

in the late Victorian period, introducing pink and white into the early hybrids.

The scientific discovery in northern Peru in 2001 of *P. kovachii*, another Peruvian species with magnificent imperial purple flowers of a size never before seen in tropical hard-leaved slipper orchids, has created further interest in the genus. Its introduction to the USA gained immense publicity in the press and the media because it was smuggled in and so arrived lacking any official documentation. The resulting court case led to the conviction of the smuggler. Fortunately, this orchid is easy to grow, and the Peruvian government has licensed a few nurseries to propagate it and to sell seedlings.

Below:
Phragmipedium boissierianum (as *Selenipedium boissierianum*) drawn by Heinrich Gustav Reichenbach for the first volume of his *Xenia Orchidacea* in 1850. This species was named for Edmond Boissier, the eminent Swiss botanist whose herbarium now resides in Geneva.

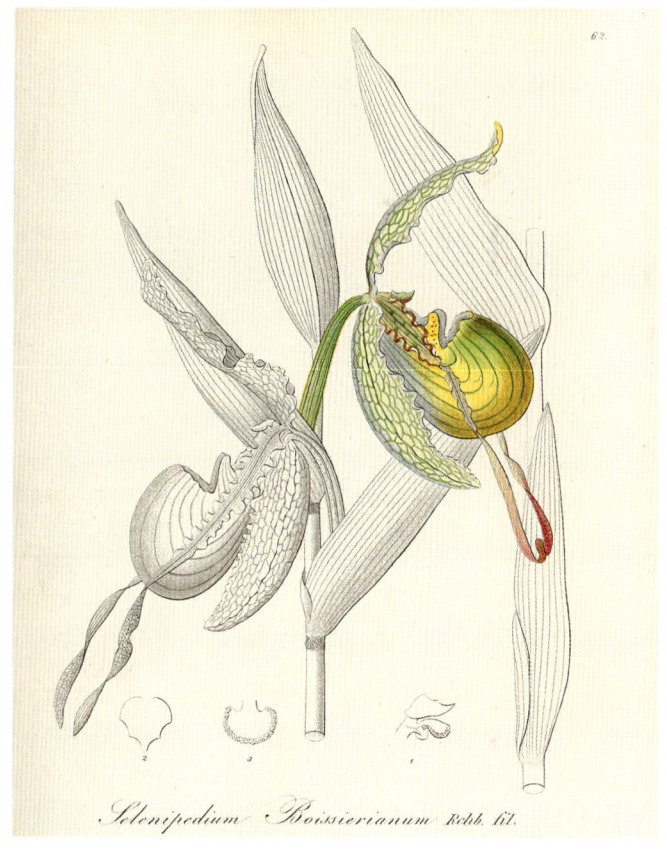

Selenipedium Boissierianum Rchb. fil.

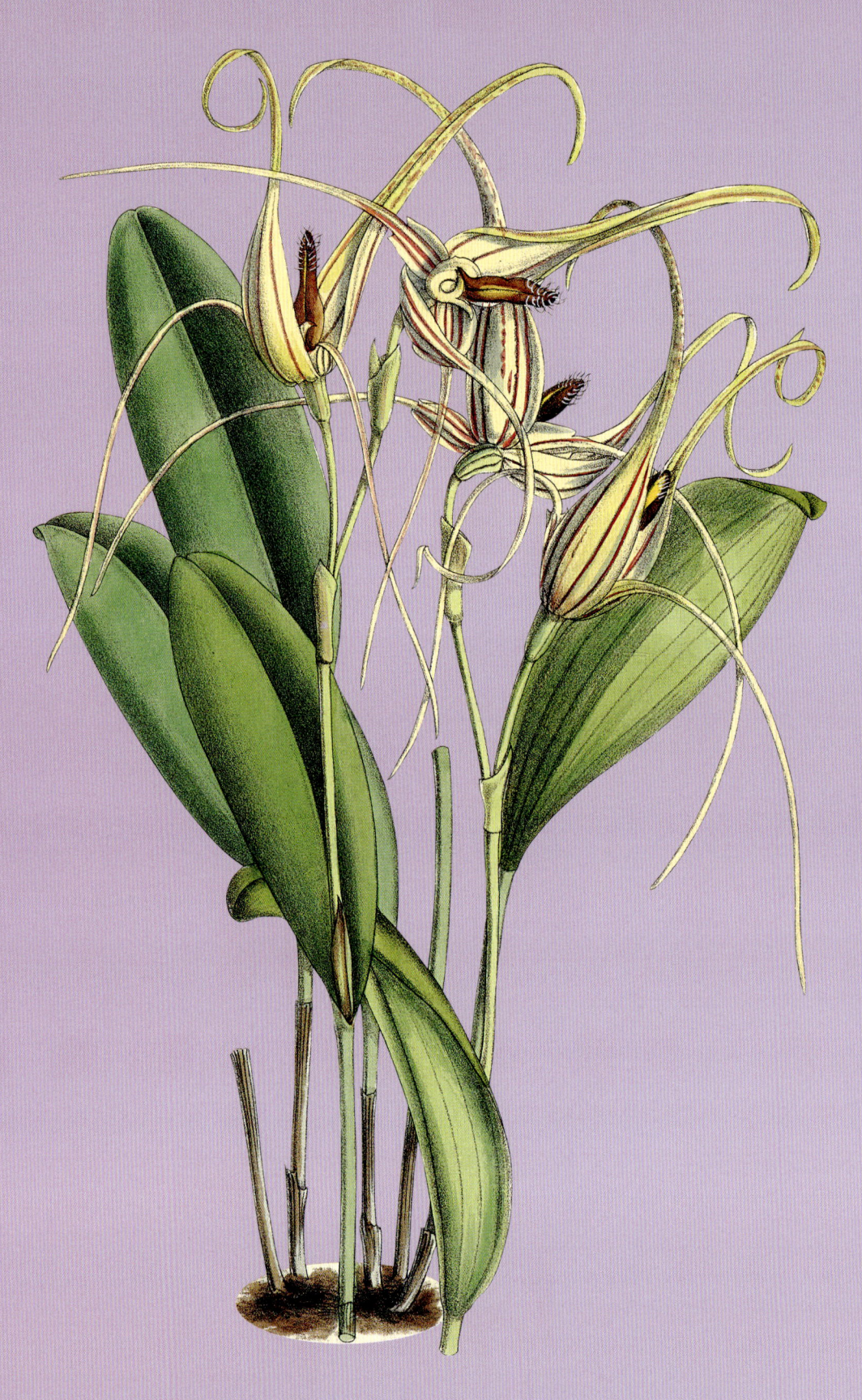

TONGUE-LIKE BEARDED PLEUROTHALLIS
PLEUROTHALLIS GLOSSOPOGON

The New World genus *Pleurothallis*, found from Mexico through Central America, the Caribbean and tropical South America, is a large genus containing at least 500 species. Previously it was considered to contain over 1,000 species, before it was carved up into a range of smaller genera based on DNA evidence, including *Restrepia* and *Stelis*. All are members of the enormous South American subtribe Pleurothallidinae, which also includes the genera *Masdevallia*, *Lepanthes* and *Zootrophion*, generally with good diagnostic characters distinguishing each.

The Greek word *pleurothallos*, meaning "rib-like branches", gives the genus its name and refers to the straight stems of many *Pleurothallis* species. Usually but not always rupicolous, referring to the tendency of these plants to form small clumps on rocks or mossy branches, the genus is vegetatively extremely variable, and species that occur in drier habitats may have almost succulent leaves.

Some *Pleurothallis* species, along with several other genera in the subtribe, have interestingly presented tiny single flowers which rest, or almost rest, on the surface of a single heart-shaped leaf. The flowers are pollinated by small *Diptera* flies. Flies are common pollinators at the higher altitudes where *Pleurothallis* species grow, where birds and insects such as butterflies and moths that require warmer climates are not found. The small but relatively open "mouths" of *Pleurothallis* flowers, which lack spurs, have evolved to allow small flies to enter and pollinate them.

The genus *Pleurothallis* was originally described and published by Robert Brown in William Aiton's *Hortus Kewensis*, the catalogue of the plants cultivated in the Royal Botanic Gardens, Kew, in 1813. The specific epithet of the first species described in that same publication, *Pleurothallis ruscifolia*, was chosen for its similarity to *Ruscus aculeatus*, "butcher's broom", with its distinctive flowers borne on flattened stems, known as cladodes, which resemble leaves.

Pleurothallis glosspogon is known as the "tongue-like bearded Pleurothallis" for its short, fat and strangely hairy labellum. Found growing at over 2,000 m (7,000 ft) above sea level in

Right: *Zootrophion dayanum* (as *Cryptophoranthus dayanus*) by John Nugent Fitch, in *Curtis's Botanical Magazine*, 1917.

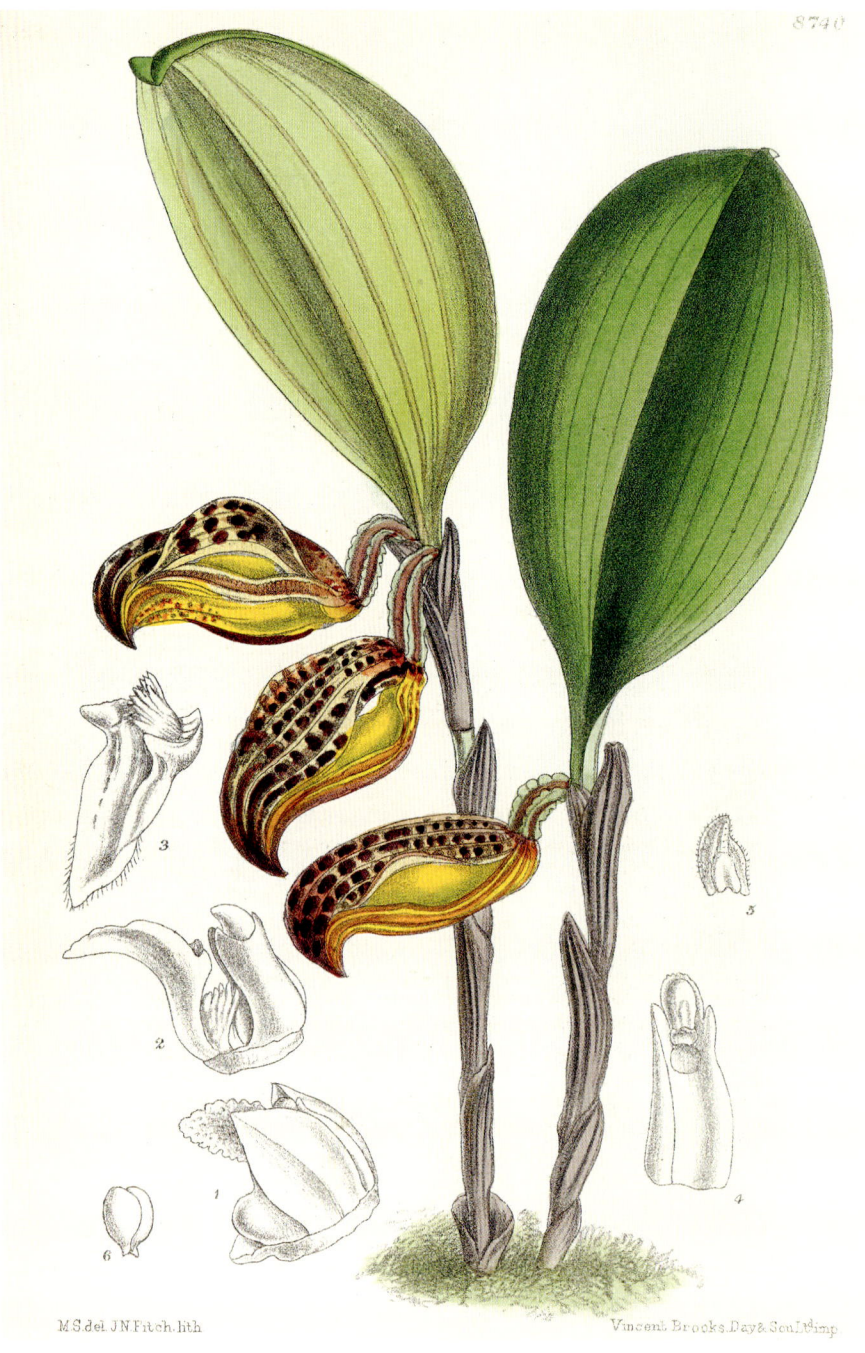

8740

M.S.del. J.N.Fitch. lith.

Vincent Brooks.Day&Son.Ltd.imp.

the Andes of Venezuela and Columbia, and the species was briefly moved into a new genus *Humboltia*, named after the explorer and naturalist Alexander von Humboldt. The name *Humboldtia* had been used by another botanist for a group of legume trees, and it was decided the two genus names were too similar, so the name *Humboltia* for the orchid genus could not be allowed.

Herbarium sheet from the Royal Botanic Gardens, Kew, showing *Pleurothallis bivalvis*

John Lindley published the newly collected species *Pleurothallis bivalvis* in 1846, basing his description on material collected in Venezuela by the young Jean Linden and commenting on its yellow flowers striped with red, as noted by Linden in the field and seen in his collection label on the specimen, written in French.

Born in Luxembourg, Linden was just 26 when he collected this specimen on his extensive travels in South America. Between 1835 and 1844, Linden collected plants, and especially orchids, in Brazil, Cuba, Mexico, the USA, Venezuela, Colombia and Jamaica. Importantly, Linden recorded extensive notes and observations on the growing conditions of plants in the wild, which were hugely important in changing the way in which tropical orchids were grown in cultivation in Europe. On his permanent return to Europe and over his subsequent career, Linden published a number of important, and beautifully illustrated volumes including *Pescatorea* and *Lindenia*.

The company he set up, L'Horticole Coloniale, introduced many exotic novelties into horticulture in Europe, including *Coffea robusta* and *Gunnera manicata*, and he ultimately rose to the rank of consul-general of Luxembourg.

The dried pressed plant Linden sent to Lindley is the "type specimen" for the species, held in the Herbarium at the Royal Botanic Gardens, Kew, and the sheet bears an illustration of the flower drawn by Lindley himself.

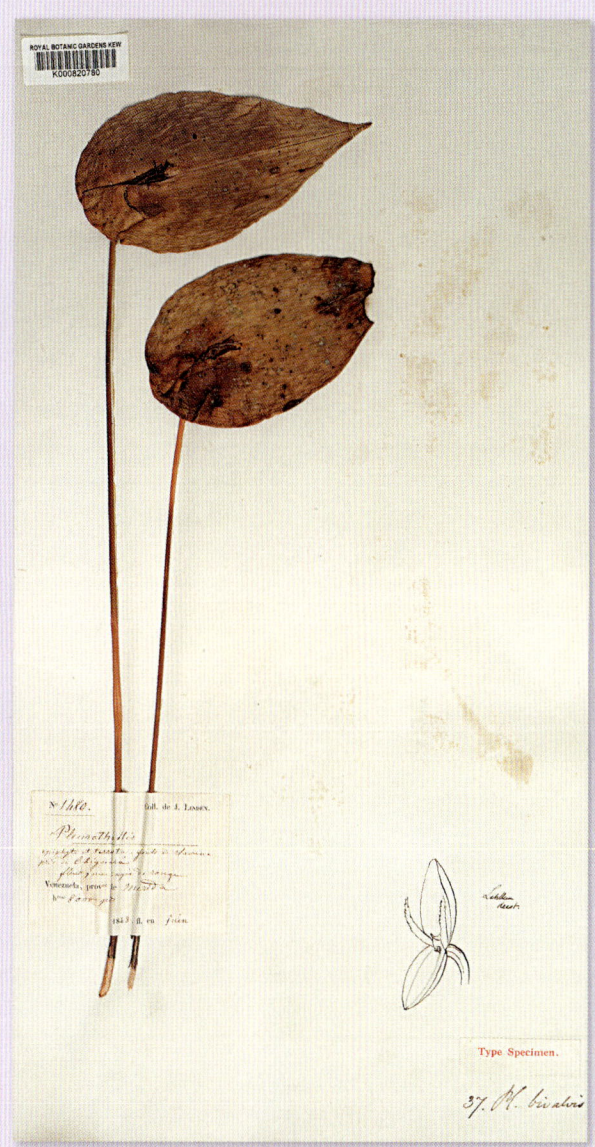

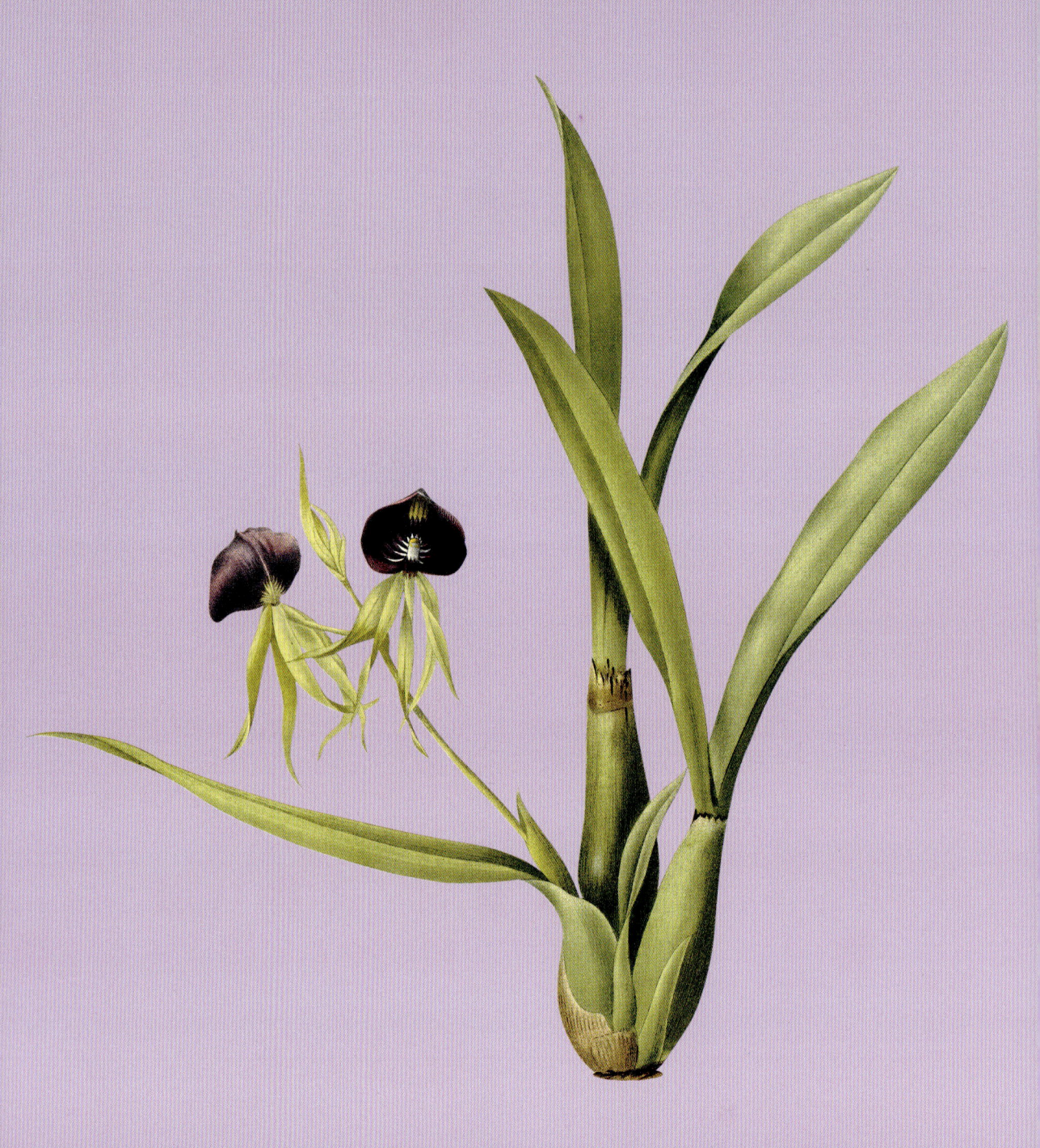

COCKLESHELL ORCHID, CLAMSHELL ORCHID OR OCTOPUS ORCHID
PROSTHECHEA COCHLEATA

Opposite:
Prosthechea cochleata
(as *Epidendrum
cochleatum*) by Pierre-
Joseph Redouté, in
Les Liliacées, 1812.

Right: *Prosthechea
cochleata* (as
*Epidendrum
lancifolium*) by Sarah
Drake, in *Edwards'
Botanical Register*,
1842.

Most orchids are technically upside down. Resupination is the scientific term for the rotation of the flower bud as it develops, so that the labellum (the modified petal that often plays a key role in the pollination of orchid flowers) is at the bottom of the flower when it opens. If you look closely at the stalk at the back of most orchid flowers (which is actually the ovary and develops into the seed pod if the orchid is successfully fertilized), you can often see twisted striations which show how the flower has re-orientated itself as it has developed. Orchids that do not rotate their flowers in this way are described as non-resupinate, and the labellum is held at the top of the flower – as in the orchid *Prosthechea cochleata*. An interesting exception is seen in some orchids that produce arching inflorescences, in which flowers near the plant initially face one way up but become resupinate, twisting to make sure that the labellum on each flower is orientated at the bottom of the flower, while those further towards the end of

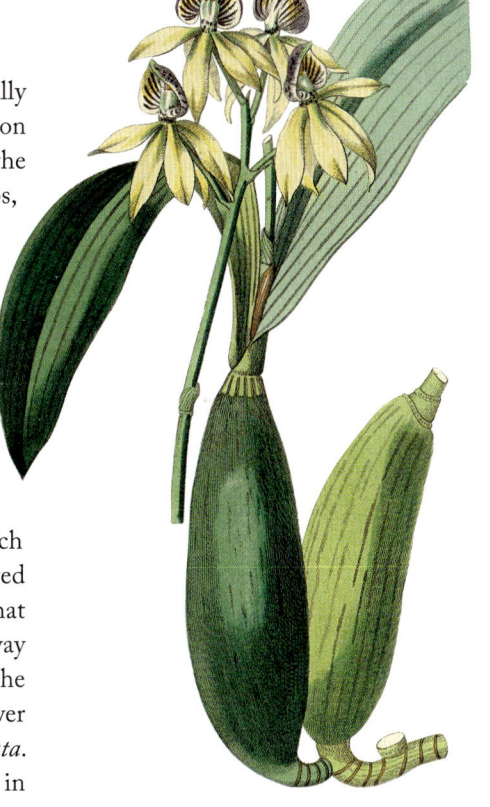

the flowering structure remain non-resupinate and do not twist, as they are already angled with the labellum at the bottom of the flower.

The long-lasting bloom of *Prosthechea cochleata*, the national flower of Belize,

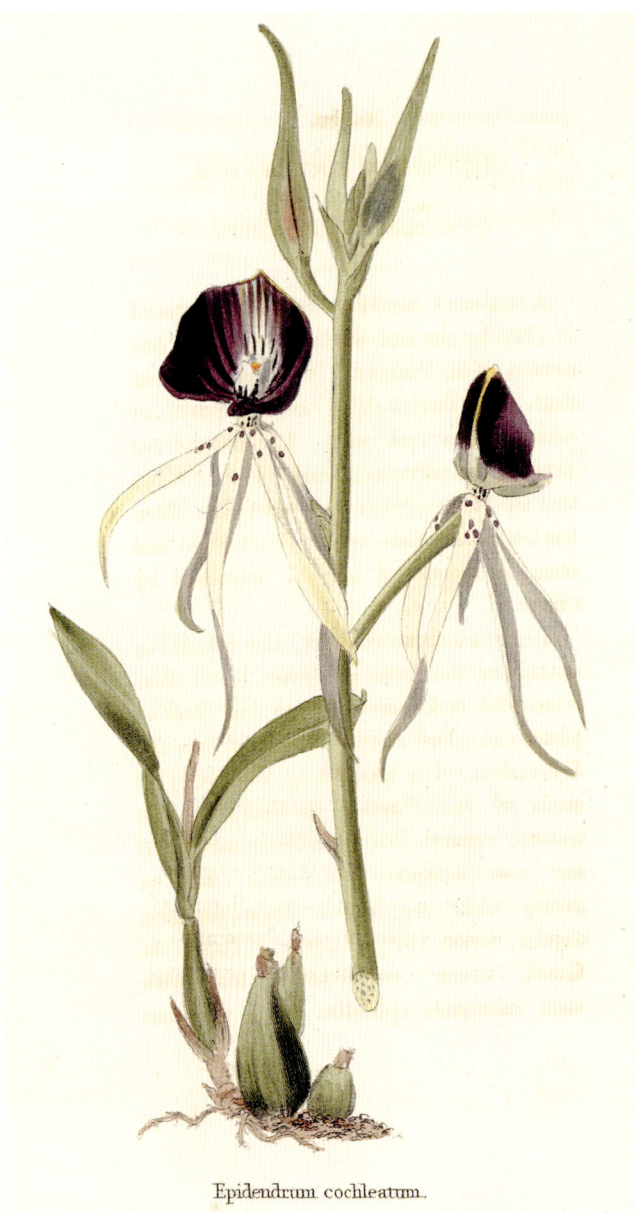

Epidendrum cochleatum.

the five long thin light-green tepals that dangle below, giving the orchid one of its other common names, the "octopus orchid" – albeit an octopus with only five legs.

The genus *Prosthechea* is distributed from South Florida, through the Caribbean, to Mexico and tropical Central and South America. The individuals found in the wild in Florida are distinctive and have been separated as a discrete variety, *Prosthechea cochleata* var. *triandra*, on the basis of having three anthers (rather than the usual one) within the central fertile organ of the typical orchid flower, the column. This adaptation is thought to have arisen naturally as a mutation, with all Floridian individuals being ancestors of that original mutant. The mutation enables the flowers to fertilize themselves, ensuring that in the absence of pollinators (as in Florida) the plant is able to reproduce and survive.

In 1787, *Prosthechea cochleata* was the first tropical orchid to be successfully flowered at the Royal Botanic Gardens, Kew. Many other orchids had been sent to Europe by collectors from around the world, but until then managing to keep them alive, let alone persuading the plants to flower, had eluded nearly all of the horticulturalists who had attempted this. Over the next 100 years, great stove-heated hothouses were built by wealthy patrons, and with the abolition of the tax on glass and the falling price of iron with increased industrialization, enormous glasshouses could now be built to try to replicate the steamy climates to which many (but not all) of the exotic new orchids being sent to Europe from tropical America, Africa and Asia were accustomed.

Above: *Prosthechea cochleata* (as *Epidendrum cochleatum*) by George Loddiges, in C. Loddiges, *The Botanical Cabinet*, 1827.

is very distinctive and an example of a non-resupinate orchid. Instead of acting as a potential landing platform for pollinators, the dark purple labellum forms a hood-like structure at the top of the flower – the "clamshell" of one of the orchid's common names. The labellum contrasts strongly with

Letter from C. H. Williams to Sir Joseph Dalton Hooker, from Bahia, Brazil, 10 May 1865

During the nineteenth century, the Royal Botanic Gardens, Kew was at the centre of a network of plants being collected, sent to England for naming and cultivation and distributed around the world for the further sharing of knowledge and often for their economic use. The first two directors of Kew, William Jackson Hooker and then his son, Joseph Dalton Hooker, were at the heart of this botanical hub, and their correspondence comprises thousands of letters (now carefully archived) which were criss-crossing the globe, at the same time as the plants they were describing.

In this letter, Williams, thought to have been a former ambassador to Bahia, in Brazil, describes the contents of two Wardian cases of plants he is sending to Kew, one of which is filled with orchids that he himself has just received – but which have not yet flowered with him. Among several other species in the consignment is *Epidendrum cochleatum* (now known as *Prosthechea cochleata*) which "flowers very freely and is sweet scented". Williams describes looking forward to receiving names for any of the unidentified plants from Hooker, along with the plants Hooker has already told him he is sending out to Williams.

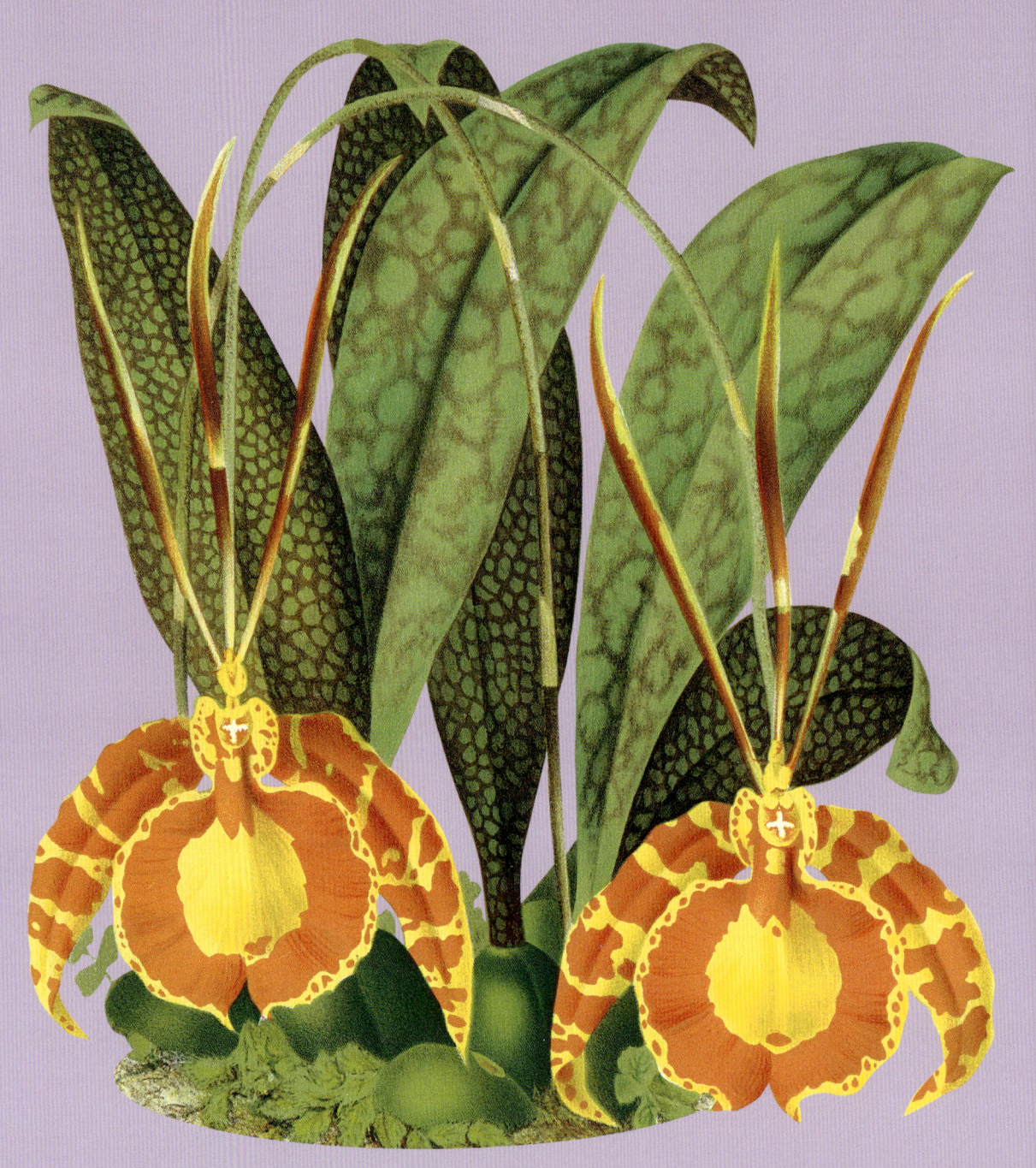

TROPICAL AMERICAN BUTTERFLY ORCHID
PSYCHOPSIS PAPILIO

At the time when this unusual orchid was described, the genus *Oncidium* included a diversity of orchids, many of which are now considered to belong to other genera, *Psychopsis* being one of them. It is one of the many genera established by the enigmatic and eccentric American botanist Constantine Samuel Rafinesque (1783–1840) in *Flora Telluriana* (1836), and one of the few to survive the studies of later botanists. The name refers to the butterfly-like flowers, *psyche* being the Ancient Greek word for "butterfly".

The genus *Psychopsis* was split from the large genus *Oncidium* by Rafinesque in 1836, but was not taken up until 1982, when the German botanists Emil Lückel and Guido Braem resurrected it. The genus, which comprises five closely allied and spectacular species, is readily recognized by its small pseudobulbs that carry a single leaf, often with red mottling on its upper surface, and its large flowers with linear-spathulate sepals and petals, and a large flat lip with a small callus at the base. The column usually has wings on either side of the stigma. The best-known species in the *Oncidium* genus are *O. kramerianum* and *O. papilio*, both of which are widely grown in orchid collections for their magnificent and unusual yellow and red-brown flowers.

The genus is found in Central and northern South America, including Trinidad. Plants grow in tall trees from sea level up to about 800 m (2,620 ft). *Psychopsis papilio* is found in Venezuela, Trinidad, the Guyanas, northern Brazil and Peru. John Day drew it three times in his scrapbooks, first in black and white on 4 December 1863, and then again twice in colour. These later drawings were made on 19 November 1868 and 23 July 1869, both of plants collected in Venezuela by Tucker for the nursery of Low & Co., and imported in July 1867.

Psychopsis krameriana is also common in cultivation, and differs in having slightly larger flowers with more heavily spotted lateral sepals and a lip with a heavily red-brown spotted margin. It is pollinated by butterflies of the genus *Heliconius*. These butterflies are territorial, patrol up and down an area, and are attracted to the flowers that flutter in the breeze and somewhat resemble the female butterflies.

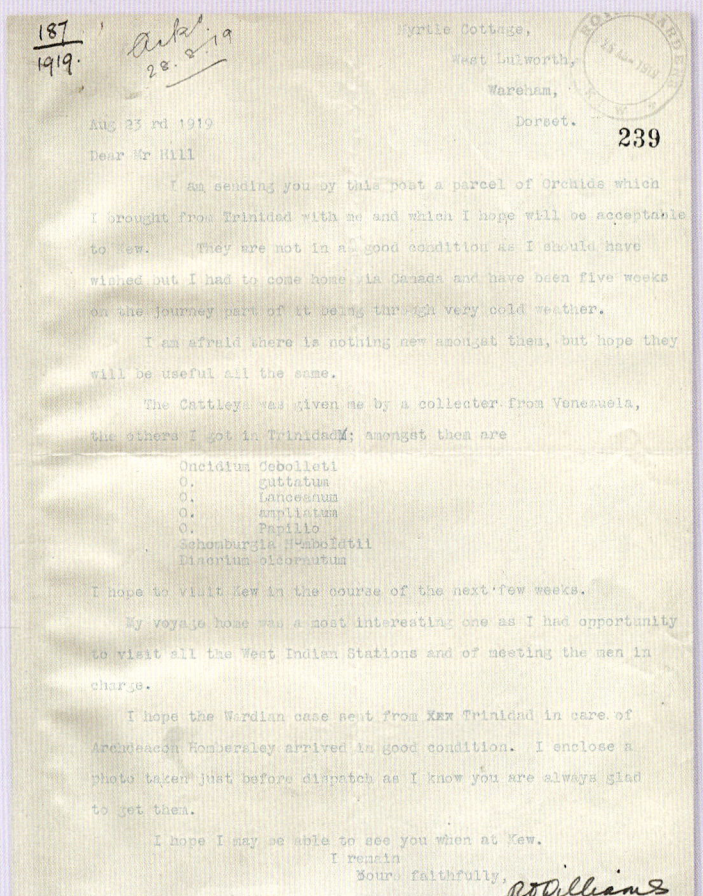

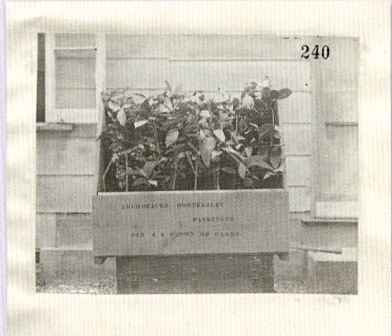

Letter and photograph from Robert O. Williams to Sir Arthur William Hill, from West Lulworth, Dorset, 23 August 1919

Mr R. Williams of Wareham, Dorset, sent to Sir Arthur Hill, Director of the Royal Botanic Gardens, Kew, a box of Trinidadian orchids that included several *Oncidium* species, including what is now *Psychopsis papilio*.

Such donations, small and larger, have ensured that Kew's remarkable orchid collection, dating back to the 1770s, has continued to grow until the present day, despite setbacks. The worst of these were during the First and Second World Wars when Kew lost many of its best gardeners and heating glasshouses was an ill-afforded luxury. A famous incident was the suffragettes' destruction of panes in the T-range orchid house before the First World War, when several dozen orchids were destroyed. Fortunately, the public's generosity and the fieldwork of Kew's staff and collaborators continues to enrich the collections.

Below: *Psychopsis papilio* (as *Oncidium papilio*) sent from Venezuela to Low & Co. and flowered by Sigismund Rucker of Wandsworth in 1868 when John Day illustrated its flower.

The male butterflies attack the flower and pick up the pollen masses on their heads.

John Day drew *Psychopsis kramerianum*, originally described as *Oncidium kramerianum* by H. G. Reichenbach in 1855 in Otto and Dietrich's *Allgemeine Gartenzeitung*, on 14 March 1868. Its flowers can reach 10 cm (4 in) or more in length. John Day's plant was a freshly imported specimen purchased at one of Stevens's sales. He exhibited it at the Horticultural Society on 17 March and it was awarded a First Class Certificate, the Society's premier award.

A number of other orchids with large and showy yellow flowers, variously marked with red or red-brown, have been distinguished in the *Oncidium* alliance. Probably the most spectacular of these belong to the small genus *Rossioglossum*. *Rossioglossum grande* lives up to its name,

having enormous flat flowers. It is native to southern Mexico and Central America, was introduced by George Ure Skinner from Guatemala in the 1830s, and was originally described in 1840 by John Lindley as *Odontoglossum grande*. It is one of the many spectacular species that were painted for James Bateman's colossal volume, *The Orchidaceae of Mexico and Guatemala* (1837–42), which did so much to popularize the cultivation of tropical orchids in Europe. In Mexico it is called "boca del tigre" (meaning "tiger's mouth") or the "clown orchid". It used to be common in the forests of *Pinus chiapensis*, *Carpinus caroliniana*, *Cojoba matudae* and laurels on the Tacana Volcano in Chiapas, but is now greatly endangered because it has been over-collected for many decades, and may even be extinct there.

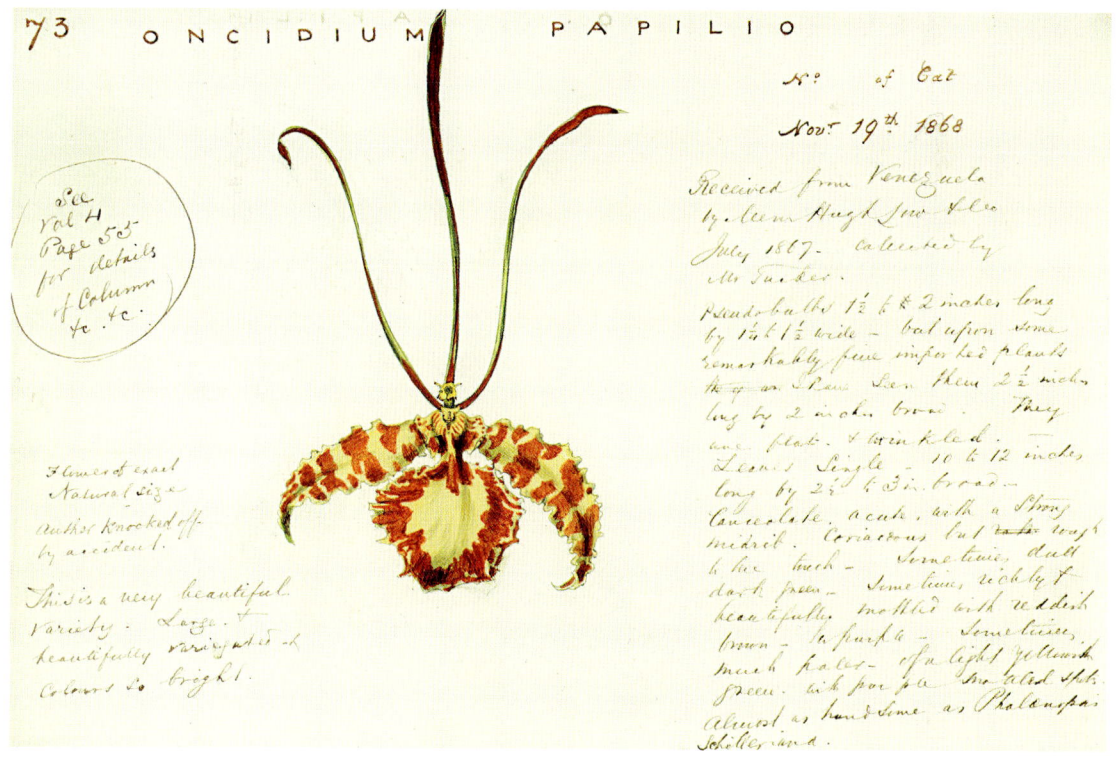

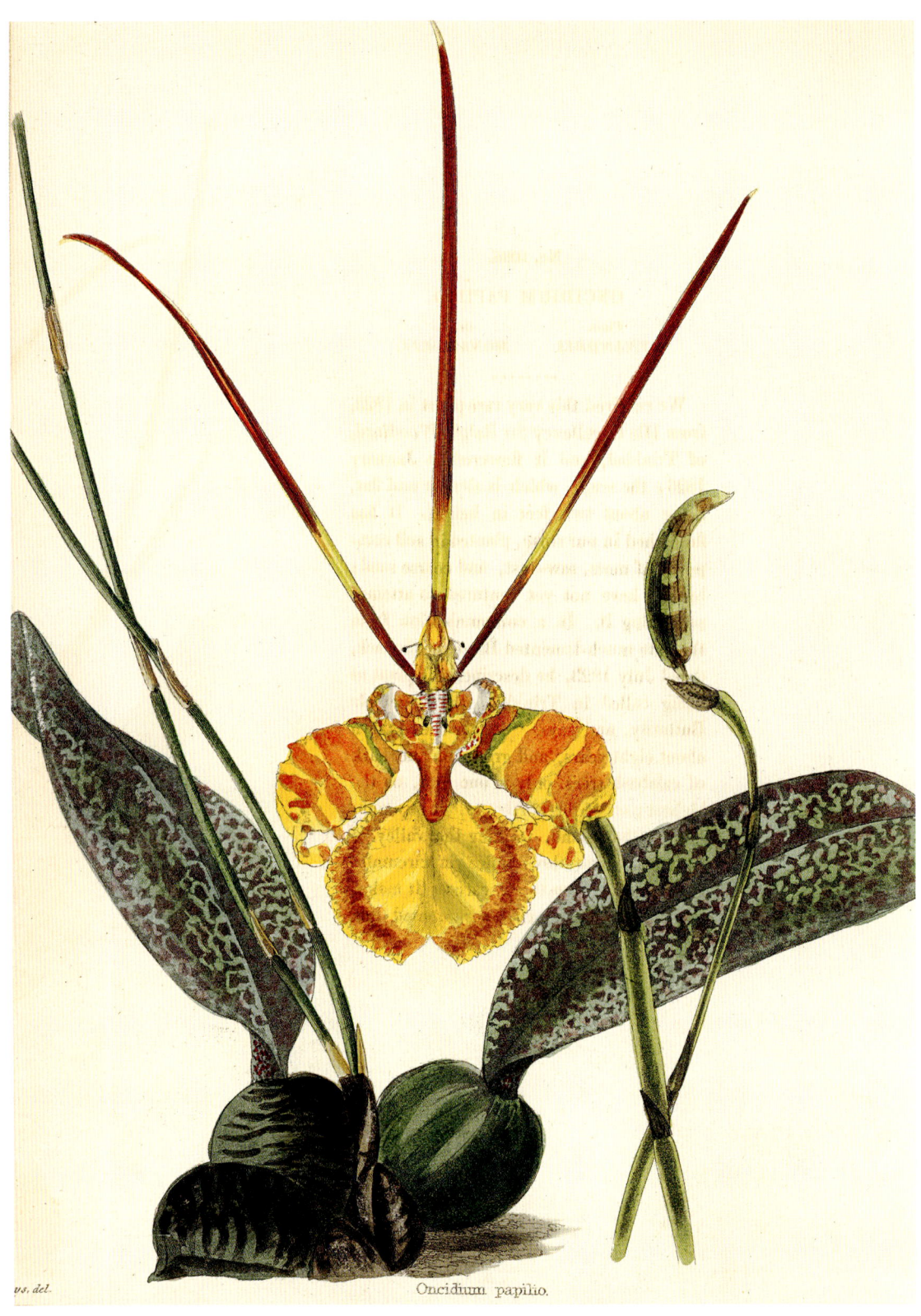

Oncidium papilio.

210　Tropical American butterfly orchid　*Psychopsis papilio*

Opposite: An early painting of *Psychopsis papilio* (as *Oncidium papilio*) from C. Loddiges, *The Botanical Cabinet* in 1827.

Right: *Psychopsis papilio* (as *Oncidium papilio*) drawn by William Hooker for *Curtis's Botanical Magazine* in 1828.

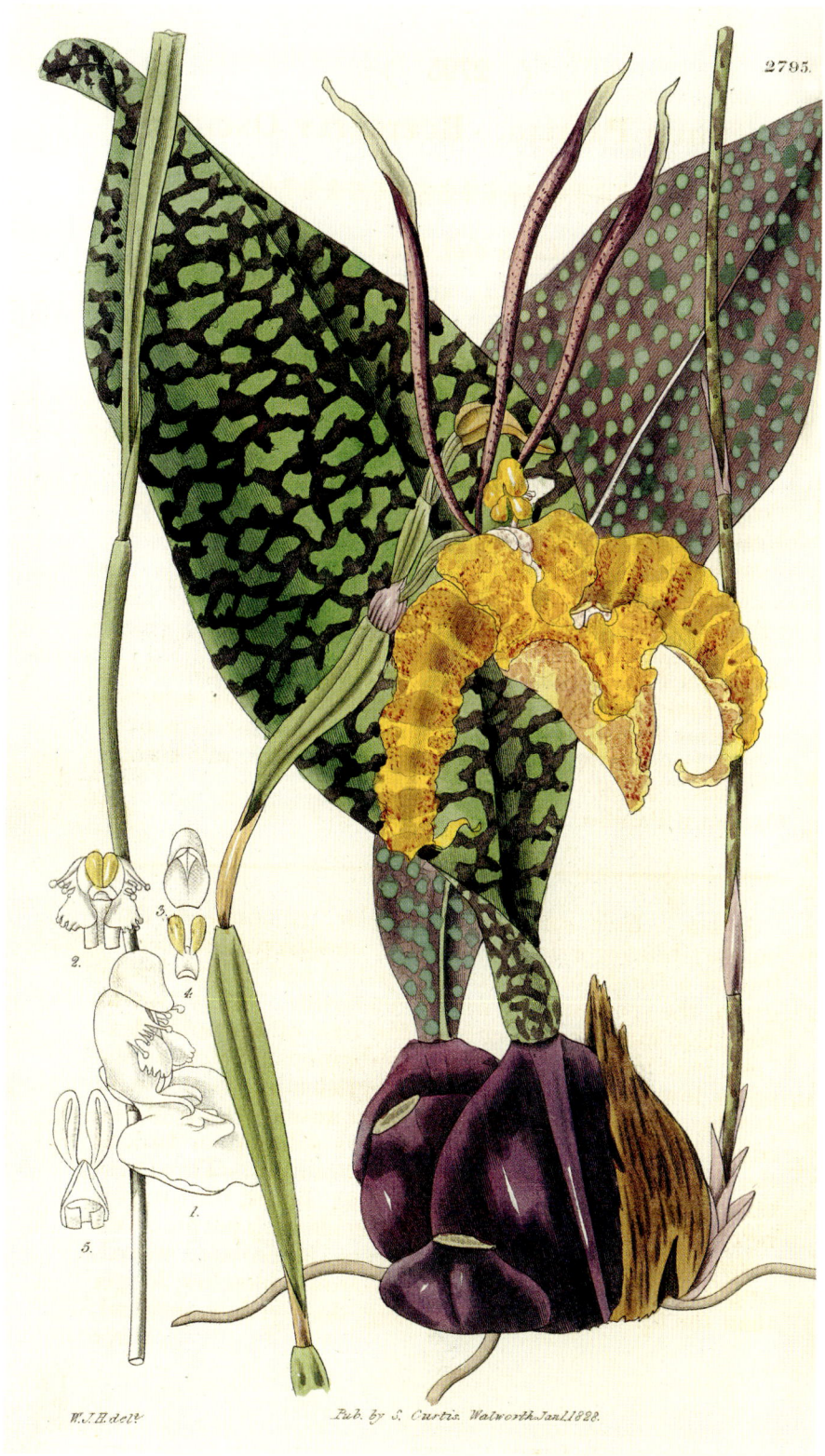

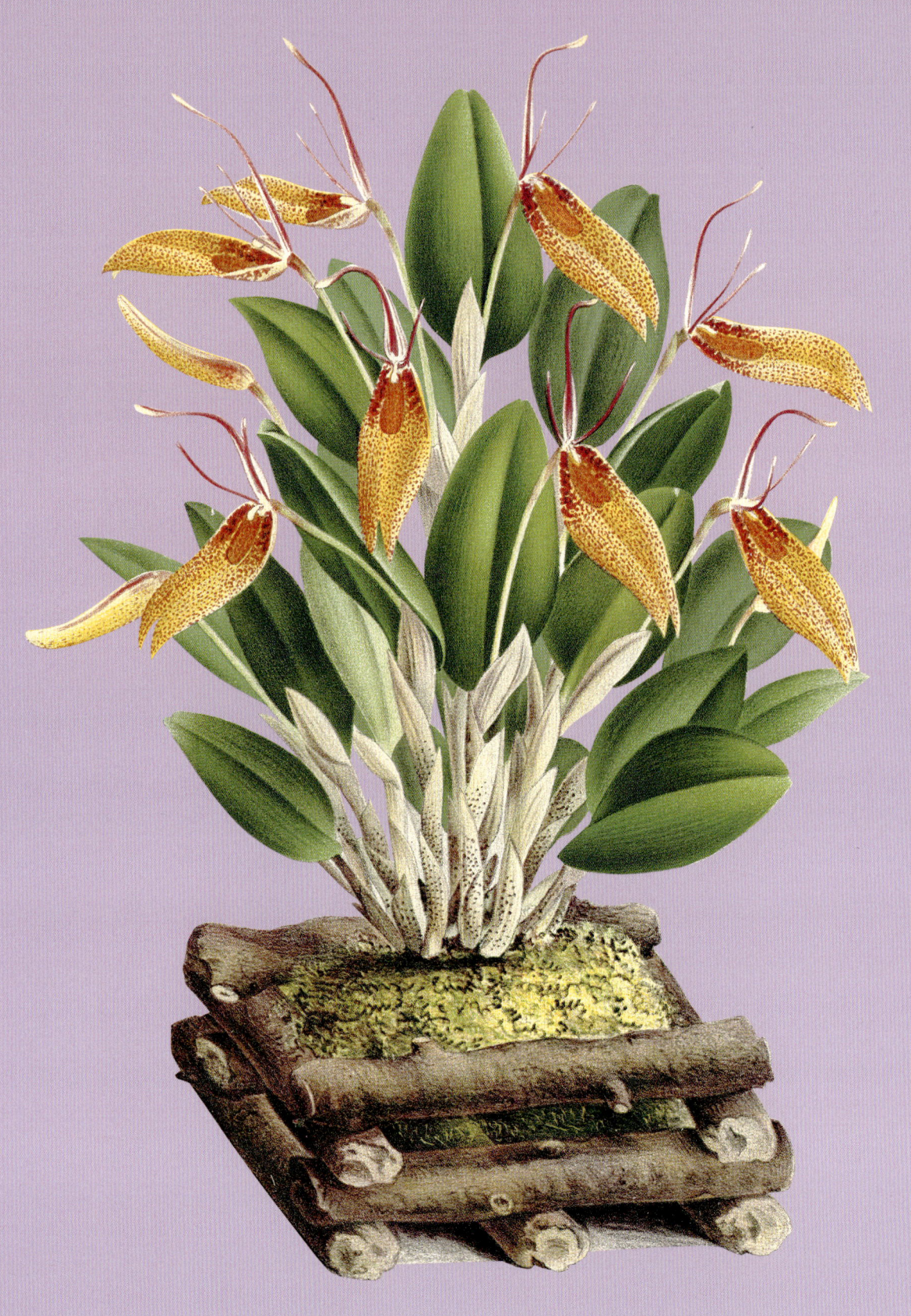

ANTENNAE-BEARING RESTREPIA

RESTREPIA ANTENNIFERA

Opposite: *Restrepia antennifera* by Pieter de Pannemaeker, in J. J. Linden, *Lindenia: Iconographie des Orchidées*, 1885.

Twig epiphytes are tiny plants growing on larger plants but which are not parasitic on them, and are so small that they can be supported by the tiniest branches and twigs. Many of the orchids that belong to the enormous orchid subtribe Pleurothallidinae (containing many thousands of species), found in the forests of Central and South America, and particularly in the mossy, perpetually damp high-elevation cloud forests of the Andes, are twig epiphytes.

The genus *Restrepia* is one such group of species and was previously considered to be part of the larger genus *Pleurothallis*. In 1815, their own distinct genus was published by the German botanists Alexander von Humboldt and Carl Sigismund Kunth and the French botanist Aimé Bonpland, and the species were transferred into it. The trio named the new genus in honour of José Manuel Restrepo Vélez, the Colombian explorer, politician and naturalist, who was one of the first to scientifically explore and document the plants of the Andes, and later became governor of Antioquia.

The genus *Restrepia* is distinctive, with larger and more brightly coloured and patterned flowers compared with other members of the Pleurothallidinae, and glandular structures at the club-shaped tips of the dorsal sepal and lateral petals of each flower. Within the genus, species boundaries are less clear, with many species being very variable, and it can be difficult to determine the identity of a particular plant. As with other members of the Pleurothallidinae – which includes the genera *Pleurothallis*, *Masdevallia* and *Dracula* – *Restrepia* plants grow in small tufts, with no pseudobulbs to store moisture, so are susceptible to drying out if the natural environment around them changes or they are not cultivated in conditions that mimic the cool damp forests of their native habitats. Each plant can produce many single-flowered inflorescences, each with a thin floral stalk originating from the base of a leaf. The dorsal sepal at the top of the flower is more slender than the lateral sepals, either side of the labellum. These lateral sepals are broad and fused together to form a large, often brightly coloured and patterned "synsepal". The labellum

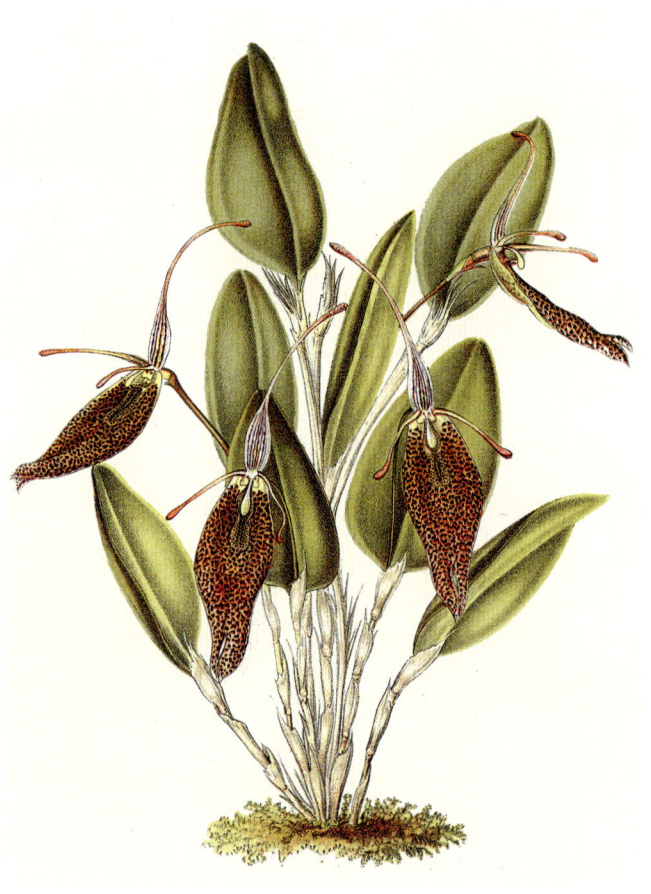

flowers, attracting and perhaps guiding insects to the flowers and into the correct position to pick up and deposit pollinia.

Restrepia antennifera is one of the largest-flowered species in the genus, each bloom being up to 6 cm (2½ in) in length. As in other *Restrepia* species the flowers are covered in intricate striations and spots, which look as if they have been painted by hand with a very fine paintbrush, and in this species the blooms tend to be yellow, with orange, red or purple striations and dots. Humboldt collected the species in the Andean mountains of Pasto, in what was New Grenada, now part of southern Colombia, but this widespread and quite variable species is also known from Venezuela, Bolivia, Ecuador and Peru. In 1877, the species was flowered for the first time at the Royal Botanic Gardens, Kew.

Restrepia species appear to be self-incompatible – that is, they need pollen from a different parent plant in order to achieve successful pollination of the flowers and produce viable seed. Recent research has suggested that as habitat destruction leads to the increasing fragmentation of *Restrepia* populations in the wild, pollinators are less likely to be able to move between plants – and may themselves be more prone to dying out – leading to a decline in the numbers of orchids, and significantly increasing their risk of extinction.

Above: *Restrepia antennifera* by P. Stroobant, in *L' Illustration Horticole*, 1869

Opposite: *Restrepia contorta* by Walter Hood Fitch, in *Curtis's Botanical Magazine*, 1877.

is much smaller and more tongue-like in shape at the centre of the flower. The lateral petals are reduced to long slender "antennae", and like the dorsal sepal have club-shaped tips, where glandular, odour-producing "osmophores" are found. The osmophores are thought to be involved in the pollination of the

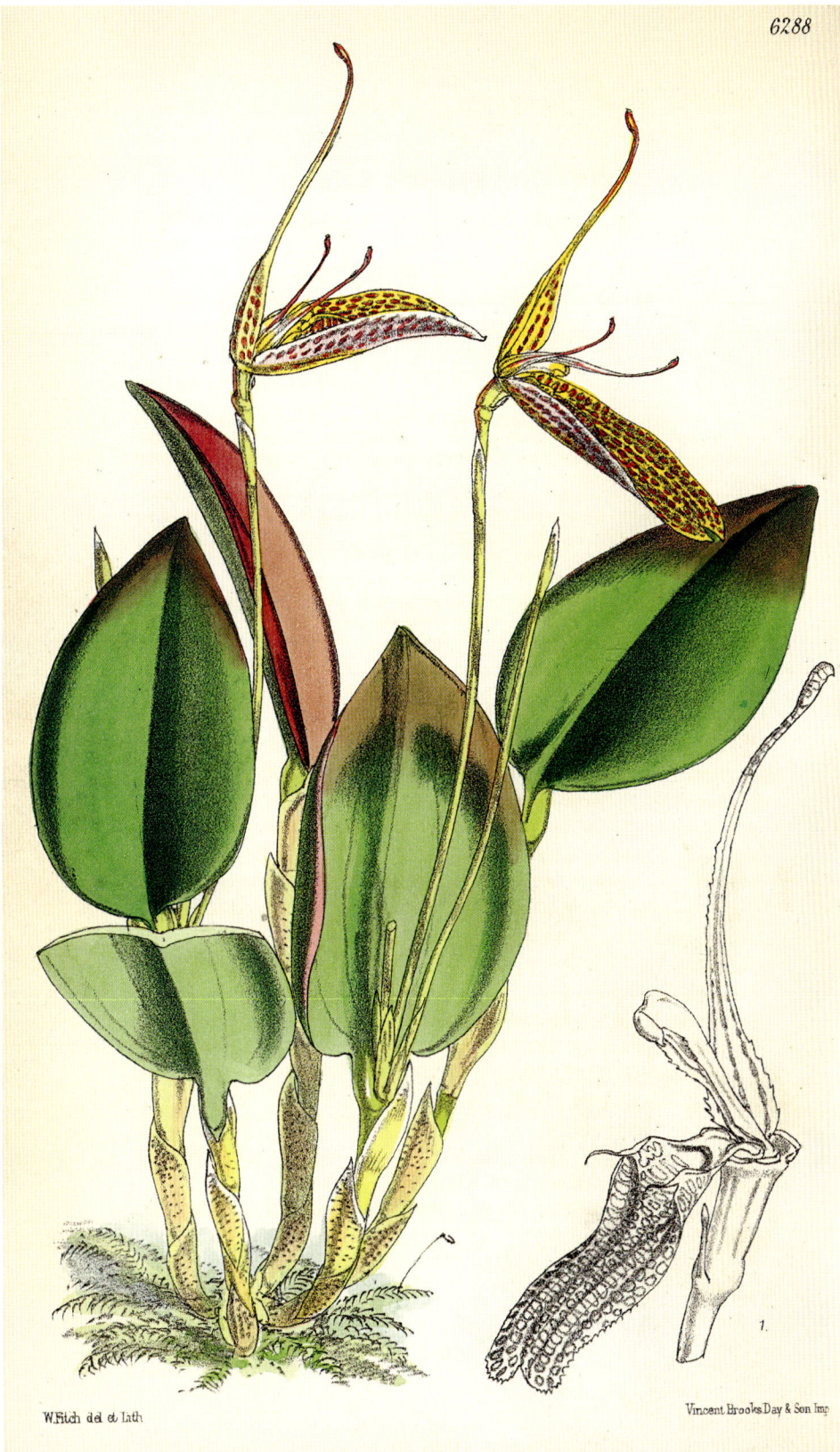

Vincent Brooks Day & Son Imp

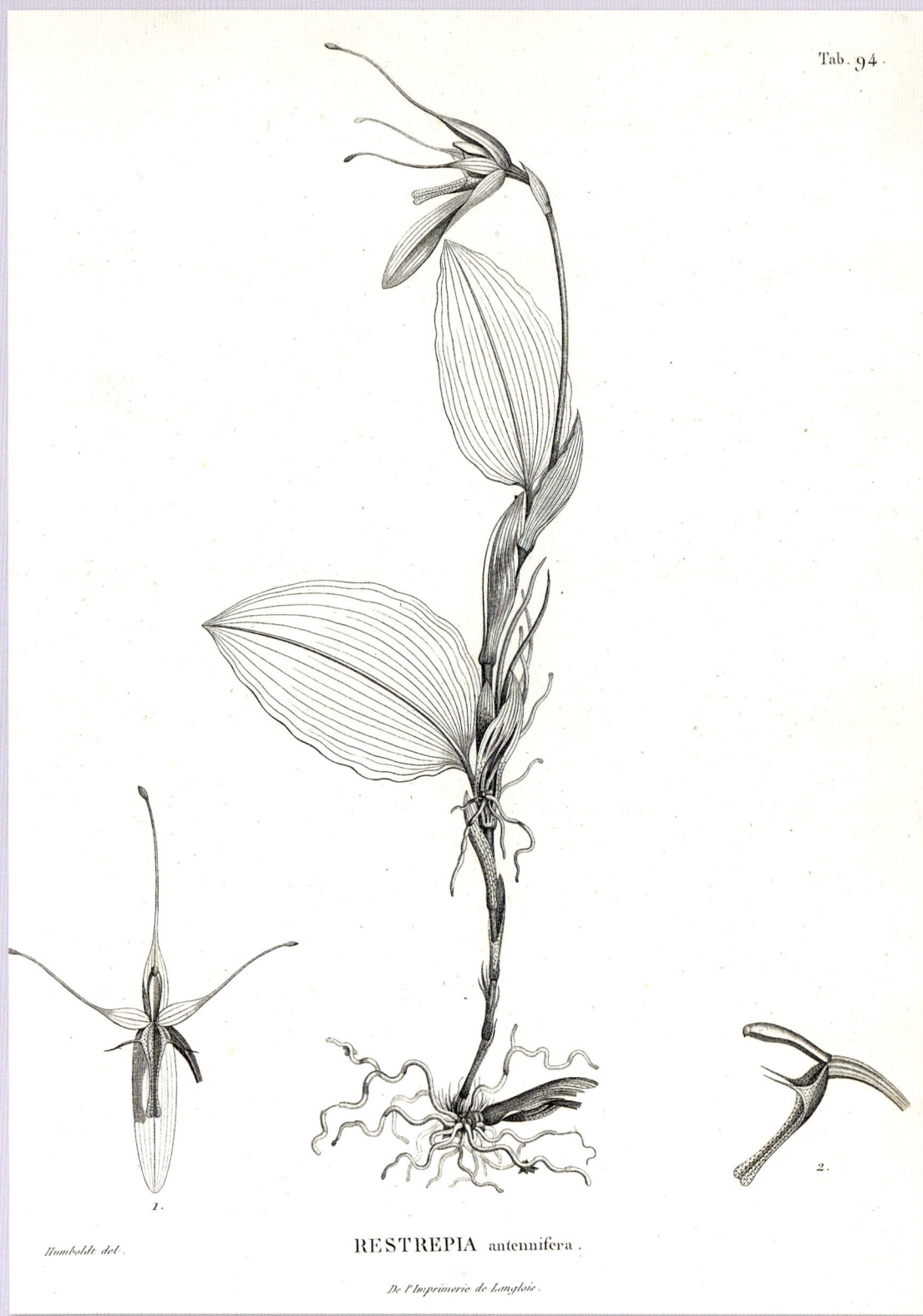

Tab. 94.

1.

2.

Humboldt del.

RESTREPIA antennifera.

De l'Imprimerie de Langlois.

Restrepii, qui geographiam et historiam naturalem Andium Antioquiensium¹ egregie illustravit.

1. RESTREPIA ANTENNIFERA. † Tab. XCIV.

Crescit in declivitate Andium Puraguayensium inter Almaguer et Pasto, ad arborum vetustarum truncos, alt. 1480 hexap. (Regno Novogranat.) ♃ Floret Novembri.

PLANTA parasitica. RADICES simplices, albidæ, glabræ. CAULIS simplex, subangulatus, superne anceps, glaber, medio radices emittens, subbifolius, vaginis tectus, sex- aut septempollicaris. VAGINÆ membranaceæ, carinato-compressæ, marcidæ, inferne glandulis atro purpureis, minutissimis conspersæ. FOLIA ovato-elliptica, acuta, basi rotundata, integerrima, plana, striato-nervosa, carnoso-coriacea, duos et dimidium pollices longa, sesquipollicem lata, alterum terminale, alterum in medio caulis, ubi radices emittit. PEDUNCULI solitarii, terni aut quaterni, ad basin foliorum erumpentes, eaque superantes, uniflori, glabri, compressi. FLOS *fig.* 1. *apertus.*) subsesquipollicaris, spathella brevi suffultus. CALYX subbilabiatus, patulus, glaber; foliolum exterius superius (labium superius) lanceolatum, concavum, superne angustissimum, filiforme, apice clavatum, rubrum, nervis coccineis pictum; foliola duo lateralia usque ad apicem in unicum oblongum, obtusum (labium inferius) connata, concava, striato-nervosa, fusco-flavescentia, interne coccineo-striata, superius longitudine æquantia; foliola duo interiora lateralia lineari-lanceolata, trinervia, rubescentia, nervis coccineis picta, ut superius apice angustissima et clavigera, multo tamen breviora; labellum planum, late lineare, basin versus dilatatum, apice truncatum, emarginatum, trinerve, flavum, nervis et punctis rubris variegatum, basin versus utroque latere processu filiformi auctum (*fig.* 2. *labellum adjecto gymnostemo.*), foliolis exterioribus triplo brevius. GYNOSTEMUM subrectum, labello brevius, canaliculatum, basin versus attenuatum, album, carnosum. ANTHERA terminalis, sessilis, bilocularis, operculata. POLLINIS massæ quatuor. OVARIUM costatum, glabrum.

RODRIGUEZIA. RUIZ. et PAV.

CALYCIS foliola quinque patula; exteriora lateralia connata; labellum liberum, basi calcaratum. GYNOSTEMUM apterum. ANTHERA terminalis, operculata. POLLINIS massæ duæ, cereaceæ.

HERBÆ parasiticæ, bulbiferæ. SCAPI spicati; floribus secundis.

1. RODRIGUEZIA SECUNDA. † Tab. XCII.

R. bulbis oblongis; foliis lineari-lanceolatis; floribus spicatis, secundis.
Crescit locis calidis et subtemperatis Provinciæ Popayanensis prope Carthaginem in truncis Crescentiæ Cujete, alt. 500 hex. ♃ Floret Octobri.

PLANTA parasitica. RADICES simplices, teretes, glabræ, albidæ. BULBI oblongi, fuscescentes, glabri, nitidi, sesquipollicares. FOLIA lineari-lanceolata, obtusa, subcarinata, coriacea, striato-nervosa, glaber-

¹ *Semanario del Nuevo Reyno de Granada.* 1809. *p.* 47.

Original description published in *Nova Genera et Species Plantarum,* by Humboldt, Bonpland and Kunth, 1816

The original description of the species *Restrepia antennifera* was published in 1816 by the naturalists Alexander von Humboldt, Aimé Bonpland and Carl Sigismund Kunth. Humboldt and Bonpland travelled together in South America at the turn of the nineteenth century between 1799 and 1804. Over five years they journeyed through Mexico, Colombia, Venezuela and Brazil. Kunth later worked with the two men to classify and describe the thousands of plant specimens they brought back from their explorations, and later went on to travel in South and Central America himself.

Published in seven volumes between 1815 and 1825, *Nova Genera et Species Plantarum* contains the descriptions of some 4,500 plant species with a huge number of illustrations. Over 3,000 of the species described were hitherto unknown to European science. The orchid genus *Restrepia* was described for the first time, with a single species, *Restrepia antennifera*, along with another 62 new orchid species in nine new orchid genera.

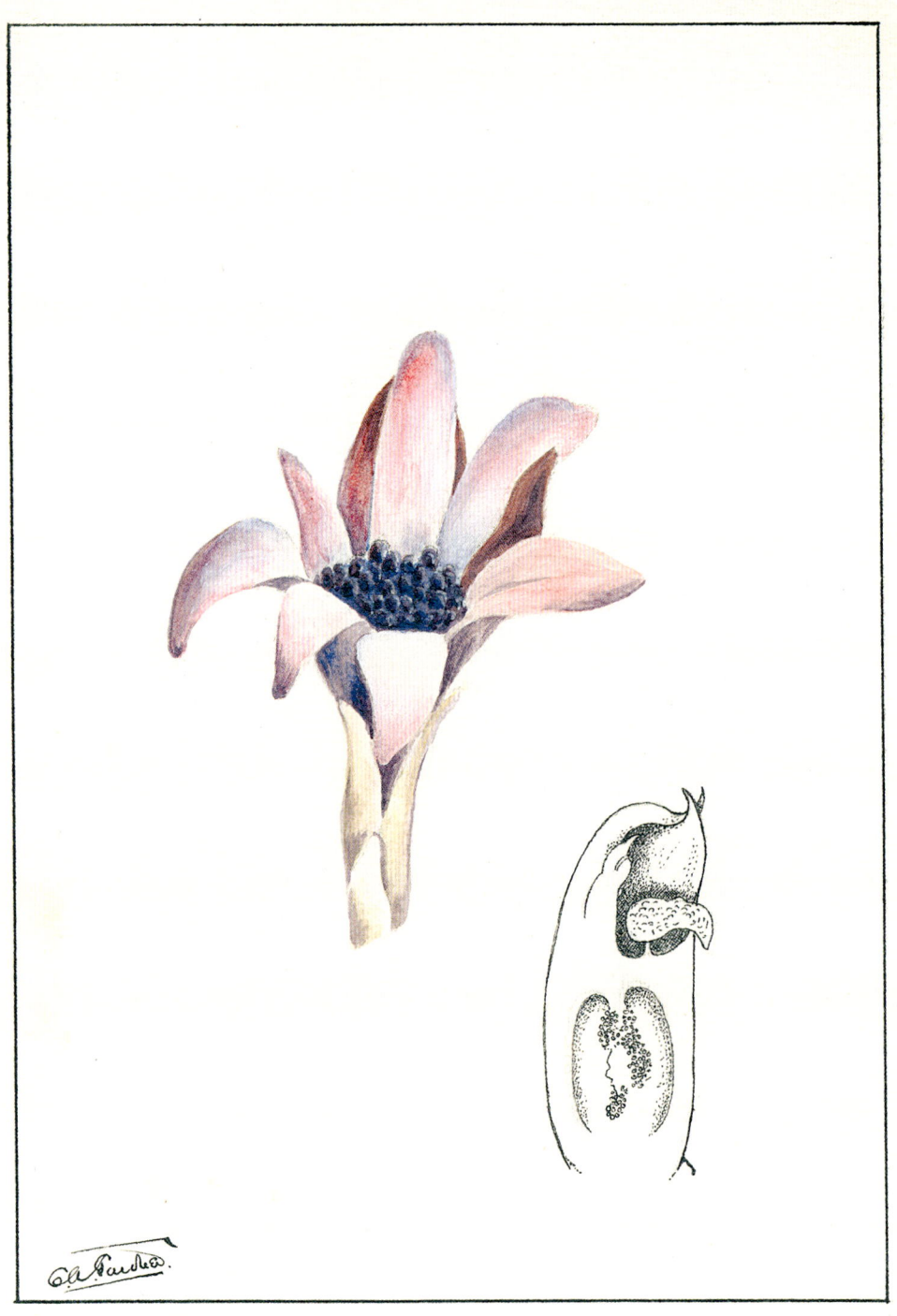

Rhizanthella Gardneri, R.S.Rogers.

WESTERN UNDERGROUND ORCHID
RHIZANTHELLA GARDNERI

The existence of an orchid that spends its entire life underground was recorded for the first time in the late 1920s. Two other species in the same genus, *Rhizanthella*, have been described since, namely *Rhizanthella slateri* from New South Wales, and *Rhizanthella omissa* from Queensland. Epiphytic orchids grow above ground in the branches and on the trunks of trees, lithophytic orchids grow on rocks, and terrestrial orchids grow in the ground – these three classes of orchid life histories are fairly well known and understood. Wholly subterranean orchids were previously unheard of, and their rarity and elusive nature continue to give these species an intriguing mystique unmatched by any other orchid. *Rhizanthella gardneri* has been described as "one of the most beautiful, strange, and iconic orchids in the world".

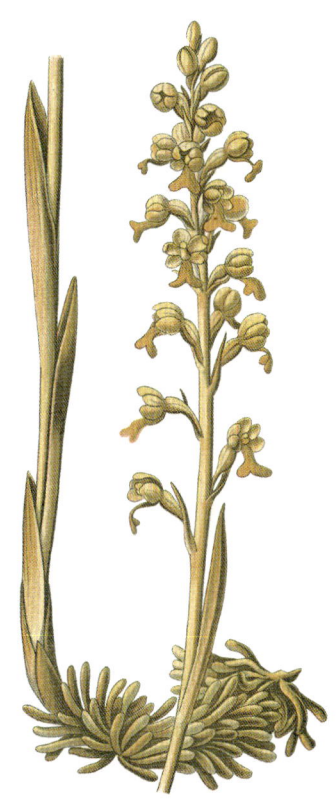

In 1928, John (Jack) Trott discovered a curious organism when he scraped away the soil at the base of a shrub on his land in the Wheatbelt Region of Western Australia, after noticing a sweet smell and a crack in the dry soil after the vegetation above had been burned. The small flowerhead he found just below the surface was unlike any plant he had ever seen. Growing entirely underground, the plant lacks chlorophyll and so is not green, and has no leaves. Approximately 150 tiny individual fleshy flowers grouped into a head 5 cm (2 in) across are surrounded by large pink-cream bracts. A thick fleshy stem that

Newspaper cutting from 1979, describing the discovery of *Rhizanthella gardneri* at a new site

In 1978, the original discoverer of a specimen of *Rhizanthella gardneri* Jack Trott offered a financial reward to anyone who found another specimen of the plant after just four other plants had been found in the intervening 50 years. In 1979, another farmer, John McGuiness, claimed his reward. Finding the curious plant on his land after turning over earth in an unused paddock, the flowerhead 6 cm (2⅓in) in diameter was giving off a sweet smell as Trott had described back in 1928. Sadly, Jack had passed away shortly before his prize was claimed, but his widow Marina, who had found another plant in 1940, continued the appeal, as described in this newspaper clipping from 1979. Five years later, in 1984, another underground species, *Rhizanthella slateri*, was described from New South Wales, and in 2006 a third species, *Rhizanthella omissa*, which was known only from a single collection made in 1958 in Queensland.

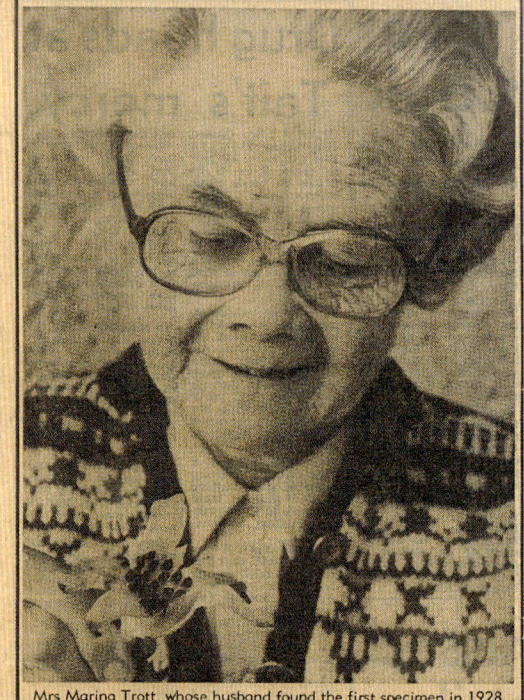

Mrs Marina Trott, whose husband found the first specimen in 1928, with the newly-discovered orchid yesterday.

Farmer finds rare orchid

By ALEX HARRIS

A south coast farmer, Mr John McGuiness, has rediscovered one of the world's rarest orchids, the subterranean *Rhizanthella gardneri*, on his property at Munglinup, between Ravensthorpe and Esperance.

The last one was found on May 27, 1959. It is listed as endangered by the World Wildlife Fund.

Only five specimens have previously been identified.

Mr McGuiness found the orchid when he turned over a mallee root in an uncleared paddock.

The orchid was delivered to the WA Herbarium yesterday in a plastic cup.

It was a perfect star-shaped bloom with a cluster of tiny dark red flowers, surrounded by five big and several smaller near-transparent white bracts.

It measured about six centimetres across and gave off a sweet smell when exposed to the open air.

The orchid's rediscovery was a big occasion for three WA people and scientists throughout the world.

For Mr McGuiness it meant he was entitled to a $100 reward offered last year by the late Mr Jack Trott, who first found it at his property—later named "Rhizanthella" —about 12 kilometres east of Corrigin in 1928.

To Mr Trott's widow, Mrs Marina Trott, now of Como, the event was a mixture of pride because she also found a specimen in 1940—and sadness because her husband was not there to share the excitement of Mr McGuiness's discovery.

"I decided to continue the reward after my husband died," she said. "But I wish he could have been here. He would have been thrilled at this latest find."

And to botanist Alex George, it was the end of 20 years' hoping and searching.

"This orchid was, like all the others, found on virgin land," he said, "But the others were discovered much farther north."

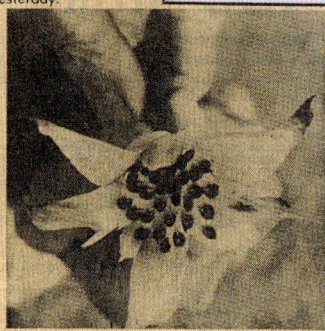

The subterranean *Rhizanthella gardneri* orchid.

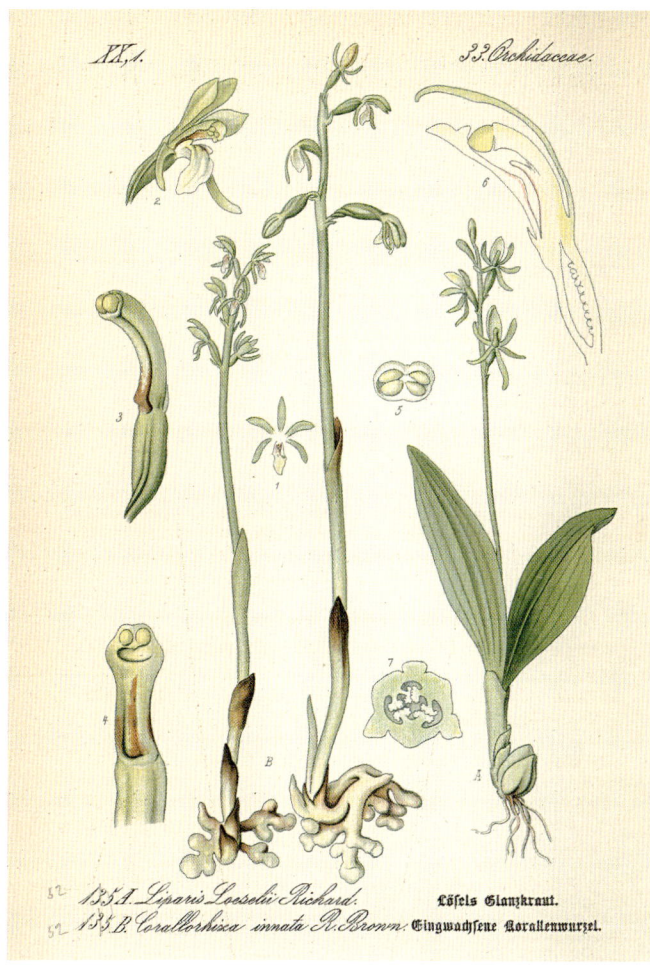

XX,1.   33.Orchidaceae.

1354. *Liparis Loeselii Richard.*   **Löfels Glanzkraut.**
135 B. *Corallorhiza innata R.Brown.* **Eingwachsene Korallenwurzel.**

Above: *Liparis loeselii* and *Corallorhiza trifida* (as *Corallorhiza innata*) by Otto Wilhelm Thomé, in *Flora von Deutschland Österreich und der Schweiz*, 1885.

lacks roots extends further below ground and acts as a storage organ.

Miniscule fungus gnats pollinate the flowers, which develop and mature several centimetres underground, with the insects burrowing through the loose soil above. It is thought that other insects, such as beetles, ants and termites, may also transfer pollen from one flower to another as they move about in the soil. The fleshy seeds are thought to be eaten by rats and small marsupials rootling below the shrubs growing above the orchid, and dispersed in their droppings.

A mycorrhizal fungus, *Thanatephorus gardneri*, links the orchid to the broom honey myrtle, *Melaleuca uncinata*, supplying the orchid with the nutrients and carbon necessary for growth. The relationship between the orchid, myrtle and fungus is obligate – *Rhizanthella gardneri* has only ever been found growing in association with the woody shrub, and death of the myrtle above ground will result in the death of the orchid below ground. Other leafless terrestrial orchids, which are also virtually entirely dependent on fungal partners, occur around the world, such as some species in the genera *Corallorhiza* and *Neottia*, but all of them emerge above ground to produce their inflorescences and fruits, unlike *Rhizanthella* species.

Only 50 individuals of *Rhizanthella gardneri* are known in the wild, in a handful of small, fragmented populations. Drought, increasingly frequent and more intensive bush fires, and habitat degradation and destruction are highly likely to jeopardize the survival of the species, as is the damage caused as a result of people searching for the orchid, digging the plants up and disturbing their subterranean environment in the process. Several of the sites where this species grows were discovered when recently burned bush was being ploughed, and the plants were uncovered in the process, ultimately being discovered at the same time as they were being extirpated. The species is so rare and is threatened by so many factors that it is considered to be critically endangered in the wild by the International Union for Conservation of Nature (IUCN), and should be afforded the highest level of conservation protection.

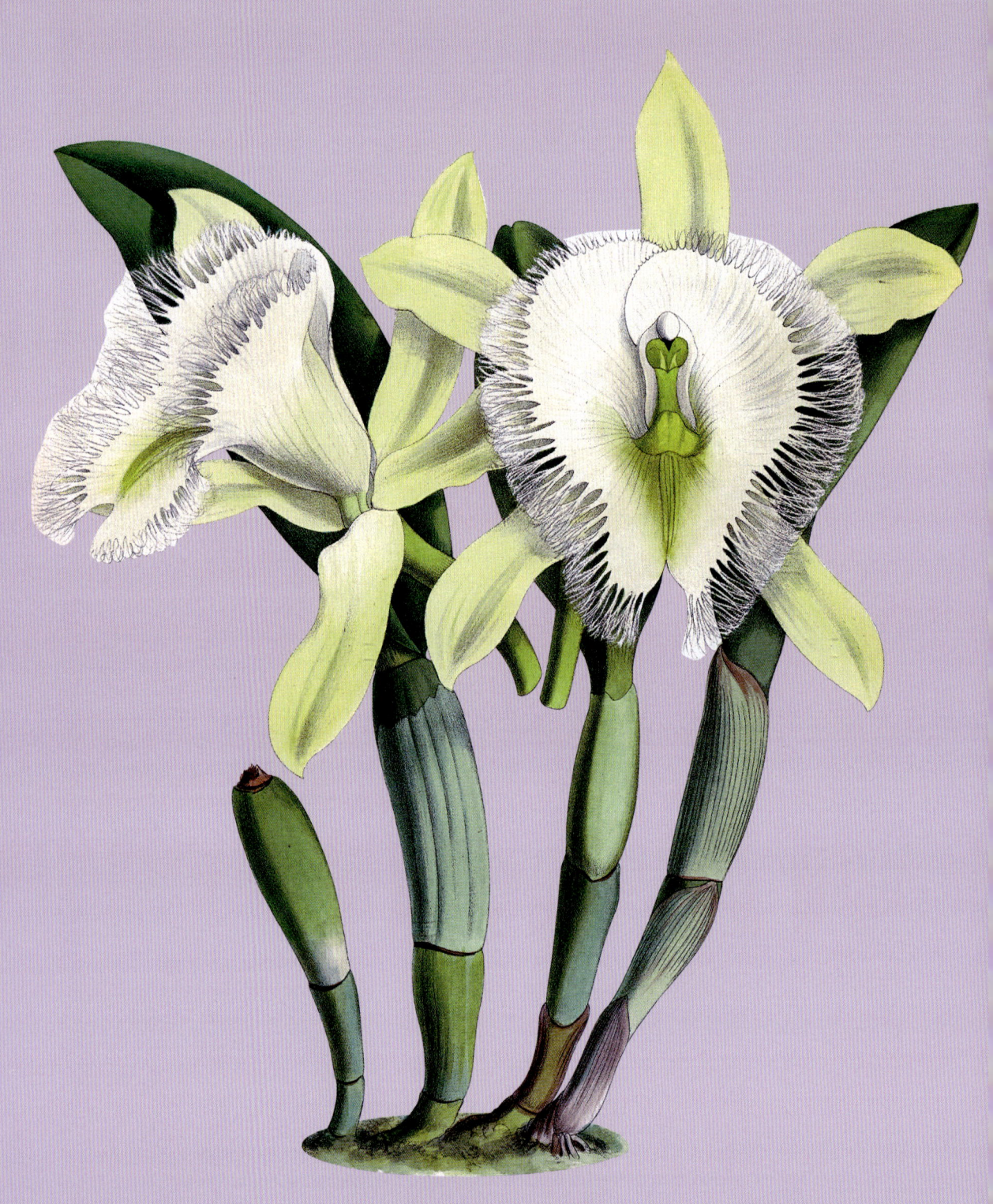

QUEEN OF THE NIGHT

RHYNCHOLAELIA DIGBYANA

The spectacular orchid *Rhyncholaelia digbyana* belongs to a small genus that contains just two species, the other being *R. glauca*, which has played a disproportionate role in the breeding of large, showy *Cattleya* hybrids – the archetypal orchids of the public's imagination. *Rhyncholaelia* is closely related to *Cattleya*, and breeders can freely hybridize it with *Cattleya* species and other orchids in the same tribe. *Rhyncholaelia digbyana* endows the hybrids with its wonderfully frilly lip, a feature that is seen in many of the resulting hybrids and that runs through many later generations of offspring.

This orchid was introduced into cultivation from Honduras by Mrs MacDonald, who gave a plant to Edward St Vincent Digby (1809–1889), 9th Baron Digby, of Minterne in Dorset, England, whose father was an admiral who fought at the battle of Trafalgar with Nelson. Digby flowered it for the first time in 1845, and John Lindley, the father of orchidology, described it as *Brassavola digbyana* in *Edwards' Botanical Register* of the same year. However, it was later realized that it did not fit well in the genus *Brassavola*. In 1881, George Bentham, an eminent botanist based at Kew, transferred it to *Laelia*, but in 1918 the German orchid specialist Rudolf Schlechter established a new genus for it, *Rhyncholaelia*, naming it for its long-beaked fruit. Apart from having a habit that differs from that of *Brassavola* and *Laelia*, it has broad leathery leaves and substantial, large flowers characterized by a long hidden nectary that is connate with the ovary. This appears to be linked to its pollination by dusk-flying hawkmoths (belonging to the Sphingidae) that have long tongues which uncoil when in use, like the spring of a watch. Recent DNA-based analyses have maintained Schlechter's genus when many other allied genera have been sunk into a greatly enlarged *Cattleya* genus.

In its natural environment this orchid is an epiphyte that often grows to form large colonies. It is found in seasonally dry woodland and thicket at low elevation near the sea. Formerly it was quite common, but land clearance and excessive collection have severely limited its distribution.

Below: *Rhyncholaelia digbyana*, a plant flowering at Kew that had been sent by Mrs O'Donnell, the wife of the governor of Honduras, drawn by Walter Hood Fitch for *Curtis's Botanical Magazine* in 1849.

The first flowering artificial hybrids that were produced using *R. digbyana*, in 1889, were *Brassocattleya* Digbyano-Mossiae (with the Colombian species *Cattleya mossiae*) by J. Veitch & Sons of Chelsea, and *BC.* Digbyano-Mendelii (with the Colombian species *Cattleya mendelii*) by C. Maron et Fils of Brunoy, France. Many more followed with crosses with *Epidendrum*, *Laelia* and *Laeliocattleya*, the last being the first trigeneric artificial orchid hybrid to be produced.

It is scarcely surprising that this spectacular orchid is the national flower of Honduras. It also has medicinal uses, and the native people in Honduras use its sap to staunch bleeding of wounds. Elsewhere, a number of orchids show pharmacological activity and have uses in traditional medicine.

The other species in the genus, namely *Rhyncholaelia glauca*, has smaller, whiter flowers than *R. digbyana*. It is native to central and southern Mexico, Guatemala, Belize and Honduras, and was collected by the plant explorer John Henchman near Xalapa in Mexico, but was introduced into cultivation by the French collector Deschamps. It grows in rather open montane forests up to 1,500 m (4,900 ft) above sea level. For example, in Mexico, it grows in *Pinus oocarpa* forest alongside a somewhat xerophytic but rich orchid flora that includes *Brassavola cucullata*, *Clowesia russelliana*, *Domingoa purpurea*, *Encyclia diota*, *Epidendrum ciliare*, *Guarianthe aurantiaca*, *Guarianthe skinneri*, *Meiracyllium trisulcatum*, *Oncidium maculatum*, *Prosthechea chacaoensis*, *Prosthechea radiata*, *Stanhopea saccata* and *Trichocentrum cebolleta*; it grows in oak forest up to 1,600 m (5,000 ft) above sea level, also with a rich orchid flora that includes many of the same species, but in addition *Lycaste cruenta*, *Maxillaria variabilis* and *Prosthechea baculus*. It has also been used in orchid breeding, although to a lesser extent, as it lacks both the flower size and the frilled lip of *R. digbyana*.

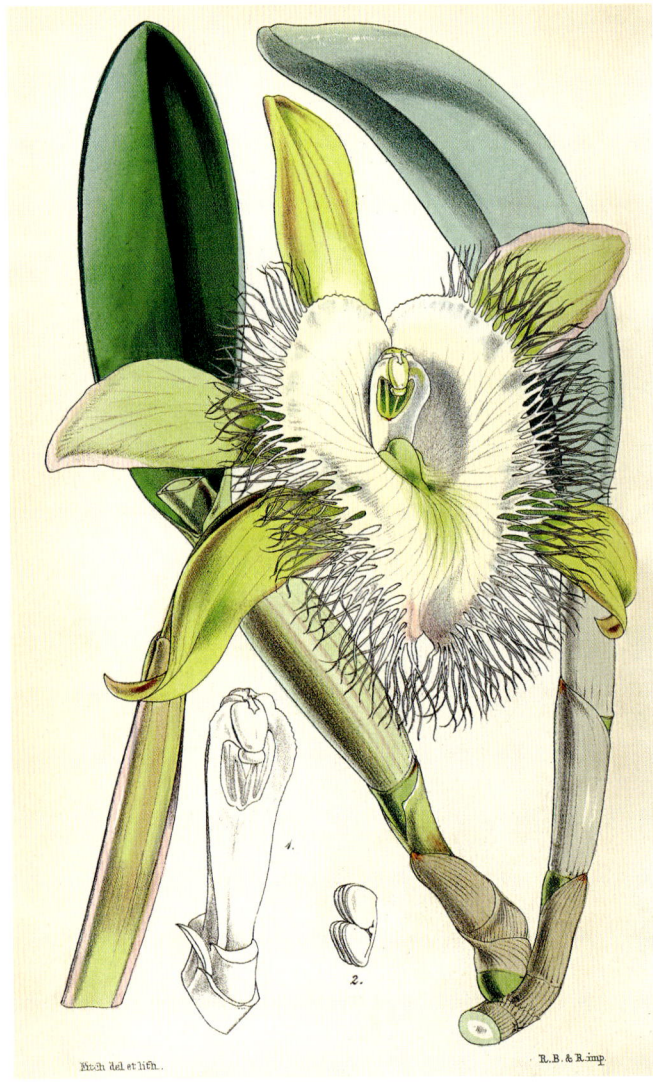

Fitch del et lith..

R.B.& R.imp

BRASAVOLA Digbyana.

Mr. Digby's Brasavola.

———

GYNANDRIA *MONANDRIA*.

Nat. ord. ORCHIDACEÆ. § EPIDENDREÆ—LÆLIADÆ. (ORCHIDS, *Vegetable Kingdom, p.* 181.)
BRASAVOLA. *Botanical Register, fol.* 1465.

———

Br. *Digbyana;* foliis ovalibus planis carnosis glaucis, labello sessili cucullato cordato subtrilobo margine in crinis longis soluto in disco callo maximo aucto, dente postico subulato incumbente.

———

This very singular plant was introduced from Honduras by Mrs. McDonald, and by that lady given to Edward St. Vincent Digby, Esq. with whom it flowered last July, at Minterne, in Dorsetshire. Its huge yellowish white flowers are as sweet as those of Aerides odoratum; and the largest measure nearly three inches in diameter. The neck of the ovary, which is cuniculate in a remarkable degree, is full four inches long.

We have not seen the pollen-masses of the plant; but it is so much like Br. glauca in habit, that we entertain little doubt of their belonging to the same genus. There are, however, some peculiarities in the structure of this plant, which must not be lost sight of. Its anther-bed has no fringes or other process at the edge, but is deeply sunk and guarded behind by a long subulate tooth, which curves over the anther (fig. 1), and the stigma has three linear foveæ, which all open into one compressed stigmatic passage.

The singular fringe that borders the lip is quite analogous to what occurs in Br. cucullata and others, only it is here extremely extended, so as to give the flower quite a shaggy appearance.

October, 1846.   U

John Lindley's description of *Brassavola digbyana* in *Edwards' Botanical Register*, 1846

John Lindley was the editor and main contributor to *Edwards' Botanical Register*, which was mainly illustrated by the exquisite watercolour paintings of Sarah Drake, his children's nanny. He used the journal to describe many newly introduced species of orchid, including *Brassavola digbyana*, which appeared in the *Botanical Register* of 1846. It was based upon an orchid introduced from Honduras by Mrs MacDonald, who gave a plant to Edward St Vincent Digby (1809–1889), 9th Baron Digby, after whom it is named.

The Botanical Register was one of a number of plant journals of the period illustrated in colour which competed directly with *Curtis's Botanical Magazine*. It was started by Sydenham Edwards, and taken on by Lindley in 1829, was successful for some years, but succumbed eventually in 1847.

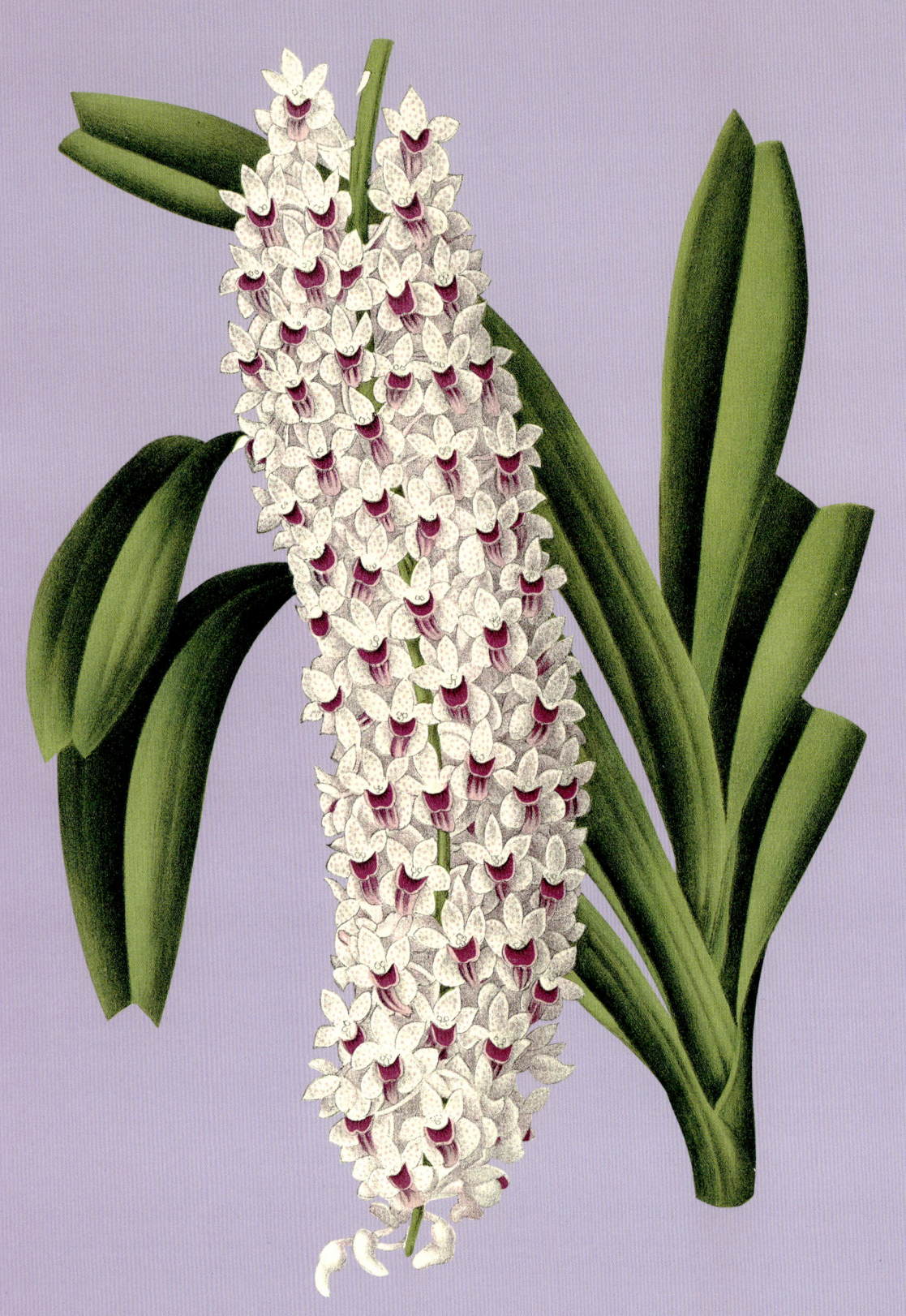

FOXTAIL ORCHID
RHYNCHOSTYLIS RETUSA

The foxtail orchid, *Rhynchostylis retusa*, often forms large clumps on trees in semi-deciduous and deciduous dry lowland forests in Bangladesh, Burma, Cambodia, China, India, Indonesia, Laos, Malaysia, Nepal, the Philippines, Singapore, Sri Lanka, Thailand and Vietnam, from sea level up to an altitude of 1,200 m (4,000 ft). The plant is similar to those of many *Vanda* species to which it is related, with stout stems bearing alternate, distichous leathery grooved leaves. Its vernacular name refers to its cylindrical, often curved, racemose inflorescences, up to 60 cm (2 ft) in length, consisting of many attractive white flowers, heavily spotted with pink on the sepals and petals, and with a rich pink lip. Each inflorescence can have more than 100 flowers. This orchid flowers in the winter and early spring.

Rhynchostylis retusa is the state flower of Arunachal Pradesh and Assam in India and of Uva Province in Sri Lanka. In India, the plant is most common in Orissa and Andhra Pradesh states, but is declining rapidly because of over-collection. The plant is considered to be a symbol of love, fertility and happiness in Assam in north-east India, and for this reason the inflorescence forms an essential element in the traditional Assamese marriage ceremony. Its inflorescences are used as a hair ornament worn by Assamese women during folk dances at the start of spring. Such is its beauty, usefulness and broad cultural significance that it is also grown as a much-loved garden plant by most Assamese.

Throughout the Indian subcontinent the root is used to treat rheumatism and as an emollient. In Malabar District in southern India, various preparations of the plant have been used to treat asthma, tuberculosis, nervous tics, cramp, epilepsy, vertigo, palpitations, kidney stones and menstrual problems. In Assam this plant has also been used to treat wounds, cuts and bruises.

Rhynchostylis retusa was among the earliest of the tropical Asiatic orchids to be described. Hendrik van Reede tot Drakenstein (1678–1703) illustrated and described this plant in his *Hortus Malabaricus* (1696), the earliest illustrated account of the medicinal plants of southern India. Based on van Reede's description, Carl Linnaeus provided it with its first binomial name, *Epidendrum*

Below: *Rhynchostylis retusa* (as *Saccolabium retusum*) drawn by Sarah Drake for *Edwards' Botanical Register* in 1831.

Opposite: Kew herbarium specimen of *Rhynchostylis retusa* (as *Saccolabium guttulatum*) collected by Robert Wight near Madras in southern India.

retusum, in his *Species Plantarum* (1753) – the genus at the time being widely used for most tropical orchids, and the epithet referring to the V-shaped notch in the leaf tip. The botanist Carl Ludwig Blume transferred it to his new genus *Rhynchostylis* in 1825 as part of his major review of tropical Asiatic orchids.

Good forms of *R. retusa* regularly fetched high prices at auction in London sales rooms. In 1855, Ashton bought a plant at auction for £22 10s, and two more were sold for £42 and £31 10s, respectively. In 1880, a plant fetched £63 at a Stevens's sale.

John Day purchased two plants as early as 1861, paying £32 and £46, respectively, for them at a sale of Dr Butler's established plants at Woolwich. On 3 July 1878 he painted a plant that had been purchased from Lady Emma Ashburton's sale at Stevens's sales rooms on 25 July 1875, and he noted that at the sale "the colour was so fine and the spike so long (27 inches) that there was a keen competition for it". He painted it again on 20 August 1878, using a plant bought in March 1863 from the nursery of Low & Co., who had imported it from Burma. Day commented that it was "an old resident of Tottenham [where he grew his orchids] and from its vigour and healthy appearance I think it will last some years longer".

Nathaniel Wallich, then Superintendent of the Calcutta Botanic Garden, collected a second species, *R. gigantea*, near Prome in Burma, and John Lindley described it as *Saccolabium giganteum* in 1833 in his *Genera and Species of Orchidaceous Plants*, the first extensive treatment of the world's orchids. It is similar to *R. retusa*, but has flowers that are half as large again as those of the latter. Henry Ridley, who introduced rubber to Malaya, transferred this species to the genus *Rhynchostylis* in 1896. It is a widespread orchid in lowland south-east Asia, being found in Burma (now Myanmar), South China, Thailand, Laos, Vietnam and Malaya. It is commonly found on large old fig trees around temples.

John Day drew it several times, and in fact it was one of the earliest orchids that he drew, under the later name *Saccolabium violaceum*, in his first scrapbook on 12 January 1863. A colour painting of a flower was added to the page on 9 February 1864. Day painted it in 1867, using a plant that he had bought at Stevens's sales rooms from a Benson collection from Burma, and again in 1881, using a plant bought from B. S. Williams.

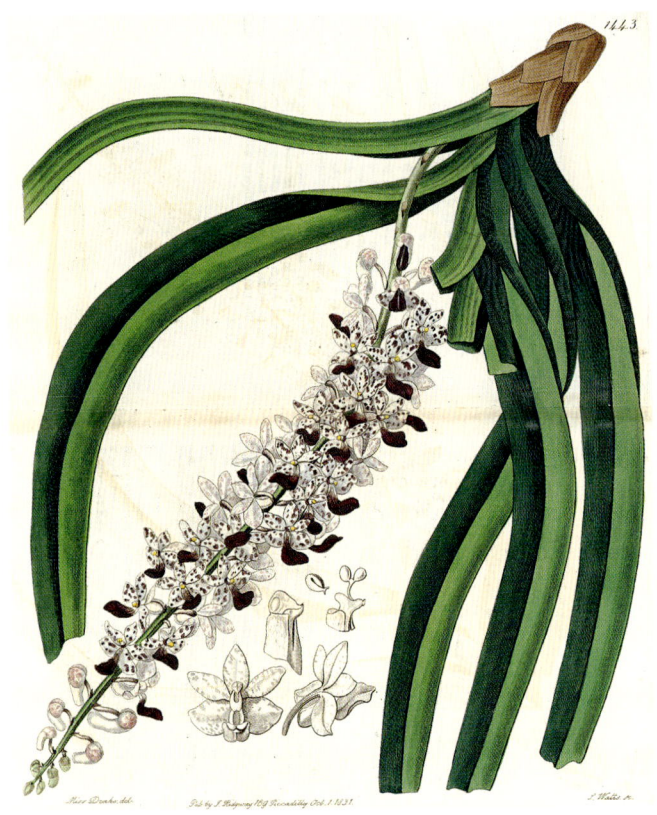

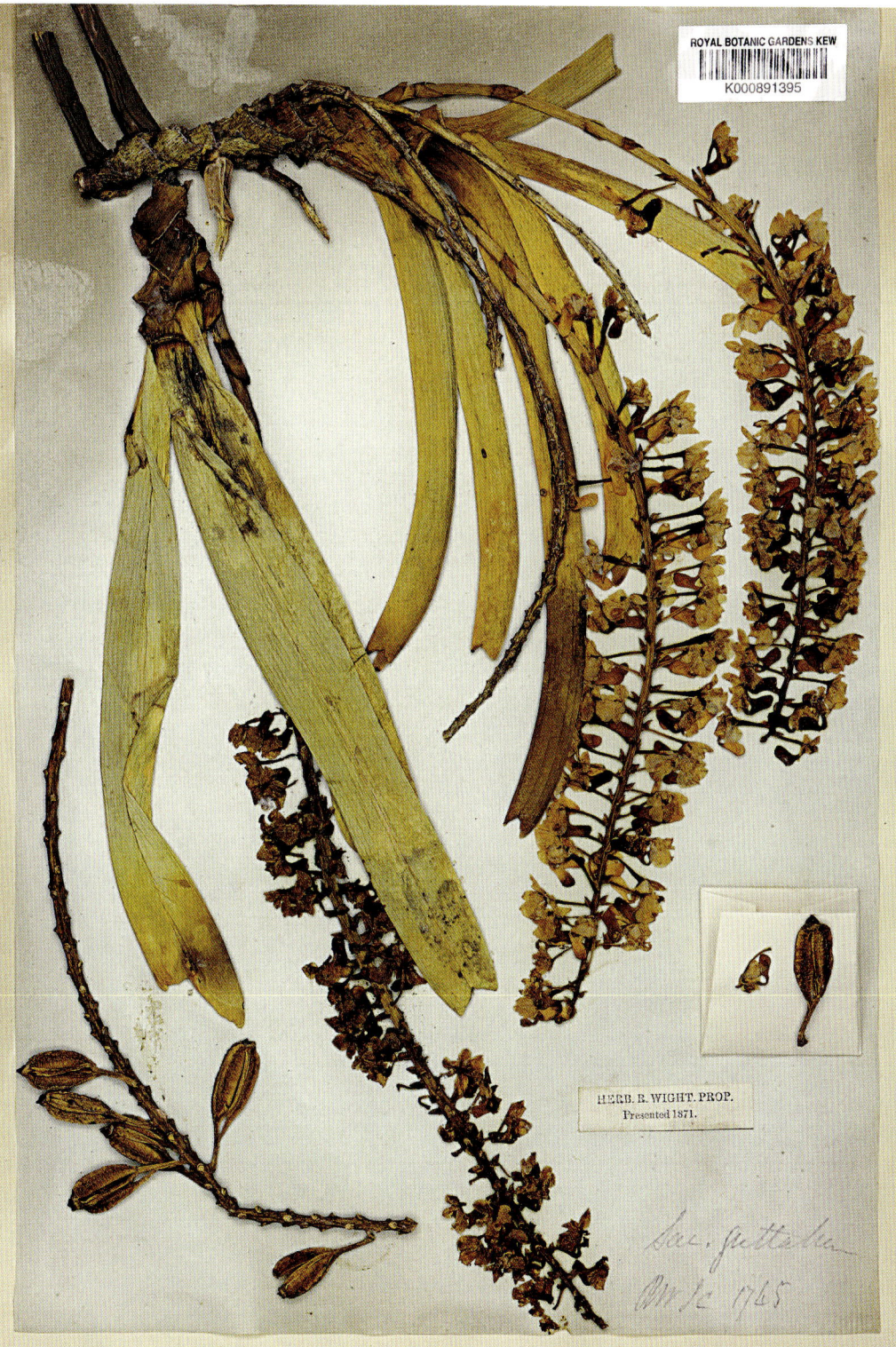

HERB. R. WIGHT. PROP.
Presented 1871.

Sac. guttatum

BM fc 1765

Rhynchostylis retusa Bl.
Flora of Madras
Det. J. Fischer
5. ii. 1927

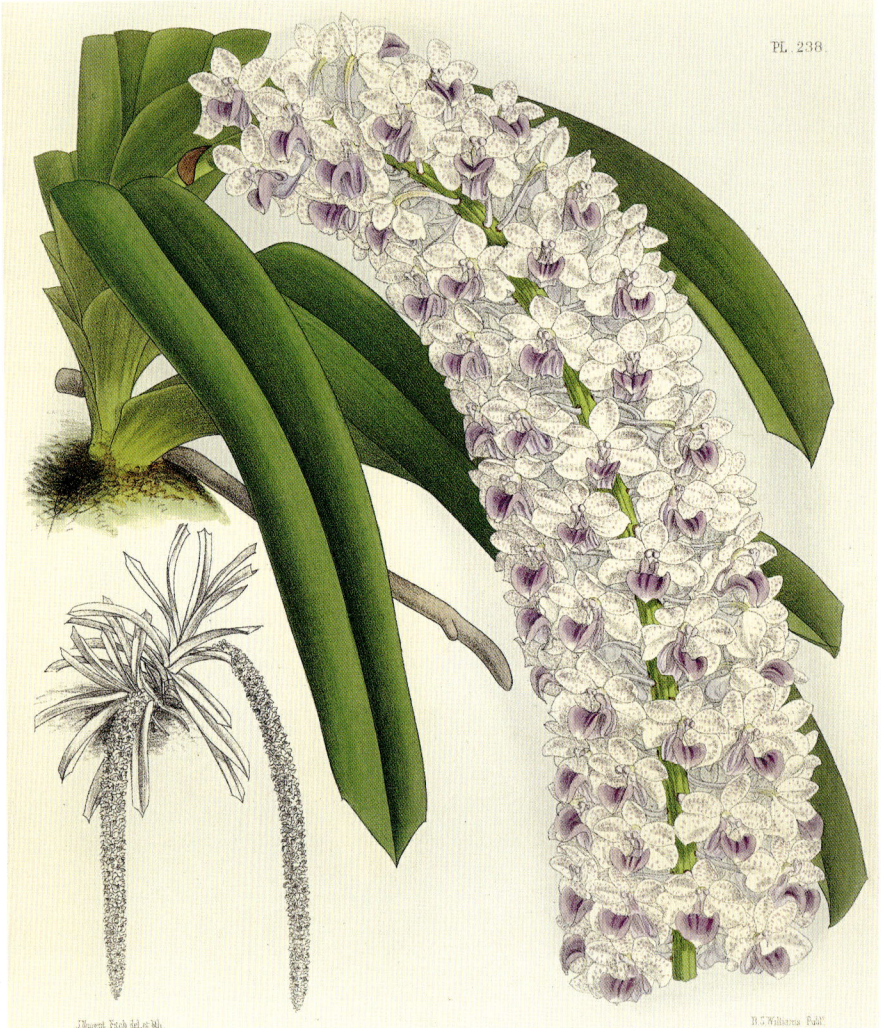

PL. 238.

J.Nugent Fitch del.et lith.

B.S.Williams Publ.

Left: *Rhynchostylis retusa* (as *Saccolabium blumei* var. *russellianum*) flowered by R. H. Measures of The Woodlands, Streatham in 1885 and drawn by John Nugent Fitch for R. Warner and B. S. Williams, *The Orchid Album* of 1886.

Day's final painting of this orchid, on 26 October 1883, depicted the albino variety, using a plant imported by the nursery of Low & Co. "from the island of Pulo [Pulau] Copang in the China Seas" and purchased by Day at Stevens's sales rooms the previous day.

Over the years, selections of both species have been made so that nowadays it is possible to find white, purple, pink-spotted and blue-spotted forms of these species in cultivation. These have become much more common in recent years because the best forms have been meristemmed, allowing the production of many plants from a single selected clone.

The genus *Aerides*, also found throughout south-east Asia and the Philippines, but in addition in the Malay Archipelago, produces similar sprays of flowers to *Rhynchostylis*. The widespread species *Aerides odoratum*, *A. multiflorum* and *A. roseum* are often found in cultivation, but the Philippine species *A. lawrencianum* and *A. jarkianum* are equally attractive and widely cultivated.

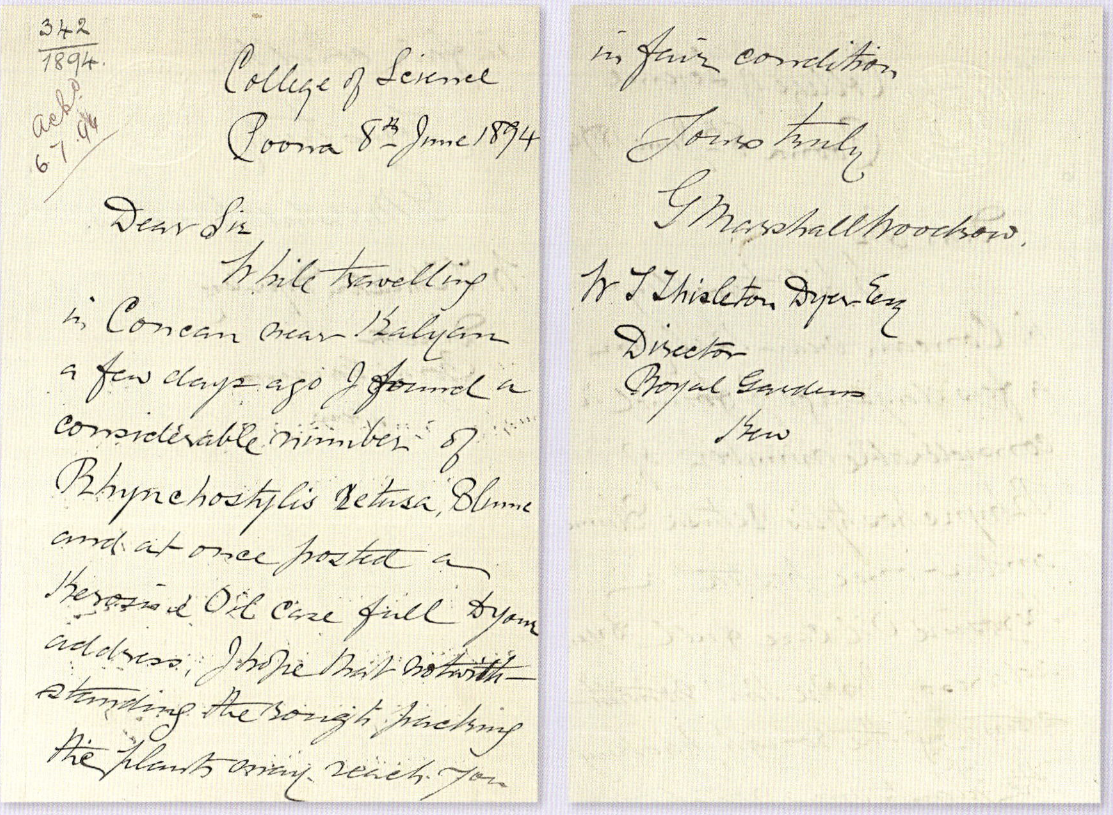

342
1894.
ackd
6.7.94

College of Science
Poona 8th June 1894

Dear Sir

While travelling in Concan near Kalyan a few days ago I found a considerable number of Rhynchostylis retusa, Blume and at once posted a kerosine Oil case full to your address. I hope that notwithstanding the rough packing the plants may reach you in fair condition

Yours truly

G Marshall Woodrow.

W. T. Thiselton Dyer Esq
Director
Royal Gardens
Kew

Letter from George Marshall Woodrow to Sir William Thiselton-Dyer, from Poona, 8 June 1894

This letter from Mr Woodrow to Sir William Thiselton-Dyer, Director at Kew, announces the imminent arrival of several plants of *Rhynchostylis retusa* collected near Concan in India.

India was a fertile source for Victorian orchid collectors. Joseph Hooker collected seven baskets of the blue *Vanda coerulea* during his expedition to the Himalayas. The Duke of Devonshire commissioned William Gibson to collect orchids for him in India. The beautiful *Dendrobium devonianum* and *D. gibsonii* commemorate his success.

Plate CIII.

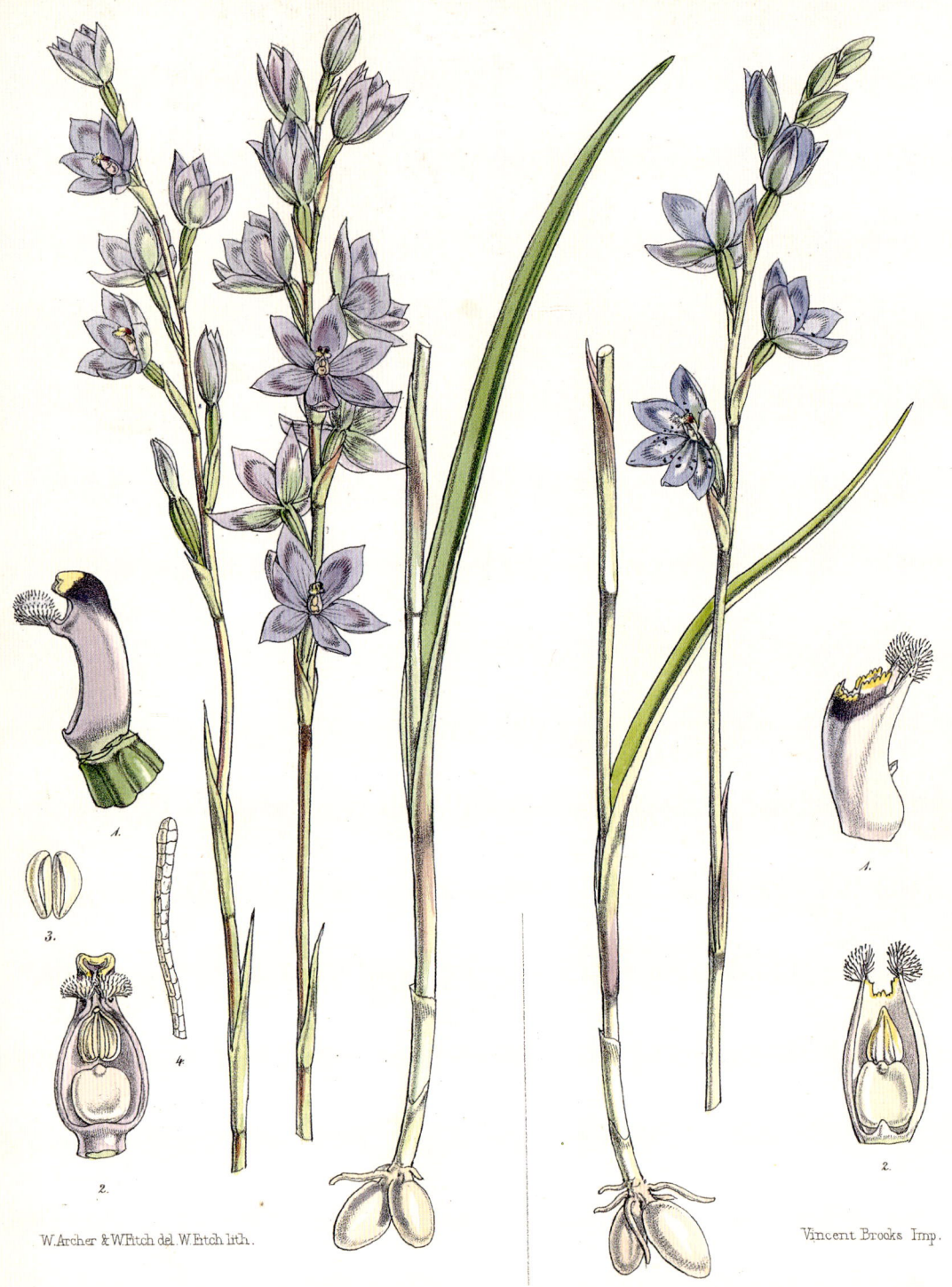

W.Archer & W.Fitch del. W.Fitch lith.

Vincent Brooks Imp.

A. Thelymitra nuda, *Br.*   *B.* T ixioides, *Sm*

SPOTTED SUN ORCHID
THELYMITRA IXIOIDES

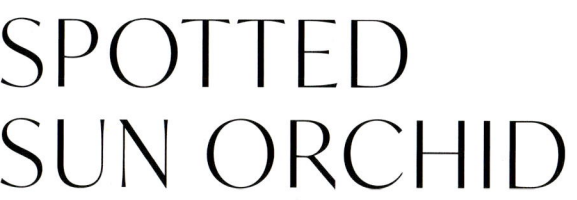

Opposite: *Thelymitra nuda* and *Thelymitra ixioides* by W. Archer and Walter Hood Fitch in *The Botany of the Antarctic Voyage of H.M. Discovery Ships* Erebus *and* Terror *in the Years 1839–1843*, 1860.

Right: *Thelymitra ixioides* by F. A. Charsley, in *The Wild Flowers Around Melbourne*, 1867.

The Australian terrestrial orchid genus *Thelymitra* is unusual in the orchid family in that it has radially symmetrical flowers, where all six of the perianth segments (sepals and petals) are essentially the same in appearance. Most orchids have bilaterally symmetrical flowers (also known as zygomorphic flowers), like those of snapdragons (*Antirrhinum*). Far less common in orchids is radial symmetry (actinomorphy), as seen in flowers of roses and cherries (both Rosaceae). Most orchids have the standard monocotyledonous flower structure consisting of three sepals, three petals and three ovules, but with five of the sepals and petals being very similar (and often referred to collectively as tepals), and one of the petals being modified, often highly and ornately, to form the labellum (the "lip"). The labellum is thought to be specialized to facilitate cross-pollination, by helping to attract a specific pollinator, often acting as a landing platform for flying insects, and guiding them into the correct orientation in which to pick up and deposit the pollen of the orchid species.

The flowers of species in the genus *Thelymitra*, members of the tribe Diurideae in the subfamily Orchidoideae, do not have a distinctly different labellum, but they do all have the structure called the column – a structure that unites all members of the orchid family. In the column of an orchid, the male and female parts of the flower (i.e. the stamens and the pistil, including the stigmatic surface)

G Y N A N D R I A

D I A N D R I A.

49. THELYMITRA.

CAL. *Spathæ* lanceolatæ, acutæ, univalves, unifloræ.
COR. *Petala* fex ovato-lanceolata, patentia, concava, tria exteriora majora.
Nectarium monophyllum, bilabiatum; Lab. *fuperius* truncatum breviſſimum. *L. inferius* erectum, trifidum,
lacinia media cucullata, lateralibus tenuibus barba ra-
diante in apice.
STAM. *Filamenta* duo piſtillo inſidentia minima. *Antheræ* ovatæ;
(juniores) tectæ duplicaturâ Labii inferioris nectarii.
PIST. *Germen* inferum. Stylus ovatus, brevis in centra nectarii
baſi cavitate mellifera inſtructus. *Stigma* obtuſum.
PER. *Capfula* clavato-turbinata, tricarinata, trivalvis, unilocularis.
SEM. plurima, ſcobiformia, receptaculis longitudinaliter parieti
adnatis, adhærentia.

O

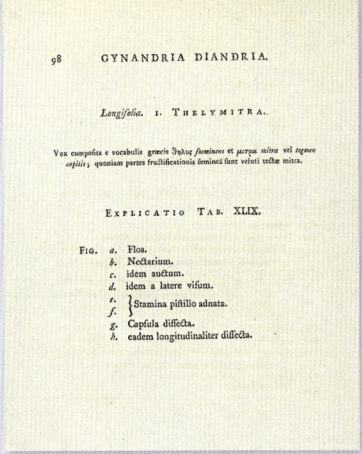

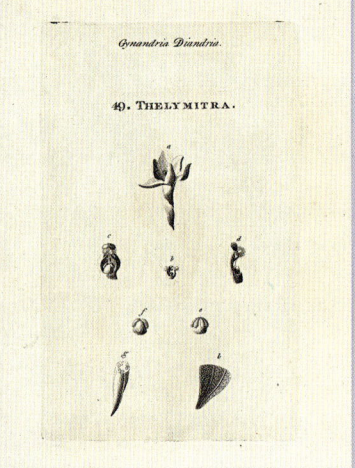

Original description of the genus *Thelymitra*, published in *Characteres Generum Plantarum, quas in Itinere ad Insulas Maris Australis: Collegerunt, Descripserunt, Delinearunt, Annis* by Johann Reinhold Forster and Johann Georg Adam Forster, 1776

Father and son Johann Reinhold Forster and Georg (full name Johann Georg Adam) Forster accompanied Captain James Cook on his second circumnavigation of the world (1772–75). As well as a substantial haul of taxa new to European science, the Forsters collected natural history specimens including plants, birds, fish and land animals, from South Africa, New Zealand, New Caledonia and Polynesia, with comprehensive observations and notes, and Georg Forster's remarkably accurate illustrations. Thousands of herbarium specimens resulted from the voyage, and the book *Characteres Generum Plantarum* was published just a year after they returned to Europe. The pair validly published some 106 species new to science from the voyage, and 77 genera, including a single orchid genus *Thelymitra* and a single species within it, *Thelymitra longiflora*, as seen here.

Right: *Thelymitra variegata* and *Thelymitra antennifera* by Robert David Fitzgerald, in *Australian Orchids*, 1875–82.

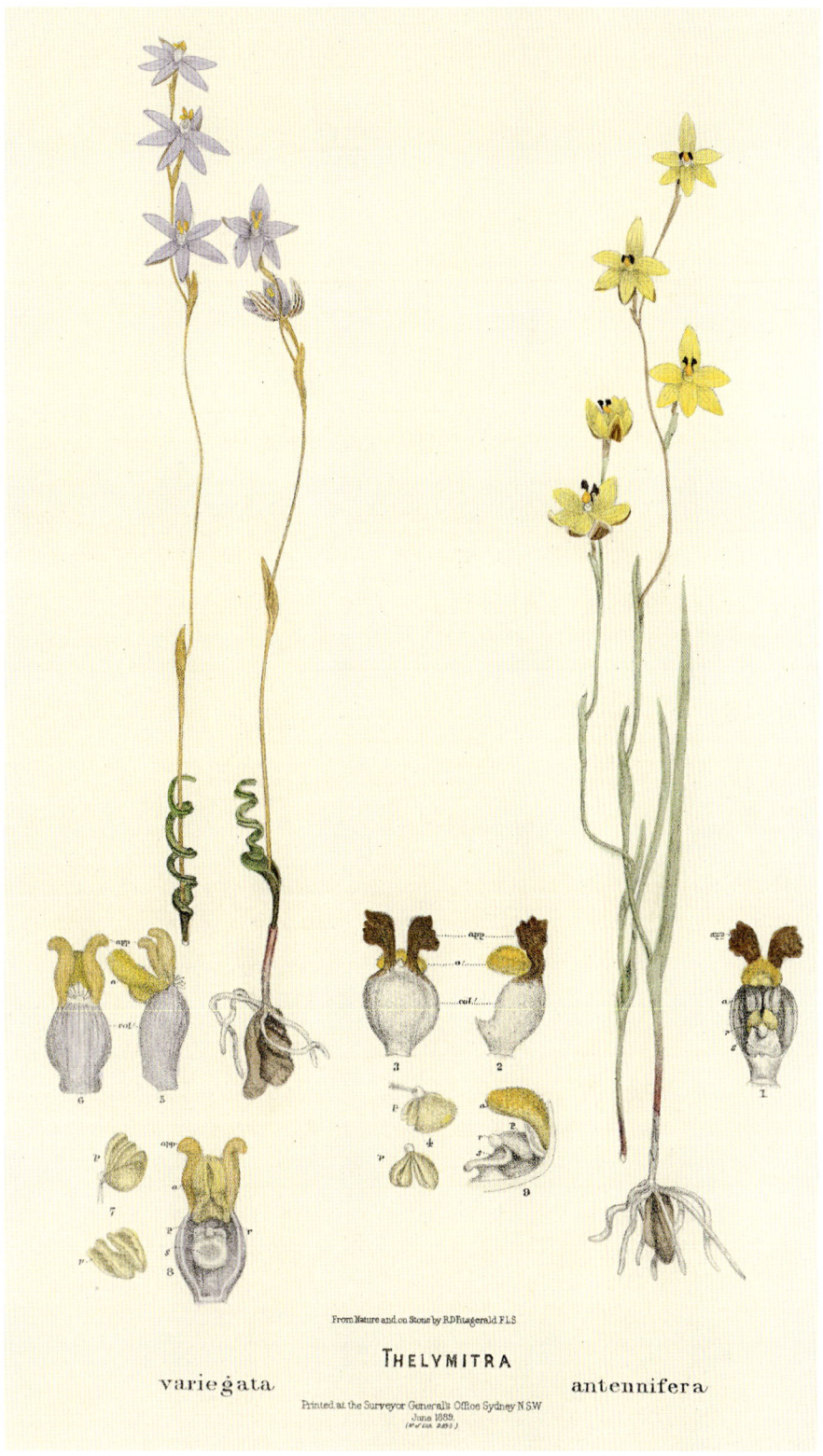

From Nature and on Stone by R.D.Fitzgerald F.L.S.

THELYMITRA

variegata   antennifera

Printed at the Surveyor General's Office Sydney N.S.W
June 1883.

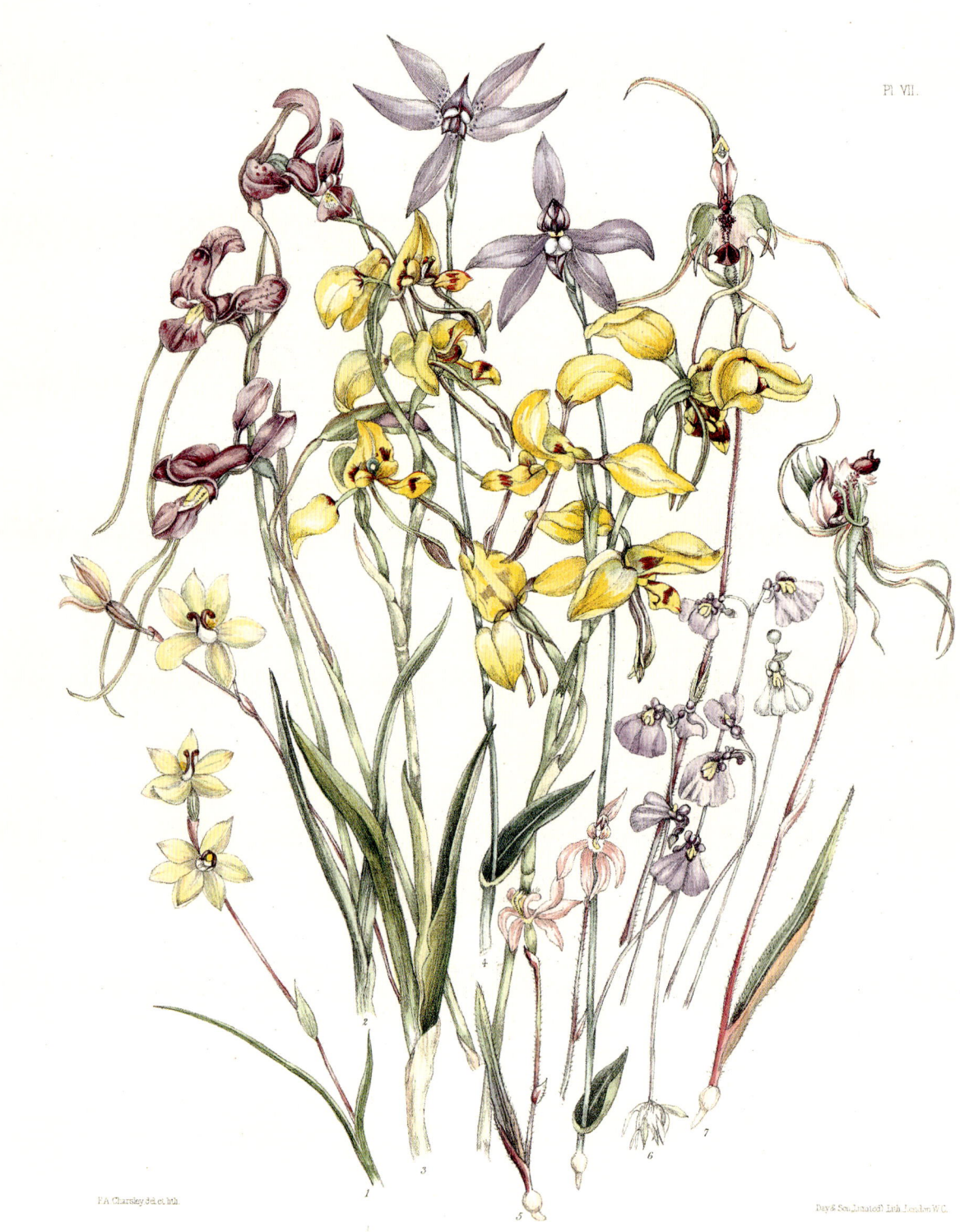

Pl. VII.

F.A Charsley del. et. lith.

1

2

3

4

5

6

7

Day & Son, Limited. Lith. London W.C.

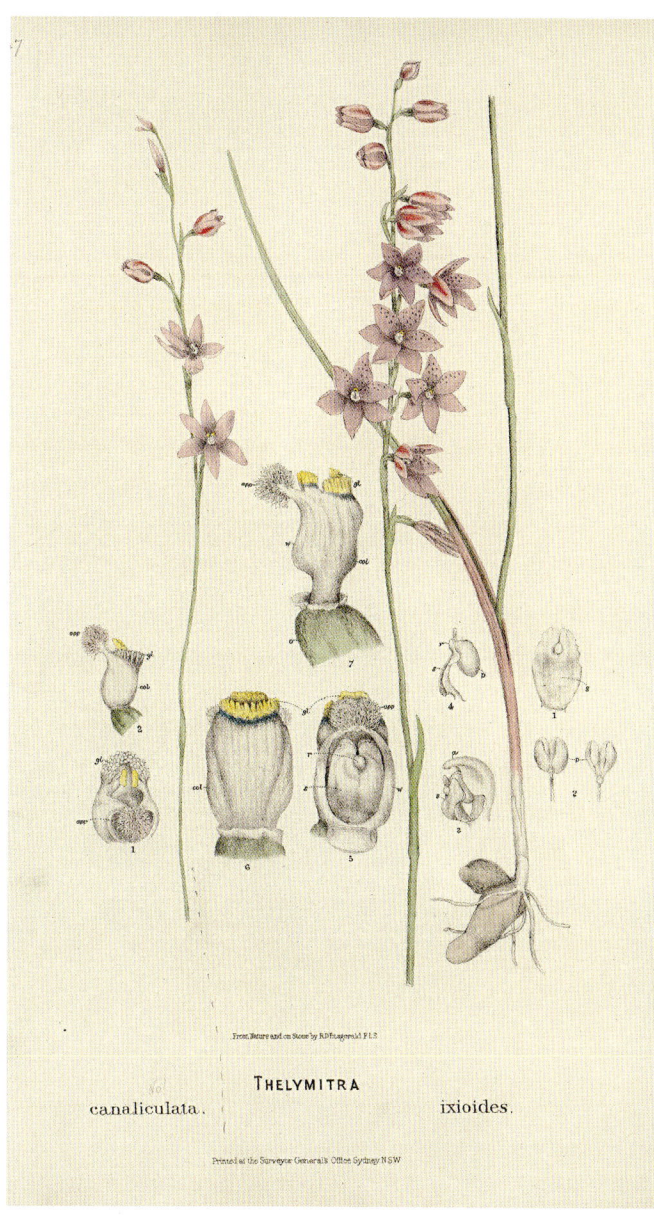

THELYMITRA

canaliculata.   ixioides.

Printed at the Surveyor General's Office Sydney N.S.W.

Opposite: *Thelymitra
ixioides* (and other
orchids including
Caladenia and *Diuris*),
as well as bladderwort
(*Utriculata*) by F. A.
Charsley, *The Wild
Flowers Around
Melbourne*, 1867.

Above: *Thelymitra
canaliculata* and
Thelymitra ixioides
by Robert David
Fitzgerald, in
Australian Orchids,
1875–82.

are fused into a single unit. Whereas
many orchid species are distinguished by
characteristics of the labellum, the
species in the genus *Thelymitra* are
distinguished based on the modifications
of the column, which may include
features such as inflated wings, fimbriate
calli, multiple lobes and elaborate glands.

Known as "sun orchids", the flowers
of *Thelymitra* open fully in the middle of
the day, in the heat of the sun. Before
late morning and after early afternoon,
and on cool or overcast days, the flowers
are closed. Blue flowers such as those
of *T. ixioides* are unusual in the plant
world, but the genus contains a number
of blue-hued species, along with a range
of other brightly coloured and strikingly
patterned species, such as *T. variegata*,
T. spiralis and *T. villosa*. The species can
readily self-fertilize or outcross via insect
pollinators, and it is thought that the
flowers mimic the appearance of flowers
of other groups of plants, including the
Iridaceae, the irises.

Joseph Banks, who was later to become
the President of the Royal Society,
collected the first specimens of the genus,
T. longifolia, from New Zealand during
Captain James Cook's first expedition
to the South Pacific (between 1768 and
1771). However, the species and genus
were not formally published until 1776,
by father and son Johann and Georg
Forster, who accompanied Cook on his
second voyage to the Pacific between
1772 and 1775, when they collected
more material of the same species. The
generic name *Thelymitra* was based on the
Greek words *thelys*, meaning "belonging
to women", and *mitra*, meaning "hood"
or "head-dress", referring to the hood-
shaped appearance of the column at the
centre of each flower.

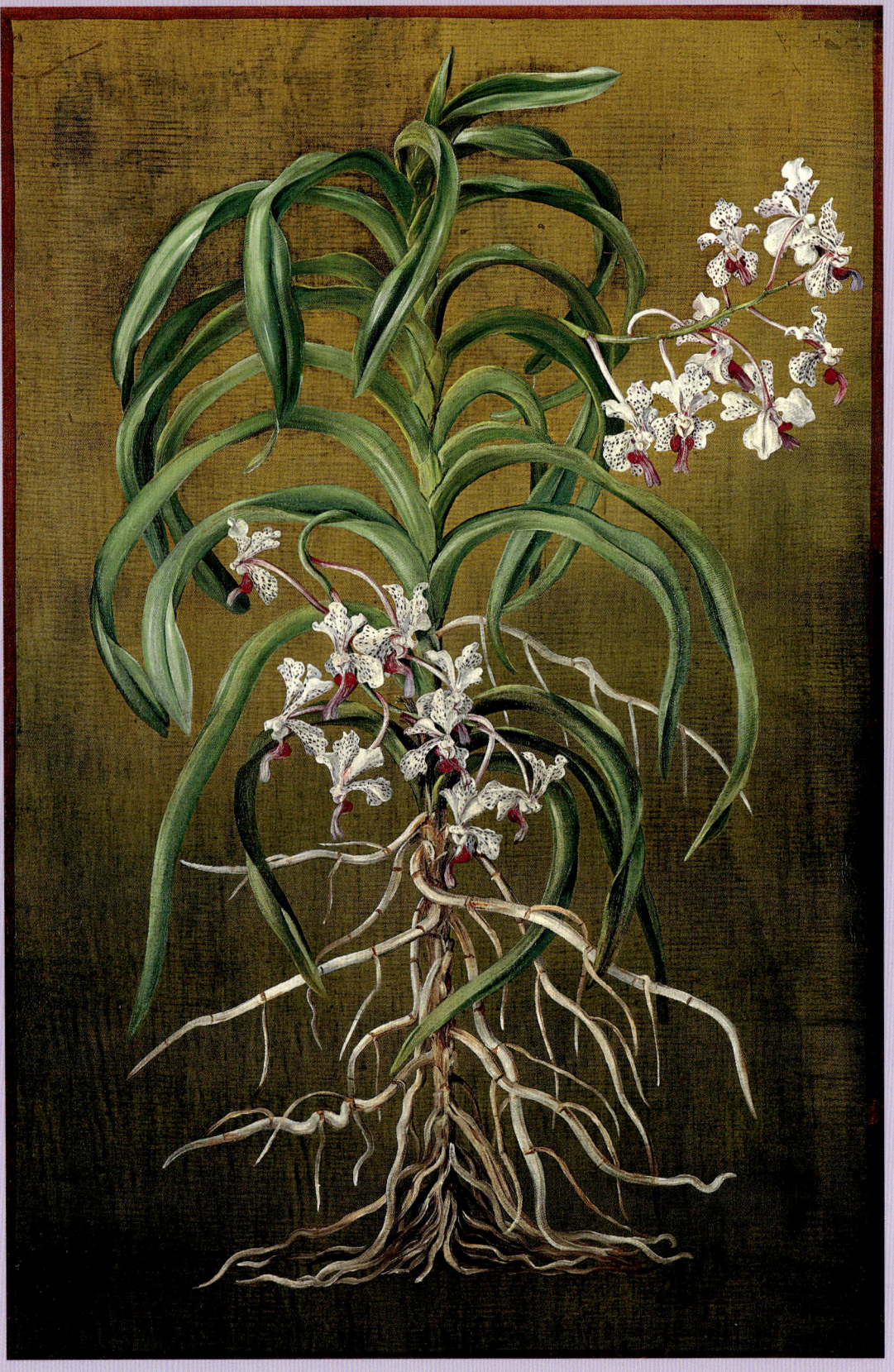

FRAGRANT TRICOLOURED VANDA

VANDA TRICOLOR VAR. SUAVIS

Species of the genus *Vanda* seem to have flowers of every possible colour – blue, white, pink, yellow, red, orange, green and brown. Combined with the enormous range of hybrids produced by artificially crossing species and hybrids from within the genus and with other genera, virtually any combination of colours seems to be possible too. *Vanda* species are found throughout much of tropical and subtropical Asia, extending to Queensland, Australia, and some islands in the north-west Pacific. They form one of the most horticulturally important orchid groups, with only genera such as *Phalaenopsis*, *Cymbidium* and *Dendrobium* accounting for more floral trade around the world.

The genus *Vanda* is a hugely diverse group of species, and some of these orchids are extremely fragrant, such as *Vanda tricolor* var. *suavis*, which is found in central and eastern Java and Bali. Originally this beautiful scrambling *Vanda* was described as a separate species in its own right, as *Vanda suavis*, by the English botanist John Lindley in 1848. The German orchidologist Heinrich Gustav Reichenbach reconsidered the taxon's placement in relation to the species *Vanda tricolor*, which Lindley had also described a year earlier, in 1847, and decided that it was actually a variety of his friend's earlier species, publishing it as such in 1864. For some time opinion was split as to whether or not *suavis* was a species in its own right, or a variety of *tricolor*. Today plants are still sometimes referred to as *Vanda suavis*, but more recent DNA evidence supports it being considered as a variety, as *Vanda tricolor* var. *suavis*. As in Englishman James Veitch's *Hortus Veitchii* (1906), where it was noted that the two taxa always occurred together in the wild, the two are extremely similar in vegetative structure and floral morphology, with the main differences in the colours of the flowers, their scent (or lack of it) and some slight differences in the shape of the labellum.

The flowers of *Vanda tricolor* var. *suavis* have a brilliant white background, whereas those of *Vanda tricolor* var. *tricolor* tend to be off-white to light yellow in colour. The variety *suavis* has deep fuchsia spots and dashes on the tepals, and the labellum narrows tightly in the middle, and is a similar deep purple-

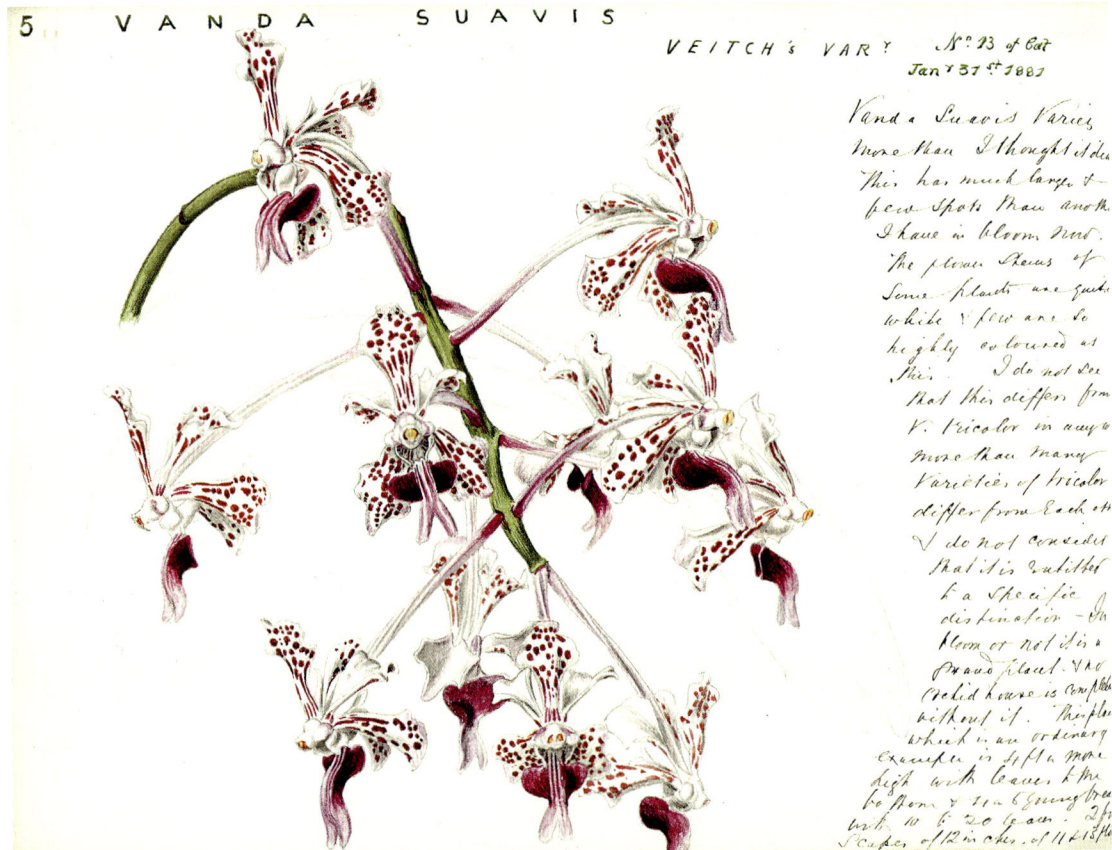

VEITCH's VAR.ᵗ N.º 23 of Cat Janᵗ 31ˢᵗ 1881

Vanda Suavis Varies more than I thought it does. This has much larger & fewer spots than another I have in bloom now. The flower shews of some plants are quite white & few are so highly coloured as this. I do not see that this differs from V. tricolor in anyt more than many varieties of tricolor differ from each ot & I do not consider that it is entitled to a specific distinction. In bloom or not it is a grand plant & no orchid house is complete without it. The plant which is an ordinary example is 5ft 11 inches high with leaves & the...

fuchsia colour, whereas the streaks and labellum of *Vanda tricolor* var. *tricolor* are much more red-brown in hue. However, it is the fragrance of *Vanda tricolor* var. *suavis* that is particularly striking and highly prized, and this attribute gave the plant its epithet *suavis*, meaning "sweet".

John Day found *Vanda tricolor* in its various forms, including the variety *suavis*, so pleasing that, starting in 1864 and over the course of 20 years, he painted it eleven times in total, writing that "In bloom or not, it is a grand plant and no orchid house is complete without it."

Both *Vanda tricolor* and *Vanda tricolor* var. *suavis* were collected in Java by the plant explorer Thomas Lobb, who in the mid-1800s worked for the Veitch family's nurseries based in Exeter and

London. Lobb collected widely in south-east Asia, and is commemorated in the names of many orchid species. Lobb sent plants back to England from Singapore, Java, Sumatra, Burma, Borneo, the Philippines and India, but his collecting exploits came to an early end when one of his legs had to be amputated while he was in the Philippines. His older brother, William Lobb, was also a collector for Veitch, but specialized in the Americas, working in Brazil, Argentina, Ecuador, Peru, Panama and Chile, and later in North America, in Oregon and California. Between them, over the two decades when they collected for Veitch, the Lobb brothers introduced a great many orchids, and exotic plants, to cultivation and botanical science.

Above: *Vanda tricolor* var. *suavis* (as *Vanda suavis*) by John Day, 1881.

Opposite: *Vanda tricolor* (as *Vanda suavis* var. *pallens*) in J. J. Linden, *Pescatorea*, 1860.

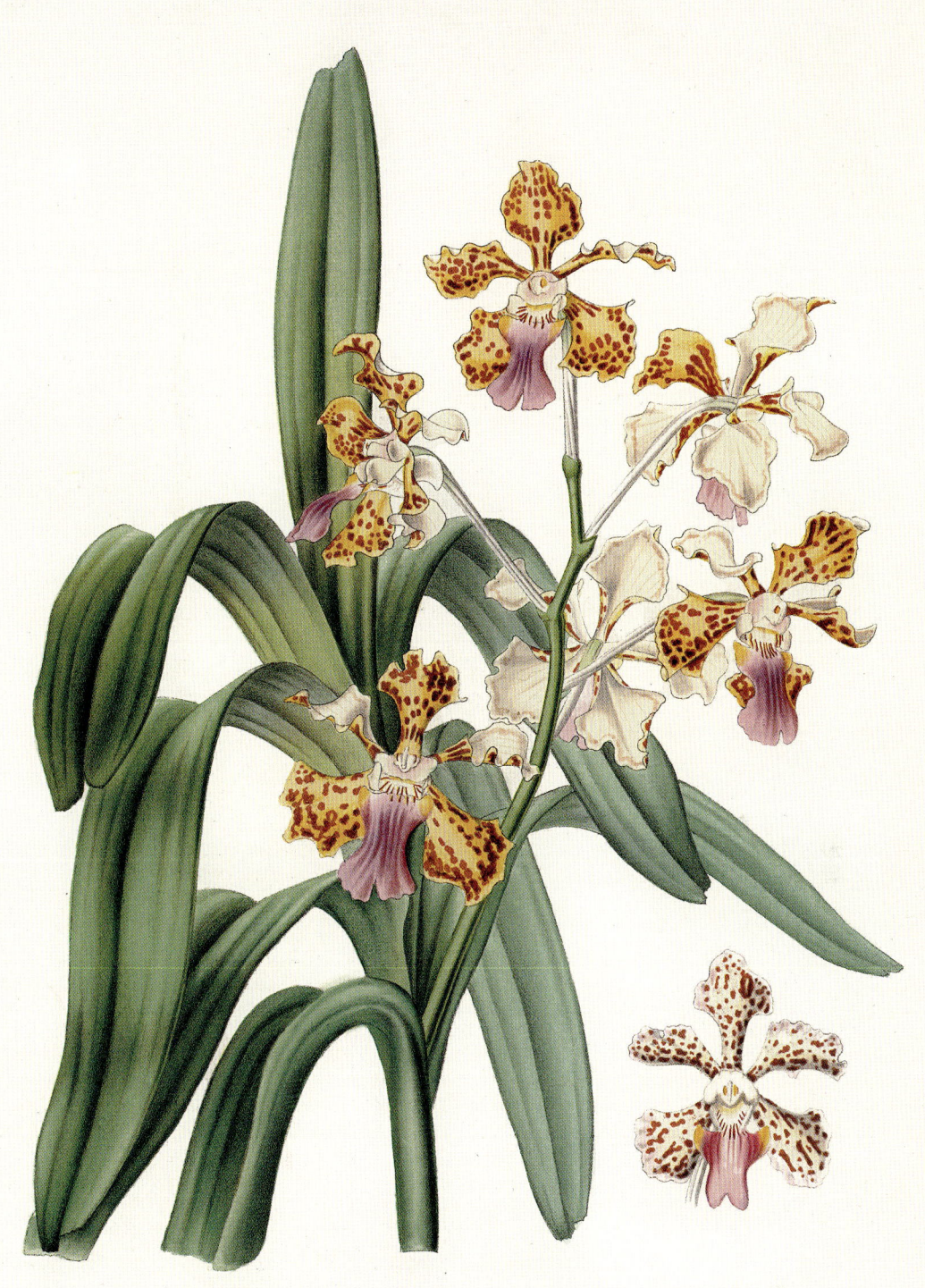

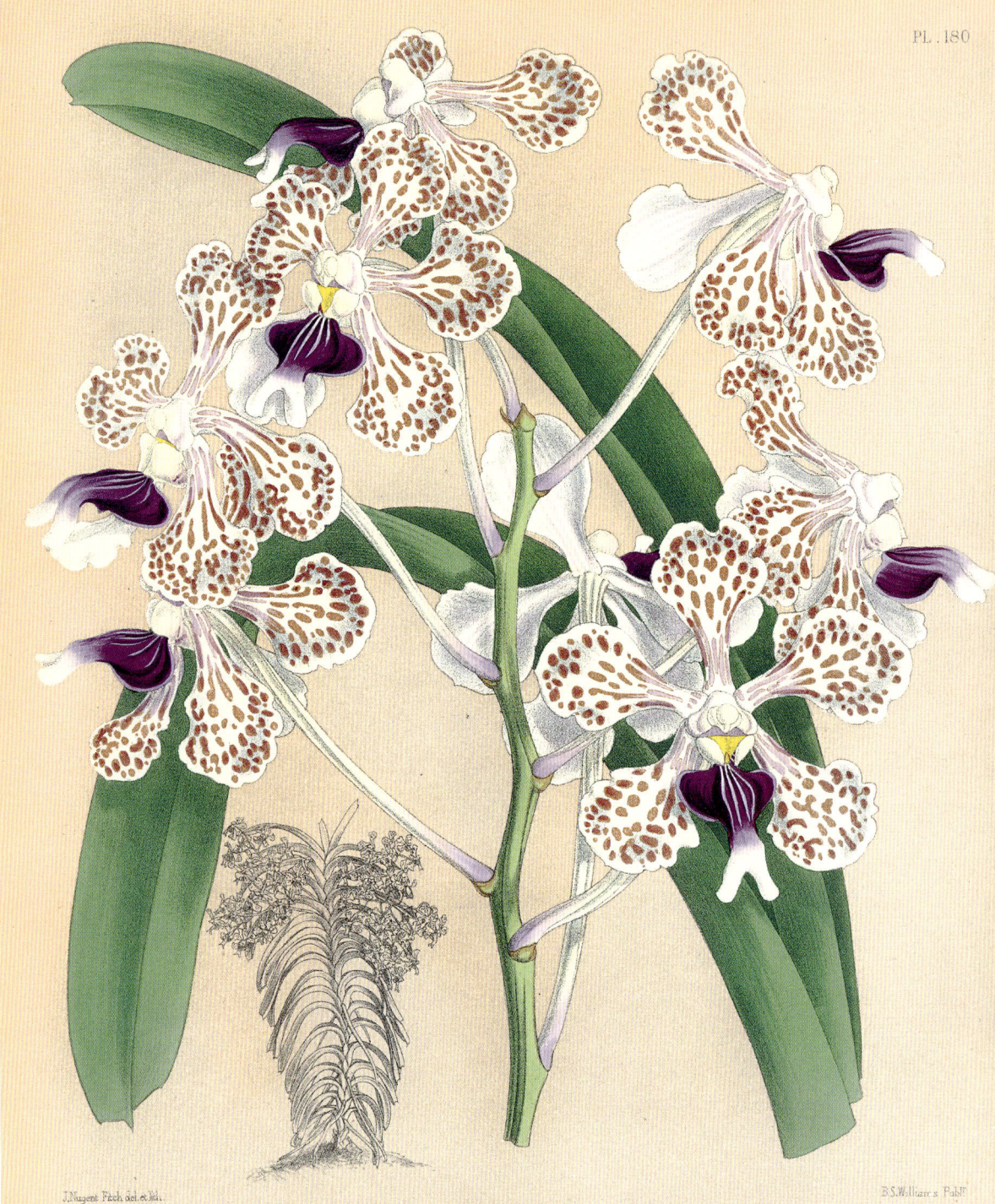

J.Nugent Fitch del et lith.

B.S.Williams Pub.

VANDA SUAVIS

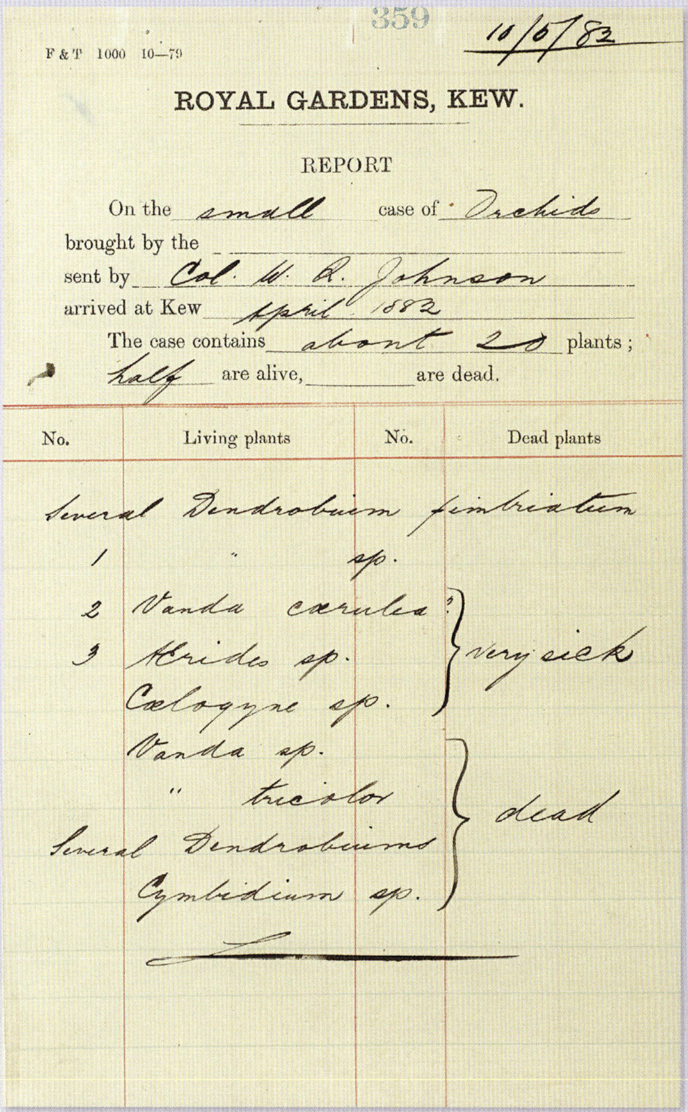

359

10/5/82

F & T 1000 10—79

ROYAL GARDENS, KEW.

REPORT

On the *small* case of *Orchids*
brought by the _____
sent by *Col. W. R. Johnson*
arrived at Kew *April 1882*
The case contains *about 20* plants;
half are alive, _____ are dead.

No.	Living plants	No.	Dead plants
	Several Dendrobium fimbriatum		
1	" *sp.*		
2	*Vanda cœrulea?*		
3	*Aerides sp.*	} *very sick*	
	Cœlogyne sp.		
	Vanda sp.		
	" *tricolor*	} *dead*	
	Several Dendrobiums		
	Cymbidium sp.		

Report from the Royal Botanic Gardens, Kew, 10 May 1882

By the end of the 1800s, the Royal Botanic Gardens, Kew were receiving and despatching consignments of plants from correspondents all over the world. Plants from distant countries were collected in the wild, sometimes cultivated in other botanical institutions, before being packed and sent by sea or land, usually in less than ideal conditions for the plants' survival. As the report here shows, many plants did not survive the journey – out of 20 plants sent by Colonel W. R. Johnson in a single small case from India, half were dead on their arrival, in April 1882. Several *Dendrobium* plants survived, but *Vanda coerulea* plants, and plants belonging to the genera *Aerides* and *Coelogyne* were described as "very sick". The casualities of the consignment included other *Vanda* plants, among them *Vanda tricolor*, as well as *Dendrobium*, and *Cymbidium* species, which all arrived dead.

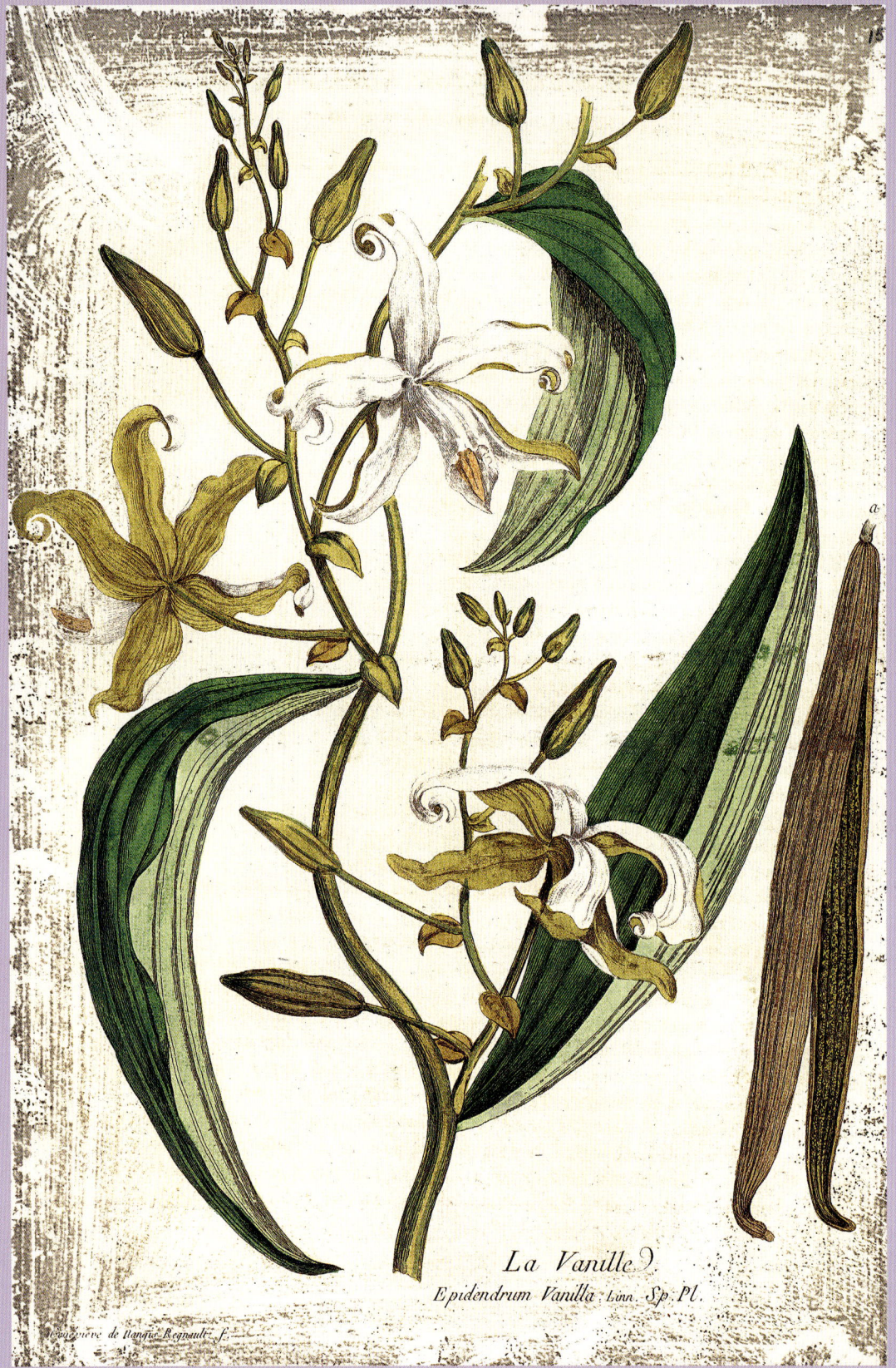

La Vanille

Epidendrum Vanilla Linn. *Sp. Pl.*

FLAT-LEAVED OR COMMON VANILLA
VANILLA PLANIFOLIA

Vanilla is one of the most commonly used "spices" in fragrances and cooking, and the most globally significant agricultural crop in the orchid family. There are over 100 species of *Vanilla* around the world, but nearly all commercially traded and used vanilla comes from the species *Vanilla planifolia*. Also known as the flat-leaved vanilla, or common vanilla, the species originally came from Mexico, Central America and northern South America. Occasionally *Vanilla pompona* and *Vanilla × tahitensis* are encountered in trade, and around the world different species may be used in the same way locally.

Growing as a vine up to 30 m (100 ft) in length, *Vanilla planifolia* is cultivated on trees or rows of stakes in plantations, and the production of vanilla pods is a labour-intensive process that does not lend itself to automation or mechanization. The greenish yellow flowers open early in the day and close by midday. If they are not pollinated during this short window of opportunity, they will die and be wasted. Most commercial vanilla is grown in Madagascar, Réunion

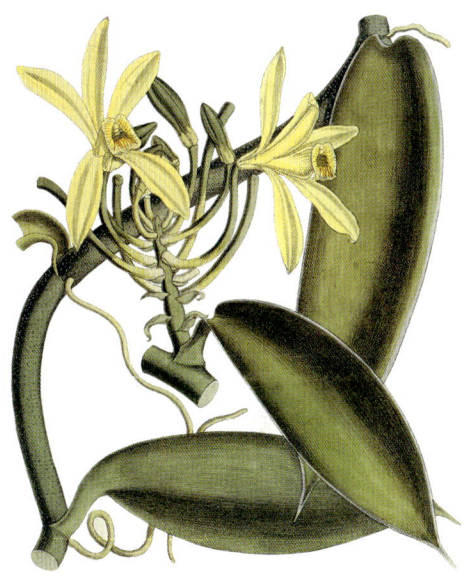

and Indonesia, but the stingless *Melipona* bees that pollinate the orchid in the wild are not present in these regions, so the flowers have to be pollinated individually by hand. The flowers develop at different rates, and only a single flower opens at a time on each vine. Hand pollination takes place very early in the morning when the flowers are most receptive, and a worker may pollinate over 1,000 flowers in a day. If pollination is successful, six to nine months later the flower will have produced a ripe seed pod. These pods are also known as "beans" but they are botanically a type of fruit called a "capsule" rather than a true "pod" or "bean". The pods are harvested by hand, blanched in hot water, and processed to develop the flavours. The maturation, or curing, process involves drying and sweating stages, again carried out by hand, and can easily take another five or six months.

The Aztec people of Mexico were the first to record their use of vanilla, incorporating it into their drink called cacahuatl, made from cocoa (*Theobroma cacao*) and vanilla, and was brought to Europe in the sixteenth century. Nowadays, vanilla is found in an enormous range of fragranced products – from expensive perfumes to cleaning products and even cigars – as well as being an important culinary flavouring in many items, including icecream, custard and chocolate.

Contrary to the common assumption, neither the flowers of a vanilla plant nor the fresh pods smell of vanilla – it is only when the pods have been cured that the flavour and scent compounds develop. These compounds are mainly found in the many tiny hairs that line the inside of the pod, surrounding the thousands of tiny black seeds. The principal component is a compound called vanillin, but a cocktail of more than 200 different compounds develop during curing, which means that vanilla pods coming from different sources or cultivars, or that have been processed in different ways, will have distinct flavour and scent profiles. Poor-quality vanilla pods, processed quickly to reduce costs, will command a much lower price than the best-quality pods. First synthesized in 1874, Vanillin – artificial "vanilla essence" – is widely used in many products and is far less expensive than real vanilla. Produced from a wide range of sources, including wood pulp from paper making, coal tar, clove oil and pine bark, artificial vanilla cannot replicate the unique cocktail of compounds found in genuine cured vanilla pods.

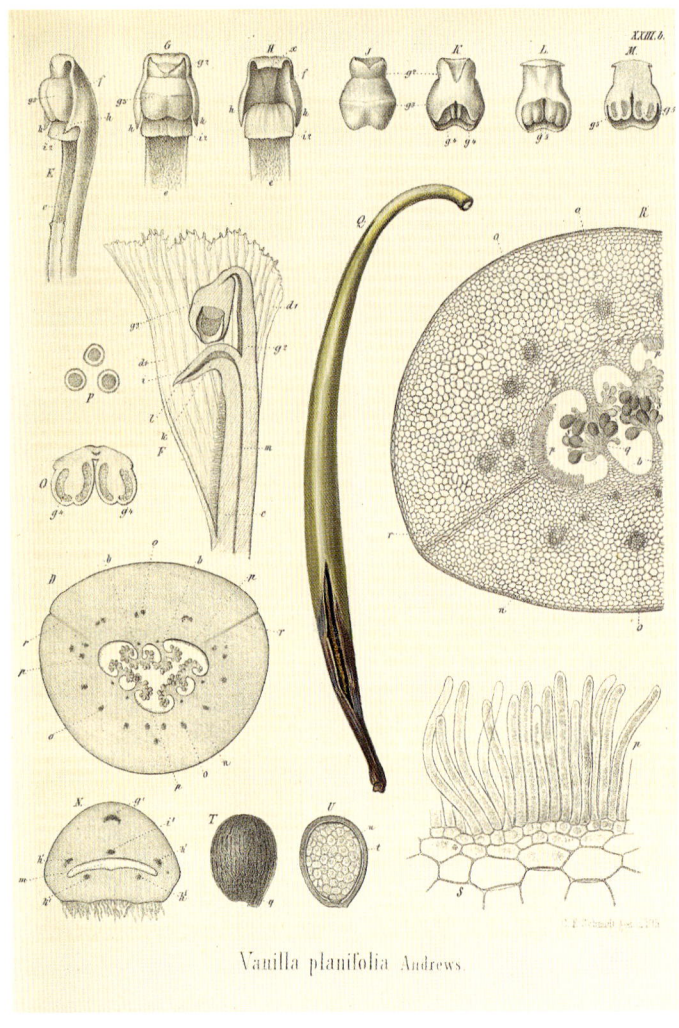

Vanilla planifolia Andrews

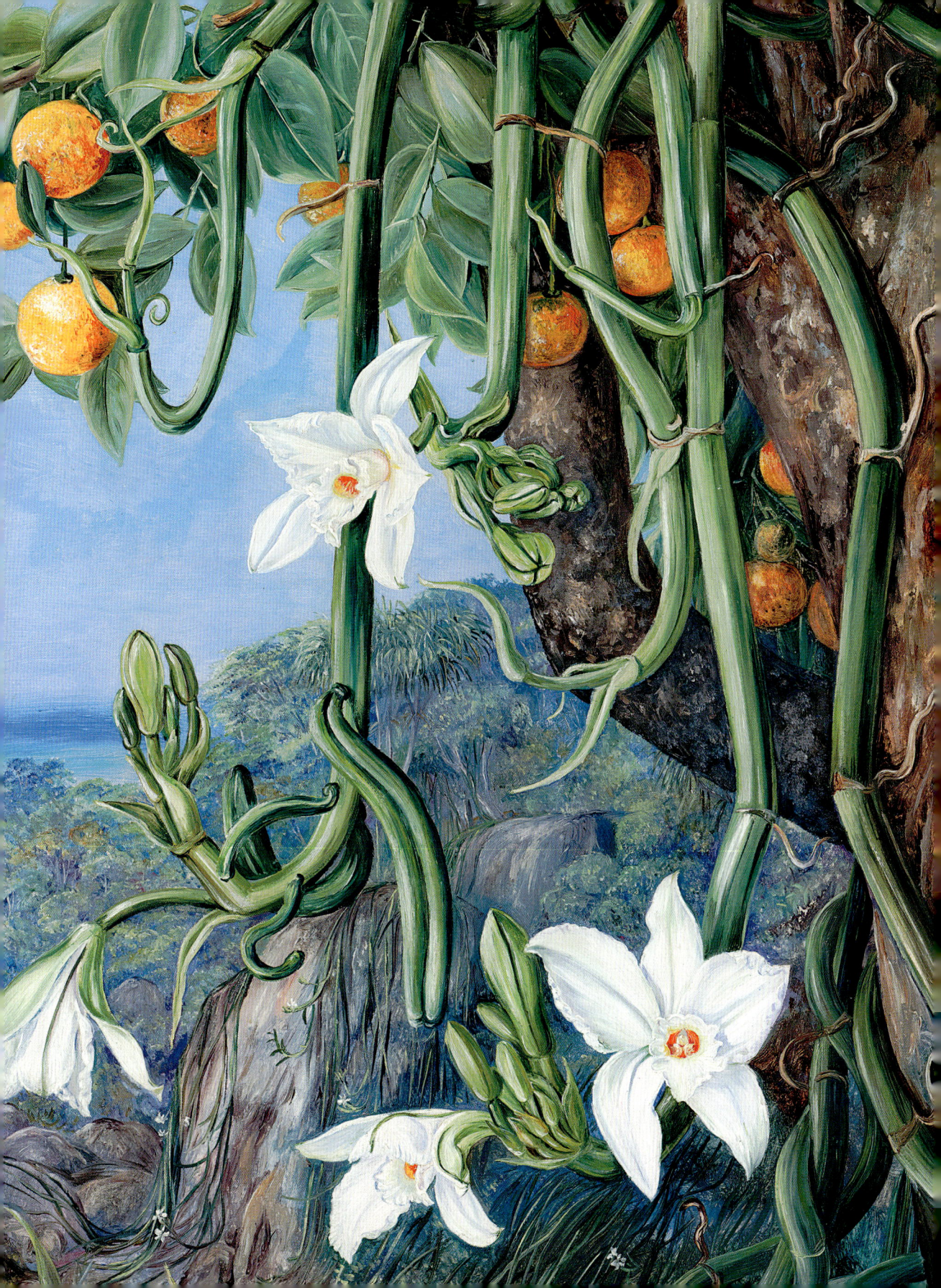

VANILLA CULTURE.

BY E. BENNETT, ENVILLE HALL, STOURBRIDGE.

As a stove climber the vanilla may safely be asserted to be one of the most interesting; its green, fleshy leaves, singular Cattleya-like flowers, delightfully fragrant fruit, and great length of roots, make it particularly well worth attention. When properly treated it is a plant of very rapid growth. A cutting placed in one of the pine pits here in August 1870, has made upwards of 240 feet of growth, and I look forward to its producing fruit this season. It grows freely in a mixture of peat, charcoal, and mortar rubbish. It may be trained in any form, and will attach itself to rough walls, wood, or iron. Having naturally little tendency to branch, I frequently stop my plants in order to make them throw out sideshoots, and in that way secure a greater amount of fruit-bearing wood. When at Osberton I tried several experiments with the vanilla, in order to find out the different temperatures in which the plants would fruit, and I came to the conclusion that for this purpose it is not requisite to keep up a high temperature. The largest plant at Osberton was planted out at the back of a succession pine stove, the temperature of which ranged from 50° to 65°, and sometimes much lower: this plant fruited freely every year. Indeed, one season I gathered off it upwards of 300 ripe pods, for which I obtained five first-class prizes. A second plant was planted in a fruiting pine stove, the temperature of which ranged from 60° to 85°; this also grew vigorously, and fruited well. A third was planted out in a house used for miscellaneous plants, the temperature of which ranged from 45° to 55°. This did not grow freely, but nevertheless bore fruit. I have therefore come to the conclusion that a temperature ranging from 50° to 70° is most suitable for the vanilla.

Major Trevor Clark has stated that the vanilla is a difficult plant to fruit; but failure doubtless occurs in many cases through want of knowledge of the art of fertilising the stigma, an operation requiring both care and skill. In the flowers of vanilla three sepals, and as many petals, surround the column which bears the anther and stigma. The first of these is attached to the summit of the column by a narrow curved neck, and contains, within a cavity on its lower surface, the pollen masses. The curved neck just alluded to bends towards the lower surface of the column, where it rests upon an organ called the retinaculum, which interposes between the anther and the stigmatic surface of the column; this latter, projecting from the column, lies immediately under the retinaculum, and terminates a bearded glandular process, which covers the lower surface of the column. The retinaculum, which is concave towards the stigma, effectually prevents all contact between that and the anther; it is therefore necessary to remove the retinaculum in order that the anther and stigma may be brought together, and this is best effected by means of a pair of narrow-pointed forceps. These should be carefully introduced sideways between the anther and stigma, seizing the retinaculum and tearing it off in the direction of the anther. The pollen masses are then drawn out, pressed down on the stigmatic surface of the column, and the operation is completed. If this is properly performed, the setting is certain; if not, the flowers will drop. Where, however, fertilisation has been effected, the flowers remain for a considerable time, or continue fixed to the fruit, which in twenty-four hours will be perceptibly elongated and in about twelve months will be ripe. It is requisite, therefore, that the vanilla should be planted and trained, so that when the flowers expand they may be easily got at. They generally open during the night or early in the morning; therefore the best time to fertilise them is in the morning, and this must be daily attended to as long as the plant is in bloom. The operation is so familiar to me now that I could venture to rely upon nearly every pod coming to maturity, although I must confess that I found artificial fertilisation difficult to accomplish at first.

I am of opinion that it would be a good speculation to grow vanilla in this country for commercial purposes, the price charged for imported produce being very high. English-grown pods are very highly flavoured, much more so than those which we receive from Mexico; a large pine stove, where the plants could be removed during the few weeks when the vanilla flowers are setting, would be all that would be needed.

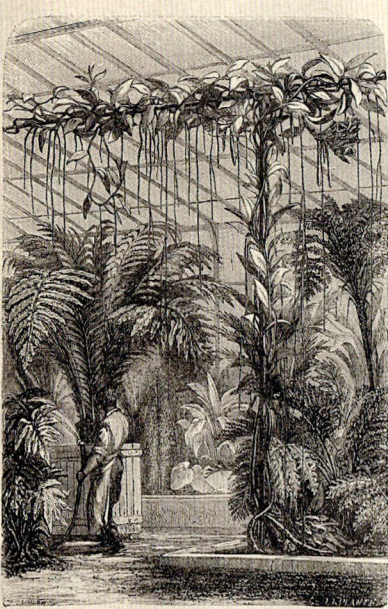

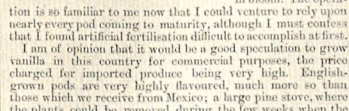

Well-Grown Vanilla in Large Plant Stove.

Article on Vanilla Culture, by E. Bennett, in *The Garden*, 10 February, 1872

Periodicals such as *The Garden* and *The Gardeners' Chronicle* gained enormous popularity and circulation in Victorian Britain, with newly described species being reported in their pages alongside articles such as this one, encouraging people to grow these intriguing, exotic plants themselves. Those who could afford to employed gardeners and built great glass-panelled stove houses, heated with boilers below to create the sweltering, steamy environments it was assumed "all" tropical plants must need to thrive.

Vanilla had been described for the first time back in 1754, and the seed pods, and the flavour and fragrance they could impart when cured properly, were well known – but the possibility of growing this expensive and highly desirable spice would have piqued the interest of many an orchidophile reading this issue. Whether or not they subsequently managed to get these difficult-to-bloom plants to flower, let alone set and develop fruits, or cure the resulting seed pods correctly, is less frequently reported upon.

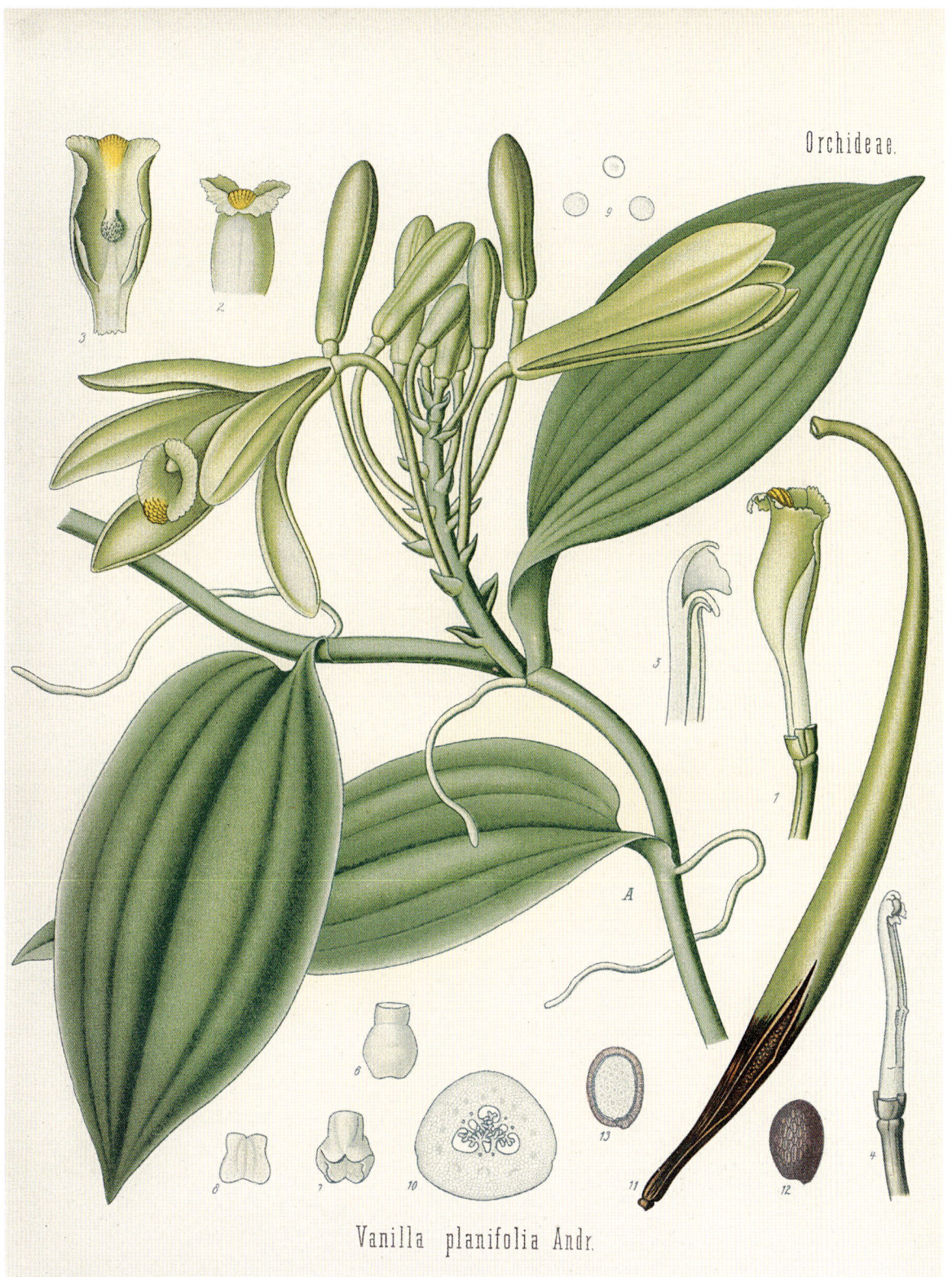

Orchideae.

Vanilla planifolia Andr.

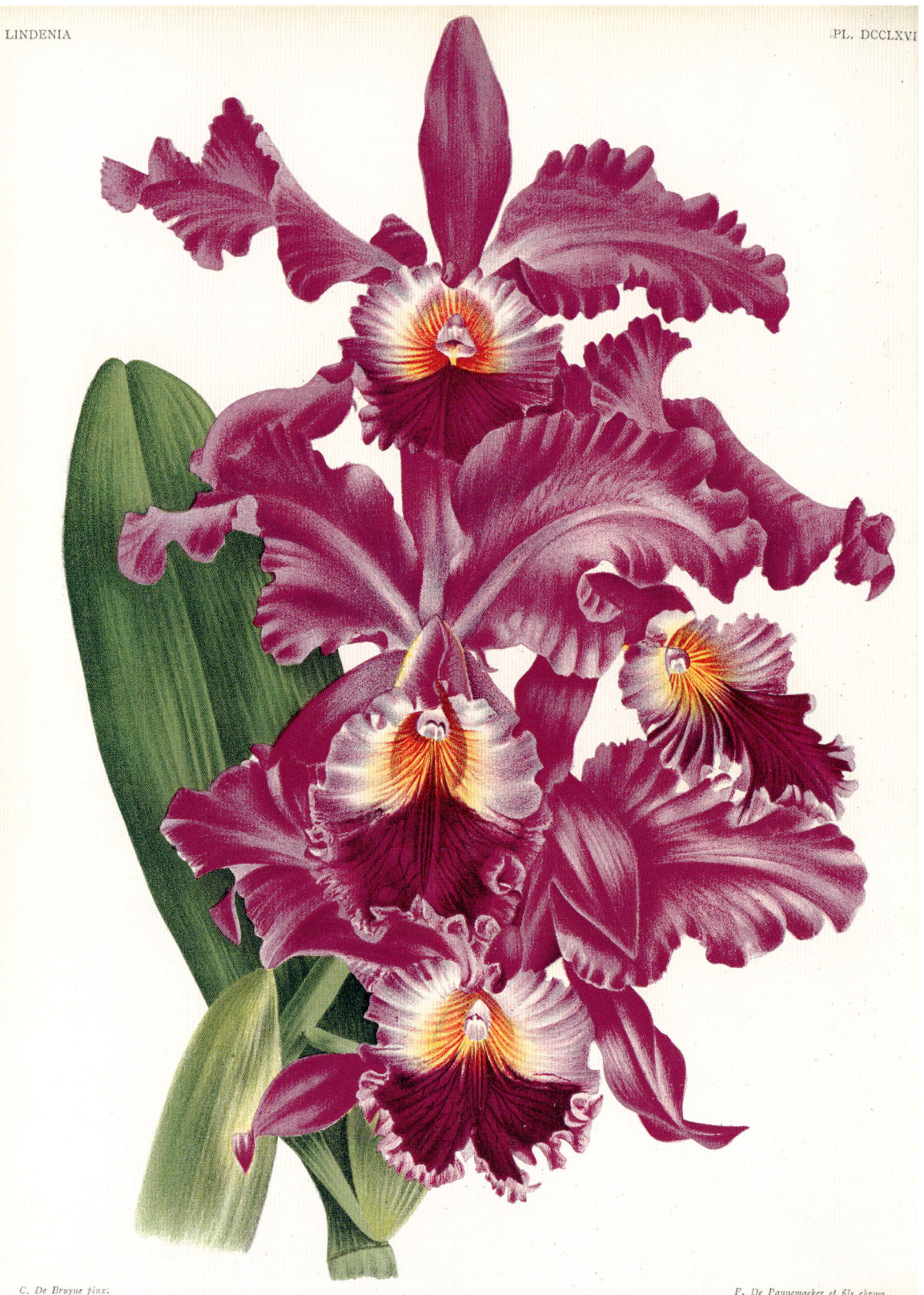

CATTLEYA LABIATA LINDL. var. PERFECTA L. LIND.

GENERAL READING

Clayton, D., *Charles Parish: Plant Hunter and Botanical Artist in Burma*, Ray Society, London, 2017.

Cribb, Phillip J. & Tibbs, Michael, *A Very Victorian Passion: The Orchid Paintings of John Day 1863–1888*, Blacker Publishing, London, 2004.

Cribb, Phillip J., *Slipper Orchids of the Tropical Americas*, Natural History Publications, Borneo, 2017.

Curtis's Botanical Magazine, continuously published since 1787.

Desmond, Ray, *The History of the Royal Botanic Gardens, Kew* (2nd edition), Royal Botanic Gardens, Kew, 2007.

Endersby, Jim, *Orchids: A Cultural History*, Royal Botanic Gardens, Kew, 2016.

Fry, Carolyn, *The Plant Hunters*, André Deutsch, London, 2017.

Griggs, Patricia, *Joseph Hooker: Botanical Trailblazer*, Royal Botanic Gardens, Kew, 2011.

Henderson, Paul, *James Sowerby: The Enlightenment's Natural Historian*, Royal Botanic Gardens, Kew, 2015.

Mills, Christopher, *The Botanical Treasury*, André Deutsch, London, 2016.

O'Brien, Seamus, *In the Footsteps of Joseph Dalton Hooker: A Sikkim Adventure*, Royal Botanic Gardens, Kew, 2018.

Payne, Michelle, *Marianne North: A Very Intrepid Painter*, Royal Botanic Gardens, Kew, 2011.

Pridgeon, Alec M., Cribb, Phillip J., Chase, M., & Rasmussen, Finn N., *Genera Orchidacearum*, Volumes 1–6 (1999–2014), Oxford University Press, Oxford.

Rix, Martyn, *The Golden Age of Botanical Art*, André Deutsch, London, 2018.

Sprunger, Samuel, *Orchids from Curtis's Botanical Magazine*, Cambridge University Press, Cambridge, 1986.

Sprunger, Samuel, Cribb, Phillip J. & Stearn, William T., *Orchids from The Botanical Register 1815–1847*, Birkhauser Verlag, Basel, 1991.

Stearn, William T., *John Lindley 1799–1865: Gardener-Botanist and Pioneer Orchidologist*, Antique Collectors' Club, Woodbridge, 1999.

Stewart, Joyce, *Orchids at Kew*, HMSO, London, 1992.

Willis, Kathy & Fry, Carolyn, *Plants: From Roots to Riches*, John Murray, London, 2014.

ACKNOWLEDGEMENTS

The Royal Botanic Gardens, Kew would like to thank the following people: Craig Brough, Julia Buckley, Anne Griffin, Kat Harrington, Patricia Long, Anne Marshall and Lynn Parker of Kew's Library and Archives; Paul Little, Daphne Maryanka; and Anna Darke, Gemma Maclagan Ram and Alison Moss at Carlton Books.

The authors would like to thank Christina Harrison, Andre Schuiteman and Thomas Walton.

INDEX

Page numbers in **bold** type refer to main entries; page numbers in *italic* refer to captions.

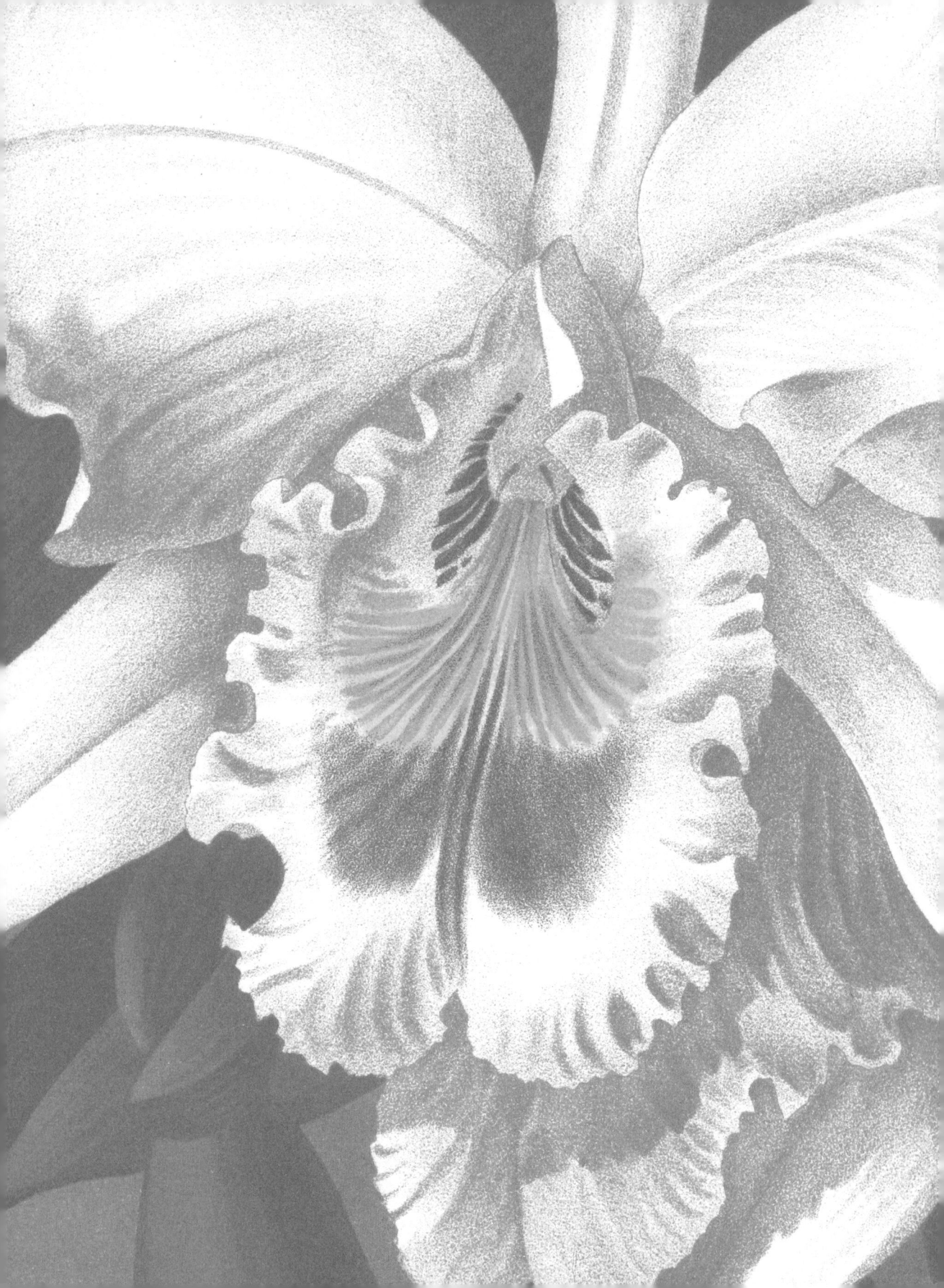